3 2

DISCARD

BLACK LITIGANTS

in the Antebellum American South

THE JOHN HOPE FRANKLIN SERIES IN
AFRICAN AMERICAN HISTORY AND CULTURE

Waldo E. Martin Jr. and Patricia Sullivan, editors

BLACK LITIGANTS

in the Antebellum American South

KIMBERLY M. WELCH

THE UNIVERSITY OF NORTH CAROLINA PRESS

Chapel Hill

The University of North Carolina Press has been a member
of the Green Press Initiative since 2003.

Jacket photographs by author.

LIBRARY OF CONGRESS CATALOGING-IN-PUBLICATION DATA
Names: Welch, Kimberly M., author.
Title: Black litigants in the antebellum American South / Kimberly M. Welch.
Other titles: John Hope Franklin series in African American history and culture.
Description: Chapel Hill : The University of North Carolina Press, [2018] |
Series: The John Hope Franklin series in African American history
and culture | Includes bibliographical references and index.
Identifiers: LCCN 2017026939| ISBN 9781469636436 (cloth : alk. paper) |
ISBN 9781469636450 (ebook)
Subjects: LCSH: African Americans—Louisiana—History—
To 1863. | African Americans—Mississippi—History—To 1863. |
African Americans—Louisiana—Social conditions—19th century. |
African Americans—Mississippi—Social conditions—19th century. |
Actions and defenses—Lousiana. | Actions and defenses—Mississippi.
Classification: LCC E185.92 .W45 2018 | DDC 305.896/073075—dc23
LC record available at https://lccn.loc.gov/2017026939

Portions of chapter 2 were previously published in "Black Litigiousness and White
Accountability: Free Blacks and the Rhetoric of Reputation in the Antebellum
Natchez District," *Journal of the Civil War Era* 5, no. 3 (September 2015): 372–98.

For

JAMES WELLS PERSON JR.

and

JANE BUSH PERSON

Contents

Figures & Map

Acknowledgments

My heart is full. This project has been a labor of love, even in those moments of uncertainty during which I wondered if I could do these incredible records—and especially the litigants who created them—justice (so to speak). I am indebted to and inspired by the people in this book.

Financial support from several institutions made this project possible, including a multiyear Law and Social Sciences Research Grant from the National Science Foundation (SES 1353231) and long-term fellowships from the Newberry Library (the Lloyd Lewis Fellowship in American History and the Monticello College Foundation Fellowship for Women), the American Bar Foundation/Law and Society Association (the Law and Social Science Fellowship), and the Council of Library and Information Resources (the Mellon Fellowship in the Humanities in Original Sources). I also received generous grants and fellowships from the National Endowment for the Humanities, the West Virginia Humanities Council, the Cosmos Club Foundation, the American Historical Association, the Dolphe Briscoe Center for American History at the University of Texas at Austin, the University of Maryland, and West Virginia University. I am particularly thankful for the three years I spent in Chicago working on this project (2010–2012 and 2014–2015). My two years as a fellow in residence at the American Bar Foundation and my year as a long-term fellow at the Newberry Library were nothing short of a gift.

This project would not have been viable without the cooperation of the county clerks' offices in Adams and Claiborne Counties in Mississippi and Iberville and Pointe Coupee Parishes in Louisiana. Mimi Miller and Trevor Brown of the Historic Natchez Foundation gave me unlimited access to the materials in the Courthouse Records Project and a space to work for months at a time. I also thank Tara Laver for her insight into the Louisiana and Lower Mississippi Valley Collection at Louisiana State University, as well as archivists at the Library of Congress, the Historic New Orleans Collection, the Mississippi Baptist Historical Commission, the Mississippi State Archives, the Louisiana State Archives, the University of New Orleans Special Collections, and the Dolphe Briscoe Center for American History at the University of Texas at Austin. Juanita Robinson gave me a place to come home to each night after hours of research in a damp basement in Natchez, Mississippi. Juanita and her daughter, Marcia Adams, also treated me as family, fed me many a southern meal, and taught me a great deal about the region.

I could not have asked for better mentors. I am especially thankful for Ira Berlin. Ira pushed me to think about the big picture, guided me when I needed help figuring out—at bottom—what was significant about this book, encouraged me to find my own voice, and helped me realize what I am capable of. Working with him reminds me of why I want to be a historian and write the kind of books people want to read. If I come to be half the scholar, teacher, and mentor he is, I will be doing well indeed. Robyn Muncy's door was always open, and she believed in me and this project from the moment I pitched it. Leslie Rowland took me under her wing from the get-go, and I have greatly benefited from her vast knowledge of southern history and from her friendship. Dylan Penningroth is a fellow traveler in the unwieldy world of local courts and has served as a source of wisdom when I needed it. Michael Ross offered me insight into the field of legal history and the world of publishing. Aaron Sheehan-Dean fed me fried chicken and offered sound advice about how and where to pitch my ideas. Laura Beth Nielsen is a mama bear in so many ways and always in my corner. Barbara Welke has been a terrific friend and cheerleader and a fine critical reader. I am a better mentor myself because of the mentorship of Peter Albert.

The friendships I have developed with my colleagues at West Virginia University and Vanderbilt University have sustained me throughout this process. For their support, good cheer, critical eye, and fierce friendship, I thank Joshua Arthurs, Jenny Boulware, Tyler Boulware, Elizabeth Fones-Wolf, Ken Fones-Wolf, Krystal Frazier, Brian Luskey, Kate Staples, and Michele Stephens. I also thank my fantastic research assistants: Samantha Yost, Francis Curran, and especially Jennifer Miller.

My interlocutors within the academy are many. For thinking with me (and for sharing meals and drinks, hotel rooms, and seats at the conference table), I thank especially Kirt von Daacke, Rachel Galvin, Joanna Grisinger, Sally Hadden, Scott Heerman, Nate Holdren, Jessica Marie Johnson, Kelly

Kennington, Christina Larocco, Michelle McKinley, Dylan Penningroth, Amy Rutenburg, Rebecca Scott, Rashmee Singh, Felicity Turner, Anne Twitty, Jill Weinberg, and Barbara Welke.

Several people read chapter drafts and proposals and offered valuable suggestions and encouragement. I thank Joshua Arthurs, Ira Berlin, Tyler Boulware, Katherine Crawford, Rachel Galvin, Joanna Grisinger, Nate Holdren, Justine Murison, Brian Luskey, Dylan Penningroth, Justin Richland, Caitlin Rosenthal, Michael Ross, Leslie Rowland, Karen Sanchez-Eppler, Rebecca Scott, Kate Staples, Felicity Turner, Jill Weinberg, and Barbara Welke. For reading the entire manuscript (and more than once), I thank Peter Albert, Ari Bryen, Scott Heerman, and Kelly Kennington. For always answering my calls, pushing me to keep going when I felt discouraged, and celebrating the high notes, I thank my dear friends Kelly Kennington and Scott Heerman. Ari Bryen talked me through every bit of this book, interpreted my thoughts when I was without words, and pushed me to think harder and clearer. Kelly, Scott, Peter, and Ari approached this manuscript with a generosity of spirit, with excitement, and with a keen eye for its shortcomings and spaces for improvement. It is hard to imagine a better support system.

For their incisive suggestions, generosity, and enthusiasm, I also thank the two anonymous readers for the University of North Carolina Press and my editor, Charles Grench. Parts of chapter 2 were first published in the *Journal of the Civil War Era*.

I could not have done this without the love and support of my friends and family. I am especially grateful for the sharp wit and ceaseless encouragement of Gabrielle Adams, Sarah Johnson Honig, Abigail Johnson, Matthew Stempson, and Jill Weinberg. The Bryen family shared their table and their home and welcomed me into their family. The Person family—Jim, Lee, Currie, and Wells—included me as one of their own from the moment I walked through their door, and I have learned so much from them. My sisters—Anna Welch, Leslie Person, Sarah Welch, and Jamie Connolly—have constantly helped me remember what is most important. They are my closest friends and confidantes. My parents, Mike and Mary Welch and Kate Fitzpatrick, neither doubted me nor judged my choices. My husband, Ari Bryen, is the best part of my life and my favorite person to think with. Our lives are filled with adventure and love. Thank you for believing in me—always.

This book is dedicated to Jimmie and Jane Person. In so many ways, Jimmie and Jane made this project possible. Jane's connections to nearly everyone in the greater Natchez area opened every door imaginable. Jimmie's family settled in Port Gibson, Mississippi, in the early part of the nineteenth century, and Jimmie himself has lived there his entire life. I learned more about Mississippi history from Jimmie—through our animated conversations, treks through old graveyards, and frequent excursions down the muddy back roads of Claiborne County—than from anyone else. Jane and Jimmie gave me a place to visit on the weekends, fed me martinis and oyster stew, and welcomed and loved me as if I were their own grandchild. They took this Yankee from Maine and made her a proud, if honorary, southerner.

BLACK LITIGANTS

in the Antebellum American South

Norman's Chart of the Lower Mississippi River. The owners of the farms and plantations along the Mississippi River (pictured here in 1858) appeared in the Natchez district courts with frequency, as plaintiffs and as defendants. Some, such as the landowners along the False River in Pointe Coupee Parish, were litigants and witnesses of color. Courtesy of the Library of Congress.

The Natchez district was home to some of the richest slaveholders in the South, as well as to nonslaveholding and poor whites, free people of color, and hundreds of thousands of slaves. Map courtesy of Danielle R. Picard.

Introduction

A BIND OF THEIR OWN MAKING

On Sunday, September 6, 1857, two white men, William Calmes and John Buford, violently seized, whipped, and attempted to kidnap Valerien Joseph in Pointe Coupee Parish, Louisiana. Empowered by their duties as slave patrollers, Calmes and Buford entered the property of another white man in search of runaway slaves. There, they came upon Joseph, a free black carpenter engaged in his work. Although Joseph had not given them any reason to believe he was a runaway, and despite the protests of onlookers and Joseph's own declarations that he was a free man, Calmes and Buford grabbed Joseph and attempted to carry him away. When others tried to intervene, Calmes yelled that he "would do what he pleased," for he intended to seize and then sell Joseph as a slave. To subdue their prey, the two men took turns beating Joseph in the head with a large stick. Then Calmes removed Joseph's clothing, forced him on his belly, and whipped his naked body with a cowhide "forty to fifty times" while an armed Buford stood guard to prevent others from assisting their bloodied captive. Eventually the onlookers helped pull Joseph from the clutches of his captors, and he managed to escape.

That two white men viciously assaulted a black man in the Deep South in 1857 is unsurprising. That they expected to do so with impunity was also not unusual. African-descended people—enslaved and free—repeatedly faced similar, unprovoked attacks. Surviving as a free person of color in a world in which blackness equaled slavery was no easy feat. By the late antebellum period, many white southerners in the region perceived free blacks as a threat to the social and racial order, and they dealt with them as such. It was not atypical for men like Calmes and Buford to insist that Joseph was a runaway slave. The presumption of slavery followed people of African descent, and

3

free blacks had to carry "free papers" as proof of their status. It is also possible that Calmes and Buford knew very well that Joseph was free. As Solomon Northup's famous tale reminds us, kidnapping and then selling a free black person into slavery occurred often enough to incite fear in free black communities throughout the country.

What is unexpected about this story, however, is that we do not learn of it from a slave narrative, such as Northup's, published for the edification of a northern abolitionist audience. We learn about it instead because Joseph chose to sue his attackers. In contrast to Northup's narrative, Joseph's case sits in a trifolded packet in a courthouse in New Roads, Louisiana. It has not been read since he filed it.

Five days after the attack, Joseph sued Calmes and Buford in the Ninth Judicial District Court, a local trial court held in Pointe Coupee Parish. He demanded damages: the "illegal and wicked acts of said Calmes and Buford," Joseph insisted, "have caused your petitioner damage to the amount of fifteen hundred dollars." To that end, he requested that the white judge, A. D. M. Haralson, summon his attackers to court for a public accounting of their offenses against him, and "after due course of law," "they be condemned" to pay him $1,500, plus interest and court costs. The defendants denied the charges against them, and the case went to trial. The court subpoenaed the testimony of several witnesses, and each verified Joseph's claims: one white man testified that Calmes and Buford "fell upon Joseph" and "pulled him out of the yard and struck him on the head with a stick." Another white man (in charge of organizing slave patrols) testified that Calmes and Buford were not in fact on patrol that day. And still other white witnesses relayed that Joseph was "born free" of an Indian mother and a black father and lived "in a negro quarter." After hearing the evidence, a white jury found for the plaintiff and issued a judgment for damages: $300 from Calmes and $200 from Buford. The judge denied the defendants' request for a new trial and ordered the men to pay their debt. Both men also faced criminal charges for Joseph's attack, but the outcome is unknown.[1]

That a black man would take his white attackers to court in the first place seems paradoxical in itself. That he would win is yet more surprising. But perhaps more interesting still is *how* Joseph framed his suit.

Joseph did not begin his petition to the court with a description of the violence inflicted on him (as one might in a lawsuit for damages). Instead, he framed the case as a debt action, using the language of property and obligation. Calmes and Buford, he insisted, owed him money: "The petition of Valerien Joseph, a free man of color, residing in the parish, Respectfully shows," he began, "That William Calmes and [John] Buford, residents of the parish aforesaid, are justly and legally indebted, in solido, unto him in the sum of fifteen hundred dollars, with interest of 50% from judicial demand until paid." They owed him this amount, moreover, for their illegal assault on his property: his body. The jury agreed and awarded him $500 for his trouble. Buford paid the $200 shortly after the trial, but Calmes ignored the judgment. When the amount remained unpaid more than a year later, Joseph initiated additional legal proceedings against him. This time, Judge Haralson ordered the sheriff to seize Calmes's property, sell it at auction, and settle his obligation to Joseph. Although Calmes absconded to Mississippi before the court could seize his property, Joseph continued to press his case. He made another white man, John A. Warren, a party to the lawsuit and pursued garnishment proceedings against him. Warren possessed property belonging to Calmes, property that could be seized and sold. He "has in his hands funds belonging to the said Calmes," Joseph relayed, "more than sufficient to pay the judgment and the costs." The judge subpoenaed Warren, requesting that he appear before him and answer Joseph's "demand." When Warren failed to attend court, however, Joseph received a judgment against Warren (in default). On April 20, 1860, mere months before Louisiana left the Union to join a slaveholders' republic, the court ordered Warren to pay Joseph $350 (the original amount plus court costs and interest). When Warren did not pay, the sheriff seized his property, sold it at auction, and provided Joseph with the proceeds. One year later, almost to the day, shots would be fired at Fort Sumter initiating a war over the right to hold black people as property.[2]

At work in Joseph's demand are a series of interlocking understandings about the relation of one's property to one's person, both in the sense of one's physical body and in the more abstract sense of one's ability to be seen at law as someone who "counts" such that he or she can make a claim. These relations between one's person, one's property, and one's legal claims form the subject of what follows. To properly understand Joseph's suit, why he went to court, why he insisted on describing assault as a matter of debt and obligation, why he won, and why he eventually managed to have a white man's property placed on the auction block, requires that we reevaluate our understandings of the relationship between black people, claims-making, racial exclusion, and the legal system in the antebellum South more broadly.

Antebellum southern courts have traditionally been understood as institutions supporting the class interests and the racial ideologies of the white planter and merchant elite. Black litigants like Joseph, however, routinely appealed to the courts to redress wrongs done to them and debts owed to them.

It appears that Joseph was right to do so. At no time during the course of the lawsuit did the court drag its feet or refuse his requests. To all appearances, the judge took Joseph's claims seriously, directed the sheriff to subpoena the defendants and witnesses, issued writs of execution immediately on request, and ordered the seizure and sale of white men's property. That Joseph, a man of color, appeared in a Louisiana court and sued two white men, claimed ownership of his body, sought not compensation for missed work opportunities but damages to repair his wounded status, and compelled the courts to seize white property to settle their obligations to him represented, in a sense, an inversion of the racial and legal order in the slave South.

This case raises questions about who had access to the power of the law and under what circumstances. Calmes and Buford certainly expected that they did. After all, they were white men, men whose race and status gave them claims to legal and political standing. They were slave patrollers, empowered by state statute to detain possible runaways. As slaveholders, they held property rights in black people. Thus, with the law on their side, they might then get away with kidnapping and selling a free man of color. Their property, however, ended up on the auction block. Joseph, by contrast, harnessed the power of the state to serve his interests and to do his bidding: he sued two white men, bound them in obligation to him through debt, and compelled the courts to seize white property and sell it at auction to settle his claims and compensate him for his degradation. The court record of the slave South is rife with stories like Joseph's.

What follows is a historical study of free and enslaved African Americans' use of the local courts in the antebellum American South. This book investigates unpublished and largely unexplored lower court records from the Natchez district of Mississippi and Louisiana between 1800 and 1860 in which free blacks and slaves sued whites and other people of color before white judges and juries in all-white courtrooms.[3] My research includes more than one thousand cases involving black litigants using the law to protect their interests, lawsuits that highlight African-descended people's involvement in a broad range of civil actions.

Court records, especially the records of the civil courts, preserve one of the great underexplored chapters in the history of black life in America. But the reasons for their neglect are not hard to come by. Researching nineteenth-century trial court records is a process fraught with technical challenges—of location, preservation, decipherment, and analysis. The bulk

The court records in many locations are still trifolded and in no particular order. Claiborne County Clerk of the Court's Office, Port Gibson, Mississippi; photograph by the author.

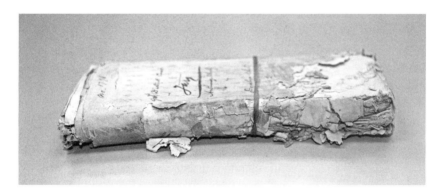

The conditions of the trial court records vary considerably. Many are deteriorating and in need of preservation. Pointe Coupee Parish Clerk of the Court's Office, New Roads, Louisiana; photograph by the author.

of these records are neither published nor housed in any traditional archive. Instead, they reside in the possession of the county clerks of the courts' offices, and most have not been processed, cleaned, or even organized. Frequently they sit in sloppy piles in the dank basements of southern courthouses or rot in unlabeled boxes in wet storage sheds on the outskirts of towns, sharing space with bugs and rodents. Unsurprisingly, they are rarely accessed. Even the employees at the clerk's offices who are in charge of them often do not know they exist. In addition, the records themselves vary considerably. Handwritten, they certainly look different from the published reports with which legal scholars are most familiar. They are often moldy, torn and falling apart, and incomplete. Over the years, they have suffered from war, theft, rot, fire, flood, and general neglect; they are rapidly deteriorating. Most are stored in settings without climate control or fire and flood suppression. Searching trial court records is also tricky. Typically they are not indexed. Docket books summarizing cases are rare. Sometimes an entire decade of cases is missing. Files might be mislabeled or disorganized. In Claiborne County, Mississippi, for instance, the trial court records are still trifolded and housed in the same drawers into which they were placed long ago (drawers that were then painted shut). These records are crumbling and in no specific order: cases from 1818 might be filed alongside cases from 1879.

Interpreting trial court records is also challenging. Lawyers, clerks, and other court officials mediated the voices of litigants and witnesses, and parsing out the division of labor between litigants, lawyers, and clerks is tough. Many petitions to the court were formulaic—with clerks simply filling in names, dates, and complaints. Some officials recorded few details about the involved parties and their grievances, while others included much more information and repeated litigants' complaints at length. It is difficult to ascertain what information court officials withheld from the record—the common knowledge and the gossip—information widely available to the local court but obscured from the twenty-first-century researcher. Often the records remain incomplete, missing relevant petitions or testimony. Final judgments are frequently absent, making the outcomes of many cases unclear.

Lastly, trial court records pose an interpretive problem for scholars interested in questions of representivity. Here, statistical analysis and sampling proves largely unhelpful because, in working with materials from these courthouses, we always work in the context of an unknown baseline. Many cases were brought but not concluded; verdicts were variable; documents went missing; we cannot see underlying processes of negotiation; we know less than we would like about enforcement; and hidden from view are the cases summarily rejected.[4]

Nineteenth-century trial court records reveal a legal system closely connected to daily life in the Old South and demonstrate the extent to which African-descended people participated in and shaped legal processes in their communities.[5] The very nature of local law and governance in the nineteenth century involved the participation of all community members—young and old, male and female, white and black, slave and free. Law pervaded the culture of the antebellum South, and as both participants and observers, southerners of all types had frequent contact with local legal processes.[6] Court day was one of the South's most important social institutions, and it drew audiences from all regions of the county. Courts met in spaces where ordinary southerners gathered—in country stores, on front porches, and under trees. As a result, a wide range of southerners understood the legal process, and this included free and enslaved black people. People of color entered local court proceedings in a number of informal ways—from spreading gossip that whites repeated in court to compelling others to prosecute wrongs done to them in an effort to maintain social welfare. But because people of African ancestry lacked many legal rights (and legal standing to bring a suit in many circumstances), they often participated indirectly or behind the scenes.[7]

Black people also came before the courts as defendants. Indeed, much of our understanding of African Americans' experience with the antebellum southern legal system stems from a focus on criminal law (black people as defendants) and restrictive legislation (black people as objects to control).[8] The emphasis on criminal rather than private law has important consequences for how we view African Americans' relationship to law and the courts, revealing a long history of linking people of color to criminality and regulation.[9] Such depictions partially reflect later, more modern concerns with African Americans' treatment by the criminal justice system writ large (the police, courts, prisons, and so forth). They also proceed from a reading of slave codes themselves—that is, draconian legislation. As a result, we sometimes have a reductive understanding of African Americans and the law: in the eyes of the law, black people are criminals (or objects) who need to be regulated; in the eyes of other, more sympathetic observers, black people are targets of a racist legal apparatus or otherwise passive.

Black plaintiffs in civil suits remain a little-known aspect of the legal history of the slave South. We have seen some glimpses of people of color using the antebellum southern civil courts, particularly as litigants for their freedom. However, we neither have a comprehensive study of the *fact* of black litigiousness in the antebellum South, nor do we have a suitable framework for understanding the *meaning* of their claims-making.[10]

People of African descent were not only observers of trials, informal participants, defendants, or objects of regulation; trial court records reveal them to be prolific litigators as well. They were parties to civil suits in their own interests and directly active in legal proceedings. They sued other people of color, certainly, but they also sued white people. What is more, they often won. This is a phenomenon that has largely been overlooked by historians.

But it ought not to be, because it speaks to the heart of the ways we understand the operation of power, law, and racial hierarchies in the slave South.

The black legal experience in America cannot be reduced to white regulation and black criminality. Examining African Americans' involvement in private law reveals a different picture. People of color appealed to the courts to protect their interests. They exploited the language of rights and property, thus including themselves in an American narrative of citizenship and privilege *in advance* of formal emancipation. When black litigants made such claims at law, they expected the courts to validate and execute those claims. Indeed, they sought accountability. Thus, seemingly mundane civil actions like debt-recovery suits complicate our notions about the sources of rights and their relationship to civic inclusion.

Reimagining both free blacks and slaves as litigators—wielders of law who successfully sued in court to protect their interests—is particularly important in today's world where black Americans' relationship to the justice system is fraught, such that "black justice" is a contradiction in terms. There remains a tension between notions of the legal system as imparting justice and liberation and the legal system as an agent of violence. This dialectic is long-standing in the history of race in the United States.

Hundreds of black people appeared before the bar in the Natchez district and used the law on their own behalf—often successfully. They sued whites and other people of color to enforce the terms of their contracts, recover unpaid debts, recoup back wages, and claim damages for assault. They sued in conflicts over cattle, land, slaves, and other property, for their freedom and for divorce, and to resolve a number of other disagreements. In addition, free people of color used the courts to register their marriages, probate wills, donate property to their children or wives, emancipate their family members, and request official family meetings dedicated to allocating resources. Enslaved men and women engaged their owners in courtroom battles over their own personal status and freedom and the status of their children and kin. Sometimes, in a few rare instances, slaves even took whites to court to recover unpaid debts for money they had loaned them. In so doing, black litigants claimed the courtroom as "an arena of possibility."[11]

In other words, long before the Civil Rights Act of 1866 and the Fourteenth Amendment in 1868, people of color in the Natchez district made and enforced contracts, sued, gave evidence, and inherited, purchased, leased, sold, held, lent, and conveyed real and personal property. Even after the 1857

Dred Scott decision established that black people "had no rights which the white man was bound to respect," the courts in the Natchez district continued to hear their claims and render verdicts in their favor.[12] Through their litigation, African Americans registered their voices in public, claimed rights, and fashioned themselves as full persons before the law.

Personhood will be central to what follows. In this book, I adopt Barbara Young Welke's definition of legal personhood. "Personhood," as Welke describes it, "rests most fundamentally on legal recognition and protection of *self*-ownership, that is, of a right to one's person, one's body, and one's labor."[13] Additional components of personhood derive from self-possession, such as "a right to the freedom of movement, to marry, to procreate (or not), to be free from physical abuse or coercion without due process of law, to contract, to inherit and devise property, and so on."[14] Making one's claim count at law, moreover, includes the right to sue and be sued. Lastly, personhood is an element of freedom that allows people to enter into certain types of obligations and relationships. At some level, in modern law at least, legal personhood is a fiction—sometimes used for convenience. In today's law, for example, corporations are persons. They have rights and obligations and can sue and be sued. But a corporation and a real person are not easily confused. This was not so for a black litigant in the antebellum Natchez district. There the assertion of legal personhood and the assertion of real personhood could merge into one. This was because of the peculiar way that the southern legal system understood rights; legal personhood was not always easily distinguished from actual personhood, because both statuses were understood in terms of gender and race. The fully vested legal person in the antebellum South was not some vague entity with rights, but rather a white man. It was an embodied notion.[15] Thus, when suing in court over their right to possess property, protect their families, and assert freedom, black litigants exercised and laid claim to legal personhood—a status both southern law and southern society reserved for white men only. Legal personhood and what we might term social personhood merged at a certain horizon and became indistinguishable. As a result, litigation simultaneously proclaimed one's contribution while it could plausibly deny such an assertion as a disruptive breach of the social hierarchy.

Consequently, when black people asserted their rights and pressed their claims in court, they also envisioned themselves as full members of their communities and pressed for civic inclusion. These were claims about who had access to the power of law, certainly. Yet they were also claims about *who counts*; these were claims to inclusion and membership. For black litigants, civic inclusion had a participatory function, one that involved the capacity to act as an independent person at law and participate in the public sphere. Civic inclusion also had a symbolic function: the recognition that this person was worthy of staking a claim.

To be sure, black claims-making and self-advocacy involved a delicate process. It also raises two larger issues. First, the evidence of black litigants' legal action raises doubts about the viability of analytical categories that scholars have long relied on to describe subordination and domination in the slave South. Free and enslaved African Americans resided at the center of antebellum southern legal culture—as the objects of white concerns about social control and racial hierarchy *and* as active protectors of their own interests. Second, and as a corollary, it places us in a stronger position to understand the centrality of legal institutions in the long struggle for full citizenship. Courts did not suddenly transform themselves from sites of oppressive regulation to sites of potential liberation in the wake of the Civil War. They were implicated in a much longer process, one that began far earlier.

An understanding of people of African descent as legal persons capable of bringing civil actions before the courts, however, ran counter to the position of many southern legal thinkers. After all, black people resided in a world of white supremacy and black slavery. As Thomas R. R. Cobb argued in his widely read treatise, *An Inquiry into the Law of Negro Slavery in the United States*, slaves, in particular, were outsiders without such rights and abilities: "Of the three great absolute rights guaranteed to every citizen by the common law, viz., the right of personal security, the right of personal liberty, and the right of private property, the slave, in a state of pure or absolute slavery, is totally deprived."[16] Free blacks, as dangerous aberrations in a social order where blackness meant being property, were interlopers outside of civil society. The condition of free people of color in the slaveholding states, according to Cobb, was "but slightly removed from that of a slave."[17] The "various restrictions" they faced placed "the free negro but little above the slave as to civil privileges."[18] The law of slavery, as one scholar has argued, was "a litany of rights denied."[19] But, as the pages that follow demonstrate, southern courts did not exclude the claims made by black litigants solely on the basis of race and condition, and people of color—free and enslaved—routinely demanded and asserted a broad spectrum of the rights inherent in personhood. In so doing, they forced white southerners to confront situations in which objects of property became subjects of selfhood.

Introduction

We cannot solely explain African Americans' presence in the courtroom, and especially their successes, by the fact that they had legal standing to sue in some circumstances or that they lived in a world in which law was woven into the community and local courts were charged with maintaining social order—although these considerations of course hold importance as well.[20] Nor did white southerners magnanimously allow black people access to the courts (however limited) because of some wish to be, or even to seem, fair. The southern courts were not an island of decency and justice in an otherwise violent world. These were the same courts that ordered the sale or execution of black people and regulated an economy based on their production and reproduction. The courts, moreover, were not instruments of white hegemony. The local court records in the Natchez district include hundreds of examples of people of color harnessing the power of the courts in the service of their own interests, challenging the notion that the law was the "principle vehicle for the hegemony of the ruling class."[21] Law is, after all, a part of society, and when examined on the ground, it reflects the messiness and the contradictions of local communities and lived experience. As this book will show, it was neither autonomous nor the province of one group of people alone.[22]

Thus, this is neither a story of "fairness" (that is, an apology for, or an indictment of, the southern legal system), nor is it a study, in the law-and-society tradition, of black people's access to justice (that is, a study of the institutional pathways through which they might make a claim and whether such pathways were relatively open or foreclosed). It is also not a study of white honor, paternalism, or hegemony (that is, a study that uses slaveholders' ideology as a framework for understanding black litigiousness).

It is, rather, a study of claims-making and the language used to that end: the language of property. The language that black litigants exploited in court helps explain their success. Black litigants claimed legal personhood through the language of property—language articulated to an audience in which an understanding of and respect for law and property rights would resonate. Through this language they were able to make whites accountable to their promises and rhetoric, navigate the world in which they lived, and exploit the inconsistencies in southern racial and economic ideologies.

On the one hand, white southerners wanted to uphold white supremacy, but, on the other, they also valued private property. Of course, for slave owners, private property and racial slavery were fundamentally linked. Slaveholders outlined their defense of slavery in the language of property rights, including the right to own people as property. These links between slavery and property, however, were not without their problems and tensions.[23] To achieve any coherence—and to make this racialized economy palatable to nonslaveholders—the law had to protect property generally.[24] Even the most marginal people tended to have something of their own, and they held it all the more dearly for it. As "people with a price," African Americans themselves had every reason to fixate on the role of property in their lives and the power it granted those who owned it.[25]

While the raison d'être of the southern legal system was the protection of the property rights of slaveholders, black litigants used that fact to protect their own livelihoods. And when left with the awkward choice between treating black people as legal persons and securing their own property rights, white southerners chose to protect their property rights, over and over again. The protection of property proved more important than upholding white supremacy and denying African Americans' claims solely on the basis of race. Black litigants exploited the tension between whites' interests in controlling people of African descent and their dedication to private property. In so doing, they created a zone of protection for themselves. Whites were caught in a bind of their own making.

By leveraging the language of property in their lawsuits, and exploiting its attendant presumptions about independence and reliability, black litigants also made claims to civic inclusion. The language of property was simultaneously necessary to describe the cases at hand, and it was bound inextricably to a broader national narrative of what it meant to be a member of the polity, to be autonomous, and to be eligible to voice one's opinion or assert one's claim. Because it was impossible to formally disentangle the two, when black litigants made a claim about property, they were also, implicitly, linking their status as owner to the ideal of a free and independent citizen.

For black litigants in the antebellum South, property rights *were* civil rights: the social and racial climate of the slaveholder's regime did not allow people of color to make their claims through the language of racial equality. Yet as the pages that follow demonstrate, people of African descent used property rights to assert a much broader constellation of rights and privileges, rights that bestowed human dignity, accountability, and claims on the state. Property rights—and the relationships such rights embodied—represented a whole host of things that made a person's world more bearable. Property relations, moreover, could be envisioned as productive of an entire system of social and civic relations.

For black litigants in the Natchez district, civic inclusion meant more than basic equality in the legal arena or membership in the polity. They were not merely seeking to belong. Registering their voices in the public court-rooms of the region also represented a means to create and protect social space for themselves and their kin. When they insisted on their "title and the rights of property to the land," in the words of one black litigant, Marie Ricard, they sought to create a tolerable community where they could enact law to, in the words of another, Pierre Salvador, "peacefully enjoy settlement of [their] property."[26]

African Americans' political claims to a public, civic identity—in the slave South—predated emancipation and formal citizenship. This pre-Emancipation experience with private law was preparation for the long battle ahead for equality and civil rights, a battle often fought over constitutional law. It was preparation insofar as it involved learning to make claims about justice, both in general and in a particular case, and to locate those claims within a common narrative of membership and independence. In the after-word, I trace one strand of this process. Many more await unraveling.

The Natchez district is the plantation region along the Mississippi River be-tween Vicksburg, Mississippi, and Baton Rouge, Louisiana. It was home to wealthy planters and nonslaveholding whites alike, as well as to hundreds of free people of color and hundreds of thousands of enslaved people. It is an un-expected place to find courts recognizing the legal claims made by free blacks and slaves. Slavery influenced every aspect of life in the region, from the reali-ties of everyday domination to its elaboration in the black codes of the period. The region's economy depended on slavery. By the early nineteenth century, the cotton counties of western Mississippi and the cotton and sugar parishes across the Mississippi River in eastern Louisiana were emphatically slave so-cieties. A number of factors combined to make the Natchez district an empire for slavery: the opening of new territory in the southern interior and the avail-ability of millions of acres of fertile land (land incorporated into the federal union through diplomacy, the removal of Native Americans, and violence); revolutions in cotton and sugar production; internal improvements; a river suited to moving goods across vast distances and to distant markets; specu-lative financial practices; throngs of eager investors; and the forced march of more than 1 million slaves from the seaboard states to the Deep South.[27]

Enslaved people drove the region's economy in multiple ways: they were the laborers who produced the cotton and sugar that made their owners millionaires, the wombs that birthed more slaves, the currency that could be liquidated and converted into cash, and the security for loans used to purchase more land and slaves. In the first half of the nineteenth century, cotton (produced with slave labor) was the most widely traded commodity in the global economy.[28] New investors arrived in the cotton kingdom almost daily, eager to buy slaves. Natchez, Mississippi, housed Forks-of-the-Road, the country's busiest and largest slave market outside of New Orleans. By the second quarter of the nineteenth century, the district's slaveholders were some of the largest importers of slaves in the booming domestic slave trade, and they were among the wealthiest people in the world. The Surget family of Mississippi, to take just one example, owned more than five thousand slaves and thousands of acres of land in both Mississippi and Louisiana; to capitalize on their investments, they worked their slaves at a killing pace.[29] Slaveholders' economic interests dominated politics, and an ideology of white privilege unified white slaveholders.

Still, white domination was not achieved by ideology or economic interest alone. Slave owners in the Natchez district applied a wide array of vicious tactics that ranged from whippings, torture, humiliation, and surveillance to forced migration, sexual predation, and threats of sale in their attempts to extract labor from and exercise power over their black slaves. In particular, bondspeople faced brutal labor practices sustained by the driver's lash. "Because I could not learn his way of hilling corn," said former slave Moses Grandy of his owner, "he flogged me naked with a severe whip, made of a very tough sapling; this lapped round me each stroke; the point of it at last entered my belly and broke off, leaving an inch and a-half outside. I was not aware of it until, on going to work again, it hurt my side very much, when, on looking down I saw it sticking out of my body. I pulled it out, and the blood spouted after it. The wound festered, and discharged very much at the time, and hurt me for years after."[30] Violence against black people—of all types and at all levels—was endemic in the Natchez district.

Violence moved along channels authorized by law. Southerners designed legislation to maintain the institution of slavery and ensure that people of African descent enjoyed few legal rights. These laws turned people into property, denied them civil and political rights, and subjected them to harsh criminal proceedings. Anyone born of a slave mother was the property of his or her mother's owner, who had the legal right, according to the Louisiana *Civil Code*, to "sell him, dispose of his person, his industry, and his labor."[31] Enslaved people could not enter into contracts, and they could not legally marry. They could not testify against whites in either civil or criminal trials.

Mississippi and Louisiana law also denied enslaved people other individual rights. In an attempt to limit their movements, the law required that slaves carry passes when they left the boundaries of their owners' plantations and farms. When they did leave their masters' property, enslaved people encountered slave patrols organized by the county and empowered by statute to whip them on the spot, arrest them, and turn them over to local authorities. Whites could corporally punish a bondsperson, but Mississippi and Louisiana law made it a crime for a slave to insult or strike a white person. Slave codes made certain acts committed by slaves criminal that were not deemed crimes when committed by whites. Enslaved people also sometimes faced harsher punishments than white people committing the same offences.[32]

For slaves charged with crimes, legal proceedings were frightening affairs.[33] In Louisiana, enslaved people were especially vulnerable because the state tried them separately and differently than it tried whites and free blacks: in special tribunals made up exclusively of slaveholders. Different rules applied to the trials of slaves. For example, Louisiana slaves did not have the right to challenge jurors either for cause or peremptorily (the right to reject a perspective juror without giving a reason), while whites and free blacks could do both.[34] In Mississippi, slaves faced special tribunals for noncapital offenses, but they were tried in the circuit court for capital crimes. Here, too, enslaved people confronted different rules than whites. For instance, the punishment for giving false testimony was excessive, and Mississippi judges issued instructions to slaves intended to demonstrate the draconian nature of the law. Court officials warned slaves not to lie or they would receive "thirty-nine lashes . . . at the public whipping post" and have their ears "nailed to the pillory" for two hours and then "cut off."[35] Mississippi slaves who appeared in court as witnesses in criminal proceedings involving other slaves met with the same warning. Moreover, whether they were tried by special tribunals or by the circuit court, white faces surrounded enslaved defendants. The judges and members of the jury were all white men. They never answered to a jury of their peers.

A culture of white supremacy conspired to strip even nonslaves of their rights: Mississippi and Louisiana laws equated free blacks with slaves to undermine their status as free people. They did this in three main ways: by formally limiting their ability to seek redress in court, by burdening them with onerous administrative and registration requirements that affected their everyday lives, and by subjecting them to heightened criminal penalties. Free blacks had legal standing in some situations and could make contracts and possess property. However, southern legislators restricted their capacity to use the courts in their own interests. Every southern state except Louisiana denied free blacks the ability to testify in court in cases involving whites. Because free blacks could not sit on juries, white men decided their fate in court. They had to have official papers verifying their free status and might be arrested as fugitive slaves if they could not provide these papers. Free people of color had to register with their local governments to prove they were indeed free and legitimate residents of the state. For example, in 1858, the Claiborne County, Mississippi, Board of Police summoned forty free black people to appear before the county court to "show to satisfaction" that they were legal residents of the county and the state.[36] Free blacks were subject to vagrancy laws. They were considered vagrants if they left their county of residence and sometimes even arrested as runaway slaves. Free people of color were banned from practicing several occupations. In Louisiana they could not operate billiard halls, coffee houses, or other establishments where liquor was sold, and they could not be employed as riverboat captains. In Mississippi they were also barred from many of these occupations, and they could not work as typesetters in a printing establishment for fear that they might publish and distribute subversive or abolitionist literature. Violations of such laws could result in criminal action, public whipping, and sale into slavery. State legislators in both Mississippi and Louisiana enacted legislation forcing free blacks to leave their states and barred nonresident free people of color from entering. Counties and towns also added their own restrictions. Indeed, Mississippi and Louisiana lawmakers and jurists expended substantial effort to foreclose African Americans' participation in the legal system.[37]

State regulatory power, brutality, and economic expansion cast long shadows over how we explain the lives of people of African descent in the Old South. These modes of explanation depict the slave South as a world of domination and subordination. But the question remains: how complete are these explanations? Enslaved people's resistance, their agency, and their formation of alternative geographies (physical, psychological, and social) limit the explanatory power that we can give to large structures such as law, violence, and capitalism.[38] These accounts of slave systems fail to account for sizeable bodies of empirical evidence—in this case, trial court records—that show people of color organizing their world in an alternative fashion.[39]

But to merely emphasize the importance of resistance is similarly unsatisfying. Not least, it replicates the same assumptions about power that the large structures account relies on. As one scholar has argued, "power"

Introduction

and "agency" (like domination and subordination) are frequently positioned against one another, "as if both terms were arrayed at the ends of some sort of sliding scale, an increase in one meaning a corresponding decrease in the other."[40] As explanatory tools these juxtapositions are confining. Framing black litigants' legal action within the power/agency and domination/subordination dialectic places white slaveholders and lawmakers at the center of black people's engagement with law. Equating black people's lawsuits with "agency" or "resistance" and the southern legal apparatus with "structure" or "power" obscures African Americans' interpretations of the law's role in their lives and the myriad ways they leveraged and manipulated it in the service of their own interests.[41] Accordingly, this is not a story of black resistance; rather, it is a story of black *advocacy*. The difference, while perhaps subtle, is important.

In other words, the emphasis is not on grading black people's relationships to slavery or racism or violence, on *whether* they succeeded or not in challenging or undermining it, but rather on *how* it was that, given its existence, they crafted a space for themselves. By space, I do not mean autonomy.[42] As Dylan Penningroth reminds us, for the oppressed, "autonomy is not a universal goal."[43] By space, I refer instead to the ways people of color expanded the boundaries of the possible. This was a space to tell their stories; a space to raise their voices; a space to make their claims; a space to have those claims recognized; and a space where their claims counted. Black claims-making, moreover, had at least two parts: first, the assertion that the plaintiff was deserving; and second, that the person listening to the plaintiff was bound to hear them and then to act. Thus, this book is a story of *accountability*, not autonomy.

In the pages that follow, I suggest that that we might get more purchase on the lives of black people in the American South by looking at their claims-making and their rhetoric in court, particularly the way they employed and manipulated the language of law and the concept of property. When discussing the language people of African descent used in court, I make no claim about the "truth" of this language, that is, about whether it authentically represents black litigants' subjectivities. Courtroom language is staged; it can be judged successful or convincing or not, but if successful, it is so precisely because it *succeeds* in cloaking one's authentic subjective state (which is always more complex and ambiguous than a well-crafted case might suggest). In the courtroom, language is used to persuade: litigants employ language to render their claims legible and thus effective. Perhaps more important, language articulated in a courtroom setting—and appealing to the bar to mediate a problem—offers an alternative to violence. For people of color in the Natchez district, employing language in court, in particular the language of property, represented a means to claim space in a violent world.

To craft this space, the language of property proved decisive. Property is not just "stuff," although of course it is stuff as well. Property is also relational; it embodies the ways people construct relationships *through* things rather than a person's relationship *to* things. The owner's privileges, powers, and immunities are linked to the nonowner's duties, disabilities, and liabilities. Thus, property rights are social in nature.[44] As such, they can be marshaled as part of a language of claims-making—claims on others and claims on the state.

Property is also a language—or a group of metaphors—that underwrites a set of white male claims about independence, membership, citizenship, and personhood. It was the language used to justify the enslavement of people of African descent—a language articulated in and supported by law. Indeed, slaveholders framed their defense of slavery in the language of liberty and property rights. But property was also the language used by black litigants to register their voices, protect their interests, and claim social space.

For black litigants, property was a mode of discourse, rhetoric that could be marshaled to make their claims recognizable and persuasive to others. Employing such language in court provided people of color with an opportunity to reconfigure their relationships in a tense society and construct a more tolerable world. When we rebalance our accounts by looking at the language and rhetoric African Americans employed in court, we see more than just overwhelming power on one hand and often futile resistance on the other. Rather, we see negotiation, tension, and the intricate volley of moves that made slave systems by turns sustainable *and* unstable. What is more, slavery, and its eventual by-product, race, are, like property, *relationships* of domination, not facts of domination.

By focusing on Mississippi and Louisiana, this book investigates both common-law and civil-law regimes. Like much of the United States, Mississippi followed the Anglo-American common-law tradition. As a result of Louisiana's civil-law history stemming from the French and Spanish colonial periods, Louisianans conceived of certain legal issues differently than their common-law counterparts elsewhere in the United States. They adhered to a written legal code rather than a legal system based on judges' decisions. When Louisiana entered the United States, many residents resisted American authorities' attempts to replace the civil law with common law. This resistance influenced the substance of Louisiana law. Louisiana lawmakers sought to eliminate judicial discretion and rejected implied law and principles of equity, important tenets of the Anglo-American common-law system. The state supreme court, for instance, had to justify all decisions by citing a specific legislative act or article in the Louisiana *Civil Code*. Louisiana also retained other remnants of its French and Spanish tradition, such as the ability of free people of color to testify against whites in both civil and criminal actions and of slaves to contract for their freedom.[45]

Still, slavery and its peculiar relationship to regimes of property and personhood served as the common denominator between the two legal systems. Despite Louisiana's civil-law heritage, I have found that the disputes involving people of color in the Louisiana courts—the kinds of litigation they initiated, the types of claims they mounted, the language they used, and the verdicts they received—resembled those in the common-law regime of Mississippi. There were moments, of course, when the laws of Mississippi and Louisiana differed—differences I raise in what follows. But by working comparatively across jurisdictions often treated as radically distinct, this book challenges the notion that Louisiana is somehow unique and thus ought to be excluded or bracketed from our discussions of slavery and law in the antebellum South and suggests that the model that I articulate for the Natchez district indeed has broader applicability for understanding the interfaces among slavery, law, and personhood.[46]

There are some important methodological "rules" when working with trial court documents. First, we ought not believe that what people say is true—that is, that their speech adequately represented the facts on the ground. Courtroom language involved performance.[47] People also lied. At times these lies are patent, but at other times, they are subtle, and their relation to "what actually happened" unrecoverable. This fact poses challenges to how we read these cases, to be sure, but it hardly invalidates their importance as records of black rhetoric and performance. A second point follows from this: we should not believe that what people said in court is somehow authentic—that is, that it reflects authoritatively people's subjective feelings about the facts on the ground, whatever those may have been. This is in part because our evidence is mediated by clerks, lawyers, and other legal professionals, but also because genre conditioned what people said. Genre, form, and the type of legal action people chose to take (or could take) also limited what they could say and do in court.

These methodological cautions are salutary not just for understanding black litigants but also for reading legal sources more generally. Yet they ought not to lead us into a sort of skepticism whereby we think that we cannot know anything about individuals from legal documents. Within the given constraints, remarkable space exists for performing all sorts of operations. Genre limits what people can say, but it also allows people to say certain things in court and make that speech recognizable as a legal claim. Speakers can sift or manipulate facts and events as they chose to (and then make a claim to what is "fact"). They can make normative claims—claims that insist that what happened is not what *should* have happened. In so doing, they can also invoke the state and demand that it take responsibility for making things happen as the claimant said it should. Finally, by making claims in court, litigants compel their opponents to answer in kind.

What follows is organized thematically rather than chronologically. While in some instances people of African descent faced roadblocks in the late antebellum period that they did not encounter in earlier years (such as difficulties manumitting family members as white southerners increasingly perceived the free population of color as potentially dangerous), black people's legal activity in civil suits (as well as the reception their legal actions received) remained consistent between 1800 and 1860.[48] Thus, the chapters in this book are organized around the tactics they used, the kinds of claims people of color made in the local courts of the Natchez district (claims to accountability, recognition, property, personhood, and family), and the language they employed when making those claims. I have divided this book into two parts. Loosely speaking, the first three chapters are devoted to tactics, that is, to how black people succeeded in court, while the subsequent four chapters are devoted to the kinds of things that they went to court to fight over and the scope and significance of their litigiousness. Of course, considerable overlap exists. Overall, I aim in these chapters to build a picture—to create, in some ways, a model—of black self-advocacy and claims-making, one that explains how people of African descent in a deeply repressive society managed to use legal institutions to make space for themselves (free and enslaved, prosperous and poor, male and female). The final chapter, an extended case study of a single family (the Belly family), attempts to show how this model worked itself out in a multigenerational sense, when law was mustered by those excluded from formal avenues of political power and participation to create a stable family, one capable of independent action even where such action might be considered deeply problematic. My conclusion looks ahead, to the postbellum period, where the links between language, law, and property made by people in the antebellum period were placed under stress as they became integrated into a national system. Here I focus on Josephine Decuir, a descendent of the Belly family and the plaintiff in the first constitutional case decided by the United States Supreme Court on racial discrimination on public transit (*Hall v. Decuir*). The case marked an important horizon in black legal advocacy, one that would eventually play out, in a differing register, over the course of the twentieth century. But that is another story.

Part

ONE

1

Telling Stories

When African Americans went to court, they told tales. And by tales, I do not mean that they presented untruths or fictions. I refer instead to the ways black litigants molded the incidents that brought them to court in the first place— perhaps a boundary dispute, an assault, or a failed business venture—into a story.[1] Storytelling held distinct power for people of color. Telling stories in court presented black litigants, whose experiences and voices white southerners frequently marginalized or silenced, with the opportunity to recount their versions of events, based on their understandings of the world around them and their place in it. African-descended people used their stories to locate themselves within narratives of American culture—stories about citizenship, property ownership, freedom, and womanhood familiar to their white opponents and audiences but that typically excluded (at least in their canonical forms) the standpoints of black people. Through narratives, black litigants reimagined their relationships to the world in which they resided and expanded the boundaries of what was possible for people of color living in a slave society. They used their narratives to try to win their cases, of course, and many did receive verdicts in their favor. But equally important, they mobilized their tales to envision and describe a world in which they were more than subordinated people dominated by slaveholders. In other words, these courtroom stories did more than just make claims; they structured moments in which white southerners were forced to confront and recognize, at least contingently, the perspectives—and claims to justice and demands for redress—of those they asserted were intrinsically other than fully human.

That judges, members of the jury, witnesses, and the audiences in the gallery recognized the legitimacy of African Americans' stories is unexpected.

White southerners characteristically assumed that black people (and slaves in particular) lied. Slaveholders were on guard against slaves' tall tales and trickery. According to their masters, slaves put on a face of deceit and stealth for whites: slaves stole, ran off, broke tools, poisoned food, and pretended to be lazy or sick to get out of work. White legislatures banned slaves' words in court because, as "liars," they could not give trustworthy testimony. Enslaved people could not testify against whites in criminal and civil cases in any southern state. As the southern legal theorist Thomas R. R. Cobb put it, "That the negro, as a general rule, is mendacious, is a fact too well established to require the production of proof, either from history, travels, or craniology."[2] "Truth," in the minds of men like Cobb, was the language of whiteness. Southern lawmakers even made deception by people of color a criminal offense. In Mississippi, for example, the punishment for people of African descent, enslaved or free, for lying in a capital case was to have both ears nailed to the pillory for two hours and then cut off.[3] But as the lawsuits I discuss below indicate, in the courtroom whites confronted the possibility of reliable black narratives. The process of disputing at law—these moments of conflict and contestation—generated a context in which white southerners would hear African Americans' stories. The legal system established the space for disagreement, and the respect for and belief in the rule of law created the possibility for the words of black people to receive credit. If white justices had uniformly discounted black people's stories on the basis of race and legal status, these conversations would not have occurred.

Trials also revealed the contests over narratives. White defendants presented the courts with counternarratives—stories immersed in the language of race and the subordination of people of color—that served as attempts to limit the opportunities and to silence the voices of free and enslaved African Americans. Yet the tales black litigants told provoked defendants to respond in kind to these stories and to account for their actions. The responses of the opponents, moreover, provide us with a glimpse into the ways the litigation of and stories told by black people affected white slaveholders.

Storytelling is omnipresent in human discourse, and "the law is awash in storytelling."[4] Telling stories in court is an attempt to organize, interpret, and direct the world in which one lives, and the stories told in adversarial processes signal the narrator's interpretation of how the world ought to operate. In adversarial stories, a tension exists between what should have happened and what occurred instead. For instance, plaintiffs tell stories about "trouble in the world that has affected the plaintiff adversely," trouble caused by the defendant. Defendants tell counternarratives that deny such wrongdoing or attribute it to someone or something else.[5] Both, however, "inhabit," in the words of Robert Cover, "a normative universe."[6] Legal stories necessarily "evoke familiar, conventional realities, if only to highlight the offending deviations from them."[7] The stories presented by black litigants in the courts of the Natchez district reflect an interpretation of how the world *should* function. Their versions, however, conflicted with the established normative order of the slave South—a world in which blackness meant enslavement and inferiority. Through their narratives—narratives in which they emerged as more than racialized or enslaved outsiders—black litigants envisioned and pressed for a new order, one that would be expanded (or transformed) to include their voices, experiences, and claims.[8]

In what follows, I offer a close reading of three cases in which litigants mediated and navigated slavery and its attendant concepts about race through contested narratives told in legal settings. The exploration of how black litigants seized on narrative structures, how they constructed competing narratives, and how opponents challenged the meanings of those stories illuminates a far more complex legal culture of slavery than any straightforward story of domination and subordination. That black litigants spoke in the register of law and told legal stories may initially seem surprising. I thus begin by exploring the ways law permeated the language of everyday life. Indeed, the ubiquity of law in the daily life of the Old South could demystify the legal process (including its more technical aspects) for people of color, as well as for other nonspecialists.

LEARNING TO SPEAK IN THE REGISTER OF LAW

In a practical sense, law consists of language, both written and spoken. Language is the substance of petitions, opinions, obligations, and statutes, as well as of conversations that occur between clients and lawyers, defendants and plaintiffs, and witnesses and audiences.[9] In the courtroom, language is also used to persuade. Litigants employ language and rhetoric to render their claims legible and convincing and thus usable and effective. Law therefore is a discourse—a shared vocabulary or a set of interlocking principles—that can be tilted in a particular direction to convey one's purpose or make one's claim. Like all discourses, including technical ones, it is anchored by a package of symbols that make it powerful, authoritative, and thereby recognizable to others, even—or especially—to nonspecialists. As such, it is necessarily permeable. In other words, in the antebellum South, legal discourse proved meaningful and authoritative in part because it was not totally unavailable to ordinary people, including free blacks and slaves.[10]

Suing in court, nonetheless, required a certain level of legal acumen, and the fact that black litigants appeared in court with regularity and told their stories raises some questions: how did black people learn to speak in the register of law? And how did their many and varied experiences with law influence the kinds of stories they chose to tell? Answering these questions requires us to think about the language of law less as a technical discourse attained by specialists after three years of law school (as we might think of it today) and to view it instead as something more organic. Even for legal professionals in the antebellum period, law was not yet a "science" spoken in a discrete, specialized language; instead, it reflected the needs and demands of local communities. Most students of law in the first half of the nineteenth century read law as an apprentice in the office of a local lawyer, and "admission to practice was less a certification of the applicant's knowledge than an opportunity for him to learn on the job."[11] In the first half of the nineteenth century, American law and legal education, especially at the local level, "remained open-ended, experimental, and practical."[12] Given the ways law manifested itself in the culture of the Old South, we would be remiss to conceive of it as something radically distinct from the practice of everyday life and therefore somehow inscrutable to African Americans—or, for that matter, to other nonspecialists.[13] A range of southerners understood the legal process intimately, could speak its language, and expected it to serve their interests.

Law was pervasive in the everyday life of the Old South, and free and enslaved African Americans were privy to a great deal of law in action. As a result of the localized nature of antebellum government, the courts operated in close proximity to all southerners. Most nineteenth-century southerners looked to their counties (parishes in Louisiana) as the constituent unit of government. Southern towns, especially those in rural areas like the Natchez district, formed around the courthouse—the social, commercial, and political center of the county. There was not yet a uniform, systematic, and rationalized body of state law, and state governments granted local jurisdictions wide-ranging authority. Most southern legal business was conducted in the lower courts: in magistrates' homes or offices; before the board of police or police juries; and in county, parish, probate, chancery, circuit, and district courts. These courts, with their broad range of duties, supervised nearly every aspect of life. They oversaw roads, bridges, and ferries. They mediated disputes between neighbors and families; probated wills; appointed executors; punished gamblers, drunks, and fornicators; sanctioned shopkeepers for opening their doors on the Sabbath; and enforced the payment of debts.

They returned runaway slaves; provided for orphans, unwed mothers, and the poor; indicted murderers; divorced adulterous spouses; and manumitted slaves.[14]

Court week represented one of the antebellum South's most important social institutions. While many people attended monthly county courts or witnessed hearings and inquests, circuit and district courts attracted residents from every corner of the county. These courts met for a week twice a year, drawing judges, lawyers, litigants, witnesses, and prospective jurors to town. Court week also attracted spectators, retailers, and performers. The courthouse steps served as a center of both business and pleasure: auctioneers sold slaves, grogshops hawked liquor, peddlers marketed goods, entertainers danced and sang, farmers and planters conducted private business, and friends and neighbors gossiped. Political parties and temperance or Bible societies frequently scheduled their annual meetings during court week. Agricultural societies held their annual fairs. Newspapers discussed court cases, announced decisions, and reported legal gossip. Local business improved when court was in session. William Johnson—a barber, businessman, and leader of the free black community in Natchez—noted in his diary that business was especially brisk during the November 1850 court session because a "Greate many Persons are in town."[15] Even those not directly involved in hearings or summoned for trials frequently turned up at court to bring testimony, offer information, or simply observe. Court week transformed sleepy, rural communities and drew diverse crowds from dispersed sections of the county—crowds that included free and enslaved people of color.[16]

Both as observers and participants, free blacks and slaves had frequent and direct contact with local legal processes, giving them ample opportunity to learn to speak the language of law. Some attended monthly county courts, watched hearings and inquests, and testified in court proceedings in cases involving other people of color.[17] Others served as carriage drivers for masters with court business and labored as marketers and hired hands when court was in session. Black people crowded the courthouse during court week—as defendants in criminal actions; as litigants in lawsuits to protect their property, determine their personal status, and enforce their contracts; and as witnesses in trials involving other people of color. Slaves appeared in court as fugitives, damaged or stolen goods, criminals to be punished, and as victims of abuse. They were objects of theft, concubines in lawsuits for divorce, and property seized to settle debts. Free blacks registered their free papers and recorded their marriages, probated their wills, manumitted family members, mortgaged their property, and sued whites and other people of color for a wide range of misdeeds. From the vantage point of the courthouse steps, African Americans observed, participated in, and gossiped about a considerable amount of legal action.

Much of the southern courts' more technical legal business concerned people of color. In Adams County, Mississippi, for example, at least half of the circuit court trials involved the commercial law of slavery.[18] Inside the courthouse, white southerners quarreled over outstanding debts for slave hires or sales; fought over "damaged," sick, or unruly slaves; and assigned responsibility for slave patrols or blame for failed partnerships. They rewarded slave catchers, disciplined runaways, penalized poor whites and free blacks who sold slaves liquor or bought goods from slaves, punished insurrectionists, and ordered the execution of slaves found guilty of capital crimes. Whites used the courts to convey the land on which slaves labored and the plantations and farms where they lived. They manumitted loyal servants, probated wills involving slave property, and sought damages for injured laborers. Slaves, then, occupied a significant portion of the court's time.

Not all technical legal business was conducted in the courthouse. Often magistrates heard complaints, conducted inquests, and held trials in taverns, fields, country stores, and other places that could accommodate large groups. As one scholar points out, "these locations pushed law physically into the community and into the lives of the people there."[19] Courts met where community members of all sorts commonly gathered.

But the kinds of legal maneuvers black men and women employed in the courtroom, and the narratives they chose to tell, stemmed as well from lessons learned in their own communities. The experiences of those around them—their families, neighbors, and fellow free blacks or slaves—also provided people of color with the vocabulary to tell legal stories. They talked to one another, told stories, and listened to the tales of others, discovering the tactics that worked and those that did not.[20] This was the kind of information sharing that Lavinia Miller, a free black woman from Louisiana, engaged in when she wrote her aunt about a family acquaintance who circumvented the laws that prohibited blacks from marrying whites. Miller herself had heard rumors of a French priest who would marry interracial couples, despite the illegality of such marriages.[21] Sharing their experiences with the legal system also provided African Americans a way of teaching and learning legal words of the more technical sort, such as when William Johnson assisted several of his free black apprentices to petition to remain in the state of Mississippi. He provided them with the legal language that would most benefit them and secured the necessary pledges of support from local whites.[22]

Slave communities served as a source of information and facilitated lines of communication. Former slaves consistently described their interactions with the legal system and their understandings of the law—information they shared with one another.[23] For instance, Jim Allen, an ex-slave from Mississippi, grieved with his fellow slaves over the injustice of a law that permitted his master to trade him to settle a whiskey debt.[24] As the narratives of ex-slaves demonstrate, many enslaved people were keenly attuned to the law. They discussed the deaths of owners and heirs' legal contests over wills, sympathetic attorneys and judges, disputes over manumissions, courtroom policies, legal gossip about town, and the laws governing their lives. They collected information about criminal trials, the executions of convicted slaves, the reach of slave patrols, and court-ordered whippings and punishments.[25] Enslaved Mississippians in the immediate Natchez area, for instance, probably discussed attorney William B. Griffith's reputation for aiding slaves in their lawsuits for freedom. Griffith was well known among African Americans in Natchez; he represented dozens of free black and enslaved litigants, and nearly all of these cases were successful. Those who had experiences with him, those who had learned a bit about the law from watching him and interacting with him, and those who had heard stories about him brought that information back to the neighborhood.[26]

Sometimes slaves even held trials of their own—trials that looked remarkably similar to those in nearby courthouses. For instance, J. Vance Lewis, a slave from Louisiana who became an attorney after the Civil War, claimed that his interest in the law began after watching his enslaved father, Doc Lewis, serve as a judge for a trial on the plantation. In a case of a stolen hog, the overseer appointed Doc Lewis the judge, and Lewis selected a jury of slaves and summoned witnesses. The site of the trial even resembled the physical arrangement of trials held in the courthouse, with the judge sitting apart from the litigants and spectators. Witnesses provided the slave court with "vague and varied" evidence, but the judge weighed the testimony from all sides carefully, intervening with questions of his own. In the end, with the guidance of the judge, the jury found the defendant not guilty. The plantation owner later declared Doc Lewis "a born lawyer," a remark that greatly pleased him as it implied a talent for the law and a sense of fairness and justice. This compliment and his father's pleasure in it planted the seeds for J. Vance Lewis's future career as an attorney and advocate for other people of color. He wrote the following about the praise his father received: "I did

Trial of Rev. Benjamin. Enslaved people had many opportunities to learn about
the workings of the law and the legal system. Some held trials of their own.
Courtesy of the Wilson Library, University of North Carolina at Chapel Hill.

not then know just what that meant, but I knew it was something big and
something good from the way Colonel Cage put it and the gracious manner
in which my father received it. So that a short time after this when the white
boys were all talking about what they were going to be, I announced that I
was going to be a lawyer. It sounded funny and they laughed at the thought
of Joe becoming a lawyer. But I had been their page boy and had learned
much from them that they had learned at school, and I did not see why I
should not be able some day to apply what I had learned as well as they."[27]
Lewis began his legal education much the same way he learned to read and
write and much the same way antebellum lawyers learned to practice law—
by observing. After emancipation, Lewis went on to study law at three different institutions and enjoyed a long career as an attorney in Michigan,
Illinois, and Texas.[28]

Attorneys also provided African Americans with opportunities to expand their legal vocabularies. Lawyers like William B. Griffith probably supplied black litigants with modes of legal reasoning and litigation strategies.
They certainly helped black petitioners navigate the legal process. Once in the
courtroom, black people listened to lawyers dispute, clarify, and interpret the

Law Office of J. Vance Lewis. In the years after the Civil War, Lewis formally studied law and eventually practiced in three states. Courtesy of the Wilson Library, University of North Carolina at Chapel Hill.

law. Yet while legal professionals provided some of the formulas, arguments, and stock phrases—as well as advice about how to shape a story—black litigants relayed highly individualized tales in their petitions. Although attorneys were coproducers of these petitions, the stories black litigants weaved in court were their own, told from their perspectives, drawn from their experiences and genealogies, and animated by their ideas of justice. Black litigants may have received help from their lawyers, but as we shall see below, they were the primary authors of their tales.[29]

Authorship, of course, should not be confused with authenticity or truth. Legal narrative, similarly, is not infinitely malleable. Genre and form condition what is sayable. The particular remedy one seeks (such as debt recovery or damages) also influences (and sometimes limits) what one can say in court. What is sayable in court at any given historical juncture, moreover, shapes what narratives a particular person can tell. In other words, there are boundaries to what can be said in court, when a person can say it, and who can speak. Courtroom language is also performed and performed according to rules. Nevertheless, within these boundaries, a lot of space for maneuver exists. Genre enables composition as much as it constrains it.

THREE STORIES

For much of the early 1840s, Pierre Salvador struggled to evict a squatter on his land in Pointe Coupee Parish, Louisiana. With the backing of the Preemption Act of 1841, Salvador, a free black man, had settled on 183 acres along the banks of the False River in Louisiana.[30] The preemption law allowed citizens of the United States above the age of twenty-one to purchase public land at a reduced rate.[31] Before registering a claim, applicants needed to reside on that land, improve it, and build a dwelling on it. To comply with the Preemption Act, Salvador had invested his time and labor by clearing and improving the land and building a small house on it. He then sent Thomas Cooley, his lawyer and representative, to New Orleans to register his claim with the land office there and purchase the lot officially. Cooley arrived too late, however, as one John C. Turner, a white man, had recently made a claim on the same lot and paid the purchase price. At Salvador's request, Cooley asked the land office to make an official inquiry into Turner's claim and declare it null and void. According to the preemption law, when two or more people made a claim on the same land, the right of preemption went to the individual who made the first settlement.[32] Salvador insisted that he had resided on the land first and improved it. Turner had arrived later, Salvador claimed, cleared only a few trees to sell as cordwood to passing steamboats, and moved into a preexisting structure. Turner, then, did not meet the established criteria to make a preemption claim. The land offices in New Orleans and in Washington, D.C., investigated the competing claims and found Turner's purchase of the land "illegal and improperly allowed." The United States Treasury office refunded Turner's money and annulled his claim. In addition, Salvador received a patent issued by the U.S. government and signed by President John Tyler for the land in question.

Despite the federal government's decision in this case, Turner remained on Salvador's property, insisting it belonged to him. He continued to fell trees to sell for timber. On March 13, 1844, Salvador filed suit against him in the local court in Pointe Coupee Parish. Salvador's petition was astutely worded. He and his attorney left nothing to chance; Salvador was careful to show that he had taken every precaution, improved the land as the preemption law demanded, and followed the procedures for registering his claim precisely. Salvador also filed two amended petitions to provide the court with additional details about his compliance with the preemption law. In these petitions, he contended that he had taken "all the necessary and legal means before the commissioners to prove his settlement and improvements and to establish his rights as the preemptioner to the premises." He was "the rightful owner" of the land. Indeed, "by virtue of the act of Congress in 1841, granting preemption rights to settlers on public land," Salvador declared, "the title to the land vested in your petitioner." However, Turner "illegally and without rights" settled on his land and filed a preemption claim with the land office in New Orleans "through illegal and fraudulent means." The "commissioner at the general land office at Washington" had recently "decided" that Salvador "had the only right of preemption on said land." Notwithstanding Salvador's "rights to the property, Turner persists in using the premises without any regard to [Salvador's] title." He repeatedly asked Turner "to leave the premises, but in vain." He wanted Turner evicted and his claim declared "unfounded" by the court, just as it had been by the U.S. government. Moreover, he requested that the sheriff take possession of the land throughout the duration of the lawsuit to keep Turner from "wasting the property." He also asked for $500 in damages and then signed the petition with an "X." In response to Salvador's petition, the court ordered a sequestration of the land in dispute (and the timber cut from that land) "until further order of this court" and set a trial date.

While Salvador mobilized the rhetoric of property rights in his petition, Turner made race the central premise of his claim to the land. Turner did not deny that Salvador had settled on and improved the land first. But Salvador had no right of preemption to this land or any other, Turner argued, because he was a black man and thus not a citizen of the United States. He requested that the court cancel Salvador's preemption claim and declare Turner the rightful owner of the land in question. Salvador, Turner argued, simply did not "have the necessary legal qualifications" required to receive a title to the lot. Because he was a man of color and not a U.S. citizen, "any patent issued" to Salvador "is null and void."

Salvador, on the other hand, neither framed his lawsuit in the language of race, nor did he cast the legal question at hand as one of race. While Turner, somewhat shrilly, insisted repeatedly that Salvador's claim was "null and void" because he was black and thus not a citizen, Salvador ignored the issue of race completely. Except in his greeting to the court at the beginning of his petition (in which he gave his name and his status as a free man of color), he never addressed it, and neither did his attorney, the witnesses who testified before the court in Pointe Coupee Parish, or the U.S. government (although his race was no secret). Instead, Salvador focused on showing the court in meticulous detail that because he complied with all the requirements of the Preemption Act of 1841, he had first claim to the land.

Turner was technically correct that the federal government granted the right to preemption to citizens of the United States only. Section 10 of the act stated that only the "head of a family, or widow, or single man, over the age of twenty-one years, and being a *citizen* of the United States, or having filed his declaration of intention to become a citizen, as required by the naturalization laws" could claim a preemption.[33] In Turner's mind, however, only whites could be citizens; black people were not fit for citizenship.

Turner was not alone in his position. The question of black citizenship played out on the national stage as those on both sides of the debate (those who argued that black people were not citizens and those who pushed for broader civic inclusion for African Americans) disputed both *who* could be a citizen and *what* rights citizenship bestowed. Many whites in both the South and the North questioned African Americans' capacity for citizenship. Southerners, like Turner, argued that people of African descent were a race suited only for enslavement and were thus not up to the responsibilities of freedom, let alone citizenship and political membership. Membership in the polity belonged to whites only. But other, more sympathetic northerners also linked whiteness to civic inclusion: even white abolitionists questioned African Americans' suitability for citizenship. Some wondered if slavery inflicted irreparable damage on the enslaved, such that living up to the responsibilities of citizenship—and embodying the virtuous, independent, public disposition of citizens—would be impossible.[34] Others, like the white abolitionist and minister, Theodore Parker, suspected that because the millions of southern slaves did not rise up in revolt against their oppressors (as the American colonists had done against the British), black people lacked the revolutionary spirit inherent in American citizenship: "Africans," Parker argued, "fail to perform the natural duty of securing freedom by killing their oppressors."[35] In this instance, however, the U.S. government implicitly disagreed and allowed a black man some of the privileges of citizenship when it granted Salvador the preemption in Pointe Coupee Parish, a privilege formalized in a patent signed by the president of the United States (a patent Salvador submitted to the court as evidence).

Just as the land offices in New Orleans and Washington had done before it, the court in Pointe Coupee Parish investigated the competing preemption claims made by the two men and summoned the testimony of witnesses—all white men. The witnesses did not engage Turner in a conversation about black citizenship. Instead, like Salvador, they focused entirely on who had settled on and improved the land first. Several men testified that while Turner had in fact resided on the land, he had not built a dwelling of his own or improved the land in any substantial way. What is more, they claimed, Salvador arrived on the land before Turner. For instance, Hypolite Decour, a neighbor who had once employed Turner, asserted that Turner did not build anything and resided in a preexisting blacksmith's cabin. Further, Turner had taken up residence in that cabin for only a few short days before traveling to New Orleans to register a claim. John Swain, another neighbor, testified that after Salvador had built the first "dwelling house" on the property, he often saw him "on the land gathering blackberries." Turner, on the other hand, neither cleared nor improved the land. Salvador, according to the witnesses, was the rightful preemptioner.

The narrative that Salvador presented in his petition reflected an understanding of himself as a property owner with a valid claim to federal land, land reserved for citizens. Thus, he implicitly rejected any race-based idea of citizenship. Rather than ask the court to assess whether or not a black man could be a citizen of the United States, Salvador and his attorney compelled the court to address a different legal question. This question involved property rights: which of the two men had a claim to the lot first? In his telling, in a story substantiated by witnesses from Pointe Coupee Parish and confirmed by the General Land Office in Washington, Salvador had first claim. It was with this question in mind that the court made its ruling. Salvador, then, succeeded in framing the debate and the official narrative as one involving property rather than race.

But even if he had addressed the question of his citizenship, Salvador might have been on firm ground—or at least firmer ground than Turner would want the court to believe. Citizenship did not become a constitutional status until the ratification of the Fourteenth Amendment in 1868. Furthermore, the citizenship of free blacks—both at the federal and state levels—before the famous *Dred Scott* decision was ambiguous.[36] The federal Constitution never defined citizenship or clarified who constituted "We the People." It left the issue of racial exclusions to national citizenship open. What rights citizenship bestowed also remained unclear, as the Constitution merely stated that "the citizens of each state shall be entitled to all privileges and immunities of citizens in the several states."[37] It did not, however, define "privileges and immunities." The 1790 Naturalization Act limited citizenship to free white persons, but it only addressed the citizenship of new immigrants seeking naturalization. It did not adequately address the status of native-born black Americans. State-level jurisprudence on citizenship was equally abstruse, especially when it came to the rights of free people of color, and the problems raised by comity further complicated things.[38] Even for white men in the South, citizenship was uneven as impediments to voting and political participation persisted, and as southern elites continued to dominate the political system well after the implementation of universal white manhood suffrage.[39]

In this space of legal uncertainty, some African-descended people took advantage of such ambiguities to press for civic inclusion. In the years after the framing of the Constitution, free people of color throughout the new nation advocated for the rights and privileges of citizenship and "to give that word a fullness of meaning."[40] Moreover, although they could not vote or hold office, free blacks in Louisiana and Mississippi had long exercised the ability to hold property, to contract, to travel out of the state, and to sue and be sued. These rights were paired with obligations, and while free black people could not serve on a jury, they were liable to pay taxes and some bore arms. For instance, members of the Belly family, a large and prosperous free family of color living in Iberville Parish, took up arms alongside whites as part of the Eighth Regiment during the War of 1812.[41] They traveled to locations up and down the Mississippi River and to France and were party to dozens of lawsuits. They used the courts with regularity to protect and convey their property, to enforce the terms of their contracts, and to adjudicate a number of other disputes.[42] In other words, free people of African descent were not uniformly excluded from the exercise of rights associated with citizenship— even in the Deep South—because the questions of who could be a citizen and what rights citizenship protected were moving targets.

Both Salvador and Turner presented narratives about citizenship. Both used legal language to support that story, and each made a claim about who was deserving and why. They also fought over who could frame the issue. Theirs was a debate over property, certainly, but it was also one over membership. At work in both narratives was a series of competing understandings about who could be seen at law as someone who counts such that he could make a claim. Both were potentially persuasive to their audiences. Yet only Turner declared that Salvador's race barred him from citizenship. Salvador, his lawyer, the witnesses, the land offices in Louisiana and Washington, D.C., and the judge in Pointe Coupee Parish all indicated that Salvador had access to at least some of the rights of citizens.

Salvador used the narrative he presented in court to affirm his relationship to the nation, as well his place in it. In his telling, he was not a black man biologically suited to slavery. His race did not bar him from civic inclusion, as Turner would have the court believe. Instead, he had rights to property and thus claims to preemption and access to citizenship. At crucial moments in Washington, New Orleans, and Pointe Coupee Parish, this narrative proved the most persuasive.

Salvador's narrative was also implicitly linked to another one: that of American progress and westward expansion. His story thus placed him at the forefront of issues central to American identity in the mid-nineteenth century. Salvador registered his preemption claim at a crucial moment in the history of the movement west, and John Tyler, the president who authorized the patent for the land, was aligned with a political agenda of territorial expansion. In the first half of the nineteenth century, the United States nearly tripled in size. Migrants pressed into this new territory, bringing with them their notions of a moral obligation to spread American democracy and progress, and, in the case of those settling the new slave states of Alabama, Mississippi, Louisiana, Tennessee, Arkansas, Kentucky, Missouri, and Texas, they also brought their slaves. Salvador capitalized on opportunities presented by American expansion. By the mid-1840s, the Old Southwest was fast becoming an empire for slavery, an empire built with and by enslaved people of African descent on land forcibly taken from Native Americans. But for Salvador (and many others) the westward impulse could bring a promising future. Salvador's tale, then, resided at the center of the narrative of American expansion, a narrative that he complicated; the patent signed by John Tyler was a symbol of his relationship to that story.

Salvador was neither an outsider to the tale of American progress and growth nor an object on which that story was based. Rather, he was a participant in that narrative. By accepting his preemption claim, the U.S. government and the local court in Louisiana consented to Salvador's interpretation.

In the courtroom, the judge in Pointe Coupee Parish, H. F. Deblieux, had listened to the testimony of the witnesses, scrutinized the patent signed by President Tyler granting Salvador the land, and examined the arguments and evidence presented by all parties. After thorough consideration and in a lengthy final judgment dated November 20, 1845, the court decided that it would not "disturb the decision" of the U.S. government. Finding that Turner had not complied with the law, it canceled his claim and declared him a "trespasser." Deblieux also had something to say about the citizenship of free blacks: it was not up to his court to "interfere" in or act on the question of citizenship, the judgment stated. And even if the court at Pointe Coupee "could be called upon to decide whether a free person of color is a citizen of the United States, one would find the preponderance of authorities is in the favor of the plaintiff." The right of preemption went to Salvador, a free black man.[43]

Salvador's deft storytelling and his success in framing the debate to reflect his version of the tale underscores his ability to navigate the world in which he lived and to exploit the contradictions within white southerners' dominant ideologies. On the one hand, whites wanted to uphold white supremacy, but, on the other hand, they valued private property. Of course, for slave owners, private property, slavery, and liberty were necessarily linked. Slaveholders defended slavery through the language of property rights. These links between slavery and property, however, had their inconsistencies. The witnesses in Salvador's case and the judge knew well the importance of private property and the role of the courts in protecting it. A number of them, including the judge, had filed their own preemption claims to public land.[44] The court could have sided with Turner. But the protection of property from usurpers and squatters proved more important than denying a black man's claim solely on the basis of race. When left with the decision between treating Salvador as a citizen and safeguarding their property rights, they chose to secure their property rights.

Salvador's story of property ownership and civic inclusion was not unique, and neither was the court's acquiescence to his interpretation of the dispute. Indeed, the implications for the status and civil standing of African Americans raised in *Salvador v. Turner* take on additional significance when placed in conversation with other cases from this time period involving black litigants in the region. The stories other people of color told in court similarly expanded the boundaries of what was possible for African-descended people in a slave society. Not only did black litigants envision a social order in which a black man could be a citizen; they also, as Aaron Cooper's lawsuit indicates, depicted a world in which the enslaved might be free.

Aaron Cooper was born a free person of color on New Year's Day 1770 in Kent County, Delaware. His recently manumitted parents, Nanny and Richard Cooper (both Quakers), and those who watched him grow up noticed his natural abilities and intelligence, describing him as "a smart boy." Apprenticed at a young age to a miller in Dover, Cooper developed a trade, learned to read and write, and even "knew his figures." He married Hetty, a free woman of color from Philadelphia, who bore the couple seven freeborn children. The family settled in Kent County in Duck Creek Hundred (an unincorporated section of the county) near Cooper's parents. Once there, Cooper set himself up in business as a miller and, like other free men, received compensation for his work, paid his taxes, and raised his family. But late one night in May 1811, Perry

Wright, Levi Goit, and three or four other men abducted and sold him as a slave to Robert Martin, a "negro trader" from North Carolina who had come to the Eastern Shore with $10,000 to buy slaves. Martin took Cooper to Dixon's Tavern in Dorchester County, Maryland, where several witnesses heard Cooper proclaim his status as a free person. Before anyone could intervene on his behalf, Martin forced Cooper onto a ship in New Castle, Maryland, along with a number of other newly purchased bondspeople, and they set sail for Norfolk, Virginia. Martin then trafficked Cooper to Natchez, Mississippi, and sold him as a slave to Parmenas Briscoe, a local planter.

Once in Natchez, Cooper immediately protested his enslavement and sued Briscoe for his freedom in the Adams County Superior Court. The story Cooper presented to the court was simple. He was free. It was this fact, his freedom, which overshadowed all others. Cooper worded his petition for his freedom concisely and deliberately. Quite plainly, Cooper said, he was a free man, born thirty-five or forty years prior to free parents in Delaware. Thomas Hanson had liberated his parents before his birth, and they "supported themselves as free people ever thereafter." Cooper too lived as a free person "from the time of his birth until he was kidnapped, was always held, esteemed, and treated as a free person in his native state." He wanted the court to recognize this fact and restore his freedom.

On September 1, 1811, the Adams County Superior Court judge ordered that a commission be sent to Kent County, Delaware, to take the depositions of witnesses who might shed light on Cooper's alleged kidnapping and his personal status.[45] The commission authorized any justice of the peace in Delaware to record the testimony of said witnesses and detailed the questions to be asked (questions approved by both the plaintiff and the defendant). Some of the questions attempted to ensure that the court had the right man: Was the witness acquainted with Cooper, and if so, for how long? Did he have any identifiable marks on his body? Did he have a family? Others attempted to clarify Cooper's personal status: Was he a free man? Was he liable to pay taxes? Still others attempted to sort out the kidnapping. Tellingly, these questions adopted details from Cooper's narrative: "Have you any knowledge of the plaintiff being kidnapped from his family sometime in the fall or winter of 1810 by several persons and carried into the State of Maryland and from there transported by a certain Robert Martin to the Mississippi Territory?" Five Delaware men acquainted with Cooper and the circumstances of his kidnapping testified before Jonathan Lowber, a Kent County justice of the peace, and their testimony would be read in open court in Mississippi during the upcoming trial.

Briscoe conducted a similar inquiry of his own. Five days after Cooper sued Briscoe for his freedom, Briscoe sent a series of letters to residents of Kent County, Delaware. In those letters he expressed concern that Martin had perhaps sold him a free man. He described Cooper physically, named his parents, and requested information about Cooper's personal status. He wanted "justice," he wrote, for himself and for "the negroe."

The witnesses from Delaware corroborated Cooper's story and told a tale of viciousness and wrongdoing. Under the cover of darkness, they testified, several armed men had forced themselves into Cooper's home, attacked him, tied him up, and carried him away. In the aftermath of Cooper's brutal beating and abduction, several white Quakers well acquainted with Cooper and his father (also a Quaker) had reassured his wife and children and went immediately in pursuit of his captors. They followed the kidnappers to Dixon's Tavern, where they heard Cooper had been taken. Members of Dixon's family described Cooper to his pursuers and claimed that Martin (who had just purchased Cooper) intended to set sail for Virginia with Cooper as his slave. In addition, they had heard Cooper insist that he was a free man. Cooper's rescue party then spread out. Some went in search of the local sheriff to obtain an arrest warrant for Martin, while others went to intercept the boat. They were one day too late, however. The vessel had set sail with Cooper on it, and they lost all track of him thereafter.

The swiftness with which Cooper appeared in court and the support he obtained speaks to the persuasiveness of his story. Within three months of arriving in Natchez enslaved, penniless, and without friends, Cooper had convinced a prominent lawyer, William B. Shields, to represent him, sued his owner, and induced Briscoe to voice misgivings about the details of his purchase. This was unusual. Attaining freedom could take years, and some kidnapped people never recouped their liberty at all. Solomon Northup's twelve-year struggle for freedom underscores the difficulties kidnapped people faced when attempting to regain their liberty. After being drugged and abducted in Washington, D.C., by two con artists who sold him into slavery, Northup, a free black man, was eventually sold at auction in New Orleans. He spent several years enslaved in Louisiana, seeking every opportunity to attain his freedom, but without success. After failed attempts to send letters home to notify his family about his condition and location, Northup eventually gained the assistance of a white carpenter, a certain Mr. Bass. After learning of Northup's predicament, Bass agreed to mail letters on Northup's behalf, despite the risk such an act posed to both his and Northup's safety. Sending clandestine letters home with details of his whereabouts triggered an extended struggle for his release. After finally regaining his freedom, Northup filed kidnapping charges against his abductors. The charges were later dropped, and Northup never received compensation for the twelve years he spent as a Louisiana slave.[46] For kidnapped people of color, attaining legal freedom was an arduous process. It is remarkable that the legal system mobilized so quickly to investigate Cooper's claim.

It is also noteworthy that Cooper's tale of freedom—a story of a kidnapping—provoked so many to come to his aid and convinced a jury to rule in his favor. Kidnapping was not unusual, and some did not consider it immoral. Whites in the Deep South frequently bought and sold kidnapped people of color. The local legal record in the Natchez district is rife with instances of free blacks claiming that they had been kidnapped and sold into slavery. For instance, in 1817, Elias, a black man from Pennsylvania, successfully sued George Bell for his freedom in the Adams County Circuit Court, insisting that he had been kidnapped from Pennsylvania, brought to Natchez, and sold as a slave.[47] With the opening of new territory, the expansion of cotton production, and the growth of an internal slave trade, more than a million enslaved people were transported from the eastern seaboard to the new states of the Deep South. By the time Cooper sued Briscoe for his freedom in 1811, plantation slavery was well established in the region and already generating an incessant hunger for slaves.[48] The trade in human property to the southern interior encouraged the kidnapping of free blacks. The potential windfall returns afforded by selling free people into slavery made their abduction financially attractive.[49]

On the strength of his story, Cooper secured the support of his lawyer, persuaded the court to send a commission to Delaware to obtain witness testimony, rallied the witnesses to substantiate his tale, and convinced a jury of local white freeholders to eventually find him a free man. Cooper's story of freedom, kidnapping, and injustice also forced Briscoe to initially concede that he might have bought a free person. While Briscoe certainly wanted to recoup his losses from Martin for selling him a free man, he also claimed to be seeking justice for Cooper. He had to find a way, even grudgingly, to define losing his property as a species of justice.

It was Cooper's story, however, that framed the terms of the debate. Of course, what Cooper could say in court—and the kind of story he could tell—was constrained by rules and conditioned by the legal remedies available to him. Yet his narrative shaped the interrogatories the witnesses answered under oath. Submitting questions that included specific details of the kidnapping forced witnesses to respond directly to his version of the story—an account they verified. Witnesses answered his questions, culled from his experiences, and corroborated his narrative. Questions that provided the date of his kidnapping, the name of one of his kidnappers, and the circumstances of his abduction sketched a template for the witnesses to complete. Every person who provided the court with testimony used Cooper's template. Even Briscoe approved of the interrogatory and did not offer questions of his own to discredit Cooper's narrative. His own investigation also closely followed the details of Cooper's story.

Moreover, Cooper told a story that the listeners in the courtroom would recognize, and he expanded it to include his perspective. Both he and the witnesses whose testimony was read in court during the trial provided considerable context for his tale of freedom. It is possible that this backdrop compelled the judge, jury, and audience in the courtroom to imagine Cooper's life as a free man. Indeed, he had a family—a free wife, seven freeborn children, and a father with extensive ties to the white Quaker community in the Delaware Valley, a community that valued his membership enough to try to rescue him.[50] His work as a miller meant that he collected wages for his labor, paid taxes, and developed connections to and networks within a broader market economy. He traveled between Delaware and Pennsylvania developing his craft. He eventually settled near his place of birth so that he could be close to his parents and set up a household of his own. He lived in a comfortable home. As a good neighbor, he helped others fell trees, build fences and outbuildings, and clear land. He worshipped, sometimes in his father's home and sometimes with the larger community. He sought to better himself and learned to read and write. He could even perform some rudimentary accounting. His story was that of a free man on the rise with a household to support.

His story was compelling to his audience because they recognized it. He told a tale that evoked familiar, normative realities. The white men in the courtroom—in the judge's robes, in the jury box, on the witness stand, and in the gallery—heard a narrative about a free householder expanding his livelihood and supporting his family. Cooper (aided by the witness testimony) thus situated himself in that familiar story. Cooper's tale, then, described a life of freedom, not of enslavement. Of course, for people of African descent like Cooper, the boundary between slavery and freedom was precarious. He resided in a world in which a free black man could become a slave in an instant. With his story, however, he depicted a world in which a man of color could be, in the words of the jury, "a free man and not a slave."

Cooper's story also incited one of his kidnappers, Robert Martin, to respond and defend his actions. Other narratives emerged from this lawsuit as well—narratives that provide us with a rare glimpse into how the lawsuits of and stories told by black litigants affected white southerners. In particular, Cooper's lawsuit for his freedom offers insight into his kidnapper's carefully crafted public image and demonstrates the ways his tale caused at least one of the players to account for his participation and distance himself (at least rhetorically) from the dirty business of slave trading.

The trial transcript includes a letter from Robert Martin, the "negro trader" who bought Cooper in Delaware and sold him as a slave in Natchez. Martin addressed his letter, dated January 7, 1812, to Jonathan Hann (one of the Delaware men who testified on Cooper's behalf). Martin wrote to Hann after Briscoe sent letters to Delaware asking about Cooper's status as a potential free person. In his reply to Briscoe, Hann detailed Cooper's abduction and named Martin the kidnapper. Martin heard of these accusations and sent a response to Hann. His tone in this letter is indignant.

Martin began by accusing Hann of treating him "with the greatest injustice" for implicating him in the kidnapping. Hann in his "heart" must know that "scoundrels" in his community committed the crime, as he, Robert Martin, was no abductor of free people. Was Hann an abolitionist, Martin wondered. Did Hann "believe that every person who buys slaves [are] the 'monsters' you mentioned, all kidnappers, all rogues?" Martin continued, "Yours was the first foul breath or pen that ever dared to associate my name with those characters." His acquaintances far and wide would agree. Martin also relayed his version of the circumstances of Cooper's sale (a sale that occurred in the middle of the night). His purchase of Cooper, he declared, was a "fair deal." In addition, when he balked at the high price Wright and the others wanted for Cooper and nearly walked away from the sale, Cooper, Martin wrote, begged him to buy him, insisting that his current master "was very hard." He questioned Cooper carefully, and at no time did Cooper claim to be free. Martin ended the letter by again accusing Hann of committing a terrible wrong against him, and he placed the blame for any wrongdoing elsewhere.

In this letter, Martin revealed much about how he presented himself publicly and how Cooper's story of kidnapping affected that image. When discussing himself as a slaveholder, Martin mobilized the language of paternalism and aligned himself with developing ideas about slavery as a "positive good." Slavery, in this view, was a relationship of family. Slave owners were benevolent fathers to their black "families" and provided necessary guidance to their enslaved "children." People of African descent, some defenders of slavery claimed, were a distinct race suited only for enslavement, because slavery offered them the direction and discipline they otherwise lacked. Slavery civilized people of color, who were not suited for the responsibilities of freedom, and kept them from descending into the savagery and debasement to which they were biologically inclined. In exchange for this guidance, the enslaved provided their obedience and labor. Martin bought Cooper to protect him from his "hard master." He promised Cooper that he would care for him well. To accuse him of anything less was despicable and an affront to his reputation and self-image.

Martin also revealed his apprehensions about the ugliness of trading in human beings. By presenting himself as a benevolent father, Martin carefully distanced himself from narratives about "negro traders." The slave trader enjoyed a sordid reputation in southern society as a dishonest and lecherous drunk who made it his business to separate families. Motivated solely by money, slave speculators were traders in diseased bodies, dealers in disorderly and criminal slaves, abductors of free people, and were generally deceitful and brutal. Unlike "those [other] characters," he was no "scoundrel," Martin insisted. Portraying the slave trader as an outcast or a "monster" served a particular purpose for Martin, however. By stigmatizing the slave trader, southern slaveholders like Martin created a figurative distance between themselves and those individuals who made it their business to deal in human beings as property.[51] With these stereotypes, slave owners in effect separated the institution of slavery from the marketplace. They conveniently ignored their own culpability in the development of the internal slave trade and insulated themselves from responsibility for the more unsavory aspects of buying and selling human beings. Yet such representations of the debauched slave speculator were myths of convenience. In reality, slave traders, like other successful business people, were often leaders of their communities.[52]

Cooper's story of kidnapping challenged the image of the paternalistic slaveholder and forced Martin to respond to his accusations. His story compelled Martin not only to account for his actions but also to defend his character. Like Cooper's petition for freedom, Martin's response was well crafted and expertly tailored. In this rhetorical performance, Martin deliberately created a moral distance between himself and the sordidness and hypocrisy of owning human beings. He was a benevolent father. The alternative—a scoundrel—was contemptible.

Cooper's narrative, however, proved more compelling. On the second Monday in April 1814, Cooper and Briscoe appeared before the Adams County Superior Court alongside their attorneys. Despite his earlier, privately expressed concern that Cooper could be a victim of kidnapping and without comment on the testimony presented on behalf of the plaintiff,

Briscoe insisted that Cooper was a slave and thus not entitled to his freedom. It is unclear why Briscoe reversed his position; it is possible, however, that he did not get compensation from Martin for buying a free person, and this lawsuit represented a potential loss of valuable property. After hearing the evidence, the jury issued the following verdict: "We the Jury find the plaintiff a free man and not a slave." They ordered Briscoe to pay the court costs ($33) and an unspecified amount in damages to Cooper.[53] Three years after Martin, Perry, and their accomplices had smuggled him out of Delaware to Mississippi, Cooper was free once again, but the perpetrators never seem to have faced charges.[54] After his release, Cooper returned to Delaware, reunited with his family, resumed his position as the household head, began to engage in agriculture, and raised his children.[55]

Both Salvador and Cooper told stories about their place as men in the political community—as citizens and as free householders. Through these stories, they made claims to membership in the polity and to civic inclusion. A third and final story involves a woman and a divorce—a scandalous one at that. Although excluded from many formal political arenas because of both her sex and her race, Jane Davis, a free woman of color born in Philadelphia, used her lawsuit for a separation from her husband and a court-ordered division of their property to direct her own life. She did so by seizing privileges usually reserved for white women.

Some thirty years after Cooper sued for his freedom and a hundred miles to the south, in Opelousas, Louisiana, Davis sued her husband for a divorce. She had married William Edmonds (a free man of color) in Philadelphia (where she lived nearly all her life) on June 19, 1835, and a few years later the couple relocated to Edmonds's hometown of New Orleans.[56] They lived together happily for a number of years, Davis stated in her petition for divorce, eventually settling in Louisiana, where they accumulated more than $5,000 in land and other property. She claimed she treated him kindly and served him obediently. But by the mid-1840s, their marriage had broken apart. Edmonds abandoned Davis for the "embraces" of another woman, she asserted, publicly denied the legality of their marriage, and accused her of selling her body to sailors in both Philadelphia and New Orleans. Davis asked the district court in St. Landry Parish to force Edmonds to appear before it and answer for his wrongdoings and his lies. In addition, she wanted a separation from bed and board (a legal separation and the first step in getting a divorce in Louisiana) and spousal support for the remainder of her "natural life."

The plaintiff and the defendant offered competing stories. For his part, Edmonds dodged the issue of adultery and abandonment by asserting that Davis was a prostitute and a slanderer. In a move similar to the one made by the superior court in Natchez, the court in St. Landry Parish sent a commission to Philadelphia authorizing a justice of the peace to take the depositions of witnesses who knew the couple and could help the court sort through the incompatible claims. The interrogatory (questions the witnesses had to answer under oath) focused almost entirely on Davis's character. As the legal record in the Natchez district demonstrates, it was not unusual for witnesses to repeat gossip and offer character evidence, and judges and juries frequently made determinations based on the personal reputations of the litigants and opinions presented by witnesses.

In late October 1847, a Philadelphia justice of the peace and alderman, John B. Kenney, deposed nine witnesses (white and black), each of whom depicted Davis as an upright and virtuous woman, a characterization the court ultimately accepted. William Nanly claimed that he "considered Jane to be a woman of chastity, of good repute, faithful to her husband and a good mother to her children." He knew her as "the wife of Edmonds." Mary Russell said that Davis was "a respectable, honest, virtuous and industrious woman" who "kept respectable company and always resided with respectable people." James Bird swore that he knew "no blemish against her character. . . . She kept company with the best of our people. She never kept company with women of ill fame." Thomas Jordan claimed that Davis "was always a gal that kept decent company—went to Church on Sunday—and was never seen in the streets at night." Eliza Smith testified that she "was never acquainted with Jane by the name of Jane Davis," but instead was "acquainted with Jane Edmonds wife of William Edmonds free man of color." Margaret McClellan, a doctor's wife who had employed Davis's mother as her housekeeper for several years, said Davis "bore a good character for integrity and industry." Robert Johnson, a Philadelphia alderman and justice of the peace, claimed Davis had a "good character" and was never arrested or jailed for a crime.

By contrast, witness testimony for the defendant from four depositions taken in New Orleans in April of the same year described Davis as a different sort of woman: a slanderer jailed for her bitter tongue who stole from her landlord, bullied her husband, and welcomed men into her bedroom at night. For instance, Cheri Roquefort, an acquaintance of the defendant, testified that Davis was not a chaste woman. She spoke "suspiciously with several men" and only agreed to come to New Orleans with Edmonds so that she could swindle him out of his money and return with it to Philadelphia. Francis Banner claimed that Davis was a "common prostitute" in Philadelphia, and that he knew several men who had had a "carnal connection with her." Edward Jones, Davis's and Edmonds's landlord in New Orleans, revealed that $200 had gone missing while Davis lived in his home, and although he could not prove it and had never filed criminal charges, Jones felt certain Davis was the thief.

In response to her husband's accusations, Davis presented herself as a virtuous wife, and her depiction of such a figure was both deliberate and familiar. She employed a formula well known to aggrieved wives seeking separations from their husbands. The very nature of the divorce process in the nineteenth century required a demonstration of fault. To be successful, litigants had to exhibit proper spousal behavior in their tales of marital discord. They needed to reassure the court that they had performed the roles expected of them. The ideal wife was chaste, obedient to her husband, and devoted to her children and her household. The ideal husband provided for his dependents, used restraint rather than violence, managed the family finances with care, responsibly represented the household in all legal and political matters, and resisted temptations such as drink, infidelity, and gambling.[57] To establish herself as the injured party, a woman needed to show that her husband had violated his domestic role as patriarch or head of household in some vital way, while at the same time maintaining her innocence. Wives did so by mobilizing the narrative of the dutiful and virtuous wife. Emilie Brout's account of her marriage to Ursin Heno, for example, was typical. In her petition to the Louisiana court, Brout, a white woman, claimed that she had "always been a dutiful wife, attentive to her business and a good mother." Despite her obedience, she had experienced "on the part of her husband all kinds of vexations, excesses, cruel treatments, outrages, and defamations."[58] Similarly, Margaret Richards, another white woman, complained that although she had been a "kind faithful, prudent and affectionate wife," her husband had "treated her in a cruel, outrageous, dishonorable and inhuman manner."[59] Ann Mather Bienville, a free woman of color, used the same language in her lawsuit for a legal separation from her husband. In her petition to the East Baton Rouge, Louisiana, district court for a separation from bed and board from her husband, St. Luke Bienville, she told the court that she had conducted herself as "a faithful dutiful and affectionate wife" and had gained the "good opinion of her friends and neighbors." She had cared for him devotedly and obediently, yet he treated her with cruelty, beating her and refusing to feed her or their four children. Despite her "patience & forbearance," living with St. Luke had become "impossible & insupportable," and Ann asked for and received a legal separation. St. Luke, then, bore sole responsibility for their marital disunity, while Ann established herself as faultless. St. Luke emerged from the narrative as the antithesis of a responsible and respectable head of household. He had failed to act as he should.[60]

While white women in the nineteenth century expertly used the formula for suing a husband for divorce, it is significant that women of color like Davis and Bienville, too, employed the trope of the virtuous wife when seeking a divorce. Definitions of femininity were intensely racialized in the antebellum South. While white womanhood emphasized domesticity, purity, and decorum, black womanhood represented debasement, hard labor, and sexual availability. Myths of black female promiscuity enjoyed an especially long history, dating back to Europeans' first contact with Africans when travelers to Africa mistook female nudity for lewdness and polygamy for uncontrolled lust. These were myths of convenience: Europeans invoked notions about African women's alleged lack of chastity and overt sexual desire as evidence of their savagery and the savagery—and enslavability—of Africans generally. In addition, many white southerners rationalized the rampant sexual abuse of black women with the conventional wisdom that women of color were naturally promiscuous and thus pursued physical relations with white men. Reflecting these stereotypes, southern laws only protected white women from rape; the rape of a black woman was deemed impossible.[61]

Davis, however, utilized her story to create an alternative definition of black female sexuality—one of purity and chastity.[62] She sought a divorce, certainly, but she also wanted the court to protect her reputation as a virtuous woman. Davis's petition focused far less on her husband's abandonment and adultery. Instead, Edmonds's "defaming and blackening" of her character troubled her most. By denying that he and Davis were ever "united in the bonds of Lawful wedlock" (denials he made in public no less), Edmonds implied that Davis was a fornicator and "of doubtful fame and chastity." Worse, he accused her of prostitution. She demanded that the court require Edmonds to appear before it and answer (also in public) for his lies. She was, as she claimed, "a dutiful and affectionate wife" who "performed faithfully" the qualities expected of a chaste woman. His aspersions jeopardized her reputation, and she would not tolerate them any longer.

To repair her reputation, however, Davis had to surmount stereotypes depicting women of color as innately hypersexual. The questions the court required witnesses to answer fixated almost entirely on Davis's alleged promiscuity. Attorneys for both Davis and Edmonds submitted these questions to the court, and the questions shared a similar preoccupation with Davis's character. None focused on Edmonds's character or crimes. What reputation did Davis have in her community, they asked. Was she known for her "chastity, integrity and general worth"? Was Davis a "common prostitute"? "Did she keep company with women of ill fame"? Had they ever heard "whispered" rumors questioning her "chastity"? Was she seen on the streets after dark? Had she been imprisoned for a crime? Yet the court also revealed its mistrust of Edmonds's witnesses—witnesses who described Davis as a lying, thieving whore. In the only question that did not focus on Davis's character and sexuality, the court asked several respectable citizens of Philadelphia to assess the veracity of two of Edmonds's witnesses (men who claimed to know Davis in Philadelphia). These Philadelphia natives asserted that Edmonds's witnesses had never set foot into the city and discredited their testimony by implying that they were liars. They also repeatedly described Davis as a virtuous woman. In the end, and with the help of people who had long known her (and whose testimony was read in open court), Davis depicted herself as a woman of irrefutable character and virtue.

Despite the images of black female hypersexuality typical of the era, Davis held herself to the same standards of womanhood as white women—at least rhetorically and for the purposes of her lawsuit. By using the court as a venue to safeguard her reputation as sexually honorable and to separate herself from Edmonds, Davis expressly rejected the white southern conventional wisdom that defined black women as biologically libidinous. Instead, she crafted an image of herself as a virtuous woman by nature and expected the court to uphold and protect that conception.

Narratives about race were not just tales that whites could use to defame black people. Rather, they were fluid rhetorical tropes potentially effective in black hands. In claiming that his wife was a prostitute, Edmonds deployed a familiar, racialized narrative about black women's sexuality. He exploited such notions of black female promiscuity to avoid responsibility for abandoning his wife and committing the crime of adultery. The tactic nearly worked. A black woman (married or otherwise) who sold her body to sailors was an image the court readily accepted—at least at first.

The final outcome is missing from the record, but a subsequent lawsuit indicates that Davis received her divorce. A year after filing her first lawsuit, she appeared in court again, this time suing Edmonds for a separation of property and a court-mandated division of the property they held in common (valued at about $5,000). In her petition, Davis referenced the divorce she received the year before. In his response to this lawsuit, Edmonds chose not to disparage her character and instead claimed (incorrectly) that because he resided in New Orleans, the court in St. Landry Parish did not have jurisdiction in the case.[63] But the court did indeed have jurisdiction and granted Davis a separation of property from Edmonds and ordered their property to be sold at auction and divided between them. Davis was finally fully separated from Edmonds. In the eyes of the court and before her community, Davis had defended her sexual honor and her reputation, eventually finding independence through divorce and property ownership.[64]

For people like Salvador, Cooper, and Davis, storytelling held a unique power. Stories told in court presented them with opportunities to link their experiences and perspectives to narratives about civic inclusion, freedom, and virtue, narratives that under other circumstances white southerners denied to black people. When black litigants told their stories, they became legal interpreters; they presented the court with narratives of their interpretations of the world around them and their place in it. It was these understandings that black litigants wanted the courts to recognize and reward.

But litigants could not go to court and just tell any story. Their narratives had to be recognizable to the other participants. They had to be plausible and fit into other narratives. These were stories that white southerners—the judges, juries, lawyers, witnesses, and audiences—had to be able to live with. So it is striking that Salvador, Cooper, and Davis depicted versions of themselves that would seem at odds with most white southerners' notions of the place of black people—as racialized and inferior others—in a slave society. Rather than crafting narratives rooted in or informed by their subordinate status, these three litigants presented themselves in ways that transcended or muted race. More important, Salvador, Cooper, and Davis used their narratives to expand the boundaries of the possible. They employed stories to lay claim to a competing normative order: a world in which a black man could be a citizen of the United States, a slave could be free, and a black woman could be virtuous. And ultimately, they persuaded the courts to recognize and accept these narratives.

Of course, Salvador's, Cooper's, Davis's stories did not convince everyone. The defendants chose to couch their counternarratives in the language of race. Although Turner did not comply with the Preemption Act of 1841, he used race to invalidate Salvador's right to preemption. He and his lawyer built on the claim that black people could not be citizens. Briscoe, despite his initial misgivings, appeared at the trial and claimed Cooper as his slave. Edmonds utilized stereotypes of black female hypersexuality to avoid responsibility for abandoning his wife for another woman. These counternarratives reflect attempts to restrict the prospects of black litigants. The defendants' focus on race and the subordination of people of African descent is unsurprising in a slave society in which people of color had limited rights and held an inferior position. The counternarratives advanced by Turner, Briscoe, and Edmonds were potentially persuasive, but the process of disputing at law also generated a context in which white judges, juries, and witnesses could credit the stories of their black opponents as plausible. Speaking through law—a shared language—created a space in which black litigants, legal officials, and even their adversaries could, in the words of Marianne Constable, "judge the world in common, or at least in common enough ways that they can speak with one another and live together and challenge one another's claims."[65] For African-descended people in the Natchez district, speaking in the register of law—and telling stories in a public courtroom—offered a means to craft a more tolerable world.

"A TYRANT'S LAW"

African Americans—enslaved and free—told countless stories that reflected their understandings of the role of law in black life. The tales they told, however, embodied a wide range of narrative arcs. For instance, the fact that Salvador, Cooper, and Davis pinned their hopes to the southern legal system might seem bewildering. The stories about the law that these three litigants (as well as hundreds of other black litigants from the Natchez district) weaved in their lawsuits—tales of a search for due process, access to justice, and confidence in the legal system—appear (at least at first glance) to differ substantially from many of the more familiar stories told in slave narratives. There, former slaves describe the draconian face of the law: southern laws turned people into property, authorized the sale of children and the separation of families, denied them civil and political rights, punished them harshly, and protected their enslavers.

Indeed, the narratives of ex-slaves (as well as their novels, speeches, and other writings) consistently demonstrate enslaved people's legal understandings of their status as chattel and the ways in which the law restrained them. As Jon-Christian Suggs points out in his study of law and narrative in African American life, the "place of law" in the narratives of slaves and ex-slaves was "totalizing."[66] Harriet Jacobs's tale in *Incidents in the Life of a Slave Girl*, for instance, is a "template for the centrality of law in the slave narrative."[67] Jacobs began her story with a declaration of her legal standing: "I was born a slave." The remainder of her opening paragraph describes a number of legalized obstacles faced by slaves: her father's failed attempts to purchase his children, her understanding of inheritance laws and slaves' unique vulnerability when an owner died, and the impossible position slave parents faced because they could not legally protect their children. Jacobs concludes her opening paragraph with a condemnation of the southern legal system and its unwillingness to provide slaves with the right to contract and hold and protect property: "The reader probably knows that no promise or writing given to a slave is legally binding; for, according to Southern laws, a slave, *being* property, can *hold* no property. When my grandmother lent her hard earnings to her mistress, she trusted solely to her honor. The honor of a slaveholder to a slave!"[68]

Similarly, William Wells Brown, a former slave and novelist, also addressed the injustice of the law in the world of a slave in his writing. His autobiography, *Narrative of the Life of William W. Brown, An American Slave*, included an appendix titled "Extracts from the American Slave Code." In this appendix Brown sought to provide a "view of the cruel oppression to which slaves are subject," ranging from enslaved people's inability to contract matrimony to the penalty for teaching a slave how to read. He began his list with an extract from Louisiana's *Civil Code*, which states: "A slave is one who is in the power of his master, to whom he belongs. The master may sell him, dispose of his person, his industry and his labor; he can do nothing, possess nothing, nor acquire anything but what must belong to his master."[69] In his later writings, Brown continued to address the law's "cruel oppression" of enslaved people. For instance, on the first page of his 1853 novel *Clotel; or, The President's Daughter*, Brown began by rebuking the brutality and inhumanity of the law of slavery: "In all the slave states, the law says—'Slaves shall be deemed, sold, taken, reputed, and adjudged in law to be chattels personal in the hands of their owners and possessors, and their executors, administrators and assigns, to all intents, constructions, and purposes whatsoever. . . . The slave is entirely subject to the will of his master, who may correct and chastise him, though not with unusual rigor, or so as to maim and mutilate him, or expose him to the danger of loss of life, or to cause his death. The slave, to remain a slave, must be sensible that there is no appeal from his master.' Where the slave is placed by law entirely under the control of the man who claims him, body and soul, as property, what else could be expected than the most depraved social condition?"[70]

In these narratives, the law emerges as a merciless taskmaster—as an institution created by slaveholders to enslave, control, punish, and dehumanize people of color. The hypocrisy of southern law is a pivotal theme in Jacobs's narrative and in Brown's novel, something each confirms repeatedly. Other former slaves, such as Harriet Jacobs's brother, John, stressed the perversity of laws that made people into property: "I cannot agree with that statesman who said, 'What the law makes property, is property.' What is law, but the will of the people—a mirror to reflect a nation's character? Robbery is robbery; it matters not whether it is done by one man or a million, whether they were organized or disorganized; the principle is the same. No law, unless there be one that can change my nature, can make property of me. Freedom is as natural for man as the air he breathes, and he who robs him of his freedom is also guilty of murder; for he has robbed him of his natural existence."[71] On this reading, southern law belonged to white slaveholders: it was created by white lawmakers, enforced by white sheriffs, and imposed by white judges and juries in all-white courtrooms. Black people could not benefit from it. As Harriet Jacobs lamented, "Pity me, and pardon me, O virtuous reader! You never knew what it is to be a slave; to be entirely unprotected by law or custom; to have the laws reduce you to the condition of a chattel, entirely subject to the will of another."[72] The southern courtroom, in the words of ex-slave Henry Bibb, was "an office of injustice" enforcing "a tyrant's law." [73]

The perspectives of Jacobs, Brown, and Bibb on the law of slavery derived from their own experience of the institution and their adamant insistence that the law should be transformed to render legalized enslavement impossible. As accounts of the relationship of law to the lives of black people, however, they necessarily remained incomplete. The stories of injustice—of the violence inflicted by law on people of color—that pervaded the writings of ex-slaves provide us with narratives about the ways law constrained people of African descent. Southern lawmakers had expended substantial effort in aiming to foreclose African American participation in the legal system. But the rhetorical power of these stories (stories that served as an important component of the abolitionists' movement to bring an end to slavery) obscured other interpretations about the role of law in black life. The draconian face of the law was but one of many narrative arcs. On the one hand, the law imposed the power of the state to enslave, imprison, and even execute people of color. Yet on the other, speaking through law could provide black litigants with a language through which to tell other kinds of stories.[74]

What is more, beginning in the 1830s, abolitionists used slave narratives (and other forms of print culture) to put "slavery on trial" in the court of public opinion. In widely circulated print culture, abolitionists consistently used the language of law and criminality to depict "the slavery debate as a vast, ongoing trial," trials that made slaveholders criminals, rendered the testimony of slaves and former slaves reliable, and found human bondage illegal.[75] In envisioning slave narratives metaphorically as trials, former slaves became firsthand witnesses to the criminality and cruelty of American slavery and their masters, the defendants. When Harriet Jacobs, William Wells Brown, and others became witnesses and slaveholders became defendants, they "provided a means to reconceptualize contemporary race relations in an alternative framework, one not based on black subjugation."[76] By appropriating the language of law and "striking the testimonial posture of the witness," former slaves established their truthfulness and authority, as well as their "right to be heard in a public tribunal."[77] In addition, by "speaking of slavery as a crime when it wasn't and portraying slaves as witnesses when they often couldn't be," abolitionists imagined a world in which slavery was illegal and people of color received due process.[78]

The court of public opinion may have exposed wrongdoing, but it did not provide actual amends. For the latter, many black people went to court. African Americans did not just rhetorically lay claim to legal personhood, due process, and the rights of American citizens. They also exercised those rights and told stories that expressed their hopes for justice through the legal system, even in the Deep South. Litigants like Salvador, Cooper, and Davis claimed the courtroom as their own. The rhetoric of due process and rights structured their petitions. For instance, in his petition, Pierre Salvador consistently referred to his "right to preemption," his confidence in the "due course of the law," and his "right to peacefully enjoy settlement of his property." He began and ended his petition with statements of respect for the court's forthcoming decision in the matter, suggesting that he would defer to the judge's fair assessment of the case.[79] The courtroom represented a site to find redress; and it represented a site in which people of color placed others under obligation to them and to make them accountable—precisely what Harriet Jacobs argued enslaved people could not do in the slaveholders' household. Through such language, black litigants envisioned and pressed for civic inclusion on one level, and on another, they reversed or problematized relations of domination that outside the courtroom were normal and unproblematic.

Law, then, was a mode of discourse, a branch of rhetoric steeped in the language of everyday life, which could be mustered to render the claims of African Americans persuasive to others. Admission to the legal arena did not necessarily require black litigants to learn a discrete, technical discipline. Rather, they learned to tilt the rhetoric of everyday life in a particular direction: to adjust the ways they spoke, the vocabularies they deployed, and their modes of persuasion in ways that made white southerners responsive to their claims. This was not a language foreign to free and enslaved black people, for they told countless stories of law, both in their slave narratives and in court. The narratives of Jacobs, Brown, and Bibb did not differ all that much from the courtroom storytelling of Salvador, Cooper, and Davis. All of these individuals sought to tell a "legal" story—the former focusing on unjust or perverted law (which presumes, after all, that there is such a thing as *just* law) and the latter expressing an expectation that the law could be used to protect their interests—to an audience with whom an understanding of and respect for law and legal rights would resonate. Southern law, while certainly oppressive, could not operate in a world where it denied African-descended people *every* mode of legal speech, for their speech was necessary to proving *other* kinds of facts in which the southern courts were likewise interested.

The narratives that Salvador, Cooper, and Davis presented in court, moreover, were "American stories"—stories about gender, freedom, property, and citizenship that fit into the recognized narratives of American culture, society, and memory. These American stories were not told independent of race; they were not race neutral. Yet black litigants appropriated these narratives and retold them to include their perspectives. Indeed, African Americans were not outsiders to or objects of such narratives but co-creators of these tales, stories that expanded by including their voices and experiences. By dismantling well-worn stories of race and creating fresh narratives about the place of black people in American society, black litigants opened up new worlds with expanded possibilities for people of color. As Anthony Amsterdam and Jerome Bruner argue in their work on narrative and law, storytelling is not "stringing together a set of 'hard facts.'" Rather, "stories *construct* the facts that comprise them." Human experiences and relationships are "not merely recounted by narrative but *constituted* by it."[80] With these stories, black litigants reimagined their relationships to and place in the world around them. Cooper, Davis, and Salvador sought to compel the courts—as the larger community watched— to recognize the validity of their stories, their voices, and their experiences, creating fleeting, hard-won moments of recognition.

2

The Rhetoric of Reputation

In September 1822, Fanny, a free woman of color and former slave, appeared before the district court in Pointe Coupee Parish, Louisiana. She was suing Francois (alias Pierre) Gueho, an "evil-minded and disgraceful" white man, for libelous attacks on her reputation. Gueho, Fanny claimed, had "wickedly, willfully and maliciously slandered" her and "endangered her freedom by insisting that she is a slave." In 1805, her owner had initiated "an act of emancipation" before Alexander Leblanc, the parish court judge, and Fanny had been living as a free person for some time, as those who knew her could attest. Archibald Haralson, a successful Princeton-educated attorney from nearby West Feliciana Parish, assisted Fanny in her lawsuit against Gueho and corroborated her claims. She behaved respectably, acted "diligently," "faithfully served" her former owner, and obeyed all "lawful commands." Nonetheless, Gueho's "acts of violence, threats and menaces" had jeopardized her reputation in the community, Fanny told the court, and caused others to question her free status. Gueho, she relayed, "intended to reduce her to slavery." He was a powerful and influential man, the "president of the Parish of Pointe Coupee." Without the court's intervention and protection, he could "greatly injure her." Fanny expected the court to hold him legally responsible for his assaults on her reputation. To that end, she requested that he be summoned to court to account for his offenses against her. In addition, she asked the court to formally "adjudge" her a free woman and award her $5,000 for damages done to her reputation, plus "general relief."[1]

We do not know what the court decided in Fanny's case. Her petition and the sheriff's return requiring Gueho to appear before the court are the only surviving documents. Yet we can conclude that not only did Fanny challenge

Petition of Fanny, *Fanny v. Gueho*. The local legal record from the antebellum South is fragmentary. Verdicts, testimony, and other materials are often missing. *Fanny v. Gueho*, Pointe Coupee Parish Clerk of the Court's Office, New Roads, Louisiana; photograph by the author.

a white man in a venue typically denied her; she also aired her complaint publicly and with Haralson's endorsement. The court validated it by ordering Gueho to respond to Fanny's charges, and the community watched. Moreover, Fanny's lawsuit indicates that she had achieved a certain degree of legal sophistication not usually attributed to an overwhelmingly illiterate people denied many legal rights. Fanny understood that she could not simply appear in court and expect to succeed without some help. She drew on a network of allies to aid her in her lawsuit, indicating that she had developed ties to local whites (including her lawyer) and activated those relationships when necessary. Finally, Fanny took great care to cultivate her reputation in her community, and legal action against a white man was a crucial mechanism for defending her good name and protecting herself and her status as a free woman.

For people of color, reputation often provided access to the local courts. For instance, all southerners (including free blacks, slaves, white women, and children) could attain the reputation in their community (or "credit") necessary to bring information to court and be believed (whether as a witness, petitioner, or defendant) by demonstrating that they had acted according to their proscribed place in the southern hierarchy.[2] Reputation was also relational. The "disorderly" actions of enslaved people (such as running away or disobedience) could signal that a particular master was unfit. A reputation as an incompetent master sometimes undermined a man's standing in his community—and his honor. Marking a man as dishonorable also affected his credibility in court, such that he might lose a lawsuit.[3] Dependents such as wives and slaves also had intimate contact with their household heads, and thus intimate information—information that once public could shape (or harm) their superiors' reputation and even influence the outcome of a court case.[4] Without a good reputation, moreover, one would be limited in the local courts, since a host of procedural annoyances and roadblocks could be mustered to stymie someone with little credibility in the first place.

One of the main rhetorical tactics exploited by black litigants in the antebellum Natchez district was to leverage the cultural scripts of reputation in court proceedings. African Americans strategically deployed the language of reputation to gain a measure of autonomy over their lives. On certain occasions, such language not only bolstered their credibility but also curtailed white authority. While scholars would no doubt agree that personal reputation was important in southern litigation, they nonetheless tend to interpret reputation as a thing that one *has* rather than as a malleable package of linguistic possibilities one *claims* or *manipulates*. An individual's reputation certainly symbolized the community's assessment and opinion about that person; but it also entailed a language that one could leverage or deploy.

People of color used two modes of manipulating language when they crafted their legal strategies: telling stories and exploiting the rhetoric of reputation. Although it is hard to formally disentangle them in any given case, they are analytically distinct. Storytelling was ostensibly historical (it explained what had happened in the past), but it was simultaneously anticipatory and future oriented. As an attempt to interpret and organize the world in which the teller—and his or her adversary—lived, storytelling in the courtroom involved imagining and then signaling the narrator's *own* interpretation of how the world should function and how the parties involved should repair a break in normal relations. The rhetoric of reputation similarly worked through an appeal to the past (that is, to the speaker's former conduct and relationships). But it evoked a *shared* and often abstract history of morals or manners (while storytelling, to be of interest, must speak to particulars) and asked its listeners to imagine themselves as participating in the same community as the speaker—a community in which the listener is supposed to be comfortable. Hence it might appear that in making these rhetorical appeals to reputation, black litigants were acceding to a discourse that painted them as inferior or subservient. Yet this is only partly true; the rhetoric of reputation was often a feint, a tactic that placed a listener in a world of black subservience only to undermine this supposedly shared truth with the story itself and its frequently paradoxical suggestion of how to achieve justice. Courtroom language leveraging the rhetoric of race and servility, in some instances, and property and reliability, in others, involved performances tailored to specific occasions, not the embodiment of stable traits. Getting this balance right proved a complex undertaking, a piece of delicate theater with potentially severe costs for any misstep. That the maneuver was often successful speaks to black litigants' ability to negotiate the world in which they lived.

When making claims in court, free and enslaved African Americans exploited the rhetoric of white supremacy and the language of race. By highlighting their reputations as obedient, respectable, and subordinate members of the community and showing that they remembered "their place," people of color shielded themselves from arbitrary punishments and restrictive laws. While, on the one hand, they needed to demonstrate that they had acted according to their subordinate position as people of color in a slaveholders' regime, on the other hand, black litigants also negotiated the meanings of their reputations as obedient and deferential to serve their own interests. They did not always win their lawsuits or achieve their desired results. Yet by forcing whites to articulate their values in a public setting, black litigants made whites accountable to the standards of behavior they set for people of color. Whites were not the only ones to deploy the rhetoric of race; these rhetorical tropes could sometimes prove effective when wielded by black people as well.

More striking perhaps, race (and the performance of the tropes of subordination associated with race) was not the sole category free blacks in particular used to claim their reputations in their communities. In some cases free black litigants could craft their reputations around a factor such as property ownership, exploiting its attendant presumptions about reliability and good faith. This narrative could prove as important as race in determining how communities treated black litigants in the local courts. By using the rhetoric of reputation to capitalize on the tension between white southerners' commitment to white supremacy and their sometimes competing desire to safeguard private property, free people of color protected themselves, their families, and their livelihoods.

"FIT SUBJECTS"

In the antebellum Natchez district, where law was localized and close to the community, an individual's reputation mattered in court. In the face-to-face society of the antebellum American South, it was paramount. After all, antebellum southern society was characterized by "personalism," a set of face-to-face, person-to-person relations.[5] In the small communities that comprised much of the Old South, very little remained private. Everyone knew or knew of most everyone else. Neighbors noticed the spendthrifts and those who worked hard to provide for their families. They observed who went to church on Sunday and who gambled and drank to excess. They distinguished the generous from the skinflints. Despite the strict hierarchies in southern society, because community members knew one another intimately, southerners became accustomed to assessing the individual measure of a man or woman, white or black.[6] Of course, personalism must not be confused with "fairness." Face-to-face societies were often cruel; people frequently distrusted their neighbors, even when they depended on them. They also lied and spread gossip—a powerful tool for marking and preserving hierarchies. Consequently, for better or for worse, communities understood litigants and witnesses as individuals, not as the "faceless members of categorical groups" found in statutes and appellate law.[7]

Personalism sometimes also stood in tension with legislation, particularly restrictive legislation (such as removal laws or laws demanding deferential behavior). This legislation expressed a collective statement about what a community—and a well-ordered society—ought to look like. In particular, restrictive legislation imagined a world in which racial hierarchies were carefully preserved and enforced. Southern laws circumscribed the lives of people of color to such a degree that local authorities could round them up and haul them into court for nearly any offense, real or imagined, from vagrancy to traveling out of state or even keeping a dog. They might also face charges for crimes of deference, such as insulting a white person or not yielding the road.

Restrictive legislation was arbitrarily enforced, both by design and in practice. By contrast, personalism (both on the ground and as an ideology) urged communities to make individualized assessments about people, to decide when they should and should not enforce the law. This posed a tension for black people. To negotiate this tension between the law on the books and community judgment they relied on claims about their own reputations, urging whites to privilege them as people and to make enforcement selective. Black litigants in the Natchez district thus leveraged and manipulated the *meanings* of their reputations to their advantage in court. In so doing, they gained a modicum of control over their lives and protected their interests. Thus, reputation provided African Americans with a language to claim space in an arbitrary world.

Acquiring a good name meant adhering to (or claiming to have adhered to) the standards of behavior expected of community members according to one's position in the social order. For instance, for free blacks in a slave society, this meant securing reputations as "good negroes"—deferential, compliant, servile, and not prone to rebellion. This language is striking in the context of a legal demand; it might easily be taken as being either purely opportunistic or as somehow assenting to one's own inferiority as the price of dealing with white courts. Such a reading gives litigants too little credit, however. It was actually a tactic, a way of locating and negotiating a problem in the practical application of law.

Indeed, in a culture in which the power of white planters seemed limitless, to shield themselves from the litany of charges that might be lodged against them, people of color needed to secure good reputations—reputations for subservience and deference—within their communities. Little wonder that Nero, a free man of color jailed in Natchez for "riotous behavior," claimed that he had always demonstrated good behavior in his community and asked the court to subpoena witnesses on his behalf. He also hired the gifted William B. Griffith as his attorney. Griffith had a reputation for fair dealing and frequently represented free and enslaved African Americans. After Nero and his attorney offered to post a bond guaranteeing that he would behave peacefully, the superior court judge ordered his release from jail.[8]

Free people of color like Nero, however, needed allies willing to affirm in court that they were indeed "good negroes," especially as they faced increasingly restrictive laws. By the 1830s, as abolitionists' attacks on slavery intensified and slaveholders' fears of slave rebellion heightened, many white southerners increasingly perceived free blacks as a threat to the social order. If slavery was the natural state of people of African descent, then free blacks were an aberration and a potentially subversive, dangerous, and unsettling example to slaves.[9] Across the South, whites escalated their assaults on free black communities. These attacks were particularly prevalent in Mississippi and Louisiana. Lawmakers in both states attempted to limit—and reverse— the expansion of the free black population and enacted laws to remove its members from the state.[10] In 1831, a Mississippi newspaper conveyed the sentiment of lawmakers in the region. "If the free coloured people were removed," it argued, "the slaves could safely be treated with more indulgence. Less fear would be entertained, and greater latitude of course allowed. . . . In a word, it would make better masters and better slaves."[11] Local whites, however, often came to the aid of free blacks wishing to remain in the state, but only if they remembered their place. In one revealing petition, twenty-one white men reminded the Mississippi legislature that while there were "vicious and evil disposed" free people of color, there were also those "who have spent a life here free from reproval, or even the suspicions of improper conduct." While the "unworthy" should be removed, these men insisted that the "good" people of color be protected. They wanted the legislature to allow local communities to make the distinction between loyal and disloyal—a distinction based on reputation and social relations.[12]

Successful petitions to remain in the state or to seek relief from suffocating restrictions required the backing of whites who knew the free black parties involved and could testify to their reputations. In their petitions, free people of color were careful to demonstrate that they were well behaved, peaceable, sober, obedient, and could offer something of worth to the larger community. To document their cases, free blacks presented evidence of support from whites in their neighborhood who verified their claims.[13] When Ann Caldwell petitioned the Mississippi legislature, she gathered the signatures of dozens of white residents of Natchez and the surrounding area to support her request for a "special act of the Legislature" permitting her to remain in the state. She pledged not to become a public charge and promised to post a bond guaranteeing "her good behavior." Her neighbors valued her skills as a healer, she claimed, and she had gained her freedom by serving as a "faithful nurse" to her former mistress.[14] Similarly, thirty-three white men of Natchez petitioned on behalf of Esther Barland, a free black woman. They asked lawmakers to allow her to remain in the state in light of her reputation for "great industry" and claimed that she was "much grieved at the idea of being driven from the Land of her home and her friends to find shelter she Knows not where."[15] Both Caldwell and Barland cultivated ties of personal obligation with local whites and called on those bonds when threatened.[16]

Enslaved men and women participated in the politics of reputation in similar ways to free blacks. A reputation as a "good negro" represented a valuable tool for enslaved people suing for their freedom. They too deployed the language of servility in their lawsuits and offered others' positive assessment of their good character and actions to support their case. In particular, enslaved people used their reputations to defend themselves against those who might object to giving them their freedom. After all, as newly freed people they might remain in the community after the conclusion of their lawsuits. They needed to demonstrate that they would not show disruptive or criminal behavior or become public charges, and that they would add something of value to the local community. Mississippi and Louisiana laws governing the manumission of slaves also insisted that enslaved people demonstrate respectable qualities or show that they had performed some kind of meritorious service for their masters to be freed. In their petitions for freedom, slaves leveraged their reputations and insisted that they were obedient, well behaved, industrious, had served their owners devotedly, and were neither prone to running away nor engaged in criminal activity. When Tom, an enslaved Louisiana man, sued René Porche for his freedom, he used his reputation to support his claims to liberty. After filing his initial petition for freedom, Tom filed an amended petition with the court simply to insist that he was fit for the responsibilities of freedom because he "had led an honest & industrious life." Several white men testified on his behalf and provided the court with positive character assessments. For example, Emile Jarreau stated that Tom was not "a rogue," "thief," or a "runaway." The assessment from reliable white witnesses like Jarreau shielded Tom from character attacks.[17] By emphasizing their positive attributes and obedient behavior, enslaved people like Tom defended themselves against potential claims that they were unfit for freedom.

When petitioning the courts, people of color also deployed the reputations of those close to them, especially family members. For instance,

Robert Colston, a kidnapped man of color suing for his freedom in Louisiana, leveraged his father's reputation as a man of "good character and merits" and his father's ties to the most powerful man in the nation—President James Monroe—to support his efforts for liberty. In his lawsuit, Colston claimed he had "enjoy[ed] the privileges of the free" until Dr. Moses Littell snatched him in Baltimore, Maryland, "by violence and force . . . and reduced [him] to a state of slavery." Littell alleged "that he had purchased Colston as a slave" and then sold him to John D. S. Arden of Louisiana. Colston asked the court to issue an order to remove him "from the illegal and forcible possession of those who hold him" and declare him a free man. Arden denied Colston's allegations and insisted that he "was a slave before and at the time" that he had "purchased him." He had bought Colston "fairly and for a good & bona fide price" from agents in Baltimore who produced a legal bill of sale for Colston. Moreover, Colston "was born a slave," Arden claimed, and he wanted the judge to dismiss the lawsuit. Colston, however, offered indisputable proof to support his claim to freedom. As evidence of his free status, Colston supplied the court with a transcript of a trial in which the circuit court of the District of Columbia had found him guilty for the theft of a congressman's gold watch. He also provided the court with a subsequent pardon document issued by James Monroe and Secretary of State John Quincy Adams. These records listed him as a "free mulatto." After examining this evidence, the Louisiana court found him a free man.

Colston relied on his father's reputation as a respectable and upright man to procure a pardon for his crime—a pardon that ultimately led to his release from enslavement in Louisiana. President Monroe knew George Colston (Robert Colston's father) personally, he stated in the pardon, and insisted that he was "a man of virtuous and industrious habits of life and well spoken of by those who had long known him." The "good character and merits" of George Colston "specially moved" Monroe to "wholly exonerate" his son, Robert. Robert Colston had engaged in "vicious practices," Monroe wrote, but his father had promised to see "to his reformation." Monroe trusted that George Colston, as an adept head of the household, would bring his son to heel.[18]

Having credible whites supporting their lawsuits certainly provided some people of color with an advantage in the courts. Yet not all white southerners' words carried the same weight. Black litigants' chances for success increased considerably if they could rally to their cause the most powerful white men in the community (or in the nation, as was the case with Colston). William Hayden gained the assistance of John Minor, a cotton planter and member of one of the most prosperous and respected families in Mississippi, when he petitioned the Mississippi legislature to allow him to remain in the state. Hayden, a free black barber in Natchez, claimed that the Mississippi act forcing free blacks to leave the state would "produce absolute ruin to his prospects." He had gained "an honest livelihood for himself" through his "sobriety and good conduct," he insisted, as "those who knew him could affirm." His reputation for "honesty," "fidelity," and "obedience to the laws of the state" made him an ideal candidate for remaining in Natchez. He owned property and ran a successful business, he asserted. But because he was in constant danger "of being driven from his home," he wanted "a special act exempting him . . . from removal from the state." Moreover, he claimed that he could produce "testimonials of his good character and honesty . . . sobriety and good conduct." Minor supported Hayden's petition and claimed to "have knowledge of [his] character" and could "testify to his honesty." Minor knew Hayden intimately and employed him for a number of years. According to Minor, Hayden's good behavior and deportment made him a "fit subject" of Mississippi. He recommended that the legislature allow Hayden to remain a resident of the state—a recommendation the state legislature followed. Calling on Minor to support his reputation as a sober, industrious, and honest businessman proved an effective strategy. Hayden's reputation protected him from "ruin" and shielded him from restrictive legislation in a social order in which the nearly unlimited power of white slaveholders could run roughshod over his "prospects."[19]

While they may have needed white allies, black litigants were the prime movers behind their cases. White men like John Minor acted at the behest of people like William Hayden. Hayden's work as a barber meant that he offered his skills to the community at large and regularly serviced white customers. By the antebellum period, black barbers in the American South had supplanted white barbers and dominated the barber trade. Successful barbers gained economic independence and constituted an important segment of the black middle class. Most were leaders in their free black communities. Black barbers' specialized skills boosted their standing, granted them more control over their work and additional leverage in their negotiations, and provided them a better bargaining position when approaching the courts to protect their interests. Such skills also gave them a level of prosperity that made it possible to initiate lawsuits, hire lawyers to represent them, and pay court costs.[20] They formed personal relationships with their white clients—clients who were vulnerable to a potential slip of the wrist and thus trusted their barbers.

Customers also shared confidences with their barbers as they enjoyed a shave, and sometimes they even socialized outside of the shop.[21] For example, over a period of five years, Minor paid Hayden fifteen dollars a month for his services and the two developed a close relationship. Their relationship began even before Hayden became a resident of Natchez, when after witnessing his talents, Minor offered to provide Hayden with "any assistance which lay in his power to render me."[22]

Men like Minor (and other clients of free black barbers) were not simply paternalistic benefactors. Barbers and their clients developed ties of *mutual obligation*—bonds that barbers activated when the opportunity arose. For instance, not only did William Johnson, a free black barber in Natchez, service white customers; he also rented buildings and rooms to white men and hired them as laborers and overseers on his farm outside of town. In addition, he lent whites money. In one year, he made sixteen loans to local whites (including Natchez nabob Adam L. Bingaman and John A. Quitman, the future governor of Mississippi), totaling more than $2,000.[23] Johnson did not have to petition to remain in the state of Mississippi. But he did help secure petitions for his free black apprentices, and he utilized his connections to local whites when doing so. He asked several of his white neighbors to sign the petitions supporting his apprentices' requests to remain in the state. As he commented in his diary, "Those names are an Ornament to Any paper—Those are Gentlemen of the 1st Order of Talents and Standing."[24]

Black people thus framed restriction as reciprocity: they had fulfilled the dictates of whites and asked to be treated accordingly. When calling on their white acquaintances to come to their aid and testify to their reputations as "good negroes," free people of color insisted that white southerners uphold their ends of the bargain.

Despite their interest in establishing a clear bulwark to protect white authority and uphold white supremacy, white southerners on the ground in the Natchez district selectively enforced the law. Many of the restrictive laws people of color faced were locally negotiated and only partially upheld. Free blacks traveling to other counties or keeping dogs did not always face criminal charges; they did not always have to petition to remain in the state. For instance, William Johnson, as mentioned, did not have to present petitions to the local courts or the state legislature asking to stay in Mississippi. His reputation as a businessman, slave owner, and friend to influential white men had earned him and his family an elevated and protected position in the larger

Part One

Natchez community. The day after Johnson's death in June 1851, a Natchez newspaper, the *Courier*, printed a tribute extolling his good reputation. It portrayed Johnson as a man with a "peaceable character" and in "excellent standing" in the community. Johnson held "a respectable position on account of his character, intelligence and deportment." The "most respected citizens" of Natchez attended his funeral, the newspaper claimed, and Reverend Watkins of the Methodist church insisted that Johnson's "example [was] one well worthy of imitation by all of his class." Johnson's "peaceable character" and his "excellent standing" shielded him from persecution.[25]

But even for men like Johnson, the benefits of a good reputation and community support had their limits. His 1851 murder served as a reminder that he was black man in a white man's regime. In spring 1849, Johnson became involved in a legal dispute with a neighbor, Baylor Winn, which ultimately led to Johnson's death. Johnson and Winn had been friendly for many years. Their relationship dissolved, however, after Winn purchased the land adjacent to Johnson's and, in disregard of the boundary lines between their properties, began cutting timber on Johnson's property. Before suing Winn in court, Johnson first attempted to compromise with him. At the suggestion of his lawyers, he asked Winn to settle the dispute by agreeing to resurvey the boundary line between their properties. Winn refused. Johnson secured a court-ordered survey, but after discovering that Winn continued to cut timber on his land, Johnson sued Winn for trespassing. In May 1851, before the lawsuit went to a final trial, Johnson proposed another compromise that included a survey paid for by both parties. This time Winn agreed, and Johnson dismissed the suit. The disagreement between the two men, however, was far from over. A month later, in mid-June 1851, Winn ambushed Johnson and fatally shot him in the presence of three black witnesses, including Johnson's son. Johnson died the next morning after implicating Winn as the shooter. Local authorities arrested Winn and jailed him, but after three trials, Winn was released from custody.[26] Because African Americans witnessed the crime, Johnson's murderer went unpunished; Mississippi law banned people of African descent (free or enslaved) from testifying against whites. While most in Natchez knew Winn as a man of color, Winn himself claimed "to be a white man, and [had] voted and given testimony as such."[27] The prosecutor could not prove his "negro blood," and in each of the three trials, the court did not admit the eyewitness testimony. Despite Winn's reputation as a "black hearted wretch" and the certainty about town of his guilt, Winn escaped conviction by claiming to be white.[28] While Johnson cultivated a good reputation, acquired skills that made him valuable to the community, and allied himself with local whites, he still remained at risk. In the end, his efforts would not be enough to obtain justice in court for his murder.[29]

Leveraging reputation might limit the scope of draconian legislation, but the results did not always benefit black people. Cultivating the wrong kind of reputation, for instance, could cost a person their case. Indeed, laws demanding deference or restricting free blacks' movements and opportunities existed to remind people of color of their place within southern society. The deferential might be exempt, but if a black person misbehaved in some way, whites could call on the law to punish the transgressor. A bad reputation and lack of support from local whites could have devastating consequences, as Lewis Burwell found in 1822 when the magistrates' court in Natchez found him guilty of "being a free negro" and refusing to leave the state of Mississippi. Because Burwell could not post a $600 security bond guaranteeing his "good behavior" and because he did not leave the state after thirty days when ordered to do so, the court ordered his sale as a slave to the "highest bidder." No one came to Burwell's aid. On the contrary, it appears that the whites in Natchez wanted to be rid of him. He had a poor reputation among slave owners. In 1818, the court twice found him guilty for selling liquor to slaves without their masters' permission, and in 1819 it charged him with assaulting a slave belonging to David Eliot, a local slaveholder. Without white allies willing to come to his aid to confirm his value to the community, Burwell himself became enslaved.[30] His enslavement points to the precarious position of many free people of color. Survival meant behaving appropriately and proving oneself worthy of the support of white southerners. It also meant putting oneself in a position to exploit the rhetoric of black servility to support one's case. Burwell did neither and paid the price.

ACCOUNTABILITY

Black litigants deliberately deployed the language of white supremacy in the service of their own interests. The tropes of subordination—deference and obedience—that people of color performed in court proceedings gave them some ground to stand on. They used the stereotypes of the "good negro" as a rhetorical and legal strategy—a strategy that granted them some additional control over their lives and safeguarded their interests. People of color knew enough about the local legal process to frame their petitions in ways that would help guarantee their legal success. That their petitions shared a similar formulaic quality in both tone and text suggests the formula was a recipe that black litigants (and their lawyers) knew well. They used their reputations for being obedient, peaceable, and industrious to protect themselves, their families, and their property and negotiated the meanings of those reputations on their own behalves.

When building a case for their good reputations in court, black litigants made many white southerners accountable to the standards of behavior whites set for people of color. They compelled whites to articulate their values in a public setting—the courthouse—and they reminded whites to honor those principles when seeking white support. In so doing, some people of color kept white power within the boundaries of its own promises and rhetoric rather than allowing it to be total—or arbitrary.

Some free people of color were remarkably blasé about the charges against them and relied on whites' selective enforcement of the law. For instance, on April 18, 1833, the district court in Iberville Parish, Louisiana, charged Jean Fleming, a free black man, with insulting Dr. Alexander Byrenheidt, a white man. Fleming, Byrenheidt told the court, had approached him on horseback along a public road in Iberville Parish and "unlawfully, willfully, maliciously insulted him . . . in a loud voice and with violent and menacing hand gestures." Fleming had continued to "abuse and vilify Byrenheidt in an angry, violent, and overbearing manner" and "threated to kill him by blowing out his brains." Fearful for his life, Byrenheidt had fled on his horse while an armed Fleming "pursued him for a considerable distance," screaming insults and threats and "waiving a loaded pistol." Fleming, however, viewed the charges against him as a waste of his time. He responded to Byrenheidt's accusations by explaining that because he had important business in New Orleans that required his immediate attention, he would not be available to appear in court for such inconsequential matters. He claimed to have several witnesses from both Iberville Parish and New Orleans who would "testify that he has always been a peaceable and well-disposed person and particularly well-disposed and respectful to the white population of the state." He listed several white men who would support his reputation as a calm and reverent man. In addition, four white men offered to act as security for him, guaranteeing that he would treat Byrenheidt courteously in the future. The outcome of the case is missing from the record, but it appears that Fleming was right to view the charges as trivial. He was never arrested for insulting Byrenheidt. Fleming used selective enforcement to his advantage.[31]

Whites did not give up their power easily, however. Sometimes whites in the Natchez district used the law to limit black people's ability to call on the cultural scripts of reputation and betrayed the standards of behavior they set for people of color—especially if those standards threatened white authority.

In 1838, Baton Rouge authorities arrested John Motton, a free black man, for heatedly screaming insults at the town's executioner while witnessing the public hanging of two slaves in the town square. In his petition for a writ of habeas corpus and release from jail, Motton admitted using "language strongly disapproving of the cruel manner in which the executioner did his duty." His anger originated from "the excitement of the moment, when the feelings of all bystanders were outraged." Understanding the gravity of the charges against him for breaching the peace and insulting a white man in the presence of others, Motton assured the district court judge that he had not used "imprudent or disrespectful expressions towards any officers on duty—or towards any other white man." His quarrel was with the executioner. A "bad feeling" existed between the two men. The arrest baffled Motton, because in his view he had behaved as he should have done. He only insulted the hangman, he insisted, as did the rest of the crowd. Executioners routinely faced insults and had bad reputations in their communities because of the infamy of their profession. Executioners, like debt collectors, ran a high risk of verbal abuse and even physical assault because of the nature of their duties.[32] The ritual excoriation of the executioner, then, was acceptable conduct, even for a free black man. The concern, however, was not simply that Motton had insulted the hangman; rather, he was arrested for "abusing the executioner in the presence of slaves."[33]

Motton's insulting language toward a white man in the presence of slaves raised the hackles of the other white bystanders because it betrayed commonly acknowledged racial and social hierarchies. One white man who witnessed the incident, William Jackson, claimed that Motton "used language rebellious in its tendency, & calculated to destroy that line of Distinction which exists between the several classes of the community of this state." With this statement to the court, Jackson revealed his apprehension about the power and reach of Motton's words. By publicly challenging a white man and calling him a "damned rascal [who] ought to be hung," Motton encouraged disrespect and even insurrection. Encouraging slave rebellion was punishable by death. The judge denied Motton's habeas request because of the insubordinate and mutinous example he had offered to enslaved bystanders.[34]

By insulting a white man, Motton had also broken the law, and in this instance, white officials enforced it. A black person's insult of or failure to show respect to a white person was a crime in Louisiana. "Free people of color ought never to insult or strike white people, nor presume to conceive themselves equal to whites," the law provided, "but on the contrary, they ought to yield to them in every occasion, and never speak or answer to them but with respect, under the penalty of imprisonment, according to the nature of the offense."[35] Elaborate laws that criminalized African Americans' speech and demanded deferential behavior reinforced the racism that accompanied slavery's entrenchment in the antebellum Deep South and the distancing of whites and blacks. The development of a rigid racial ideology and efforts to make whiteness synonymous with freedom, and blackness with slavery, depended on the everyday practice of racial difference. With his affidavit, Jackson reminded Motton of his inferior standing within southern society.

While laws demanding deference reinforced racial boundaries, they also betrayed the uneasiness of white lawmakers and their white constituents about African Americans' speech and the place of free people of color within a slave society. When white southerners prosecuted blacks for insulting whites, they revealed their anxiety about the impact and scope of African Americans' words. By claiming that Motton's actions were "calculated to destroy that line of Distinction which exists between the several classes of the community," Jackson implicitly acknowledged that Motton had the power to upset racial hierarchies. Motton may not have achieved the results he desired when he petitioned the court for his release from jail, but his actions reminded white southerners of his words' influence and potential danger.

That the court adjudged him guilty does not obscure the fact that he participated in a legal system in which he had a voice. Yet in that moment in the town square, Motton believed he could speak up *not only* because the local legal culture provided him with opportunities to do so but also because he believed that he had, in fact, behaved appropriately. By insisting that *everyone* insulted the hangman, Motton attempted to make white authorities accountable to the standards they set for acceptable behavior.

THE LANGUAGE OF PROPERTY

Petitioners like William Hayden and Ann Caldwell reveal the ways people of color manipulated the meanings of their reputations as "good negroes" and exploited the rhetoric of white supremacy and black servility to protect themselves and their interests. Yet free blacks also moved beyond the tropes of deference when leveraging the language of reputation in court. Jean Fleming, for instance, did not simply use the rhetoric of servility to respond to Alexander Byrenheidt's accusations. He also used the language of property and wealth: important business in New Orleans kept him from attending court. Moreover, a disagreement over property triggered the confrontation between Byrenheidt and Fleming in the first place. A few days before the two met along the road in Iberville Parish, Byrenheidt had sued Fleming to recover an unpaid debt, a debt Fleming disputed and a lawsuit he resented. Rather than behaving deferentially, Fleming subjected Byrenheidt (a man to whom he did in fact owe money) to quite a tongue-lashing.[36]

Factors such as property ownership sometimes proved as important as race when determining how Natchez district communities assessed reputation. After all, William Johnson's standing did not stem from obsequious or servile behavior. Rather, Johnson's reputation as a fair-minded businessman and property holder long offered him and his family an elevated and protected position in the larger Natchez community, allowing them privileges often denied free people of color. Johnson was born a slave in Natchez, the son of a slave woman and her white master, and his father manumitted him in 1820 and set him up in business as a barber. Johnson swiftly became one of Natchez's most prosperous and respected free blacks. At the time of his death, he had accumulated more than $25,000 in property. This figure included three successful barbershops in Natchez, a farm south of town called Hard Scrabble, townhomes, slaves, farm tools, and livestock. He filled his home with mahogany chairs, mirrors, art, musical instruments, and books. He set high standards of respectability and conduct for himself, his family, and his apprentices. Although he could not vote or hold office, Johnson paid close attention to party politics and was involved in local government. He read voraciously, educated his children, and attended art exhibits and musical concerts. Johnson engaged in a good deal of business with local residents, white and black. His associates included Colonel Adam L. Bingaman, a wealthy and respected white man and prominent politician. Johnson's neighbors included the banker Gabriel Tichenor (who was the former owner and father of Ann Battles Johnson, Johnson's wife) and Peter Lapice, a businessman and owner of Whitehall and Arnolia plantations. In personal and business matters, Johnson conducted himself much like other men of the merchant class—white or black.[37]

Race (and the performance of the qualities associated with one's race) did not solely determine someone's reputation or position in his or her community. Instead, a person's reputation could be multiple, varied, and contested. The rhetoric of servility (obedience and deference) conveyed blackness and subordination. But this language was unstable, as the litigation between Antoine Lacour, a free black planter from Iberville Parish, Louisiana, and the overseer of his plantation, a white man, suggests.

Lacour's reputation as a responsible, independent property owner provided him with the necessary leverage to defeat white men in court repeatedly.

Lacour was a wealthy landholder. In 1830, his household consisted of eighteen slaves.[38] Like white men of similar financial standing, he bought and sold land, slaves, and other property, ginned cotton, rented out bondsmen, and, when he went to court, hired white attorneys to represent him. Lacour's illiteracy did not bar him from legal action. He made extensive use of the legal system to increase his wealth, protect it, and bequeath it to others. Between 1831 and 1844, Lacour was embroiled in at least nine lawsuits—all but one involved litigation against white men. He won each case.[39] In early 1838, he hired a white man, Weyman Ingledove, to serve as overseer on his cotton plantation. A slave-owning free black planter who employed a white overseer made for a rare figure in the antebellum South. This curious arrangement, however, lasted less than a year; between 1839 and 1840, Ingledove sued Lacour four times, twice for back wages and twice for slandering him as a horse thief. He even attempted to have Lacour arrested. Ingledove's persistent pursuit of Lacour proved a costly mistake: he lost each case. Although Lacour could not serve on a jury, hold office, vote, or participate in a number of other civic acts reserved for white men, he repeatedly outmatched Ingledove.

In the late summer of 1839, Lacour's legal troubles with his overseer began when Ingledove sued him for back wages. In his petition to the Iberville parish court, Ingledove claimed that Lacour had hired him in April 1838 to serve as a "Labourer and overseer" on his plantation for a "term of nine months." According to Ingledove, near the end of the contract, Lacour had evicted Ingledove from his plantation and refused to pay him. Lacour intended to depart Louisiana, Ingledove claimed, "without leaving sufficient property to satisfy the judgment which he suspects to obtain against him." Witnesses for Ingledove (one of whom Lacour had sued successfully in 1831) testified that Lacour planned to sell his property for $100,000 and go to France where "Negros" had "rights" and "were admitted as Generals in the Armies." Ingledove wanted Lacour "arrested and confined" to ensure that he would not flee the state. In early December 1839, the parish judge ordered Lacour's arrest but suspended the warrant shortly thereafter when Lacour denied the charges against him and filed a motion to dissolve the arrest. While Ingledove (and witnesses for him) repeatedly used the language of race to refer to Lacour (reminding the court that Lacour was a "negro" who sought the same "rights" as whites), Lacour used the language of property and wealth. Indeed, Lacour admitted that he planned to move to France, but he claimed that he had "plenty of . . . slaves, movables and credits" in Louisiana, enough to "satisfy" Ingledove's "demand."

In the trial that followed, witnesses established the source of the men's disagreement. Some months prior, Lacour had lent Ingledove a horse and sent him, in his capacity as overseer, in search of runaway slaves. When Ingledove returned fifteen days later without the horse, claiming he had lost it, Lacour had terminated his employment and refused to pay him unless he returned the missing horse. After listening to the witnesses' testimony, the parish court judge ordered Lacour to subtract the value of the horse—some $50—from the $200 he still owed Ingledove. Lacour swiftly appealed, claiming that Ingledove's theft of his horse justified terminating his employment without pay. Two months later, the district court in Plaquemine overturned the parish court's decision and dismissed Ingledove's case entirely.[40]

The controversy between the two men was not over. In the spring of 1840, Ingledove sued Lacour twice more, this time for slandering him as a horse thief. In both of his defamation lawsuits, Ingledove professed himself a man "of irreproachable honesty, character, and reputation" and "a good neighbor and good friend." Notably, he used rhetoric similar to that employed by Fanny and other free blacks and claimed to exhibit "harmless and inoffensive deportment toward all and every persons." Despite these qualities, Lacour had "falsely, maliciously, and slanderously" accused him of dishonesty and of stealing and then gambling away his horse. These accusations "render him contemptible and suspicious to the public and . . . deprive him of his honest reputation," he lamented. Lacour also had made threats against Ingledove in "both the English and [F]rench languages" and had warned that if he approached his plantation again, he would "shoot him & make his negroes throw his dead body in the river." The district court dismissed the first lawsuit because of lack of evidence, requiring Ingledove to pay court costs and non-suited him (fined him for filing an inadequate case) in the second.[41]

Lacour's success hinged on both men's reputations in their community. Each summoned witnesses to testify on his behalf. Community members frequently provided the court with verbal accounts of the controversies at hand, descriptions of physical evidence, speculation about the circumstances of a given case, and personal opinions about the litigants involved. The community constituted a discriminating audience—weighing in, providing information, and passing judgment. Such testimony sometimes shaped the outcome of a case.[42]

In many ways, Ingledove faced an uphill battle when he sued Lacour. While white men had the greatest claim to a good reputation as a result of their superior position in the southern hierarchy, formal determinants such as race and gender did not fully define a person's status. Indeed, Lacour's race was not the only factor determining his place in his community. Although a man of color, he had significant influence because of his position as a wealthy planter and slave owner. Despite Lacour's race, his neighbors and acquaintances viewed him as a fair-minded and self-sufficient householder. Because he performed effectively the qualities expected of a man of his economic stature—honesty, rationality, reliability, and independence—he enjoyed an elevated status, which provided him with additional leverage in court.

For Lacour, cultivating a good reputation did not mean behaving deferentially. He had to act decisively. Proving himself worthy to his white neighbors meant demonstrating the willingness to protect his property, both in and out of court. Propertied white men would not respect another man who did not safeguard his property, and they would not respect a man who allowed his overseer to steal from him. By custom and law, southern men handled the economic aspects of their households. Part of being a competent householder meant prudently managing one's property. To demonstrate that they were capable of heading households and able to handle the responsibilities of freedom, free men of color had to go to court to defend themselves and their livelihoods. Their reputation as adept heads of households depended on it.

Not a single witness, however, uttered a word in favor of Ingledove's character or reputation, even those who testified on his behalf. One even reported rumors of Ingledove's gambling as an explanation for the alleged horse theft. Thieves had particularly ignoble reputations in southern society: to be called a thief implied a lack of trustworthiness. In a face-to-face culture in which a man was known by his word, charges of dishonesty could not be left uncontested. Trust was essential in a society where many were illiterate. Lenders often extended credit on little more than a handshake or the borrower's oral promises to pay the debt. A damaged reputation might result in the loss of crucial sources of livelihood and opportunities for employment. Charges of theft, fraud, frequent gambling, and dishonesty could have ruinous consequences and jeopardized a man's position in his community.[43] With his social and economic standing on the line, as well as his prospects for future employment, Ingledove could not afford to disregard such an allegation. Ignoring an accusation of theft was tantamount to admitting that it was true.

Worse, by calling him a thief, Lacour publicly shamed and dishonored Ingledove. In so doing, he damaged Ingledove's reputation. Notions of honor held a central social and cultural place in the slaveholding South, and white men were especially sensitive.[44] Accusing a man of being a dishonest and unprincipled thief was a serious offense; it was the worst insult of all.[45] But to be denounced as a thief by a black man was a particularly humiliating offense to a white man, as Ingledove claimed when Lacour accused him of horse theft. By raising the possibility that Ingledove was a lying thief, Lacour dishonored him before other white men. Ingledove felt the sting of his accuser's words all the more sharply because his defamer was black. Indeed, Ingledove repeatedly (and indignantly) reminded the court that Lacour was a "man of color."[46]

Lacour's accusations of dishonesty and theft were not the sole threats to Ingledove's reputation. Whatever his economic stature, Lacour was still a black man, and Ingledove was white. The danger derived from the repetition of Lacour's words. Lacour's version of events gained additional credibility as propertied white men repeated it. Because of the superior social standing of white men of property, their voices and opinions were thought inherently more believable and authoritative than those of all others.[47] Repetition among reliable and impartial white men thus validated the accusation of theft. Lacour's allegation became, in nineteenth-century parlance, the "common fame" or "common report." It became fact. In each of the trials involving the two men, no one questioned whether Ingledove had stolen Lacour's horse; all assumed he had. Once Lacour's words circulated among whites, they attained power—the power to dishonor a white man before other white men.

Lacour's position among his neighbors, his ability to speak, and his use of the local courts to protect his interests were not determined solely by his being a man of color in a slaveholder's regime. As a landholder with a reputation for rationality, independence of mind, fair-dealing, and self-sufficiency, he was expected by the members of his community to act decisively rather than deferentially.

What is more, by describing himself as "harmless," "inoffensive," and well-behaved, Ingledove echoed the rhetoric of servility used by free blacks like Fanny—a racialized rhetoric that implied blackness and dependence. Strikingly, Lacour did not. Instead, he utilized the language of property, a rhetoric that implied whiteness and independence. The rhetoric of reputation, then, was not always stable, and people of color capitalized on that.

Lacour was not unique. People of color repeatedly used their reputations as responsible property owners and creditors (coupled with their ties to their communities) to sue whites and other people of color to enforce the terms of their contracts, recover unpaid debts, recuperate back wages, and claim damages for assault.[48] Some, like Lacour, even sued whites repeatedly. Suing whites, of course, was dangerous. They risked appearing insolent. When initiating lawsuits, they needed to strike a delicate balance between deference and self-assertion. They could not forget their position within a southern racial order dedicated to white supremacy, but their very survival might mean using the courts to protect themselves, their families, and their property. Having the courage to seek redress in court against a white person might have increased their standing in their communities, especially since courts often found in favor of black litigants.[49] But much of their legal success relied on contradictions within white southerners' competing ideological beliefs. Whites wanted to control people of African descent, but they also valued private property. Black litigants like Lacour took advantage of the tension between whites' interests in upholding and enacting white supremacy and their dedication to private property, and in so doing, they protected themselves and their resources.

When black litigants went to court in the antebellum Natchez district, they exploited a local culture of law and governance in which they had a voice. Through their litigiousness, people of color searched for an immanent tension between the legal system and social relations in their communities and a way to expose and exploit those tensions. They did this by engaging in the politics of reputation. They depended on their ability to leverage the cultural scripts of reputation and their ties to their community to defend themselves and improve their situations. A good name could shield them from attack, as it did in the case of Fanny, and sometimes even allowed them privileges often reserved for white southerners, as it did with Antoine Lacour. What is more, the language that black litigants exploited—the rhetoric of servility, the language of property—(and knowing when and under which circumstances to use that language) demonstrates their ability to negotiate the realities of the world in which they lived. They were individuals—not anonymous black faces—in a legal system intimately connected to the community. Black litigants made their communities accountable to the standards of conduct whites set for people of color and used those standards to their advantage. In certain circumstances, they even kept white authority in check.

3

Advocacy

In 1830, Ann (alias Jane) Corbet, a free woman of color from New Orleans, petitioned the district court in Iberville Parish. She sought the return of her two young children, Catherine and Alexander, who were being illegally held on a plantation belonging to one François Duplesis. She hired as her "true and lawful attorney" Edmund Green, an illiterate free man of color, sending him to represent her interests in Iberville Parish and collect her children to bring them back to New Orleans. The trial record repeatedly referred to Green as both her "lawful attorney" and her "attorney in fact," and he signed his name to the petition (with an "X") as her legal representative.[1] In spite of what we might surmise to be his lack of formal training, he advocated for Corbet in the Iberville Parish court and helped her secure a writ of habeas corpus demanding that Duplesis bring the children before the court and return them to Corbet's custody.

A free black advocate like Green was a rare figure in antebellum America, not just in the Natchez district.[2] Here a qualification is necessary; information on Green is thin, unfortunately. It is doubtful that he submitted to an examination and was formally admitted to the Louisiana bar. It is more likely that his legal practice, if he had one, was ad hoc. Although he could not read Blackstone or Kent, he must have learned to speak the language of law as many ordinary residents of that place and time, including white lawyers: by observing and participating in the local legal culture. Whether or not he had a license to practice law, which was unlikely, the court in Iberville Parish recognized Green as Corbet's legal representative and permitted him to proceed as such. He was successful in helping her reclaim her children.

Both Green and Corbet—a black advocate representing a black plaintiff—implied a shift in the existing legal order in the cotton South and created a dissonance between what was said in court and who was speaking. For whites in the courtroom, the scene probably appeared jarring or farcical. The very notion of a "black litigant" is paradoxical and points to a tension in the way that white southerners understood objecthood and legal agency in a slave society.

Suing and acting in court in the service of one's interests and to protect one's livelihood, one's body, or one's family involved a claim to legal person-hood and a property-based selfhood. "An action," according to the Louisiana *Code of Practice*, "is the right given to every person, *to claim judicially* what is due or belongs to him." It also involved "*the exercise of that right*, that is to say, a judicial demand founded on a contract, or given by law, by which the plaintiff prays that the person against whom he proceeds, be ordered to do that which he has bound himself towards him to perform."[3] In particular—as the Louisiana *Code* envisioned—white men took action and made judicial claims. By using the courts to protect their own interests, black litigants exercised a legal personhood usually reserved for white men only. As Barbara Welke demonstrates, "personhood, citizenship, and nation were imagined in abled, racialized, and gendered terms."[4] What is more, the legal authority of white men was vital to the shape American law took in the nineteenth century, for it defined those who were full members and those who were not.[5] White men's privilege and their superior claims to independence, personhood, and citizenship (all accorded by law) rested on the exclusion (as well as the domination and ownership) of others.[6] Thus, when black litigants like Corbet made claims in court, Natchez district judges, lawyers, and other whites in the courtroom confronted situations in which objects of property became subjects of selfhood.

That a black man represented Corbet was equally illogical. Like the "black litigant," the "black advocate" was an oxymoron. Most white southerners believed black people were intellectually inferior to whites and suited only for slavery; they were neither advocates nor active participants in civil society. They could beg for things but not advocate for them—an important distinction. They did not, in the minds of many whites, have the capacity for interpretation, rational thought, or the reasoned analysis required of advocates. This line of thinking had a distinguished pedigree. In *Notes on the State of Virginia*, Thomas Jefferson points to the intellectual deficiency of people of African descent to justify denying them civic equality: "Comparing them by their faculties of memory, reason, and imagination," Jefferson writes, "it appears to me, that in memory they are equal to the whites; in reason much inferior, . . . and that in imagination they are dull, tasteless, and anomalous." They could recite and mimic, but, as Jefferson continues, "never yet could I find that a black had uttered a thought above the level of plain narration."[7] Black advocacy was not just incongruous, however. It was also potentially dangerous to the social and racial order of the slave South, for it could provide an entry point into the larger system of governance. Black people—as litigants and advocates—were outsiders, subjects of law rather than agents of it.[8]

Nonetheless, on significant occasions, many African Americans managed to bend the southern legal system to their will. In some cases, they could do this through their own initiative, or through the initiative of another legal amateur acting in their stead—such as Edmund Green. In most cases, however, the more effective strategy for achieving their goals was a very contemporary one: hiring a lawyer. To employ a lawyer, to get him to stand in public and stake his reputation on the claims of a black person, was, in its own way, an act of self-advocacy.

The region's many lawyers who represented people of color were white men, law's normative persons. More than two hundred white lawyers from the Natchez district represented black clients in the first half of the nineteenth century. Black clients were a regular and ordinary part of the region's attorneys' practice, and with the fees lawyers collected from their clients (black and white), many became rich. Local lawyers served all manner of clients, and representing people of color neither damaged their reputations nor depleted their bank accounts.

What was profitable or even routine for a lawyer, however, could ultimately be troublesome for a judge. People of color suing on their own behalf also appeared by the hundreds in the courtrooms of Natchez district judges. While lawyers advocated, judges had to find a balance between the individual claims made by people of African descent and the integrity of legal doctrines and the slave system as a whole. The claims-making of black people, moreover, pressed judges to confront situations in which the central pillars of their society—white supremacy and private property—came into conflict.

This chapter turns away from the linguistic strategies people of color mobilized in court to investigate white lawyers' incentives to represent black litigants and white judges' motivations when deciding cases involving African Americans' claims. It assesses the role of white people in the story of black litigiousness. Of course, rhetoric remained important, but rhetoric rarely led to results without a particular institutional makeup. Understanding the institutional framework of the Natchez district bench and bar—in this case, the makeup of the legal professionals, the internal hierarchies and values, the incentive patterns, and the pressure points and tensions—provides insight into how and where marginalized peoples inserted themselves and under what circumstances.

Yet an account of white southerners' motivations only takes us so far in explaining black legal action. People of color did not go to court because whites "allowed" them to; they went because they understood their relationships through a particular prism, and because they felt entitled to make demands on others and that their demands should be executed. Law, moreover, is a complex social practice neither captured by one group alone nor dependent primarily on a single group's ideological commitments. As I shall suggest by way of conclusion, this relatively straightforward insight has substantial consequences for how we understand the dynamic interplay between race, rights, and law in the antebellum South more generally.

I begin, however, with a discussion of the Natchez district bar and legal education in the first half of the nineteenth century. Examining how white lawyers learned law is, in some ways, proxy evidence for how black people learned to speak in the register of law. Far from showing mastery of a discrete body of knowledge, legal practice in the antebellum South proved highly variable, with diverse levels of technical skill. Most important, knowing "the law" meant learning on one's feet and tapping into a discourse of everyday life.

THE BAR

The Natchez district bar was lucrative and crowded.[9] The Old Southwest, with its rapidly expanding economy, attracted many men looking to capitalize on the opportunities presented by the booming markets in cotton, sugar, and slaves. John A. Quitman, for example, moved to the Deep South to practice law because, as he wrote in a letter to his father, money there was "plenty" and "their cotton, sugar, tobacco and rice are always in demand, and the world will not do without them."[10] "No part of the United States," Quitman continued in another letter, "holds out better prospects for a young lawyer."[11] Ambitious lawyers like Joseph Glover Baldwin—a man with only two years of formal schooling—considered the region a "legal Utopia, peopled by a race of eager litigants, only waiting for the lawyers to come on and divide out to them the shells of a bountiful system of squabbling."[12] Lawyers moved to the Natchez district by the dozens, having been drawn there by "exhilarating prospects of fussing, quarrelling, murdering, violation of contracts, and the whole catalogue of *crimen falsi*—in fine, a flush tide of litigation in all of these departments, civil and criminal."[13] The Lower Mississippi Valley's booms and busts—its enormous wealth built with speculation, unmanageable debt, ruthless competition, and violent exploitation—provided lawyers with an endless supply of bickering clients. In such a place, Baldwin promised, "all the floodgates of litigation were opened, and the pent-up tide let loose upon the country."[14] If "defective titles," "unsound negroes," "universal indebtedness," "hard and ruinous bargains," and "an elegant assortment of frauds construc-tive and actual" could not drum up enough clients, then the criminal docket would. As Baldwin wrote with glee, "what country could boast more largely of its crimes? What more splendid role of felonies! What more terrific mur-ders! What gorgeous bank robberies! . . . And in Indian affairs!—the very mention is suggestive of the poetry of theft—the romance of a wild and weird larceny."[15]

While many lawyers serviced regular clients, they did not specialize in just one area of law. According to Baldwin, "the range of practice was large. The lawyer had to practice in all sorts of courts, State and Federal, inferior and Supreme. He had the bringing up of a lawsuit, from its birth in the writ to its grave in the sheriff's docket."[16] There was no separate plaintiffs' bar or defense bar. Most accepted all types of cases and did not distinguish between clients. Many of those clients were people of color.

In the first half of the nineteenth century, national standards for legal education were inchoate. Most prospective lawyers studied law by apprentic-ing in the law offices of practicing attorneys. Thus, lawyers learned law-office law—local law that suited the needs of their communities. Although some received additional training at the few colleges with recently created law lectureships (the College of William and Mary established the first in 1779, followed by Brown in 1790, King's College in 1795, and Transylvania Univer-sity in 1799), real instruction took place on the ground in local law offices and courtrooms. Students read law in the offices of lawyers in good standing, usually for a period of two to three years (although this varied). For instance, George Winchester, a prominent Natchez attorney, politician, and judge read law for two years in the office of the Salem, Massachusetts, lawyer Joseph Pickering. On completion of his studies he received a certificate from Pick-ering verifying his abilities and character: "I hereby certify that Mr. George Winchester of this town has been a student at law in my office for about two years past, during which period he pursued his studies with much affinity; and I further certify, that his exceptionable character and his acquirements in professional learning are such as entitle him to the confidence of the pub-lic."[17] Others read law on their own. As Abraham Lincoln wrote in an 1858 letter, "the cheapest, quickest, and best way" to become a lawyer was to "read Blackstone's *Commentaries*, Chitty's *Pleadings*, Greenleaf's *Evidence*, Story's

Equity and Story's *Equity Pleading*, get a license, and go into the practice and still keep reading."[18] The Natchez attorney Thomas Reed and his brother, James, read law together, and to aid him in his training, Thomas wrote a "Key to Blackstone," a small, handwritten notebook that he used to make sense of various principles explored in Sir William Blackstone's *Commentaries on the Laws of England*.[19] Some, like John T. McMurran, had little education and read law in the office of his uncle. Despite his modest beginnings, McMurran eventually practiced law in the largest, busiest, and most respected law office in the region. There he continued to learn on the job and became particularly adept at handling commercial litigation.[20] Each method—apprenticeship and self-education—emphasized hands-on experience. Most law-office education focused on the practical skills of litigating and teaching students to argue cases before a court. Students learned by doing and observing.[21]

Others acquired additional training. Edward Turner, for instance, supplemented his practical, law-office education with a more formal legal education at Transylvania University in Kentucky, one of the first universities to implement a law lectureship. At Transylvania University, he read Blackstone's *Commentaries* and developed a vision of the law as a cohesive body of rules and principles. This vision of the law (as a unified set of principles) was newly developing in the post-Revolutionary era, as (mostly) elite, state-level legal professionals throughout the nation sought to create a uniform, clearly defined, and universally applicable body of law to supplant the more flexible system of "localized law" (law that "emerged from the daily lives of actual people") practiced on the ground in most communities.[22] As a student, Turner began exploring the notion that the study of law was a science—a set of universally applicable principles resulting from reason, not passion. He applied his practical skills and his reading of treatises in written compositions that explored legal issues of the time, such as his thoughts on civil government.[23]

Learning to speak in the register of the law, however, did not require formal education. Some spoke it more fluently than others. As Joseph Glover Baldwin relayed, "practicing law, like shinplaster banking or a fight, was pretty much a free thing."[24]

At the end of their training or reading period, prospective lawyers gained admission to the bar after appearing before a committee of local lawyers or judges and submitting to an oral examination. After completing his law-office education, Thomas Reed passed an exam administered by Mississippi judge George Coulter and received a certificate granting him permission to practice law. It read, "The State of Mississippi, Be it Known that the undersigned having Examined Thomas Reed touching his knowledge of the law and finding him duly qualified to practice as counselor and attorney and the said Thomas Reed having produced satisfactory evidence of his moral character I do hereby authorize the said Thomas Reed to practice as an attorney and counselor in the several courts of the first Judicial District of Mississippi."[25]

The rigor of such examinations varied, as did the lucidity and quality of the prospective lawyer's answers. Joseph Glover Baldwin described witnessing one aspiring attorney's examination by a Natchez judge. The candidate, Thomas Jefferson Knowly, "was not encumbered with any learning," Baldwin confided. When the examining judge began by asking, "what is a *chose in action*," Knowly answered clumsily, "A chosen action? eh?—yes—exactly—just so—a chosen action? Why, a chosen action is—whare a man's got a right to fetch two of three actions, and he chuses one of 'em which he will fetch—the one that's chuse is the—chosen action; that's easy, squire."[26] His answers only grew worse over the course of his examination, and he did not receive a license to practice law. Most candidates for law licenses were not as ignorant as Knowly, and those with a cursory knowledge of Blackstone's *Commentaries* usually passed their examinations. Entry to the bar was not necessarily a reflection of a student's formal knowledge of legal theory; instead, because the nineteenth-century lawyer was primarily a litigator, admission to the bar gave him the go-ahead to learn through practice.[27] Practical, on-the-ground training was especially important in the frontier atmosphere of the Old Southwest where lawyers and litigants needed to adapt legal principles to local, rapidly changing circumstances.

In the midst of the bonanza of fees for Natchez district lawyers, it is no surprise that attorneys took clients both black and white. Black clients were a regular and ordinary part of their practice. At least 211 lawyers in the region represented people of color. Moreover, such attorneys were not lawyers working exclusively for black communities; rather, they represented both whites and blacks. The Louisiana attorney and sugar planter Charles Poydras, for instance, established a lucrative law practice representing all manner of clients in cases that ranged from land disputes to divorce. At least twenty of his clients were people of color.[28] Nathan Meriam, an Iberville Parish lawyer and judge, often represented free women of color in their debt-recovery lawsuits, and Thomas Nichols, another Iberville Parish attorney, represented black women in their lawsuits for divorce.[29] Between 1840 and 1860, Auguste Provosty, a successful Harvard-educated attorney practicing in Pointe Coupee Parish, represented at least thirty black clients. For instance, he repeatedly aided

Martin Juge, a free man of color, in his debt-recovery lawsuits. He also represented the interests of Antoine Decuir, a wealthy, free black sugar planter.[30] While many lawyers accepted people of color as clients, they just as often served as attorneys for those challenging black people. Although Archibald Haralson often represented Isabella Hawkins, he also represented others in their lawsuits against her.[31] Natchez attorneys Cowls Mead and William B. Shields frequently faced off against one another in the Adams County courtroom, alternatively representing blacks and whites. They also represented both enslaved people and slaveholders. For instance, in 1808, Mead served as the attorney for Coleman Grymes and his brother London in their lawsuit for freedom against a white slaveholder, Thomas Foster. Shields represented Foster and lost the case. A few years later Shields served as Aaron Cooper's attorney in his successful freedom suit against the white planter Parmenas Briscoe. This time Mead represented the losing defendant.[32]

Representing people of color did not harm attorneys' law practices, and they enjoyed successful and profitable careers. Some went on to serve as judges and politicians, and a number transitioned from lawyer to large-scale planter. This seems unexpected, because the little we know about the lawyers who represented black people in the region is negative. In particular, Judith Kelleher Schafer argues that one New Orleans attorney who represented enslaved litigants was a "sleazy" and "inept" bottom-feeder.[33] Schafer traces the life of the attorney Jean Charles David, who represented nineteen enslaved people in their lawsuits for freedom. In her portrayal, David emerges as a corrupt man living at the bottom of the social ladder. According to Schafer, because David represented slaves, he alienated prospective white clients of superior wealth and standing. For this reason, he spent his life in debt.[34]

In the Natchez district, however, some of the most powerful and respected men in the region (and even the nation) represented both white and black clients—enslaved and free. They were leaders in their communities and beyond, men who actively shaped the legal and political culture of the slave South.[35] Representing people of color did not appear to affect their reputations, and it certainly did not jeopardize their bottom line.[36] Nearly all were slaveholders, and many were wealthy. For instance, William B. Shields served as an attorney for a number of enslaved clients as well as wealthy white planters. His successful law career secured him a position as a judge on the Mississippi Superior Court, and in 1818 President James Monroe nominated him as a judge for the U.S. District Court, District of Mississippi. He served in that position until his death in 1823. Others who represented black clients enjoyed similar success. John A. Quitman served as governor of Mississippi, a judge on the Mississippi High Court of Errors and Appeals, and a general in the Mexican-American War; Powhatan Ellis was a U.S. senator from Mississippi and a federal judge; and Walter Leake was both a Mississippi senator and governor.

Attorneys representing black clients were not abolitionists: indeed, lawyering in the Natchez district provided most practitioners with the money to speculate on land and slaves. For instance, the legal careers of John A. Quitman and John T. McMurran set the stage for a windfall of riches; they owned hundreds of enslaved laborers and thousands of acres of land.[37] Charles Poydras was one of the wealthier sugar planters in Pointe Coupee Parish. In 1860, he possessed ninety-six enslaved laborers, and he owned real and personal property valued at $220,000.[38] Those who became judges started as lawyers, during which time they also became planters and large-scale slaveholders. For instance, the Natchez lawyer turned judge and planter, Edward Turner, began acquiring slaves in the 1820s, and by 1850 he owned 220 enslaved laborers. Others owned fewer slaves, but still attained planter status. Before he died in 1823, William B. Shields owned forty-one slaves, and John Dutton, an Iberville Parish judge, owned twenty-eight slaves in 1820.[39] Although they did not accumulate the same degree of wealth as Turner, Shields and Dutton resided firmly within the ranks of the planter class. Representing black clients limited neither lawyers' opportunities for professional success nor their potential to amass enormous wealth.

Even for the less prominent, serving black clients did not damage their reputations or hinder their ability to attract white clients. One such attorney, William B. Griffith, commanded respect throughout the region. A native of Maryland, Griffith relocated to Natchez around 1818 and soon gained distinction as a talented litigator. Although he did not acquire great wealth, he was comfortable. When he died in 1829, his estate consisted of five slaves and some luxuries, including a few hundred books.[40] His clients ranged from wealthy, white planters such as Adam L. Bingaman and Bingaman's involvement in civil litigation to Lewis Burwell, a free man of color who repeatedly faced criminal charges in Adams County. He ran a thriving law practice, first alone and then alongside his partner, John A. Quitman. Griffith's reputation as a talented and successful lawyer, as well as the opportunities presented by practicing law in the Old Southwest, attracted Quitman to the region. On arrival in Natchez in 1821, Quitman borrowed money from Griffith and read law in Griffith's office. When he passed his examination a year later, Griffith made him a partner. John T. McMurran joined the firm in 1828, a year before Griffith died of yellow fever.[41] After Griffith's death, Quitman and McMurran continued to represent both white and black clients, just as Griffith had done before them.

Over the course of his ten-year career in Natchez, Griffith represented at least two dozen free and enslaved African Americans in a wide range of criminal and civil cases. He defended free blacks and slaves charged with larceny or insulting a white person; he helped black creditors recover unpaid loans; he aided free blacks in their lawsuits to claim damages for assault; and he represented enslaved people suing for their freedom.[42]

Griffith used his connections in both Natchez and his native Maryland to aid his clients. For instance, John Hamm, a man of color suing for his freedom in Natchez, hired Griffith as his attorney, and Griffith rallied the support of several influential white men in his efforts to help Hamm secure his liberty. In his petition to the Adams County Superior Court in 1819, Hamm told the court that he was an indentured servant and the son of a white servant woman, Elizabeth McGuire, and an unnamed black slave. His mother had died "shortly after his birth" in Kent County, Maryland, and he "was bound as an apprentice" to a local man named William Sutton until his twenty-first birthday. With the permission of his master, Hamm relayed, he had attended an evangelical "camp meeting" in the woods of Kent County in August 1816. During the meeting, however, Hamm's cousin (also a man of color) and two other unsavory characters kidnapped him. They then "forcibly . . . brought him down the river to Natchez where he was transferred from one to another until . . . James H. Steele" bought "him as a slave for life." He asked the court for his freedom from enslavement by Steele and Charles B. Green, two local men.

Griffith went to great lengths to help Hamm gain his freedom. He began by seeking out Sutton, Hamm's master in Maryland (the man Hamm was allegedly bound to as an indentured servant), and sent him a letter requesting his assistance. Griffith asked him to secure the depositions of several local witnesses familiar with Hamm's status as an indentured servant and privy to the events in question. He gave Sutton precise instructions on how to conduct the depositions for them to be admissible in the circuit court in Natchez. Griffith also called on his own professional and personal networks to support Hamm's bid for freedom. He suggested that Sutton seek the council of Ezekiel Chambers, a Maryland lawyer and the brother of James Chambers, a Natchez resident and an acquaintance of Griffith's. Chambers, Griffith believed, would "see that everything [was] done in due form" and "immediately." Moreover, with Hamm's story and his description of his kidnapping in mind, Griffith requested that the witnesses address the following questions: Was Hamm the son of a white woman and a slave father? Was he an indentured servant? If so, indentured to "whom and for how long a period?" Was he "forcibly taken away or kidnapped from a camp meeting held in the forest of Kent County?" What was Hamm's reputation "in the neighborhood?" Did anyone in the neighborhood think of Hamm as "as slave for life or was he ever claimed as such by anyone?" Did he have any identifiable marks on his body? Griffith insisted that the witnesses provide "full & explicit . . . answers, and state everything which [they] thought [would] be material" in order to help "rescue a fellow from an unjust & cruel state of slavery."

Both Sutton and Chambers swiftly came to Hamm's aid. Sutton wrote to the judge in the case, William B. Shields, and provided him with a copy of Hamm's indenture agreement. Sutton insisted that Hamm was his apprentice and his responsibility. Whether motivated by human feeling for Hamm or by a desire to recover his indentured servant, Sutton pledged to do anything in his "power to [help] release him from the unrighteous bonds which the inequity of his fellow man forced him to wear." Chambers, the Maryland attorney, also wrote a letter to the judge, assuring him that Hamm was an indentured servant born of a white mother. Hamm's cousin, "a negro man named Phil," kidnapped him and sold him to a slave trader. "His freedom," Chambers continued, "was not in the least degree controversial." The evidence, he claimed, "will be found entirely satisfactory and fully sufficient to afford Hamm's liberation—I have no doubt." In addition, Chambers sent the court the depositions of twelve witnesses familiar with Hamm. Most had known him since his birth. The witnesses claimed that Hamm was an indentured servant and not a slave, the son of a white mother and a slave father, had been kidnapped in Maryland, and illegally sold into slavery. The lawsuit was suspended in 1822 without explanation. But it is likely that the parties resolved their dispute outside the courtroom. Given the evidence in Hamm's favor, Griffith's stature in the Natchez community, his success in helping other wrongfully enslaved people secure their legal freedom, and the number of whites who offered their assistance, it is quite possible that Hamm obtained his liberty.[43]

Assessing why Griffith (and white lawyers more generally) went to such trouble to represent black clients like Hamm is tricky. That black people's networks included white lawyers or patrons does not adequately answer the question (although presumably white lawyers sometimes represented black clients for this reason). Certainly black people cultivated relationships with white people, including lawyers, and called on those bonds when necessary.

But enslaved plaintiffs in freedom suits in the Natchez district were most often the victims of kidnapping and trafficking and thus strangers to the community.[44] Hamm, like many enslaved litigants, was unknown to Griffith. It could be that Griffith served black clients out of respect for or protection of the law. If they were illegally detained as slaves, Mississippi law permitted enslaved people to sue directly for their freedom in the circuit courts.[45] Griffith's contemporaries described him as "a man of much and varied learning," a man who had "mastered the science of law in all of its branches."[46] He held the legal system in high regard, and there were moments when the law protected the rights of the oppressed. It is also possible that Griffith viewed representing wrongly enslaved black clients as a species of justice: Hamm was a free man illegally held as a slave, and thus Griffith dutifully followed the law to safeguard a free person from the injustice of enslavement. His law partner, John A. Quitman, described him as a "noble man" of the highest order: Griffith, Quitman relayed, "has every quality to command respect . . . he pursues a steady and undeviating course in the true road to professional eminence. . . . Hard application and severe logic, thorough preparation of his cases, and astonishing energy of will are his characteristics."[47] He may also have represented black clients as a matter of honor, statesmanship, or even paternalism: as a member of the bar governed by a code of ethics, perhaps he viewed it as his duty or his burden to protect and represent the weak, as a master would his slave.[48] Members of the Mississippi bar saw themselves, in the words of another Natchez attorney and contemporary of Griffith and Quitman, as "a body of gentlemen distinguished then, as now, and at all times, for their integrity, patriotism, scrupulous honor, and high-toned courtesy."[49]

The desire to act as a man of honor with a sense of protectionism or paternalism, however, also does not sufficiently address why white lawyers took black clients. The very claims black people made in court—to freedom, property, self-direction, civic inclusion, and civil rights—challenged the system of racial hierarchy and black slavery from and on which white men's honor and paternalism derived and depended. In the slaveholders' republic, subjugating and dishonoring black people enhanced white men's honor.[50] Importantly, dishonoring people of African descent included casting them as outsiders and denying them any standing in civil society.[51] Representing black clients in civil suits, moreover, would make for a strange way to bolster honor—particularly in more routine cases like debt recovery or a suit for back wages: it is far from the kind of highly charged symbolic behavior that makes honor and dishonor visible to others. Instead, standing up in court and advocating on behalf of black people's claims was, in its way, recognition that these clients were more than just racialized outsiders suitable only for en-slavement. It meant acknowledging black membership in civil society. Aiding an enslaved man in his lawsuit for freedom or a free black woman in her claim to a plot of land also meant working against the social and material interests of a slave society. While it is tempting to attribute the actions of white lawyers to a particular set of values or a worldview such as honor or paternalism, to do so is problematic. Not least of all because it assumes that people always act in accordance with their values and that one's values are stable and shared with others.[52]

To return to Griffith for a moment: while he sought to "rescue" Hamm from his "unjust & cruel state of slavery," he was a slaveholder himself and probably not motivated by anti-slavery feelings. He also married into a wealthy slaveholding family: his father-in-law was the planter and judge Edward Turner. In representing people of color, Griffith was not mounting a challenge against the institution of slavery. As Griffith knew well, the laws allowing illegally enslaved people to sue for freedom were not intended to protect the rights of slaves. Instead, they protected free people from illegal enslavement. As the antebellum legal theorist Thomas R. R. Cobb wrote, "the suit for freedom is allowed only to those who are actually free, and are wrongfully detained in bondage."[53] The lawyers who represented people of color were not abolitionists or early cause lawyers, and they certainly were no saints. For instance, one of the defendants in Hamm's lawsuit for freedom, Charles B. Green, was also a lawyer. He and his partner, Christopher Rankin, represented both black and white clients, and they even represented enslaved people in their lawsuits for freedom.[54] It scarcely needs to be emphasized that when talking about legal professionals we ought not to be quick to suspect altruistic motives.

Lawyers left few clues as to why they took black clients, leaving the matter open to speculation. In the extant personal papers and letters of lawyers and judges from the region, no references exist to any of their black clients or to black litigants more generally. Griffith and the other attorneys probably rep-resented black clients for a host of reasons, including patronage and human feeling. But given the sheer number of black litigants present in the region's courts and the wealth of Natchez district attorneys, money may have been a top motivator.

Griffith, Green, Rankin, and the two hundred other attorneys who represented people of color did not work for free, and serving black clients could prove lucrative. Few lawsuits listed attorney's fees among the court costs, and most lawyers' account books from the region have not survived.

Thus, the evidence does not reveal what kinds of fees Natchez district lawyers charged black clients specifically. One extant attorney's account book, that of the Claiborne County, Mississippi, lawyer Alonzo Snyder, demonstrates that attorneys' fees ranged, however. Sometimes Snyder charged his clients a percentage of the final judgment (typically 10 percent); in other cases he levied a standard fee, such as ten dollars for filing a suit and twenty dollars for drawing up a deed.[55] Frederick H. Farrar, a Pointe Coupee Parish lawyer and district court judge, also charged his clients a 10 percent fee and sometimes struggled to get them to pay up. After serving as Sarah Connor's attorney for five years in a lawsuit in which she received a judgment for $28,000, she refused to pay his $2,800 fee. In a heated exchange of letters between them, Farrar and Conner disagreed over both his fee and the unpaid balance. Eventually Farrar offered to have "the amount of my fees to be fixed by any three gentlemen of the profession, one to be selected by each of us and then to be selected by an umpire."[56] It is unclear if Conner agreed to such an arrangement. Like white clients, free people of color hired attorneys and probably paid similar fees. Although some free people of color in the region lived hand to mouth, many free black people owned property and had the means to obtain a lawyer. Yet like clients everywhere, they did not always pay their attorney's fees. Lewis Viales sued the free black descendants of Pierre Belly three times for failing to pay him for his legal services after he had helped them settle the estate of the deceased.[57] Sometimes the courts added the attorney's fees to the overall court costs and ordered the losing party to pay the balance. This proved helpful for enslaved people suing for their freedom who might not be able to raise the capital to pay an attorney. For instance, when John, a man of color, sued George Williams, a white slaveholder, for his freedom, the court issued a verdict in John's favor, found him to be a free man, and ordered Williams to pay the court costs. The costs included John's attorney's fees—ten dollars to be paid to William B. Griffith.[58]

Black clients, however, were susceptible to their lawyers' lack of scruples in ways that white clients were not. In a region with a social order dedicated to black slavery, lawyers sometimes took advantage of their black clients' particular vulnerabilities. For instance, because she was enslaved and could not pay her lawyer's fees in her freedom suit, Phoebe, a woman of color in Natchez, promised to indenture her son, Harrison, to her attorney until Harrison turned twenty-one. After helping her secure her freedom and the freedom of her children, her lawyer, Spenser M. Grayson (who occasionally represented black clients), took possession of Harrison and sold him to one Abner Mardis. A year later, Harrison, aided by his mother, petitioned the court for

CLERK'S COSTS.

Writ and Docketing, ———— *25*

Entering return, ———— *12*

    appearance, ———— *25*

    continuances, ————*1. 00*

Filing papers, ————

Judgment by default, ———— *1. 75*

    rules, ———— *71*

    motions, ———— *41*

    orders, ———— *21*

Swearing and impanelling jury, — *25*

Swearing witnesses, *verdict* *34*

Venire facias, ———— *25*

Judgment final, ———— *25*

Recording judgment, *3. 50*

Taxing cost and copy, ————*71*

Execution and filing, ————*1. 50*

Issuing   subpœnas,

Issuing commission, ————*1. 25*

Copies   sheets,

Witness' certificates. ——*12* *0 75*

SHERIFF'S FEES.

Serving writ and copy,

Entering and return,

Taking bail bond,

Summoning   witnesses,

Venire, ———— *50*

ATTO. *Griffith* *10*

Tax, *2*

$ 25 .25

On occasion, the court costs document the attorneys' fees. *John v. Williams*, Historic Natchez Foundation, Natchez, Mississippi; photograph by the author.

a writ of habeas corpus, claiming that Mardis held him as his slave and kept him from "exercising the rights and privileges of a free born person." Mardis brought Harrison before the court, as the writ demanded, but after he explained that Phoebe indentured Harrison to Grayson because she could not pay her legal fees, and he bought the indenture from Grayson for $100, the court dismissed the case.[59]

Harrison's case reminds us that we should be wary of imputing to lawyers who represented people of color benevolent motives or anti-slavery sentiments: for just after Grayson had helped to free a family, he turned around and took a property interest in a member of that family and liquidated that property interest as soon as he could. Grayson, an attorney who on occasion represented enslaved people suing for their freedom, bought and sold his former client, demonstrating no evident qualms about treating black people as chattel.[60]

White men like Grayson represented black clients for the money, but others took matters a bit more personally. Edmund Green, whom we met at in the beginning of this chapter, was not the only man of color advocating for another before the Natchez district courts. Consider the case of Norman Davis. Davis, an illiterate free black man from West Feliciana Parish, represented a white man, John L. Collins, as his "attorney in fact," a designated legal representative not necessarily licensed to practice law. But when representing Collins, Davis also advocated for his own interests. In 1840, Collins petitioned the court in West Feliciana Parish, represented "by Norman Davis, a free man of color, his attorney in fact." Collins wanted to manumit Catherine and her children, an enslaved family owned by his recently deceased brother, for her "meritorious services and faithful, honest, & discreet conduct." Catherine, Collins added, was "acquainted with the rights of white people and the duties of People of Color," and he insisted that she would "conduct herself and raise her children to such discreet, honest, & industrious habits that the interests of society will not be injuriously affected by granting the request." The court permitted Collins's request, and, in 1841, allowed him to manumit Catherine and her children. Davis repeatedly appeared in court on Collins's behalf (as his "agent and attorney") and he signed his name with an "X" to various legal documents as Collins's legal representative. In addition, both Collins and Davis offered themselves as security, posting a $1,000 bond guaranteeing that Catherine and her children would not become public charges or wards of the state. Davis, however, had a familial interest in this case and in Catherine's manumission. The 1850 federal census shows that he, Catherine, and the children lived together in Shreveport, Louisiana.[61] So we might suspect that Collins and Davis were colluding to manumit Davis's family. Yet Davis could have guaranteed the transaction and posted a bond on behalf of Catherine and her children without serving as Collins's attorney in fact. For instance, he could have served as a surety (a person who takes responsibility for another's performance of an undertaking, such as an appearance in court or the payment of a debt) guaranteeing the bond. Formally neutral parties acted as sureties for many transactions before the courts. Among them were free people of color who were sureties in lawsuits in which they were not parties, guaranteeing the transactions of both white and black people.[62] But Davis was more than a surety; he took on a formal role in the case. Although it would be surprising if Davis had been examined before a judge and formally admitted to the Louisiana bar, the West Feliciana Parish court allowed him to represent a white man in his request to emancipate an enslaved woman and her children. While it is not clear why Collins and Davis made such an arrangement, maneuvering before the bar was possible for many people in this society, regardless of how much technical law or legal theory they knew or whether or not they were literate. Davis's interest in this case, however, was familial, as opposed to the more overtly material interests of many lawyers in the region who represented black clients.[63]

While it is difficult to separate black clients' voices from the mediation of their lawyers (as well as that of court clerks who recorded their testimony), what emerges from the documents are personalized tales of self-advocacy told by black litigants. Indeed, if lawyers alone shaped the lawsuits, then the stories presented would be more formulaic. The cases, however, were co-produced: while attorneys certainly provided their clients with litigation strategies, legal arguments, and advice about how to shape their testimony, the cases reflect the differing perspectives and varied personal histories of black litigants. The interrogatory in John Hamm's freedom suit, for instance, followed his version of the kidnapping and his genealogy. Thus, we might deduce that black clients compelled their lawyers to work for them in ways that reflected their interests, their version of the events in question, and their claims to personhood, property, family, and freedom. The extant evidence does not permit us to see how black clients chose their attorneys, the deals they made with them about payment and representation, and the specific division of labor between client and attorney. Yet they had many lawyers to choose from. Some, like Griffith, probably had better reputations for success than others. But regardless of the lawyer they chose, black litigants persuaded their attorneys to make sure their personal requests and needs were heard and met in the courtroom. What is more, lawyers may have represented black clients for a range of reasons, including financial ones. But they had access to those clients *in the first place* because there were black clients to be had—a multitude of people who knew their rights had been violated and who sought to press their claims in court.

THE BENCH

Attorneys throughout the region took property interests in black people—as clients and as slaves. Many of the lawyers in the Natchez district became wealthy. Becoming wealthy meant putting their earnings in the most potentially lucrative investments of the time: land and slaves. Nearly all Natchez lawyers became planters, and they identified with the values of the planter class.[64] Many, like John A. Quitman, turned opportunities before the bar into profitable investments and used the returns on their investments to support a certain type of lifestyle: one that included "fine horses," "well-dressed and very aristocratic servants," and "costly Port, Madeira, and sherry."[65] "Cotton-planting," according to Quitman, "is the most lucrative business that can be followed. Some of the planters net $50,000 from a single crop."[66] It was men like Quitman, moreover, who became not only great holders of property but also the primary regulators thereof: judges.[67]

In the antebellum Natchez district, at least half of the courts' daily business involved the commercial law of slavery and the regulation of black people as property.[68] Yet judges confronted people of African descent as property (property they both owned and regulated from the bench) *and* as litigants in their courtrooms. Hundreds of the disputes that came before the region's courts involved claims made by people of color. While litigants of color were not unusual, they were also potentially problematic, as were their claims to property, family, and freedom. The claims-making of people of color caused judges to grapple with the civic standing of those whom southern law made into property. When black litigants sued in court, they asserted a legal personality usually exercised by white men, and their actions forced judges to think about the far-reaching consequences of their claims.

Evidence of judges' attitudes on the place of black litigants in their courtrooms and their everyday decision-making is slim. Civil litigation in Mississippi involved jury trials, and the voices (or words) of judges rarely made it into the lower court record.[69] Most civil trials in Louisiana were bench trials administered by a judge (although plaintiffs could and sometimes did request a trial by jury in any civil suit except those involving debt recovery), but judges' final pronouncements tended to be routine and formulaic and rarely revealed their position on people of African descent acting at law.[70] Just as often, final judgments went missing from the trial record. On occasion, however, Natchez district judges used their judgments and other writings to work through their uncertainty about the tensions inherent in black litigants' claims to property, personhood, and civic identity. Given their background as lawyers and their social position as planters, one might predict that judges would either act like the region's attorneys who disregarded the race of their clients in favor of fees *or* like slaveholders who might be generally ill-disposed to black litigants. But their thinking proved more complex.

In the 1820s, Edward Turner, the prominent Mississippi lawyer turned judge and planter, presided over at least forty-five cases involving African Americans (many of them freedom suits) as a circuit court judge in Natchez. While the trial records themselves reveal little of Turner's thinking about black litigants, people of color found some redress in his courtroom and many won their lawsuits.[71] Turner owned hundreds of slaves in his lifetime, but his early writings as a student at Transylvania University provide some insight into his uneasiness regarding slave ownership, and more revealing, his thoughts on the civic identity of people of color. It was before the bar, Turner argued as a young man, that black people should lay claim to property and personhood—and by extension, to civil rights.

In 1799, Turner wrote and delivered a "Composition on Slavery" to his fellow students and professors at Transylvania University. In it, he made arguments unexpected for a man who would later become one of the larger slaveholders in Natchez. His thoughts in the "Composition" demonstrate, however, that at least one legal official in the Natchez district grappled with the entanglements of race, property, and the legal personality of black people and came to the conclusion that the courtroom represented a site in which they could air their grievances and make their claims. He made such arguments by appealing to the language of natural rights and property ownership.

Turner began his "Composition on Slavery" by asking his listeners to keep an open mind, "exercise patience," and not "condemn" his "opinion" until hearing him out. He understood that he had "long-established principles to combat and deep-rooted prejudices to defeat . . . but I do not fear surmounting all those obstacles in the course of my argument in the common cause of Justice and humanity." He then embarked on a powerful denunciation of slavery and the slave trade: "The transporting of slaves from their native country to America was contrary to human nature and a disgrace to our country. I need not at this enlightened period labour to prove. The mind that has adequate *Ideas* of the inherent rights of mankind, and known the value of them, must feel its indignation against the shameful practice of our forefathers, of making mere goods and chattels of human beings." Yet while, "by the eternal principles of human Justice, no master in the state has a right to hold a slave in bondage for a single hour," "the law of the land . . . has authorized a slavery as bad or perhaps worse than ever England knew." Positive law, Turner argued, contradicted and undermined the laws of nature. It was manmade law, after all, that transformed people of African descent into objects of property. Turner was not alone in his reasoning. Other legal professionals of the time grappled with the tensions between natural law and positive law and their relationship to slavery. For instance, when arguing before the Supreme Court in the *Antelope* case (in February 1825), Francis Scott Key, the attorney representing the interests of several hundred African captives, insisted that "by the law of nature all men are free," and positive law that made people into property was hypocrisy.[72] Similarly, Turner reminded his listeners to remember the principles of the Revolution and their joint commitment to natural rights: "We may talk of liberty in our public counsels, and say we feel a reverence for its dictate and flatter ourselves that we detest the ugly monster—but so long as we cherish the poisonous weed of partial slavery amoung us, the world will doubt our sincerity.—In the name of heaven, with what face can we call ourselves the friend of equal freedom and the inherent rights of our species, when we pass laws contrary to each, and are using our utmost endeavors to prevent our government's legislating in behalf of the oppressed. Today we may be aroused as one man against the invader of the rights of his fellow creatures: tomorrow we may be guilty of the same oppression which we reprobated and resisted in another."

Why, Turner asked his listeners, deny people of African descent rights to life, liberty, and property? "Is it because the colour of those victims is not quite so delicate as ours? Is it because their untutored minds (humbled and debased by the hereditary yoke) are less capacious than ours? Or, is it because we have so long been habituated to their deplorable situation, as to have become callous to the horrors of it—that we are determined to keep them and their offspring until time shall be no more, on a level with the brutes?"

Turner then asked his listeners to imagine for a moment what one such "unhappy victim"—a slave—might say when "pleading at the bar of justice, the cause of himself and his fellow sufferers—what would be the language of this oration of nature?" Here Turner alluded to John Locke's formulation of the "state of nature," a place where all are born equal in regard to their rights to life, liberty, and property. By ventriloquizing a slave using the language of property and natural rights in particular to speak before the bar about his condition—and making a reasoned argument when doing so—Turner revealed his position on black people and the law: "This my imagination tells me he would address his hearers: 'We belong, by the laws of the country to our masters, Subject to our rigorous doom—We do not wish them to lose their property—We do not wish you lawmakers to compel an immediate emancipation of us or our posterity, because Justice to their fellow citizens forbids it." Respect the laws of property, Turner reminded his listeners, but remember your moral duty. "We only supplicate you not to restrain the gentle arm of humanity which it may be stretched forth in our behalf," said Turner's "unhappy victim," "not to oppose that moral or religious conviction which may at any time incline a majority of you to give freedom to us or our unoffending offspring—not to interrupt legislative interference to the course of voluntary manumission . . ." Turner continued, "We have not (would he argue) rebelled against our masters—We have wielded our necks, submissive to the yoke, and without a murmur remained satisfied, in the destruction of our natural rights."

"What could we answer to arguments like these," Turner asked his audience. How does extending "equal rights" to the oppressed impede the rights of others, he wondered. Is "our vanity and self consequence wounded at the idea of a darky African participating equally with ourselves in the rights of human nature, and rising to a level with us, from the lowest point of degradation? Prejudice of this kind, my hearers, are often so powerful, as to persuade us that whatever countervails them is the extremity of folly, and that the peculiar path of wisdom is that which leads to their gratification."[73]

In this composition, Turner did not explicitly argue for an end to the institution of slavery, gradually or otherwise. He was more interested in stopping the passage of laws limiting voluntary, individual manumissions. He remained, after all, cognizant of the property rights of slaveholders, as did the slave he ventriloquized. But Turner also delivered a powerful argument for the extension of natural rights to people of African descent—rights he defined as not simply "inherent" but also "equal" and endowing "equal freedom." Most important, he imagined that the place where one would advocate for those rights was before the "bar of justice," by availing himself of the rhetoric of law. Such a person, moreover, would do so by appealing to the language of property rights—the same language that southern slaveholders used to defend their right to hold people as property. What is more, in asking his listeners to imagine an enslaved person appealing to the "bar of justice," Turner invited his audience to recognize people of color as legally responsible persons rather than property.

As he got older, however, Turner's worldview and values evolved. In 1860, more than sixty years after delivering this composition and near the end of his life, Turner revisited his early work and wrote the following notation: "This was spoken by me at the Tra. University on 24th May 1799. Sensible of my incompetency to speak with propriety on any subject, but particularly that of slavery cause me to rise with diffidence and distrust."[74] It appears that his thinking changed over the years—how quickly is hard to say. Within a decade after delivering his "Composition," he started to acquire slaves himself. Nonetheless, Turner began his legal career with doubts about the exclusion of people of African descent from civil society, and throughout his tenure as a lawyer and a judge—and even as he accumulated slave property—he treated black litigants as if they had a legal personality (as did his son-in-law, William B. Griffith). It was before the bar, after all, that Turner had imagined that people of color should make such claims.[75]

The civic identity of people of African descent and the restrictions on their right to participate as equals before the "bar of justice" troubled other judges in the region as well. When faced with black litigants in their courtrooms, litigants who claimed rights to property and self-possession, judges had to face head-on the contradictions in the values they held most dear—specifically, the tensions between race and property. Consider, for example, the position of the judge in Pierre Salvador's 1844 lawsuit against John C. Turner (a lawsuit I discussed at length in chapter 1). In that lawsuit, Salvador, a free man of color, sued Turner, a white man, in the district court in Pointe Coupee Parish to evict him from his land. With the backing of the Preemption Act of 1841 that provided settlers with the opportunity to buy public land at a reduced price, Salvador had settled on nearly two hundred acres in Louisiana. Turner, however, had also made a claim on the same lot and argued that Salvador had no right of preemption because he was black and thus excluded (in Turner's mind) from citizenship. Turner was not alone in sketching a picture of the normative American citizen as white and male. For instance, Joseph Lumpkin, the chief justice of the Supreme Court of Georgia, spent a good deal of his time on the bench denying that free blacks ever were or ever could be citizens of either Georgia or the nation.[76] In late 1845, however, the court in Pointe Coupee Parish ruled in Salvador's favor and declared Turner a trespasser.[77]

In his final judgment, Judge H. F. Deblieux thought carefully about whether or not personhood and civic identity could be extended to free people of color. Ultimately he decided that it was not up to his court to "interfere" in or act on the question of citizenship, and even if his court "could be called upon to decide whether a free person of color is a citizen of the United States, one would find the preponderance of authorities is in the favor of the plaintiff."[78] Before rendering this judgment, however, Deblieux had turned to others with authority on the matter. In particular, he cited a section of James Kent's *Commentaries on American Law* in which Kent explored the ambiguity of the citizenship status of free blacks. Deblieux appeared to follow Kent's position that "in most of the United States, there is a distinction in respect to political privileges between free white persons and free coloured persons of African blood; and in no part of the country, except in Maine, do the latter, in point of fact, participate equally with the whites, in the exercise of civil and political rights."[79] But, as Kent indicated, the rights afforded to citizens differed according to gender, race, and jurisdiction. Free blacks, like white women, were citizens but barred from holding office or voting according to the laws of their state of residence.[80] Free people of color faced legal restrictions on their full participation in civil society, yet they were not excluded from citizenship. Because both the questions of who could be a citizen and what rights citizenship entailed remained inchoate in this time period, Salvador's lawsuit forced Deblieux to confront the possibility that people of color could lay claim to legal personhood, if not citizenship.

What is more, Deblieux could not ignore black public presence; indeed, in the 1840s, he presided over many lawsuits involving people of color. Like Edward Turner, Deblieux also acknowledged the legal personhood (and the rights associated with it) claimed by litigants of color, for in his courtroom they routinely sued to protect their rights to property, family, self-ownership, and self-direction.[81] Such lawsuits compelled judges like Turner and Deblieux to formally assess the relationship between race and civic identity.

Yet lawsuits like Salvador's also pressed judges to choose between the two most important foundations of their society: racial hierarchy and private property. When faced with this paradox, Natchez district judges found themselves in good company. As Adrienne Davis has shown in her study of race, sex, and private law in the nineteenth-century South, inheritance cases involving the transfer of wealth from white men to black women and children forced southern judges to figure out ways to preserve property rights without upsetting racial hierarchies. But protecting the testamentary freedom of white men meant walking a thin line, for these cases, as Davis argues, "threaten[ed] antebellum economic and social hierarchies predicated on race, gender, and (enslaved) status."[82] Judges like Turner and Deblieux were well aware of the tension between whites' dedication to controlling people of African descent and their commitment to private property—the very same contradictions black litigants exploited when they went to court to protect their interests. At the level of practice, however, this tension remained difficult to resolve.

The courts, then, found themselves caught in a bind. At stake was the primacy of private property; undermining property rights meant undermining slavery. As one southern state constitution put it, the "right of property is before and higher than any constitutional sanction ... the right of the owner of a slave to such slave and its increase is the same and as inviolable as the right of the owner to any property whatever."[83] When the sanctity of property was on the line, extending rights to people of African descent sometimes proved more palatable than upholding the social and cultural norms of racial hierarchy.

While on the bench, many judges from the region invested considerable time and resources in assessing the claims of black litigants. They did not dismiss the charges made by litigants of color out of hand; rather, many took African Americans' claims to self-possession and self-direction seriously and made a concerted effort to get to the bottom of a dispute. In so doing, they demonstrated that even in a racially and economically stratified society, white people were not the sole arbiters of knowledge or truth.

The "commission," for instance, demonstrates that under certain circumstances, white judges privileged African American knowledge. On many occasions, judges in both Mississippi and Louisiana issued a commission to take the depositions of witnesses from outside the county. In some cases, such testimony came from witnesses in a neighboring county within the state; in other cases, judges sought witness testimony from places as far off as Pennsylvania, Ohio, Virginia, and "the Island of Domingo."[84] Sometimes an authorized commissioner (such as a notary) would travel to take the depositions. Yet more typically, the judge allowed any local official with the capacity to administer an oath to take the depositions. Along with a request for testimony, the judge would also send an interrogatory. After the depositions were taken and returned, the judge read the testimony in open court during the trial. Commissions were expensive and time-consuming.[85] To get one, plaintiffs had to appeal to the judge and demonstrate that their case would be strengthened by testimony from distant witnesses.[86] Doing so meant convincing the judge that the case had merit. Although on occasion judges sent commissions for black litigants in cases involving divorce or debt recovery, most commonly judges issued commissions in enslaved people's lawsuits for freedom.[87] By sending commissions in freedom suits in particular, judges put considerable work into assessing the legal personhood of the enslaved plaintiff. Rather than readily assuming that black litigants were slaves (and thus objects of property moving through the economy rather than legal persons), judges conceded (at least temporarily and during the suit) that they were legal subjects.

When requesting commissions, black litigants compelled judges to acknowledge that there were some circumstances in which the words and stories of people of color could be credited. The witness testimony taken by commissions played a central role in helping determine outcomes in such cases because they provided details about events outside the courts' jurisdictions. Without local knowledge of the people and circumstances involved a given case, courts frequently turned to testimony offered by distant witnesses. In general, the information witnesses provided, their testimony about the events in question, their assessments of the character and actions of the people involved in the disputes, and their opinions on the matters at hand helped weave together a story about the circumstances of a case. These narratives aided the court in its attempts to assess the litigants' competing claims. Through their use of witnesses, black litigants wielded their ties to their communities—both local and distant—to their advantage and employed their extensive social networks on their own behalf. For instance, in Frank Irwin's freedom suit, witnesses from outside of the local community helped the district court in West Feliciana Parish determine his status as a free man. In his 1837 petition to the court, Irwin contended that he was born a slave in Pennsylvania and gained his liberty at the age of twenty-one. He then moved to Cincinnati, Ohio, and lived there for several years as a free man before he was "seized and delivered as a slave" by a man named Harris. Harris had "carried" him to Kentucky, Irwin recounted, and "after much cruel treatment," sold him as a slave to Thomas Powell, a Kentucky man temporarily residing in Louisiana. Powell denied Irwin's allegations and insisted that he was his slave.

Here were two parties, with irreconcilable stories, one black and one white. One of them was lying. The district court judge, Thomas Jefferson Morgan, issued two commissions to examine witnesses in Ohio and Kentucky and establish Irwin's "true" status. The witnesses offered their testimony to justices of the peace and notaries public from their home jurisdictions, which then sent the depositions to the court in Louisiana.

If, as some legal scholars suggest, we find "the truth" in the courtroom by telling the most believable story, it is significant that the stories told by black people were heard and credited. To be believable, stories must be familiar.[88] White men—particularly property-holding white men—could "literally create truth with their words."[89] By virtue of their position in the southern hierarchy, they were considered the most credible. By contrast, the significance of this procedure (sending a commission to uncover the truth) was that it conceded the possibility of a white man lying and, more important, that there was no racial monopoly on truth and knowledge.[90]

Irwin and the circumstances that brought him into Powell's possession were not well known in the greater West Feliciana Parish community. Thus, witnesses from outside the area proved central for the local court to determine Irwin's status, his personal genealogy, and the course of events that brought him to Louisiana. Moreover, for those not familiar with Irwin, descriptions of physical characteristics from the witnesses ensured they were dealing with the right man. Witnesses portrayed him as "dark but not very black," "tall," "large boned," "with blunt & heavy features," and a "clumsy looking negro." The court then matched those (racialized) descriptions to the man petitioning for his freedom in West Feliciana Parish.

The witnesses' accounts, however, painted a blurred picture. Indeed, in his final judgment, Judge Morgan remarked that he had "no small difficulty in reconciling their testimony." Witnesses on Irwin's behalf claimed that although he had been born a slave in Pennsylvania in 1809, his master freed him when he reached the age of twenty-one. Several white men from Kentucky, however, recounted a different version of the story. These men claimed that Irwin was born a slave in Pennsylvania in 1809 and brought to the state of Kentucky shortly after his birth. He had remained in Kentucky as a slave on the farm of General James Taylor until he ran away in July 1830 to Ohio, where he lived for several years. Taylor had found Irwin in Cincinnati a short time after he "eloped," although due to his age and infirm condition, he did not capture Irwin himself. Thus, Irwin remained in Cincinnati and lived as a free man. In 1836, however, Taylor sold Irwin to his son-in-law, a Mr. Harris. Harris promptly traveled to Cincinnati, seized Irwin as his property, brought him to Kentucky, and sold him to Powell.

After sorting through the various accounts from faraway witnesses, Judge Morgan drew the following conclusions: Irwin was born in 1809 in Pennsylvania and lived in Cincinnati from 1830 to 1836 with his master's knowledge. All of the witness testimony supported these suppositions. Thus, Morgan deduced, Irwin was a free man because he was born in Pennsylvania and lived in Ohio in the years after the 1787 Northwest Ordinance prohibited slavery north of the Ohio River. Moreover, Morgan continued, "even if he was born a slave, having resided in the state of Ohio with the knowledge, consent, and approbation of his owner at that time, he is therefore free." Taylor, Morgan argued, in essence consented to Irwin's residence in Ohio because he did not take any legal action to recapture him. Therefore, the judge found Irwin a free man and ordered Powell to pay the costs of the lawsuit. Although Powell appealed, the Supreme Court of Louisiana affirmed the lower court's decision and again ordered Powell to pay costs. While the witnesses offered competing accounts, the judge uncovered the corresponding pieces of the story and used that testimony to determine Irwin's rightful status as free.[91]

The commissions Judge Morgan sent on behalf of Irwin provide tangible evidence that he took the claims of people of color seriously and invested material resources and time in resolving them. What is more, Irwin's lawsuit indicates that judges were open to the idea that people of African descent had privileged forms of knowledge, especially of their personal histories and genealogies. Whites did not have a monopoly on truth, knowledge, or reason.

Judges in the region also devised ways to deny black litigants' claims to self-possession and self-direction. Thomas Jefferson Cooley, a lawyer turned district court judge from Pointe Coupee Parish, was one such figure. Throughout the late 1830s and early 1840s, Cooley practiced law in the parish alongside his son, William Henry Cooley. Both father and son represented white and black clients in lawsuits over unpaid debts, land disputes, back wages, and other disagreements. As their black clients frequently won their cases, Thomas and William probably put similar effort into representing their black clients as they did their white ones.[92] In the mid-1840s, the governor appointed Thomas Cooley as a judge in the Ninth Judicial District Court in Pointe Coupee Parish. In that capacity, he began to preside over cases involving black litigants and occasionally issued verdicts in their favor.[93]

While Cooley's final judgments tended to be brief and formulaic or (most often) missing from the trial record, one extant opinion reveals his attitudes on the place of black litigants in his courtroom and the position of free people of color in a slave society. In 1854, Tom, an enslaved man, appeared in Judge Cooley's courtroom and sued his owner, René Porche, for his freedom. Tom claimed that Porche was "contractually obliged" to grant him his liberty. In his petition, Tom informed the court that five years earlier, he had entered into a self-purchase contract with Porche for $200.[94] He had fulfilled his end of the bargain and paid Porche the agreed-on amount, Tom contended, but Porche refused to live up to his promises and continued to hold him as a "slave for life." Tom asked the court to enforce the terms of his contract and "condemn" Porche to "liberate & emancipate him according to law." Moreover, several white men testified on Tom's behalf, supporting his assertion that Porche had publicly acknowledged his "contract to emancipate Tom." William Cooley (Judge Cooley's son) served as Tom's lawyer and testified that "Tom had come to him to ask him to sue Porche for his freedom," and because he knew that Tom had paid him the agreed-on price, William Cooley thought Tom had a "clear case." His father, however, disagreed and dismissed the case as a nonsuit, claiming that the contract was not in compliance with new state laws governing manumissions. In particular, he argued, Tom's master did not post the now-required "bond with good security" in the event that "the slave if emancipated and allowed to remain in the state, shall not become a public charge." Because of this and other violations, the contract did not conform to the law and was now invalid. To that end, he wrote that Tom "has a right to his freedom by virtue of the contract with the defendant—but the defendant is protected by the repeal of the law which existed at the time of the contract." Tom remained enslaved, and he probably never recovered the $200 he paid Porche for his freedom.

Cooley's final judgment in this case, dated June 6, 1855, was long and detailed, and he used it to undermine the claims of people of color—ostensibly in the name of maintaining public order. To demonstrate that the contract did not comply with current state law, he spent considerable time describing the changes in the manumission laws that occurred after Tom and Porche had entered into an agreement. Yet he also used his judgment to comment on the manumission of slaves and the role of free people of color in a slave society—opinions that he used to support his decision to deny Tom his legal liberty. "As a general rule," he wrote, "it is a dangerous thing to emancipate a slave . . . it adds to an intermediate class, the very existence of which had a tendency to create discontent among those who are left in the inferior state." Free blacks were potentially treacherous, and while Tom might have had a claim to freedom, "the public safety and the public policy must sometimes override individual rights." Here Cooley appealed to a vision of the legal system that restricted individual liberties in favor of protecting the public order and maintained patriarchal hierarchies (what Laura Edwards has called, "the peace").[95] Indeed, it appears that Cooley found the use of the courts to create an "intermediate class" of free blacks distasteful and dangerous. In Tom's case, he sought technicalities in the law that could be marshaled to deny Tom's bid for freedom. Cooley may have represented black clients on occasion, and he may have allowed them an audience in his courtroom. Yet his maneuvering in Tom's lawsuit indicates that he only did so because the structure of the law (which allowed people of color to sue in certain circumstances) said that he must. When he had the opportunity to deny African Americans' claims to freedom and to personhood, he took it.[96]

Cooley's language in *Tom v. Porche* points to the contradictions inherent in black people's claims to a legal personality and to self-possession. While black litigants were both frequent and common, they were also potentially problematic and in the eyes of Cooley, threatening. When faced with people of African descent as litigants in their courtrooms, legal officials confronted situations in which objects of property became legal subjects. Judges in the Natchez district had their eye on these contradictions and struggled with them.

When assessing the role of white judges and lawyers in black people's lawsuits, we might ask how best to integrate them into our account of black litigiousness. This is ultimately a question of how much weight we should assign to particular factors in our accounts of causation. There can be no doubt about the importance of legal expertise, even though, as I have demonstrated, such expertise sometimes remained underdeveloped. Lawyers were important co-producers of black people's lawsuits. Judges pose a harder problem. But at the very least I would urge that we avoid a common metaphor for the judge, that of the gatekeeper. Not only does this not adequately capture the ways that judges struggled with the presence and claims of black litigants; it also raises a knotty interpretive problem. Viewing black litigiousness and claims-making through the framework of what whites would allow or what they wanted makes a number of assumptions. First, it assumes that people share an ideology and that ideologies remained stable over time. Judge Edward Turner's "Composition on Slavery" provides evidence not only of the complex, variable, and contradictory nature of a person's thinking but also shows how it might evolve or change over the course of his life. Second, this framework assumes that people will act in accordance with their ideology. Yet judges consistently made decisions that did not align with their values and found ways to justify them or set aside their own distaste. White southerners were capable of acting in ways seemingly contrary to their ideologies and sometimes even temporarily suspended their intolerance in the context of their daily lives.[97] Third, examining black litigiousness through a framework of what whites would permit also makes assumptions about the consistency or even autonomy of law: law reflects culture, and certainly white slaveholders wrote the laws and peopled the courtrooms, but they were not of a single mind and not without their internal contradictions. Finally and most important, this framework assumes that knowledge and power are centralized and hegemonic. Yet the legal action of black people in the antebellum South—scores of people mounting claims in court—demonstrate that whites did not have a stranglehold on power, knowledge, and truth, or for that matter, a stranglehold on the law.

Black litigants were not present in the southern courts simply because white people allowed it; and indeed, many, like Thomas Cooley, would have banned their presence if possible. These were the same courts, governed by the same laws, that ordered the hangings and whippings of black people, policed all aspects of their lives, and regulated an economy centered on the commodification of their bodies and their labor.

Black litigants were present because they understood that law is not a resource monopolized by one group of people. Instead, it reflects the contradictions, tensions, and messiness of people's lived experiences and daily interactions. People of African descent were acutely aware of the world in which they lived and of those contradictions, and they knew when to exploit them to their advantage. What is more, they were litigants, claims-makers, and clients because they envisioned themselves as such—as a people with rights (even if limited), rights that had been violated.

Perhaps, then, we might raise another set of questions: What is the significance of black litigiousness? Or more precisely, what did it mean when the men who shaped the slave economy and the legal and political culture of the South took black clients and heard the claims—and demands—of black people in their courtrooms? When white judges and lawyers recognized black people as legally responsible persons, not property—even temporarily—they gave the lie to one of the most important components of the proslavery ideology: that people of African descent were natural "children" incapable of self-government and self-direction. And even if they did not intend to, even if they just wanted to take cash out of black people's pockets, even if they felt they were in a bind—when they stood up in a public courthouse beside a black litigant who demanded to direct aspects of his or her own life, they helped that person claim rights. For the white slaveholding South, this was part of its own undoing.

In the first three chapters of this book, I have tried to provide a framework for the claims-making of people of color in the Natchez district—the stories, strategies, and points of entry. The second half of this book examines the scope and significance of their litigiousness. The final four chapters turn to the specific types of claims black litigants brought before the courts—claims to property, freedom, and family. When appearing in a public courtroom to assert the right to recover debts owed to them; to own, inherit, and dispose of property; to contract; to enjoy the fruits of their labor; to protect their family and family resources; to ensure their futures; and to demand freedom, black litigants (male and female, single and married, young and old, wealthy and poor) proclaimed and exercised a civic personality and in the process expanded the boundaries of the possible.

Part

TWO

4

Your Word Is Your Bond

In 1828, Ben Lewis, a free black man, sued Samuel Patterson, a white man, in the circuit court in Natchez, Mississippi, for the sixty-two dollars Patterson borrowed from him the year before. As evidence of the debt, Lewis provided the court with a promissory note signed by Patterson pledging to pay Lewis within sixty days. Despite Lewis's repeated requests for the money, the loan remained unpaid nearly a year later. Lewis asked the court for the balance of the loan and $150 in damages for his trouble. The court found for Lewis and ordered Patterson to pay him sixty-two dollars, plus interest and court costs.[1]

Lawsuits like Lewis's were familiar to the local courts of the Natchez district; debt actions represented one the most common types of lawsuits people of color initiated. Black moneylenders were regular participants in the credit economy of the slave South. Free people of color, in particular, repeatedly extended loans in various amounts to both white and black people. When the sums went unpaid, free black creditors sued borrowers to recoup the money owed. Regardless of whether or not the defendant was black or white, free black creditors won nearly all of their debt-recovery lawsuits: of the extant ninety cases, black plaintiffs only lost twice. The loans free people of color extended could be lucrative, particularly when borrowers repaid them with interest. To protect such investments, free black creditors took several steps to ensure that they could appeal to the force of the law to guarantee repayment and, failing that, to compel the state to intervene on their behalf—by ordering the debtor to pay or even by seizing and selling his property at auction to satisfy the debt.

Debt represented an obligation, a relationship that bound the debtor to his creditor. The image of binding, however, troubled many. Debt signaled dependency on and subordination to a lender, and borrowers throughout antebellum America (both in the North and South) consistently invoked the language of slavery when describing indebtedness and insolvency. To enter into a debt was to assume a dependent position, the position, some lamented, of a slave. For many, debt potentially carried a stigma: it was simultaneously necessary to compete in the increasingly complex and competitive marketplace and could even be lucrative; but it also signified failure—both moral and financial.[2] To avoid the shame of debt, white planters sometimes disguised debts as private gifts offered among friends and peers. But white southerners could not describe their debts to black lenders in the language of friendship and bequests offered by peers—for that would mean recognizing a person of color as an equal. Because these particular relations of obligation were commonly understood as forms of "bondage," being indebted to a black creditor put white borrowers in an uncomfortable position: being bound to a black person was always potentially problematic, for it represented an alteration of the racial and social order. It was one thing to borrow from a free black creditor; but the bonds of obligation were even more discomforting when the lender was a slave.

In the Natchez district, a world in which blackness symbolized dependency and whiteness independence, white debtors were bound to black creditors. The legal mechanisms involving debt collection favored lenders—even when those lenders were black. Under such circumstances, the courts could serve as a place where the social and racial relations of a slave society were temporarily suspended, insofar as their suspension furthered the goal of preserving private property. This chapter examines debt recovery from its inception (the loan) to its discharge (whether through payment or execution). The process itself was loaded with symbolic weight, for in the antebellum South, it invoked a set of highly charged ideas about virtue, ethics, membership, and race.

THE FACT OF LENDING

Debt was omnipresent in the antebellum United States. At some point in their lives, most free people faced indebtedness of some form or another—rich and poor, rural and urban, young and old, white and black. As one scholar put it, "the antebellum economy was structured as much around borrowed money and promises of payment as it was around the routes of rivers, roads, canals, and, by the 1840s, railroads."[3] While debt and even insolvency were inescapable facts of life for many throughout the country in the nineteenth century, the configuration of the agricultural economy in the cotton South meant that few southerners could avoid it. Smallholders and planters alike faced an income gap between the months leading up to the harvest (when they laid out significant expenses) and the harvest (when they could expect payment for their crops). Many came up short in the interim, and loans from banks, merchants, suppliers, friends, and neighbors tided them over until the sale. In addition, because the limited supply of circulating coinage fell far short of financial requirements, credit instruments—such as promissory notes and bills of exchange—circulated throughout the economy in place of hard currency. Thus, many southerners did business on credit. For instance, one study found that antebellum southern farmers purchased nearly three-fourths of all merchandise through credit.[4]

Yet in the Natchez district, credit and debt took on special meaning. Slave-grown cotton was the most widely traded commodity in the global marketplace, and the region's slaveholders were some of the wealthiest people in the world. Planting cotton, however, required significant capital investment, and farmers and planters were frequently cash poor; their money was tied up in the most productive investments of the time: land and slaves. They relied on credit for liquidity. To obtain credit, they planted cotton and borrowed against their crop. People, too, were collateral. The enslaved not only produced millions of pounds of cotton worth billions of dollars; they could also be borrowed against to attain more land and slaves. Natchez district planters expanded their holdings through credit and speculation. Credit came easy, and opportunity appeared limitless. The insatiable demand for cotton, a land bonanza, slave laborers sold to the region in the hundreds of thousands, and state and local banks willing to issue generous loans on little more than promises created a rush of investment, production, and growth. Yet with the booms came the busts: this frenzy also encouraged business practices akin to gambling, the overproduction of cotton, overinvestment in slaves, and dependency on credit.[5] It also meant significant (and unsustainable) debt, debt that often went unpaid. Debt actions, unsurprisingly, represented the most common type of lawsuit found in the Natchez district's courts.

Credit came from many sources. Banks provided loans, and investors—both local and distant—supplied capital. Yet southerners also borrowed from one another. Planters offered their acquaintances gentlemanly "gifts." Local merchants floated short-term loans. Kin, friends, and neighbors borrowed from each other when times were tight. Out of this credit economy, however, emerged an unexpected figure: the black creditor.

People of color were more than just property and labor in the southern economy; they were also essential arteries for capital. Much of the extant evidence of black moneylending stems from debt actions in the local courts (actions only taken when sums went unpaid); thus, it is unclear how many people of color were involved in the credit economy of the region and how much capital they controlled. There is evidence to suggest that black lending was widespread in the Deep South, however.[6] These transactions do not reveal the individual motivations of lenders and borrowers; court proceedings involving unpaid loans evaluated the legitimacy of the debt, not the broader credit relationships between the involved parties. Debt actions cannot explain why whites, for instance, chose to borrow from black people. Nonetheless, it is clear that free blacks throughout the Natchez district extended loans, large and small, to both whites and other black people. At least ninety black men and women in the region were creditors, and they lent money to planters and smallholders alike.

Debt actions indicate that as sources of capital, free blacks drove the local economy and the credit system in the Natchez district in important ways. For instance, Manuel Britto, a free man of color and merchant from Pointe Coupee Parish, extended loans to his many of customers, ranging from small amounts to several hundred dollars.[7] Rose Belly, a free woman of color from Iberville Parish, lent even larger sums, sometimes as high as $2,000.[8] Free black barber William Johnson kept detailed account books listing the sums of money his acquaintances borrowed from him, the payments made on their accounts, and the dates of their final installments. Johnson served as a creditor for a broad segment of the Natchez population, lending money to wealthy white planters such as Adam Bingaman and John Quitman and former governor George Poindexter as well as his nephew, William Miller, and his mother, Amy Johnson. He lent money to scores of people each year, and the amounts varied. His largest single loan was for $1,000, and others ranged from $100 to $660. Many, however, were short-term loans for under $100, and some for just a few dollars: for instance, Johnson noted in his diary on October 31, 1835, that he "loaned Dr. Benbrook $3.00."[9] A number of borrowers took multiple loans. Over the course of 1840, for instance, one Isaac Leum borrowed money from Johnson several times, money Leum paid back in increments. At the end of the year, Johnson noted in his ledger that "the whole amount of his bill is now paid and closed—Enough Said."[10] Johnson's barbershop doubled as a kind of bank—a place where members of the Natchez community could go for a loan. Moreover, Johnson also served as a broker. He exchanged currency and charged brokerage fees.[11] According to his accounts, his borrowers rarely failed to pay him the money they borrowed. For example, between March 31, 1836, and March 30, 1837, Johnson lent a total of $4,700 and by September

12, 1839, all but $925 had been repaid. When the sums went unpaid, however, Johnson appealed to the legal system.[12]

Because many borrowers eventually repaid their debts without the threat of litigation, the lawsuits between black creditors and their debtors only represented a small proportion of the loans extended by free people of color. Elizabeth Pilard, a free black woman, lent money to a number of people in her Pointe Coupee Parish community and sued to recover debts that ranged from $100 to $200. For instance, in early 1812, Pilard used the courts to recoup payment for loans extended to various white men.[13] Yet these lawsuits probably reflect only a fraction of the individual loans she floated that year. Most loans were probably not delinquent, and as one scholar has shown, many southern creditors also preferred to deal with delinquent debtors in private.[14] Thus, lawsuits represented moments when credit relationships had gone awry. Still, creditors—both white and black—appealed to the force of the law when borrowers did not meet their obligations.

THE ACT OF SUING

Lawsuits between creditors and debtors concerning unpaid loans represented one the most common types of civil actions involving free black plaintiffs. Yet for many creditors (black or white), litigation was not expedient; it could delay payment while the lawsuit made its way through the courts. Creditors pursued other avenues—such as appealing to a borrower's honor and sense of obligation, extending deadlines, or requesting that borrowers secure the loan with a lien on their property—before appearing in court.[15] But the law was always implicated in credit relationships; lenders knew that it could be brought to bear when a debt went unpaid. Litigation, moreover, was an attractive option because courts could draft a repayment schedule or seize and sell the debtor's property to satisfy the creditor's claim. Thus, when their requests for payment went unheeded, free black lenders like Johnson and Pilard sued both whites and blacks to recoup the money owed to them.

Free black plaintiffs used the courts to recover sums both great and small. Some debt-recovery suits involved wealthier free blacks and large amounts of money, ranging from hundreds to thousands of dollars. For instance, in 1858, a free man of color, Oscar Leduff, sued in the Pointe Coupee Parish court to recover the $600 he lent another free man of color, John Baptiste Leduff—a lawsuit Oscar Leduff won.[16] In 1850, Antoine Decuir, a free black sugar planter, sued Victor Dupperon, also a free black man, for a

$2,300 debt and received a judgment in his favor in default when Dupperon did not show up in court.[17] Many other lawsuits, however, involved amounts of as little as a few dollars. In 1840, Margueritte, a free woman of color, sued in Iberville Parish to recoup money she lent Andeau Roth, a white man, and the court ordered that he pay her nine dollars.[18] Margueritte lent sums of money under $100 to several people in her Louisiana community and sued when they did not repay her. For instance, in 1831 she sued another white man, Simon Allain, for the sixty-four dollars she lent him and received a judgment for that same amount.[19] Margueritte used the courts consistently to settle small debts and resolve various disagreements over property.[20] Going to court was costly; the attorney's fees, court fees, and travel costs could add up quickly. With large sums of money at risk, the potential gains outweighed the costs. Yet for those suing to recover a few dollars, it might be cheaper to use other means to force a debtor to pay. Litigation involving amounts under $100, however, was not uncommon.[21] Thus, lawsuits over small sums further expose a culture of expecting the courts to intervene and order the payment of debts.

Lawsuits to recover debts followed a similar formula and produced similar results. Plaintiffs detailed the amount of money lent, the date of the loan, and the date the debtor promised to repay the sum, and they included a statement about an "amicable" and ultimately unsuccessful request for repayment before resorting to litigation and a promissory note or notes as evidence of the debt. On October 6, 1817, Phillis, a Louisiana free woman of color, sued Antoine Langlois, a local white man, to recoup the money she had lent him several months prior. Her petition was short and to the point. Quite simply, she told the court that "on the tenth day of April in the year 1816, Antoine Langlois of the said parish of Iberville did make his certain promissory note in writing bearing the date aforementioned. He then promised to pay to the order of your petitioner the sum of two hundred and seventy eight dollars on the tenth day of April 1817—for money lent.—Yet the said Antoine Langlois, although requested, hath not paid the sum but refuses so to do. Wherefore your petitioner prays that the said Antoine Langlois be cited to appear before this honorable court and be condemned to pay the above sum with interest and costs of suit." She included Langlois's promissory note as evidence and then signed her petition with an "X." The court issued a verdict in her favor and ordered Langlois to pay her the $278 he owned her, plus interest and court costs.[22] This was not first time Phillis sued Langlois either. In a similar case that same year, Phillis sued Langlois to recover a $330 loan. She won that lawsuit too.[23] Phillis's lawsuits against Antoine Langlois resembled thousands of other debt-recovery cases from the region (including those involving white plaintiffs and defendants).

Free black plaintiffs nearly always won their debt-recovery cases. Indeed, between 1800 and 1860, black plaintiffs lost only two debt-related cases out of ninety in the region's courts. Two-thirds of these cases (sixty-one) involved white defendants.[24] Sometimes borrowers simply came to court to "confess" to the debt and agree on a timetable for repayment. After failing to repay the $175 he borrowed from free black Paulin Verret, John Kelly, a white man, appeared in court in 1855, admitted that he owed the money, and agreed to pay the sum promptly.[25] Some defendants fled the area to avoid repayment and moved beyond the jurisdiction of the court. Absconding, however, was not always the best tactic as plaintiffs often pursued those who owed them money. For example, in 1837, shortly after Rachel, Elizabeth, and Ellen Rapp (sisters and free women of African descent) successfully sued John Fletcher (a white man) in Louisiana for a $500 debt he owed them, Fletcher fled to Mississippi to avoid repaying them. The three women pursued him doggedly from New Orleans to Natchez, attempting to recover the money. Once in Mississippi, they finally pinned Fletcher down and demanded repayment. Getting nowhere, they sued him again—this time in the circuit court in Natchez. The court issued a verdict in their favor, and they received a judgment for $800 plus interest and court costs—three hundred dollars more than the first verdict. In 1838, Fletcher paid the debt and covered the costs of the lawsuit.[26] Other borrowers, such as Victor Dupperon, did not show up for their court dates, and the plaintiffs won judgments in default.[27] Some debtors denied the plaintiffs' allegations and contested the debts supposedly owed: George Troxeler denied owing Augustin Borie fifty-seven dollars. But when Borie, a black man, produced a promissory note signed by the defendant, the court ordered Troxeler, a white man, to pay up.[28] If the plaintiffs proved that the debts were legitimate and still outstanding (typically with a promissory note signed by the debtor) then the courts consistently issued verdicts in their favor.[29]

The nature of credit relationships provided black creditors with a measure of power over others. Debt might make someone have to flee the state, for instance, and live in exile. Even then, as the case of the Rapp sisters suggests, one was not safe from one's creditors. Black creditors not only appealed to the courts as a potentially neutral party; they could also use the threat of litigation to put debtors on guard and convince them to pay and avoid the humiliation of seeing their private failings exposed in public. In addition, promissory notes, like the one Borie produced in court as evidence against Troxeler, contained the power to adjudicate relationships. Promissory notes represented an important piece of material culture that held the power to cause the court to decide who was a liar and who was not. Paper evidence, then, gave black creditors authority over others, black and white. In keeping with what I have suggested in chapter 3, we have here another example of how whites did not have a monopoly on the truth.

CHARACTER AND CREDIT

Credit, then, was more than a financial arrangement; it also involved a complicated social performance. The fact of lending was connected to the act of suing in complex ways. When deciding whether to extend a loan, free people of color made character assessments about their neighbors and acquaintances and appraised the reputations of both white and black southerners. These facts became central to their attempts to use legal institutions to collect their debts. Creditors—free black or otherwise—did not lend money to just anyone. Free blacks carefully evaluated the creditworthiness of potential borrowers, inquiring into their reputations and their ability to pay. In the face-to-face society of the Natchez district, borrowers' reputations were well known. Creditors' decisions to extend loans rested on their own experiences with the borrowers or second- or third-hand information from those they trusted. When they did not have a credit relationship with a potential borrower, lenders listened to gossip and gathered information from others or through their own observations. They might visit a potential borrower's place of business and observe the number or type of customers entering a store or the condition of the crops in a field. Newspapers also provided useful information, as they reported notices of insolvent debtors requesting meetings with their creditors, the dissolution of partnerships, and the formation of new businesses. For instance, when he had trouble meeting his obligations, Maximillion Ricard, a free man of color, petitioned the court in Iberville Parish requesting a meeting of his creditors. To alert his creditors to the meeting and to Ricard's financial trouble, the date of and reason for the meeting was published in a local newspaper (as was required by law for all insolvent debtors, black or white).[30]

Without modern credit-reporting systems used to ascertain an individual's payment history, the totality of his or her debts, or a person's financial history and standing, antebellum lenders calculated creditworthiness (and the probability of default) by assessing the character of potential borrowers. The criteria for creditworthiness included traits such as honesty, punctuality, economy, and temperance. Creditors valued reputations for honesty and transparency because without publicly available balance sheets, debtors could easily hide the true condition of their finances. In the world of antebellum commerce, there were rules, and it was up to borrowers to apprise lenders of any looming trouble that might keep them from paying their debt.[31] Late payments might make it difficult for creditors to meet their own obligations. An extravagant lifestyle might mean a borrower lived beyond his or her means, and vices such as heavy drinking or frequent gambling might represent moral deficiency.[32]

Black lenders certainly appraised the character and creditworthiness of other black people. But they also made judgments about the character of whites. When Antoine Langlois, a white man discussed above, appealed to Phillis for a loan, she must have assessed whether or not he could be trusted to repay it. Was he a man of good character and fair business habits? Did he have a reputation for honesty? Did he meet previous obligations on time? Had he defrauded creditors in the past? Did he live extravagantly? Was he a gambler or a drinker? She must have received satisfactory answers to these questions because she lent him large sums of money on at least two occasions. In the end, he failed to live up to her expectations when he neglected to repay his debts, and she appealed to the law to protect her investments. As lenders, black people consistently made moral judgments about the character of whites. If white people were unworthy, then presumably black creditors would not extend them loans.

Extending a loan to a white neighbor or a free black acquaintance might also establish or strengthen a relationship between the creditor and debtor— as a patron, peer, or subordinate, depending on the borrower. For instance, when Rose Belly, a free woman of color, lent Joseph Orillion $2,000, she did so because the two had a mutually beneficial relationship. Orillion, a prominent white slaveholder, consistently served as a witness and signatory to the land transfers, slave donations, and official acknowledgments that Belly and her family members registered in the Iberville Parish courthouse. When she needed an ally, he stepped up; when he needed a loan, she stepped in.[33]

But the loans people of color extended were more than just "social debts"—loans that represented "relationships, not transactions . . . governed by rules of etiquette, not law."[34] Borrowers' reputations as creditworthy were not solid guarantees that they could repay the loan, especially if they got into financial trouble at a later date. These loans were also business transactions and lucrative undertakings, particularly when borrowers repaid them with interest.[35] Lenders did not extend credit as a mere favor or as charity; rather, they intended to make a profit. When credit relationships broke down, creditors appealed to the courts to protect their investments.

Black people also conducted business on credit; they, too, were debtors and defendants in debt-recovery lawsuits. Free blacks borrowed money just as their white neighbors did, and when they could not or would not pay their debts, they also found themselves in court. White plaintiffs also almost always won their cases against black defendants (just as black plaintiffs did). Some free black borrowers repeatedly faced litigation for failing to pay their debts to white creditors. For instance, between 1833 and 1834, Jean Fleming, a free man of color, appeared in court in Iberville Parish as a defendant in ten debt-related cases. Each case involved a white plaintiff, and Fleming lost all but one of these lawsuits.[36]

Race—and character assessments associated with race—was not necessarily a barrier to credit. While white supremacist ideology marked black people as natural dependents incapable of taking care of their own affairs (and thus unworthy of a loan), some white lenders consistently extended loans to black borrowers. White creditors—like black ones—did not lend money to those they believed to be high credit risks. They assessed the reputations of free black borrowers and their ability to pay their loans. Free black borrowers repeatedly emerged as creditworthy. Past behavior, experience with the borrower, and a reputation for economy and punctuality sometimes proved more important than racialized stereotypes. Francois Dormenon's white acquaintances continued to lend him money throughout the 1830s and 1840s, despite the occasional difficulties he faced repaying those debts.[37] Although Jean Fleming was a defendant in several debt actions, numerous white men consistently vouched for his character.[38]

Debt actions only allow us to see the credit relationships that had broken down. What we cannot see are the ones that never started. When black people made character assessments about potential borrowers, when they made judgments about others, there were moments (invisible to us by nature of the evidence) when they told some white people no.

EXECUTION

Black creditors took several precautions to limit their risk—precautions that had legal ramifications. While on the one hand, they assessed the character of potential borrowers to determine credit risk, they also took measures to ensure that they could appeal to the institutional power of the courts to enforce repayment. In a society with a legal regime dedicated to protecting black slavery, black people harnessing the power of the state to further their own ends—especially against whites—reversed power relations.

To protect their interests, free black creditors took several steps to ensure that they could appeal to the law as a mechanism to ensure repayment. For instance, some debt-related lawsuits involved oral promises to pay, but most debtors and creditors appearing in the courts of the Natchez district relied on promissory notes to record the loan and guarantee repayment. Requiring that the borrower write a promissory note for the loan provided plaintiffs with evidence to use in court. The promissory note resembled an IOU—a slip of paper on which a debtor promised to pay a creditor a specified sum either on demand or by an agreed-on date. Like debt-related lawsuits, promissory notes also followed a simple formula and included the date of the loan, the amount borrowed, the interest rate on the loan, a promise to repay, the deadline for repayment, and a signature of the borrower. For instance, Manuel Britto's promissory note stated, "$177 New Orleans, May 5, 1857. Six months after this date I promise to pay to the order of Nathan Folger at his counting room one hundred and seventy seven dollars with eight percent interest after maturity for value received. Due November 5/8/57. Signed Manuel Britto."[39] Most borrowers wrote promissory notes on scraps of ripped paper.

These scraps of paper were an important component of the credit system in the Natchez district. Promissory notes had many purposes. They served as evidence of the loan, of course, but they also circulated in the local economy. Unlike someone's oral promise to pay or a loan recorded in William Johnson's ledger, promissory notes could be assigned to someone else. In other words, creditors could transfer a note by signing it over to a third party, a third party who could then collect the amount due from the borrower or assign it again to another party.[40] Creditors in the Natchez district used promissory notes like currency, assigning them to others to pay their own debts, acquire credit themselves, or to make purchases. Just like the theft of a slave, a horse, or other property, stealing a promissory note was a crime. The Adams County circuit court, for instance, found George Miler, a free black man, guilty of stealing a $500 promissory note drawn on a Louisiana bank. Apparently he fled to Mississippi with the note and tried to sell it there, but his actions drew the suspicions of others, and he ended up in jail.[41]

Free black creditors endorsed promissory notes to third parties, white and black. When these loans came due and the debts went unpaid, third parties sued the borrowers and often made a profit on the interest. For example, in 1811, Jean Baptiste Lorrie, a white planter, borrowed $1,600 from Rose Belly. The debt went unpaid for several years, collecting interest, and in 1816 Belly appeared before the Iberville Parish Court and "transferred and assigned . . . a certain obligation with mortgage" to Antoine Dubuclet, a free man of color and her son-in-law. When the loan came due in 1820 and remained unpaid, Dubuclet sued Lorrie for $1,765, the balance of the loan plus "legal interest" and stood to make a $165 profit. The court found for Dubuclet and ordered that Lorrie pay the amount by October 20, 1820 (a mere fourteen days after Dubuclet filed his lawsuit).[42] As Dubuclet's lawsuit suggests, black creditors capitalized on legal mechanisms involving debt collection that favored lenders—even when those lenders were people of color.

In addition, black creditors took measures to ensure that they could appeal to the institutional power of the state to enforce repayment. While some free black lenders in the Natchez district lent money without requiring that the borrower secure the debt (perhaps because the amount was too low to warrant it), many creditors requested a lien against a particular item of the debtor's property in exchange for the loan. If the borrower repaid the debt, the creditor would release the lien. If not, and the creditor received a judgment in his or her favor, the creditor had the right to "execution" on the borrower's property (a right to confiscate the assets of the debtor). The local sheriff would seize enough of the debtor's property necessary to pay the debt and sell that property at auction to repay the loan.

Debtors in the Natchez district mortgaged land and slaves as collateral for their debts. Mortgages were contracts in which the debtor granted a particular creditor a right to real property (as security for the debt), property that could be sold to satisfy the creditor's claim if the debtor defaulted on the loan. Mortgages provided creditors with the security that helped ensure the repayment of the loan because it guaranteed that creditors had first dibs.[43] When James Rutledge, a white man, borrowed $600 from Cupid Hawkins, a free black man, he mortgaged a tract of land to secure his debt. After he failed to repay the debt, Hawkins sued him for $600 plus interest and requested that the court seize the land and sell it to satisfy his claim. The court issued a verdict in favor of Hawkins and ordered Rutledge's land to be seized and sold.[44]

Black creditors also had property interests in other black people and sometimes took execution on slaves as collateral. For instance, the free black planter Augustin Borie sued a white couple, Phillip Roth and Marie Joseph Orillion Roth, for the $600 he lent them. To secure the loan, Borie told the court, the Roths mortgaged an enslaved woman. He wanted the sheriff to seize her, sell her, and provide him with the profits necessary to settle the debt and the mounting interest on the loan. Marie Roth, however, claimed that she was not indebted to Borie because her husband incurred the debt, a debt that in fact her husband denied owing. Yet the court found for Borie and ordered the enslaved woman to be taken and sold at auction to satisfy the debt.[45]

When they received verdicts in their favor and the debts remained unpaid (whether because the borrower did not have sufficient property to satisfy the debt, had fled the jurisdiction of the court to avoid repayment, or had refused to pay), black lenders also initiated garnishment proceedings against third parties: people who either served as security for the loan or people who had possession of property belonging to the debtor. For example, when William Calmes, a white man, fled the state of Louisiana and refused to pay the $300 he owed Valerien Joseph, a free man of color, Joseph initiated garnishment proceedings against another white man, John A. Warren. Warren, Joseph claimed, "has in his hands funds belonging to the said Calmes, more than sufficient to pay the judgment and the costs." The court subpoenaed Warren, requesting that he appear before it and answer Joseph's "demand." When Warren did not appear, however, Joseph received a judgment of garnishment against Warren (in default), and the court ordered Warren to pay Joseph $350. When he failed to pay, the sheriff seized his property, sold it at auction, and gave Joseph the amount due to him.[46]

Here we might pause and savor a bit of irony: the auction block sits in the midst of a highly charged symbolic field, for blacks and whites alike. Seizure of a debtor's property and its sale at a sheriff's auction was a common result of Natchez district debt actions. However, the image of white property on the auction block—property put there by the claims of a black person—is striking. The auction block was a visible symbol of the white ownership of black slaves and a looming threat that served to enforce slave discipline. It was no accident that when black people theorized freedom, they included the refrain "no more auction block for me." The auction block had complex resonance for whites as well, both as a symbol of their domination over black people and as a reminder that their things, too, might be sold in public, the ultimate in financial failure, which carried strong moral overtones about a white person's good faith, reliability, and ultimately, their honor. When a black person initiated a lawsuit that resulted in the seizure and sale of white property, it signaled the disruption of the existing order. After all, it was black people who stood on the region's auction blocks; as people with a price they were the objects of auctions, not instigators of them. Thus, white indebtedness to black people—and black people harnessing the power of the state to enforce those obligations—posed a number of real problems for whites.

"THE BORROWER IS SLAVE TO THE LENDER"

Debt also posed symbolic problems for white people. Debt connected people. In particular, credit bound lenders and borrowers together in relationships of obligation. The ubiquity of antebellum indebtedness caught many in webs of credit: cotton planters depended on their buyers, importers on goods from wholesalers, wholesalers on local producers or retailers, retailers on payments from consumers, and consumers on loans or guarantees from kin or friends.[47] For many, such bonds were the cost of doing business in antebellum America. But for some, the chains of obligation were uncomfortable.

Debt actions took place within a social order (and a symbolic universe) that assigned certain moral characteristics to debt—and to race. But to what extent was it problematic for a white person to borrow from a black person? Debt-recovery lawsuits themselves do not provide adequate evidence for answering this question; nor do the extant personal papers and letters from Natchez district whites. Yet a variety of other cultural discourses do.

Southern planters, as I mentioned above, sometimes disguised their credit relationships and lending and borrowing through a masquerade of gift giving. When one white planter issued credit to another, they couched their transaction in the language of gifts rather than the language of loans; borrowers requested that lenders "send" along money (and did not spell out a repayment schedule), while lenders depended on the honor of their peers to repay the loan.[48] In addition, credit relationships among planters were a form of patronage and represented, in the words of one scholar, "reciprocal commercial friendships."[49] Using the language of gift giving or friendship allowed planters to avoid (or mask) the stigma of debt—a stigma that signaled dependency on and subordination to creditors.[50]

When a white planter "borrowed" a gift of money from someone of his social class (and from the same race), he was bound by honor to a peer. But when a white person borrowed from a black person, they were bound in obligation to a subordinate. For whites, these bonds must have at times proven unnerving, for they could not avoid the shame of debt by invoking the language of gifts and patronage that they used with their peers; white borrowers could not describe black creditors as their friends or equals without disrupting the hierarchies inscribed by white supremacy and black slavery. What is more, debt meant dependency on and subordination to a creditor. When that creditor was black, the white borrower's world tilted. To some white southerners, the black creditor and white borrower probably evoked a feeling of disorder.

Nonetheless, in a society in which black people were bound to white people—in every way possible—white borrowers had a legal obligation to honor their promises to black creditors. Debts were pledges; they were agreements to pay. Black lenders appealed to the force of the law to make whites accountable to their commitments. When Phillis went to court to call in her loans to Antoine Langlois, she publicly announced his dependence on her and his obligation to her—a position usually reserved for the enslaved. And the court recognized that bond as valid.

Moreover, the language of binding—to be bound in obligation to someone—was reminiscent of slavery. The image of debtors as slaves was common in the antebellum United States. Antebellum politicians, social commentators, moralists, and debtors and their sympathizers characterized indebtedness and especially insolvency as a form of slavery. After all, in older societies, unpaid debts often led to enslavement, and in early nineteenth-century America, debtors could still be imprisoned in many states. Debtors, these commentators claimed, were in perpetual bondage to their creditors.[51]

For many antebellum Americans (northern and southern), indebtedness also was the antithesis of republican virtue and independence. Debtors threatened the social and moral fabric of the new nation and compromised both individuals and the state: as one newspaper from the Natchez district lamented (and in sexualized language), "Debt is the curse of our age. . . . Debt cheats honesty and drives out virtue. It sneers at purity and pollutes innocence. . . . States are weakened and made the prey of the money-changers by debt."[52] Debtors were subordinate to and dependent on the indulgence of their creditors. As dependents, debtors lacked self-direction. Most problematically, debtors were not free to make the independent, impartial decisions so important to the success of a republic: according to one historian, debt was a "formidable barrier to autonomous evaluation of public matters or manly participation in public debate."[53] Indebtedness made a man impure; and it symbolized a loss of manhood, for an indebted man could neither provide for his dependents nor properly manage his household.

In their newspapers, sermons, and other writings, white southerners in the Natchez district compared indebtedness to slavery and condemned such dependency. For instance, the editor of the *Southern Sentinel*, an Iberville Parish newspaper, frequently published such warnings: "Live Within Your Means," one editorial opined, "Next to slavery of intemperance, what slavery on earth is more galling than that of poverty and indebtedness? The man who is everybody's debtor is everybody's slave, and in a much worse condition than he who serves a single master."[54] In this editor's opinion, debt slavery was a fate worse than the hereditary, perpetual bondage faced by those who served "a single master": people of African descent. In another issue, the *Sentinel* published a poem, "Don't Run in Debt," which ended with a final verse invoking the debt slave: "The chain of a debtor is heavy and cold, Its links all erosion and rust; Gild it over as you will—it is never of gold—Then spurn it aside with disgust. The man who's in debt is too often a slave, though his heart may be honest and true; Can he hold up his head, and look saucy and brave, When a note he can't pay becomes due?"[55] The debtor's "heart might be honest and true," but he could not confidently show his face in public. Debt also could pollute an "honest and true" nature: as the *Woodville Republican*, another local newspaper, put it, "debt makes a man a slave and robs his toil, his contentment, his independence, and too often his integrity."[56] Debt circumscribed his independence and his ability to participate in the polity as an autonomous individual free in his choices.

The image of the debt slave, however, had particular salience in the Natchez district. The structure of the economy of the cotton South encouraged indebtedness and speculation. Credit offered opportunity. For some, credit was the path to upward mobility, even enormous wealth. Yet while white slaveholders relied on slaves as a liquid form of credit and assumed debt to buy slaves, they simultaneously recoiled at the idea of debt because they associated dependence with slavery. Thus, they faced a paradox. Debt was a necessary part of conducting business, but it also forced the debtor to enter into a state of bondage.

Black lending took place within this symbolic matrix in which the relationship between debt and slavery was frequently invoked. The irony of becoming the "slave" of a black creditor—a person naturally suited to dependency (according to the ideology of white supremacy)—was probably not lost on white borrowers. But borrow they did.

Borrowing from a free black creditor was one thing. Yet the threat to southern racial hierarchies became amplified when whites owed debts to (and were thus bound in relationships of obligation with) slaves. Consider the case of Milly. In early November 1824, Milly, a slave, successfully sued a white man, Peter Brown, twice for sizeable debts he owed her. The first time Milly went after Brown, she used the Adams County, Mississippi, circuit court to recover

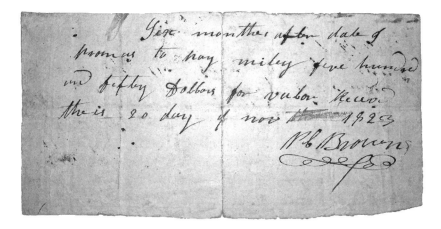

Promissory notes, including those involving enslaved lenders such as this one, followed a similar formula. *Milly v. Brown*, Historic Natchez Foundation, Natchez, Mississippi; photograph by the author.

the $110 she had lent him. One David Lawson, a white man and her owner, helped her recover the money and served as party to the suit. As evidence of the debt, Lawson and Milly provided the court with a promissory note signed by Brown indicating that he had borrowed the money from her and promised to repay her "without delay." The case went to trial, and the jury issued a judgment for $127.[57] Milly also initiated a second lawsuit against Brown in her own name (filed on the same day as the first lawsuit). This time she sued Brown to recover a debt of $550. Once again, she presented the court with a promissory note signed by Brown. Despite the evidence against him, Brown claimed that he had not "undertaken any promise" to pay Milly the specified amount. This time the jury awarded Milly a verdict of $584, and the judge overruled Brown's motion for a new trial.[58] Although a slave, Milly must have acquired considerable capital (both financial and social) to be able to lend out such large amounts of money, capital she successfully protected in court despite her personal status.

Milly was not the only enslaved woman to extend credit to whites. In 1800, Elizabeth, an enslaved woman belonging to one Domingo Loreno, sued Maria Williams, a white woman, for the sixty-two dollars she had recently lent her, and the Natchez court ordered Williams to pay the debt plus 10 percent interest. The court record listed Loreno as Elizabeth's owner, but he was not a party to the suit.[59] Harriet Jacobs's grandmother, moreover, lent her mistress $300, money she scraped together over a period of years and set aside to purchase her children. Unlike Elizabeth and Milly, however, Jacobs's grandmother did not or could not protect her interests with a promissory note as evidence of the loan and its terms. Even if she had a promissory note, she did not have legal standing to protect her investment in court.

On a few occasions, however, enslaved people circumvented the statutory prohibitions that denied them access to the courts and initiated debt actions. Yet because enslaved people in Mississippi and Louisiana could not be parties to suits (they could only be parties to lawsuits for their freedom if illegally enslaved, and even then they were limited), the court had to find a workaround. For instance, in Milly's second lawsuit, the clerk of the court described her as a free woman of color. Yet in the first (where Lawson was a party to the suit), the clerk listed her as "Milly, a negro woman slave." These cases were filed simultaneously: on the same day and dictated to the same clerk of the court. Moreover, the same lawyers, William B. Griffith and John A. Quitman, represented the plaintiff in both cases. I have not found any evidence that Milly was a free woman. Thus, because Milly was an owner of property (property her owner knew she possessed and perhaps had an interest in) and a signatory to a promissory note, it is possible that in this second case, the court allowed a temporary, workable legal fiction about property ownership that provided her access.[60]

Cases like Milly's prove maddening for the twenty-first century researcher because so much information is missing from the record. Her lawsuits—like debt actions generally—were formulaic, and there is no indication of the local knowledge that must have played a role in the court's decision. Milly's litigation also leaves many questions unanswered; everything we know about her we know from these lawsuits. Many enslaved people left little written documentation behind. But from this seemingly elusive and tantalizing piece of evidence, we can learn some things: Milly used the courts to sue a white man twice. And twice she won when she was not entitled to be in the courtroom to begin with. Furthermore, Milly's case is exemplary rather than exceptional. Her lawsuits shared many of the same characteristics of those involving other black litigants, from her ability to harness her community networks to her expectation that the courts would hear her claims. Milly's litigation offers additional evidence that people of African descent enjoyed considerable legal knowledge. Moreover, not only did Milly challenge a white man; she also aired her complaints publicly. By insisting he sign a promissory note and appearing in a courtroom to protect her interests, Milly compelled Brown to meet his commitments. The court validated her claims, and the community watched. If debt was indeed a form of slavery, as many in the region claimed, then Brown was bound in obligation to Milly—a woman and a slave.

An action, as the Louisiana *Code of Practice* outlined, involved "the right given to every person, to claim judicially what is due or belongs to him." Actions also bound people to their obligations: "the exercise of that right, that is to say, a judicial demand founded on a contract, or given by law, by which the plaintiff prays that the person against whom he proceeds, be ordered to do that which he has bound himself towards him to perform."[61] In the antebellum South, it was white men who took action and made claims, and as the enslavers, they could not be bound to black people. Yet being indebted to a black creditor put white borrowers in an awkward position: in a relationship of obligation to a black person, often described as a form of bondage. When black creditors stood up in court and called in the loans they extended to white people, debts many whites described as a form of slavery, they created a dissonance between who was speaking and what was being said: in a social order in which blackness meant bondage, whites were bound to blacks. When the courts found in favor of black creditors, as they almost always did, they recognized those bonds as defensible.

But cases like Milly's also remind us that slavery was first a system of property. This is not to deny the role of race and racial violence in the enslavement of African-descended people. White southerners of course used race as a tool of oppression, and property, liberty, and race were closely linked. But these links were not without their tensions. The raison d'être of the southern legal system was to protect private property—particularly the property rights of slaveholding, white men. This reality, however, gave free blacks and sometimes even slaves a set of tools that they, too, could use to secure their own advancement and ensure their own futures.

Their litigiousness, moreover, was a form of political engagement. For when black people approached the courts in the service of their own interests, they made claims on the state. And when black litigants compelled the courts to take execution on the property of others—including seizing and selling the property of whites—the state did their bidding. In the absence of formal political or individual rights, they used property rights as a stand-in for a broader constellation of rights. For black people in the antebellum slave South, property rights *were* civil rights. Property relations, as the next chapter demonstrates, could be generative of an entire system of social and civic relations.

5

The Sanctity of Property

Property, in the case of the antebellum South, was a system of ownership that enabled or underwrote a large-scale slave system. Slavery itself was "a set of property rights" supported by a legal apparatus that defined slaves as property and an owner's authority over his slaves as a right of property.[1] Slaves were a form of wealth, a source of credit, and a mode of exchange. They could be sold, rented, traded, and bequeathed. A slave mother's children were the property of her owner. As property, slaves could not contract for wages or determine their own hours or the type of work they performed; owners could assign them to any task, at any time, and in any setting where slavery was legal.[2] Southern masters defended slavery on the grounds of liberty and the right to property. In the words of one slaveholder, "As an owner of slaves (and one whose income is derived almost entirely from their labor), I assert an unquestionable right to my property, and protest against every attempt to deprive me of it without my consent."[3] Property rights were a gift from nature. Without them, in the language of the new republic, there could be no liberty. A master's right to his property was inviolable; it was the essence of his freedom. It was the source of his political authority.[4]

Property was also tied to an analytically separable (although often re-lated) set of issues: the ownership of things formed part of a narrative about autonomy and supported a set of claims about one's eligibility for self-governance and one's participation in a regime of common governance. Ownership provided the pathway to independence, and rights to property (considered fundamental and natural) conferred power, authority, and in-clusion in a republican society. Property was more than a means to acquire wealth or achieve comfort; it was also a way to anchor a person to a system of power.[5] Property ownership was tied to membership in the polity: in Jeffersonian terms, the owner, as economically independent, impartial, virtuous, and politically vested in the country's future, represented the ideal citizen in the new nation.

When people of color went to court to claim their rights to property and protect their livelihoods, they exploited white southerners' commitments to private property. Whether they owned a large plantation and dozens of slaves or their carpenter's tools and a few heads of cattle, hundreds of free blacks in the Natchez district used the local courts to protect, recover, enhance, and bequeath their property. In addition, people of African descent played multifunctional roles in the southern economy: as property themselves, certainly, but also as creditors, investors, and owners. The relationship between their economic roles and their use of law to protect those positions served to create chinks in the armor of southern white supremacy.

While the principal mandate of the southern legal system was to protect the property rights of white slaveholders (including the right to own people as property), people of color used this tendency to safeguard their own property. To achieve any consistency—and to convince or appease nonslaveholders— southern jurists and legislators had to protect the irrefutable rights of free proprietors. While lawmakers occasionally sought to deny free blacks the right to property ownership, their attempts were met with reproach, as critics claimed that doing so could divest all freeholders of their property rights.[6] In this world of white freedom and black slavery, race and property went hand-in-glove; but there were moments when the actions of black litigants forced some white southerners to choose between these two pillars of their society. Time and again, the protection of property rights (rights that unavoidably extended to free people of color) proved more important than denying African Americans' claims solely on the basis of racial status. Whites could not deny or invalidate such claims, because to do so would upend the legal foundation of a slave society: the sanctity of private property.

By leveraging the language of property in their lawsuits, and exploiting its associated presumptions about autonomy, independence, and reliability, black people registered their voices in public and exercised a civic personality. The language of property was required to describe the circumstances surrounding a particular case, certainly, but it was also tied to a larger narrative about membership in the new republic and, ultimately, citizenship. Thus, as owners, black litigants claimed a right to personhood and civic inclusion.

Yet they also made other claims. For people of African descent—a people with limited formal rights—property rights represented a broad constellation of rights and privileges related to the protection of human dignity. Black people used property rights to leverage a host of other rights tied to ownership and possession, rights that allowed them to direct aspects of their own lives and make demands on the state. Property was a way of regulating relationships more generally.

Free blacks went to court with full knowledge of their rights to property, and they expected the courts to deal with them fairly and protect those rights, just as they would with white southerners. They sued whites and other people of color in disputes over real and personal property. They also appealed to the courts to protect the dignity of their labor and sued to protect labor contracts or recover back wages. Like many antebellum Americans, free people of color viewed their labor as a form of property; it, too, represented a path to economic independence. Property ownership, however, sometimes rendered free people of color vulnerable to the greed of unscrupulous individuals. Free blacks' precarious position in a social order dedicated to white supremacy sometimes meant they were the victims of fraud—or worse. When cheated, they appealed to the courts to intervene. This chapter focuses its attention primarily on the property disputes of free people of color, as the southern legal apparatus did not acknowledge or protect the slaves' economy, although on occasion even those held as property went to court and sued.

FREE BLACK PROPERTY OWNERS

When the free black barber William Johnson died, he left behind an estate that included land in Adams County, Mississippi, a small plantation, two townhouses, three barbershops, a bathhouse, slaves, livestock, farm tools, and a number of personal items, including a violin and a large collection of books. Johnson's wife, Ann, took control of his estate after his death, managed his holdings, paid the required taxes, and bequeathed what remained to the couple's children on her death.[7] The Johnson family was not unique. Free blacks throughout the Natchez district owned property and achieved a measure of economic stability and even prosperity. They even constituted some of the Natchez district's most successful and wealthy sugar and cotton planters. The women of the Belly family of Iberville Parish owned estates that rivaled those of the region's richest whites. The daughters of Pierre Belly, a Frenchmen and planter, and Rose Belly, Pierre Belly's former slave, managed to carve out a place for themselves in a white man's world and prosper. Belly manumitted Rose and their six daughters and legally recognized the girls as his "natural children," born of Rose, "commonly called Rose Belly free negro woman."[8] Rose lived with Belly as his wife, and their community accepted them as married. In the years before his death in 1814, Belly, the wealthiest planter in Iberville Parish, passed much of his property to Rose.[9] Later in his will and in accordance with Louisiana law, Belly bequeathed half of what remained of his estate to his surviving brother and sister, both residents of France, and bestowed one-fourth to Rose and one-fourth to his daughters. When he died, Belly's holdings included more than five thousand acres of land, five plantations, ninety-six slaves, a house, cabins, a corn mill, a kiln, cattle, and considerable personal property.[10] Rose died fourteen years later, in 1828, leaving her property to their daughters.[11] The Belly daughters conducted their lives much like whites of equal economic status. They married free black men of similar Afro-French backgrounds, prosperous men who fought alongside whites during the War of 1812. They educated their children with private tutors and sent them to France for additional schooling. They bought slaves to labor on their enormous plantations. With the land, slaves, and money they inherited and accrued, coupled with their influence in the community, their talent for business, and their skills as litigators, the Belly daughters and their husbands amassed substantial estates. In 1860, a handful of Pierre and Rose Belly's descendants owned more than fifty slaves each. By the eve of the Civil War, the Belly family formed one of the most affluent free black family groups in the United States.[12] Not all free people of color in the Natchez district acquired such wealth, of course, and many owned little more than their barber's tools. However, according to one study of black property ownership in the South, all but a few free people of color owned some property.[13] The ownership of that property, both real and personal, represented a hallmark of their freedom.

Free blacks in the Natchez district acquired property in a number of different ways. Some, like the Johnsons, inherited it from their parents and spouses. Many, like the Belly daughters, inherited real and personal property from white fathers or received donations from other white relatives. Although whites and blacks could not legally marry in Louisiana or Mississippi, many interracial couples (usually white men and free and enslaved black women) lived together as married and produced children. After his white wife died, the Natchez planter Adam L. Bingaman began a decades-long relationship with his slave, Mary Ellen Williams. He manumitted Williams, and she bore him several children. In 1841, he moved Williams and their children to New Orleans to live among other prosperous free black families. On his death in 1869, Bingaman and Williams's daughter, Elenora, inherited his estate.[14] While technically the mixed-race children of white men and black women were bastards, fathers could legally acknowledge these children as their own, which provided the children with additional inheritance rights. In the years before he died, Adam Bingaman appeared before a Louisiana notary to recognize his free black offspring as his "natural children." Louisiana children recognized legally as natural children could inherit up to one-quarter of a parent's estate.[15] Inheriting large estates from their white fathers made several free families of color some of the wealthiest people in the Natchez district. Other free people of color had white parents who set them up in business before they died.[16]

Free blacks acquired property in ways other than inheriting it. Many free people of color in the region owned productive farms and plantations and raised sugarcane, corn, and cotton. These farmers and planters also possessed horses, sheep, hogs, cattle, and farm machinery. In Iberville Parish, for example, Augustin Borie, Antoine Lacour, George Deslonde, St. Luc Ricard, Cyprian Ricard, and Antoine Dubuclet, all free men of color (and some related), owned sugar and cotton plantations that dwarfed many of the holdings of their white neighbors. A number of black and white farmers in Iberville Parish and the surrounding area paid Borie (the owner of a cotton gin) to gin their cotton. Dubuclet owned and operated Cedar Grove, a successful sugar plantation.

In contrast to the landholding class, many free men of color acquired skills such as barbering, carpentry, masonry, and kettle-making and worked for wages. They also worked as mechanics, coopers, shoemakers, and cigar makers. Some developed such skills as slaves and relied on them once free. Free people of color operated successful businesses such as grocery stores and barber and tailoring shops. Free black women ran a number of boarding houses and inns that accommodated and fed travelers and steamboat workers who disembarked along the Mississippi River. Some of these inns doubled as bordellos and gambling houses, operations that sometimes ran their proprietors afoul of the law. For instance, in 1843, Clarissa Bartlett faced charges for "keeping a disorderly house," a house that attracted people of "evil name and fame" day and night and encouraged debauchery and "dishonest conversation."[17] Free women of color also peddled goods at market (goods they made or purchased wholesale) and operated mercantile shops. Ann Johnson produced and then sold the goods she made in the markets around Natchez. Some free women of color such as Ann Caldwell labored as nurses and others worked as seamstresses, cooks, and laundresses.

Although many free blacks exhausted their incomes on daily necessities, some used the capital they received for their goods and services to purchase real and personal property, including land, cattle and horses, farm equipment, and luxury items such as pianos, books, and china. Following the pattern whites set in the Natchez district, they also bought slaves. Slave ownership was widespread among the free blacks of the Natchez district. In Louisiana, roughly one out of three free black families owned slaves. In 1830, for example, 965 black slaveholders owned 4,206 enslaved people.[18] Many free people of color used a portion of their income to buy and then manumit enslaved friends and family. For instance, Henriette, a Louisiana free woman of color, spent many years saving her money to buy her son, Charles. After purchasing him in 1847, she petitioned the court in Pointe Coupee Parish to emancipate the fifty-year-old Charles. The court granted her request and gave Charles permission to remain in the state of Louisiana.[19] Manumission became more difficult in the late antebellum period, however, forcing free blacks to keep their family and kin as slaves. But slave ownership also represented an opportunity to gain a level of prosperity and wealth, and some free people of color purchased and then exploited slave laborers. For instance, Amy Johnson bought several slaves over the course of her lifetime to serve in her household and peddle goods in Natchez markets. When Claire Pollard died, she left behind an estate valued at $82,000, including $27,000 in slave property.[20] Like their white neighbors, free blacks bought, sold, traded, mortgaged, and sometimes mistreated enslaved people.[21]

In addition to material comfort, property ownership provided free people of color with access to the courts. In regard to property, both Mississippi and Louisiana allowed free blacks the same rights and privileges as whites. In particular, free black men in both states could make contracts and possess property, including slaves. Single free women of color shared the same property rights as free black men; once married, however, free wives of color faced the same legal handicaps as white wives.[22] Free blacks sued whites and other people of color to recover stolen goods; demand compensation for damaged property; recuperate back wages; enforce the terms of contracts involving land rentals, slave hires, and partnerships; and resolve a multitude of other disputes involving property ownership and possession. "Black Ben," a free man of color living in Natchez, sued several white men to recover the money they owed him. For example, he sued William Brooks twice for sizeable amounts (once in 1814 for $870 and again in 1816 for $902), money Brooks owed him for cotton purchases. In both cases, the court found for Ben.[23] In 1831, Antoine Lacour, a free man of color, sued Valery Landry, a white man, for shooting and killing his horses "without cause or provocation." Landry denied legal and financial responsibility for the death of Lacour's horses.

These were "mischievous horses that no fence could stop and keep," Landry testified, and Lacour refused to keep them from damaging Landry's crop and frightening his cattle. The court, however, found Landry responsible and ordered him to pay Lacour ninety dollars plus court costs.[24] Free blacks' property suits were commonplace in the local courts of the Natchez district, such that court clerks frequently neglected to identify the litigants as people of color (despite Mississippi and Louisiana laws that required officials to do so in court documents). Manuel Britto, a free man of color and a merchant, sued several times to recover debts for the goods he sold on credit, and court officials neglected to label him as a person of color in nearly half of his lawsuits.[25]

NARRATIVES OF PROPERTY

Property ownership supplied free blacks with both the capital and confidence to sue; it also provided them with a language to employ in court—language black litigants could mobilize to make their claims recognizable and thus persuasive to others. For white audiences, the image of black litigants (people held as property) availing themselves in the language of property must have proven unsettling, for many whites in the slave South had claimed the language of property as a marker of the privileges of whiteness. Yet in some circumstances, the language of property—a language linked to a discourse of inclusion and autonomy—proved effective in black hands. Consider the case of Augustin Borie. In September 1818 in Iberville Parish, Louisiana, Borie, a free man of color, sued Jean Baptiste Lorrie, a white cotton planter, for his share of a cotton gin. Two years prior, Borie and Lorrie had contracted to build a cotton gin "in community" and situated the gin on Borie's land. But, Borie claimed, some "difficulties" had arisen between the two men, which had made it "disadvantageous to continue their community" and co-ownership. Because Borie and Lorrie held the gin "in equal proportion," Borie wanted it sold and an "equal division" of the profits distributed to the two men on "equitable ... terms and conditions." Lorrie, however, claimed that the cotton gin should belong to him because he alone had provided the materials and the labor. In his defense, Lorrie summoned two witnesses, Jacques Rivere and Jean Trapper, both free men of color. While the cotton gin resided on Borie's property and "both parties were equal sharers in all the expenses that accrued, of every kind," Rivere and Trapper recounted, Lorrie had supplied the wood to construct it and the labor "of three of his negroes" to build it. Furthermore, they claimed, Lorrie "worked as hard as one of his negroes himself." Other witnesses testified that while the two men had entered into a contract to build and share the cotton gin as "equal partners" and in "equal portion," Lorrie provided the lion's share of the capital to construct and maintain it. After considering the evidence, the jury found for Lorrie and awarded him ownership of the cotton gin; although Lorrie had agreed to let the cotton gin reside on Borie's plantation rather than his own, because he had provided most of the labor and materials for its construction, the jury declared that it belonged to him. Shortly thereafter, however, Borie and Lorrie mended their relationship and agreed to keep the cotton gin as common property on Borie's plantation, continue to share the profits, and work as partners.[26]

The language that Borie used in his petition reveals his expectation that the court would safeguard his interests and provides some insight into his interpretation of his relationship to Lorrie. Borie leveraged the language of property and consistently referred to his rights of possession: the gin was on his land. He helped pay for its construction and maintenance. Both he and Lorrie had rights to the gin; thus they should sell it and divide the proceeds. Throughout the entire process, Borie used the terms "equitable" or "equal" to describe his partnership with and relationship to Lorrie. Borie repeatedly insisted that the courts protect him equally in what he called his "mutual bargain" with Lorrie and demanded an "equitable division" of the property. Ironically, however, while Borie used the language of property to describe his right to the gin, witnesses for Lorrie described his rights to the gin in the language of race. Indeed, Lorrie ultimately gained possession of the gin because he "worked as hard as a negro" to construct it. In this instance, labor (and "negro-like" labor at that) created ownership.

Although he lost this lawsuit, it appears that Borie was neither reluctant to sue a white man nor intimidated by the formality or mystery of the judicial process. Instead, he understood the specifics of the southern legal system and expected it to work to his advantage—and to protect his property—just as it would for a white man. Borie, moreover, was no stranger to the courts. He sued several white men in his lifetime. Between 1815 and 1840, he was involved in more than twenty lawsuits, most of which he won.[27] He was not alone. Many other Natchez district free people of color sued whites in similar fashion using similar language.

It is perhaps unsurprising that Borie presented himself as Lorrie's equal and expected the court to treat him as such. Both men were planters and on similar footing, at least economically. But in labor disputes and lawsuits over broken contracts and back wages, free people of color of lower financial standing proved similarly forceful. The language Louis Cadoret used in his lawsuit against his white employer was particularly inflammatory and stood in striking difference from the more deferential tone taken by free blacks who appealed to their reputations as "good negroes" when approaching the courts. Instead, Cadoret publicly accused his employer of dishonesty; by defrauding him of his wages, his employer stole his property, and Cadoret demanded equal protection and justice from the court.

In his 1821 petition, Cadoret, a free man of color in Pointe Coupee Parish, claimed that Joseph Decuir, a wealthy and prominent white planter, had hired him as "laborer and overseer" on his plantation for a year and contracted to pay him $300 for that labor. Although Cadoret had "faithfully performed his duty, and never gave cause for complaint," Decuir dismissed him after a few short months and paid him only part of his promised salary. Then, when Cadoret complained about the broken contract and demanded the money owed him, Decuir offered to allow him to remain on the plantation picking cotton at a far lower wage. Cadoret, being a man "without money, and without employment," wanted the court to enforce the original terms of his labor contract and compel Decuir to pay him for the remainder of the year. Because of Decuir's "perfidy in hiring [Cadoret] with the intent to cast him out on the world when it would be difficult to find employment," he wanted the $244 still owed him. And because he "suffered great injury in being deprived of the opportunity of hiring with some planter of known integrity," Cadoret also wanted $1,000 in damages.

For Cadoret, the courtroom represented more than a site of dispute resolution; it was also a site of public reprimand. When suing Decuir, Cadoret sought more than his wages. He used his lawsuit to unleash a scathing condemnation of Decuir. To that end, he concluded his petition by reminding the court that "he had the happiness of living in a country governed by laws that protected the liberty and rights of a poor overseer, no less than an opulent planter, that having once dismissed him, the contract was dissolved and could not be renewed without mutual consent." More important, Cadoret continued, "he would never contract with a man who, wallowing in his riches, hired an overseer by the year, during the busy season, and when he had less to do, perfidiously dismissed him, thru. . . avarice; as if he had acted thru ignorance of the law, yet his religion must have taught him that to defraud a laborer his salary, is one of the four sins that cry to heaven, equally with willful murder." Despite the potential risks that using such language against a white man might pose, Cadoret let Decuir know what he thought of him—in public, no less. He accused Decuir of dishonest, greedy, and criminal behavior. In Cadoret's estimation, Decuir was not an honorable man, and he wanted everyone to know it. Cadoret rebuked Decuir before his peers. What is more, he also reminded Decuir of his responsibilities as an employer and expected the court to enforce those responsibilities.

Cadoret positioned himself as person with rights to defend and demanded equal protection of his property—his labor—from the courts. In his view, the "poor overseer," white or black, enjoyed the same rights and protections as the "opulent planter." This property was his natural right; it was sacred. Antebellum Americans well understood the sanctity of property in one's labor. When claiming his rights to his labor, Cadoret inserted himself into a tradition dating back to Adam Smith: "The property which every man has in his own labour, as it is the foundation of all other property," Smith wrote in *Wealth of Nations*, "so it is the most sacred and inviolable. The patrimony of a poor man lies in the strength and dexterity of his hands; and to hinder him from employing this strength and dexterity in what manner he thinks proper without injury to his neighbour is a plain violation of this most sacred property."[28] Decuir deprived Cadoret of his most fundamental right—a right that many believed no person or government could infringe upon. He also fused that understanding with Christian tradition: defrauding the worker was "one of the four sins that cry to heaven." Cadoret viewed his labor as his own property, a property his employer had "perfidiously" and "sinfully" disregarded. As the owner of his labor, he was entitled to put that labor up for sale and benefit from its rewards. It was property that he expected the courts to help him protect, especially since Decuir was an untrustworthy man without "integrity." He insisted the law come to his aid and safeguard his interests.[29] For those free people of color who worked for wages like Cadoret, the ownership of their labor proved critical to their status as free persons. Free blacks' right to contract, to possess property, to own their labor and themselves, and to sue to protect these rights represented crucial features of their freedom and placed them in stark contrast to slaves.

The court dismissed the case at the plaintiff's request before it went to trial, and the reasons for its dismissal are lost from the record. Nonetheless, Cadoret employed a narrative in court—of property in one's labor—that other free people of color would use with great success. Many free blacks shared Cadoret and Borie's expectations that the courts equally protect the property rights of people of color, and they too expressed this perception in the language that they used in their lawsuits. Indeed, in 1853, just two years after being manumitted from slavery, Cadoret's own son, a skilled carpenter also named Louis Cadoret, successfully sued Henry Demouny and Samuel Jones, two white men, for $150 in back wages and insisted on prompt payment. As a former slave who surely felt the injustice of laboring without compensation, Cadoret would not work for free any longer.[30]

Even those free people of color living hand-to-mouth at the margins of southern society approached the courts with the expectation that their interests would be served, and they leveraged the language of property and self-proprietorship. Wealth did of course provide free people of color with important material and social benefits, but poverty was neither a bar to court action nor a barrier to courtroom success. Consider, for example, Rosalie's lawsuit against Jean Duclos, a white man. In 1839, Rosalie, a free black woman, sued Duclos for the thirteen dollars she had lent him and fifty dollars in back wages. Rosalie claimed that she had lived with Duclos for six months as his "hired servant." During that time, Duclos had asked her "to act in the capacity of a wife" and provide him with sexual and household services. After securing certain guarantees, Rosalie had consented to do so, and she also had agreed to lend him thirteen dollars. However, their relationship soon soured, Rosalie claimed, and she sought the help of the parish court to force Duclos to return the money and pay her wages for the months "he engaged her as his wife." Those services, in her estimation, were worth fifty dollars. Although the parish court judge expressed distaste at this informal and "unfortunate marriage," he ordered Duclos to pay Rosalie thirteen dollars and the court costs. She did not get paid for her services.[31] But by going to court to claim what was due and what belonged to her, Rosalie demonstrated that she understood herself as providing important services—both sexually and with her household labor. Her body was a tool; it was her property. It provided her with a legal interest such that she could use it to mediate relationships. While she did not receive compensation for her labor, the language that she used to describe it demonstrated that she endowed that property with value.

PROPERTY RIGHTS AS "CIVIL RIGHTS"

Like their white neighbors, some people of color invested in land and slaves. Black litigants' disputes over real and personal property were common in the local courts of the Natchez district. They sued to recover unpaid debts for land and slave sales and to recoup payment for slave rentals. They sued in disputes over injured bondspeople and to evict squatters on their land. They sued to over damaged goods and stolen cattle. For free blacks, the acquisition of such property provided them with a measure of independence, and the right to protect that property in and out of court was a symbol of their freedom and their relationship to the polity. Their right to ownership was a right they defended vociferously and one they linked to a broader constellation of rights and relationships.[32]

Like their white contemporaries, free people of color understood that land ownership could bring economic independence as well as greater personal autonomy. Many free blacks in the Natchez district acquired real estate, and they showed little hesitation when taking legal precautions to safeguard their land. They commonly sued to recover unpaid debts for land deals, to protect real estate from sale or seizure, and to receive compensation for damage done to their property or resources extracted from it without their permission. While land ownership did not secure the vote for people of African descent in the antebellum South—as it did for propertied white men—free people of color nonetheless insisted on their right to own land and demanded that the courts protect these rights. Claims to land and the protection of landownership in court also meant exercising a civic identity, a status ordinarily reserved for white men.[33]

For many free blacks—especially former slaves—using the courts to protect their real estate signaled to the larger community that they were competent householders and capable of handling the responsibilities of freedom. John Sandy's reputation as an adept household head depended on his willingness to take legal action to safeguard his property. In his 1841 petition, Sandy, a free man of color and former slave, relayed that for the previous five years he had possessed and occupied "as owner unmolested" a tract of land along the Mississippi River in a community known as "Bakers Settlement." He "expended" great effort and "considerable expense" to improve the property by "building cabins, clearing land, and establishing a wood yard" with the intention of filing a request with the "Land office at Greensburg" for a preemption claim to the land, preemption rights he stated were guaranteed him by "Acts of Congress" in 1838 and 1840. Moreover, "since he became a free man, he has conducted himself in an orderly and respectful manner" and thus "deserved the good will of the citizens of Bakers Settlement." But to his "great damage and annoyance," Charles Barnes, a white man, had "illegally, forcibly, and fraudulently taken possession" of his property. He had repeatedly and unsuccessfully asked "Barnes to leave the premises" and to "desist" from cutting timber on his land, an act that "prevented him from pursuing his occupation of cutting cordwood for steamships." Barnes's illegal possession of Sandy's land had kept Sandy from "enjoying his Civil Rights secured to him by Law." He wanted Barnes to leave his property and pay him $300 in damages. One month after filing his petition, however, Sandy requested that the court dismiss his lawsuit.

Why he did so is unclear, but it is possible that Sandy and Barnes settled the matter outside the courtroom.[34]

As a former slave, Sandy's land ownership was both a symbol of his freedom and a pathway to economic independence. It also represented his principal means of subsistence. Protection of that property, both in and out of the courtroom, was important to his very survival. As the master of his domain, Sandy had not only the right but also the responsibility to sue. Suing whites, however, could prove dangerous. But Sandy demonstrated an astute understanding of his position in a racial order dedicated to white supremacy, and he employed a scrupulous mix of deference and self-assertion when prosecuting his lawsuit. He simultaneously showed the court that he had "conducted himself in an orderly and respectful manner," *and* he displayed his willingness to take legal action to protect his "Civil Rights" to property. Part of proving himself worthy of the respect of the "citizens of Bakers Settlement" meant demonstrating his ability to run his household and protect his livelihood. Sometimes prudent household management involved going to court. For Sandy, property ownership and a good character were linked.

There was much more at stake than just his reputation, however. It was no accident that Sandy framed his rights to property as a matter of civil rights. While arguably one of the most important expansions of civil rights occurred with the Fourteenth Amendment to the Constitution in 1868 (particularly the rights of former slaves to due process and equal protection under the law), black litigants in the antebellum Natchez district used their lawsuits to argue for the extension of civil rights to people of color. They did so, however, not in the language of racial equality, but in the language of property.

For free blacks in the antebellum South, property rights *were* civil rights. In the absence of other rights, free people of color used property rights to claim and wield a host of rights linked to possession, rights that tied them to a narrative of inclusion within the polity (membership they were otherwise denied).[35] Property rights, moreover, represented something far more capacious then simple ownership.

Ownership is not merely possession; it is not a single right. Instead, ownership is comprised of what some property theorists have termed a "bundle of rights."[36] Ownership refers not simply to a person's relationship to a thing, but instead to "rights or relationships among people with respect to things."[37] Property, then, is relational. For people of color like Sandy, this constellation of rights and the relationships they embodied was far-reaching. By insisting on his right to possess the track of land at Bakers Settlement, Sandy not only claimed the right to have exclusive physical control over the property. He also claimed the right to manage that property; the right to use it as he saw fit ("unmolested," he avowed); the right to obtain an income from it and benefit from its fruits (in this case, to cut timber and sell it as cordwood to steamboats); the right to its security (such that men like Barnes could not enter it and use it without his permission); the right to sell or rent it to others (if he needed or wanted the income); and the right to transmit it (and bequeath to his children, wife, or kin as inheritance or a gift). Moreover, Sandy insisted that these were "civil rights" and "secured to him by Law."[38]

Wielding property rights as civil rights helped Sandy construct a more tolerable world for himself and his family; these rights encapsulated the essence of his self-determination. For a man once enslaved, self-determination carried a special meaning. Protecting his property rights represented far more than his right to the exclusive possession of the land: it also meant he could direct his own life, make choices, keep others in check, and secure his future and the future of his children and kin. Sandy could not access the social and political equality that civil rights provided white, slaveholding men. But, like Augustin Borie and hundreds of other people of color in the Natchez district, he did claim an equal right to property and the other rights that ownership entailed, not least of all the ability to access the courts and demand that the state enforce these rights and adjudicate relationships. Indeed, in the aggregate, property rights could stand in for a whole host of things that made one's world more bearable.

Free people of color also expanded property rights to include the protection of human dignity. For Sandy, this meant membership in and access to a particular community. Property rights also signified his relationship to others—in this instance, the "citizens of Bakers Settlement," people he interacted with daily and people whose respect he had gained.[39] While it is unclear who comprised the other members of the community, it is evident that Sandy's connections to the residents of Bakers Settlement provided him with important networks and support, networks that he drew on when he went to court to challenge a white man. Membership in a community might also offer him protection and solace; it helped ensure his future. For other people of color in the region, like free black landowner, Pierre Salvador, property rights included, in his words, "the right to peacefully enjoy settlement of his property."[40] To Salvador, ownership conveyed a right to carve out a space for himself, to work his own ground, and to live in peace. For people like Salvador and Sandy, ownership also entailed the power to create and enforce boundaries, both real and symbolic, because it included the authority to exclude people. For others still, ownership—and the protection of ownership—offered opportunities to register one's voice in the public arena and make one's story known. It also forced others to contend with or answer to those stories. It meant that they were people whose claims counted.[41] Property relations, then, could be imagined as productive of an entire system of social relations.

It was not just black men who claimed property rights as civil rights; free women of color also exercised the constellation of rights and relationships associated with ownership and expanded those rights to include privileges they might not readily have access to by virtue of their skin color and sex. In so doing, they, too, asserted a civic identity. When Marie Ricard, a free woman of color from West Baton Rouge Parish, Louisiana, and the owner, "in her own right," of tract of land on the Mississippi River, appeared in court alleging "that a certain Charles Hubeau, a free man of color . . . has taken illegal and forcible possession of the land and settled there without [her] consent," she expected the court to respect her rights to property ownership. She insisted that Hubeau vacate the property, return the "title and the rights of property to the land" to her, and condemn him to pay her $200 in back rent. She did not just assert her title to the land; she also claimed all the rights associated with ownership, including her right to use and to security. What is more, Ricard was a married woman; technically, she could not sue in her own name. Nonetheless, she insisted that the court hear her claim and protect her right to handle the economic business of her own life just as it would other free (and male) property owners.[42] She was not the only married woman to do so. Despite their status as legal dependents and in spite of prohibitions against married women's property ownership, many married women of color in the region owned and controlled property and went to court to safeguard it as de facto single women. Local court records from the region show married women (both black and white) playing fast and loose with the doctrine of coverture—ignoring it when convenient and hiding behind it when necessary.[43]

Sandy's and Ricard's claims to land and property rights linked them to narratives about independent proprietors well known to their white, male audiences—indeed, they played upon white expectations. To many white men in the antebellum South, landownership evoked a vision of a citizenry who provided for themselves and their families and could not be bought or unduly influenced by bosses, landlords, or political operators. Such independence was a prerequisite for political inclusion. But in the U.S. South, the narrative of the independent, politically vested landowner was a narrative of white privilege—and one that was gendered male. White men did not include black people (or white women) in this narrative of autonomy. In particular, white men used law to keep women and racialized others from making claims to land, membership, and independence. Through the law of slavery, whites claimed people of African descent as property, and as property black people could not own land or other property themselves. The law of coverture, furthermore, provided men with the right to ownership of their wives' personal property, and men served as managers of their wives' real property. While a husband could not sell her land without her permission, he could rent it out and extract resources from it. Both women and black people were dependents. Thus, the normative litigant and citizen was a white male.[44]

But Sandy and Ricard used their lawsuits to include themselves in these privileged categories of legal personhood and citizenship. By leveraging the language of property and their status as owners, and by exploiting its associated presumptions about independence, people of color like Ricard and Sandy made claims to civic inclusion. As these were claims to land, the language of property proved necessary to describe the case. Yet that language was also bound to a broader narrative of what it meant to be a member of the polity, to be someone who counts such that he or she could register his voice or assert her claim. When Sandy and Ricard made a claim about property—and insisted the court protect, in the words of Ricard, their "title and the rights of property to the land"—they were also, implicitly, linking their status as proprietor to the ideal of a free and autonomous citizen.

PROPERTY IN PEOPLE

Free blacks' property claims moved beyond land ownership; among their rights, some insisted, was a right to and authority over the property within their households: slaves. Claims to property rights as civil rights were not necessarily liberatory; indeed, sometimes people of color took property interests in human beings. For some, slave ownership represented economic advancement and an opportunity to gain a level of prosperity, if not wealth. By buying and selling slaves, they were not merely acquiescing to the demands of a white slaveholders' republic or signaling that they did not threaten the racial status quo. Rather, they were investing in the currency of the time; while many free black people bought enslaved kin and friends with the intention of freeing them, some free people of color—including former slaves—acquired slave property to support their various economic endeavors. Skilled artisans and shopkeepers bought enslaved apprentices and helpers to assist in their businesses; landowners bought field hands and house servants to work their farms and plantations. Some aggressively pursued human property and accumulated substantial numbers of enslaved laborers. Many of these black masters were once enslaved themselves. Rose Belly, for instance, formed part of a shipment of thirty slaves sent to Pierre Belly from Jamaica to Louisiana. Pierre Belly later freed Rose and bequeathed half of his estate to her and their daughters, an estate that included ninety-six slaves. The Belly daughters and their families continued to acquire additional slave property throughout the antebellum period.

Just as they did with other types of property, free people of color showed little reluctance to involve the courts in their disagreements over slaves. They sued to recoup debts for slaves purchased from them; to retrieve slaves stolen from them; to get compensation for sick, unruly, or otherwise "damaged" slaves they unwittingly bought; and to receive payment for slaves injured or killed by others. Maria Theresa, a free black Mississippi woman, sued Josiah Martin, a white man, for the $450 value of a slave she claimed he stole from her.[45] Eliza Bossack (alias Carter), a free black woman, and John Holden, a white man, spent much of the mid-1830s in the Mississippi courts fighting over the ownership of an enslaved woman named Kitty.[46]

Free people of color also sued in disputes over slave hires. Hiring out slaves was commonplace across the American South. As one study of slave hiring has shown, enslaved people were more likely to be hired out to someone else than sold to a new owner.[47] For both owner and renter, slave hiring could be lucrative. Hiring out slaves, especially those they did not immediately need, allowed masters to extract as much profit as possible from their human property, and it also allowed large numbers of southerners who could not afford to buy slaves themselves to benefit from slave labor. But because both owners and hirers sought to maximize their investment, and because both simultaneously laid claim to mastery over the slaves in question, slave hiring inevitably involved conflict.[48] Frequently, those conflicts meant a trip to the courthouse.

Slave owners hired out their slaves for a number of reasons, ranging from efforts to extract revenue from unneeded and idle slaves, to discharge debts, to provide a slave with training as a carpenter or bricklayer, and to punish or banish a recalcitrant slave.[49] Whatever their motivation, hiring was profitable, and slaveholders—black and white—sought to increase their returns on slave capital. But renting out valuable property to someone else was also risky, and when deals went sour, free black masters used the courts to protect their investments. Sometimes renters, for instance, declined to return hired slaves. In 1816, Marguerite Ove, a free woman of color, sued Arnaud Lartigue, a white man, to recover possession of her slaves and $3,000 in damages. In her petition, Ove stated that one Louis Gourgis agreed (in a written contract) to rent her slave, Francine, and Francine's children for six dollars a month. This arrangement had continued for twelve years. But Gourgis had recently died, Ove asserted, and the executor of his estate, Lartigue, refused to return the slaves to her. In his answer to her petition, Lartigue denied Ove's allegations, insisted that she did not have "any right or title" to Francine and her children, and asked the court to dismiss the lawsuit. After considering the evidence, however, the court issued a verdict for Ove and ordered Lartigue to return her slaves and pay the court costs.[50] Other hirers neglected to pay owners the rental fees. In an 1822 lawsuit, Marie Simien, a free woman of color, successfully recouped payment for renting her slaves on several occasions to Jacques Nicholas, a free man of color.[51] In an effort to extract every penny in profits from her bondman's labor, Margueritte, a free black woman, hired out her slave, Urbin, to work for Simon Janes on Sundays—after Urbin had completed six days of work for her. When Janes (a white man) failed to pay her the hiring fee, she sued, and the court ordered him to pay his debt.[52]

Free people of color also sought redress for damage done to their slaves while in the custody of another. Owners expected that at the contract's end hirers would return their slaves in the same condition or without noticeable depreciation. Yet in order to increase their profit margins, hirers had the incentive to demand long hours from the slaves they rented, beat them when they did not labor hard enough, require them to work in dangerous conditions, furnish them with inadequate clothing and shelter, and feed them poor-quality food. Thus, when their property was in danger, owners took ruthless and negligent hirers to court. In 1851, Aimeé Porche, a free woman of color, sued Ebenezer Cooley, a white man, for $440 after a slave belonging to Cooley stabbed her slave, Hypolite, while in Cooley's possession. Hypolite's injuries were such that he could not work, and Porche sought compensation for his lost labor, doctor's fees, and the damage done to her property. It appears that Porche and Cooley settled the matter outside of the courtroom, as both parties agreed to dismiss the lawsuit, and Cooley paid the court costs. While on the one hand Porche sought payment for damaged property, on the other hand she reminded Cooley about the boundaries of white violence. By compensating Porche for Hypolite's injuries, Cooley implicitly acknowledged that sometimes whites were limited in their relationships to and authority over certain black bodies.[53]

Like slave owners, slave hirers were also profit-minded, and they too used the courts to enforce their contracts and guarantee the labor of the slaves they rented. In an 1860 lawsuit, free man of color Simon Bonnefoi claimed that he had paid Julie Labry, a white woman, $130 to rent her slave, Bill, for one year. Three months into the contract, however, Labry retrieved Bill and refused to return him to Bonnefoi. He "had the right," he told the court, to Bill's "services," and because of the labor he had lost, he wanted $500 in damages. Labry, however, contended that she attempted to return Bill to Bonnefoi, but Bonnefoi "refused to receive him." The court dismissed the case and ordered Bonnefoi to pay the court costs.[54] A battle between an owner's long-term property rights and a renter's short-term profits resided at the center of disputes between owners and hirers. Both viewed the slaves in question as capital assets, and both looked to the court to safeguard their investments. Black renters, like black owners, also laid claim to their rights to property and their command over the human property within their households. In the absence of other individual or political rights, property rights—whether to land, slaves, cattle, or clothing—represented broader rights, rights black people insisted the courts defend.

PRODUCING INDEPENDENCE

Claims to legal personhood and inclusion also involved claims to one's body and one's labor. Property ownership came in many forms; not everyone had access to land and slaves. Many free blacks worked for wages and viewed their labor as a form of property—property they expected the courts to protect. In this view, they were not alone. As land grew more expensive (and in the case of areas such as the urban Northeast, more scarce), many Americans began to work for wages, and members of the producing classes—laborers, mechanics, artisans, small businesspeople, and so forth—throughout antebellum America insisted on the dignity of that labor.[55]

Free black men and women pursued lucrative vocations as skilled carpenters, blacksmiths, kettle makers, brick masons, seamstresses, and retailers and sold their labor and services in the busy commercial and agricultural sector of the Natchez district. As it did in other parts of the antebellum United States, sex defined occupation, and men and women, in large part, practiced different trades. Whereas free black men worked as artisans and laborers in the manufacturing and agricultural sector, women monopolized the service sector and occupied positions as seamstresses, laundresses, and nurses and operated commercial establishments such as boarding houses and market stalls. Free black men also worked as overseers for both white and free black planters. Although their wages and earnings varied by gender as well as occupation, free blacks' skills and abilities provided a measure of economic security for themselves and their families. Some even prospered.[56]

Property in one's labor was a valuable form a security because it was evidence of a good character—of reliability, accountability, and industry. Free blacks' marketable skills enhanced ties to their communities and helped them forge favorable relationships with their neighbors, black and white. Skilled people of color offered something of worth to their community. Artisans like blacksmiths, tailors, or barbers performed indispensable services for whites, in particular, and these services had important legal and material benefits. The valued position of skilled laborers in their communities helped free black workers to successfully petition to remain in Mississippi and Louisiana, especially as lawmakers passed legislation requiring free blacks to leave each state. William Hayden's skills as a barber earned him the respect and support of local whites, support that proved important when he petitioned the legislature to remain in the state.[57] In 1859, Ann Caldwell used her proficiency as a nurse as a justification to remain in the state of Mississippi. Over one hundred white residents of Natchez co-signed her petition and claimed she was a faithful nurse with a good character.[58] Free blacks' expertise increased their positions in their community, gave them opportunities to meet a variety of people, allowed them some control over and choice in their work, provided them some leverage in their negotiations for hire, and even offered them a better bargaining position when approaching the courts to protect their contracts.

If property was indeed a sacred and natural right, then those who deprived laborers of their wages were guilty of theft. While, as the cases of Hayden and Caldwell suggest, clients came to the aid of skilled black laborers, sometimes deals went sour, and free blacks engaged their customers and employers as legal foes. Free black men and women consistently sued over broken labor contracts and wages owed them, lawsuits they frequently won. In 1835, for example, John Hardes, a free black Mississippian, sued William Mosby, a white man, for the $240 Mosby owed him for carpentry work he had performed on Mosby's cotton plantation. Although Mosby claimed he had already paid Hardes and denied he owed him anything further, the jury found for Hardes for $240.[59] In 1859, Leandre Decuir, a free black Louisianan, received a judgment for $519 plus interest and court costs from a white man, Patrick Gleason, who hired him to raft and run timber.[60] Honoré Roth, a Louisiana mason, brick-maker, and kettle settler, often sued his white employers to recover the money they owed him for the labor he performed.[61] In 1859, Josephine Degruise, a free woman of color, sued the white children of her recently deceased employer for $2,000 in back wages "for eighteen years of long and useful services" as a nurse and "faithful servant" to their father. She was particularly attentive to him "in the last years of his life, when he was old, infirm and sick, requiring [her] attendance." His will, she claimed, included a provision for "payment of the wages for services rendered," but his heirs refused to pay. While the court ordered an inventory of the estate to see if it could meet her demand for back wages, the outcome of the case is not known.[62]

Free blacks like Degruise and Roth viewed their labor and skills as valuable property, and they expected the courts to come to their aid and help them recover and protect that property. Black people possessing and directing their own labor, however, proved problematic in a society that made blackness synonymous with unfree labor. Their sense of the value of their labor was all the more revolutionary because it proclaimed a politics of ownership at odds with the material interests of white slaveholders.

WHEN PROPERTY SUED

Although property owning property sounds like a contradiction in terms, throughout the Natchez district (and the American South more generally), enslaved people also acquired property. And while Mississippi and Louisiana laws dictated that slaves could only hold property with their owners' permission, the enslaved in both states acquired property—sometimes even substantial amounts—with and without their owners' consent. They did so in a number of ways. For instance, many planted gardens of their own to supplement their diets, raising fruits and vegetables such as sweet potatoes, collards, beans, tomatoes, and pears. They often sold their garden surplus to their masters, mistresses, and neighbors and in local markets. Some even cultivated cash crops like cotton and sold those crops to local merchants at the end of the harvest season. Other farm and plantation slaves raised hogs and chickens, kept horses, and tended livestock. They sold poultry, eggs, fish, oysters, and game to free blacks, poor whites, and others in their neighborhoods. Many acquired small amounts of cash by selling their services and hiring out their labor in their free time—as skilled carpenters or kettle makers, as healers and nurses, as fortune-tellers, and as peddlers. Enslaved men and women used a portion of the money they earned to buy items such as clothing and furniture—and sometimes even their own freedom and the freedom of their loved ones. Of course, slave owners could—and did—restrict the slaves' economy. Enslaved people had a limited amount of time to work for themselves, and they did this work late at night or on Sunday afternoons after they completed an exhausting amount of labor for their owners. Selling eggs a dozen at a time in no way produced great wealth, although it may have conferred great dignity. Property ownership—however little—was common among the slaves in the Natchez district and elsewhere.[63] Moreover, as one scholar has shown, because southern laws neither protected slaves' property nor recognized their property rights, enslaved people used extralegal means to claim and display property and to solve conflicts over it. For instance, bondspeople made their property publicly visible as their own (and their kin's) through gift giving at marriage ceremonies or displaying it in the slave yard.[64]

Sometimes local authorities recognized enslaved people's claims to property and prosecuted instances of theft on the behalf of slaves. In 1854, Daniel Smith, a Natchez resident, faced larceny charges, a warrant for his arrest, and $3,000 bail for stealing a gold watch and several coins that belonged to an enslaved man named Bill. Because of his status as a slave, Bill could not pursue the case himself. However, Joseph Hawk, a white man, brought the theft to the attention of the justice the peace on behalf of Bill. Five additional white witnesses appeared before the justice of the peace to claim that the property belonged to Bill and to provide evidence that Smith had "carried it off." The case never made it to trial, however. Shortly after his indictment Smith died of cholera, and the court dismissed the case.[65] In Mississippi and Louisiana, slaves could not testify in cases involving whites, making it all the more difficult to prosecute those who committed wrongs against them. But as this case suggests, enslaved men and women might sidestep the statutory bans on their testimony and their ability to own property and protect it in court by getting a white witness to pursue the case for them.

On a few occasions, as we saw in the previous chapter, enslaved people circumvented the prohibitions that denied them access to the courts and themselves brought lawsuits in disputes over property and debts owed them. In November 1800, for example, Elizabeth, an enslaved woman belonging to one Domingo Loreno, sued Maria Williams, a white woman, for the sixty-two dollars she had recently lent her. As evidence of the debt, she produced a promissory note signed by Williams indicating that she had borrowed the money from Elizabeth and had promised to repay the loan promptly. Despite Elizabeth's requests for the money, the loan remained unpaid for several months. She asked the court for the balance of the loan and $100 in damages for her inconvenience. The Natchez court ordered Williams to pay the debt plus 10 percent interest and court costs. The court record listed Loreno as

Elizabeth's owner, but he was not a party to the suit. Elizabeth did not have legal standing to sue Williams. As an owner of property and a signatory to a promissory note, the court allowed a temporary, workable legal fiction about property ownership that provided her access.[66]

Litigants like Elizabeth sought to compel their audience to confront (and perhaps even rethink) a narrative about property ownership, legal personhood, and independence that was gendered male, white, and free. Suing in court had effects that reached well beyond the courtroom, insofar as the mere act of recognition similarly was an acknowledgment of the potential for people of color to be more than objects of regulation. By holding property, being a signatory to a promissory note, and appearing in a courtroom to protect her interests and register her voice in public, Elizabeth exercised a civic identity.

VULNERABILITY

Just as free people of color were plaintiffs in disputes over various types of property, they were also defendants in similar kinds of lawsuits. They borrowed money and did not pay their debts. They failed to make their payments on their purchases of real and personal property. They made contracts with overseers and skilled laborers and neglected to pay them for their work and services. They hired lawyers to represent them and tutors to educate their children and failed to pay the fees. Free blacks also faced court action in these conflicts and often lost the lawsuits (although certainly not always). For instance, in 1822, Eugene Lacroix, a white Louisiana man, sued Maximillian Ricard, a free man of color, twice for debts Ricard owed him, and Lacroix won both cases. Soon after, at least three other white men successfully sued Ricard to recover unpaid loans. In early 1823, Ricard petitioned the court with a claim of insolvency and requested a meeting with his creditors and a temporary halt to all the judicial proceedings against him.[67] In 1849, Jacob Meyer recovered the $110 Victor Dupperon owed him for the purchase of calico, books, bridles, and stockings.[68] Augustin Borie was arrested and jailed for failing to pay a debt after the court issued a judgment against him, but he swiftly sued the justice of the peace and the sheriff for false imprisonment and eventually won the case.[69]

But free black people's precarious position in the slave South left them vulnerable, and sometimes those around them took advantage of that vulnerability. Whites might attempt to cheat free people of color. For instance, Ellen Wooten, a free woman of color, sued George Harrison for interest on a $2,000 debt owed to her—interest she claimed he tried to defraud her of because she could not read or write.[70] Rachel Hicks took a property interest in her own

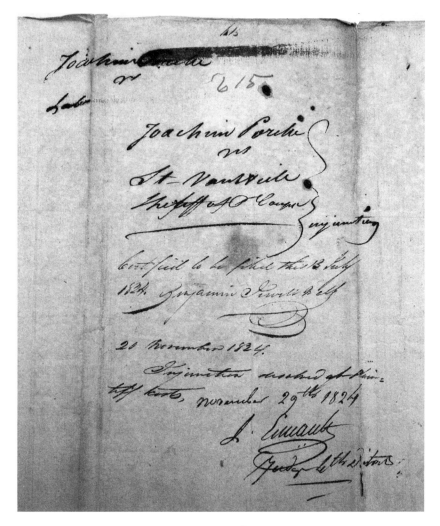

Local court records have a material culture of their own. Even the front matter tells a story, with details added at different times by various hands. *Porche v. Van Winkle*, Pointe Coupee Parish Clerk of the Court's Office, New Roads, Louisiana; photograph by the author.

son (whom she held as her slave) and mortgaged him to secure a loan from a white man named Evans. However, she sued Evans after he took advantage of her illiteracy and tried to force her to pay more than she owed.[71] In both Wooten's and Hicks's lawsuits the courts issued verdicts for the free women of color, protecting them potential fraud (although Hicks's son remained at the mercy of a mother who would use him as security for a loan).

Swindlers used more than just illiteracy to cheat free people of color. They also capitalized on some free blacks' uncertain status as free when trying

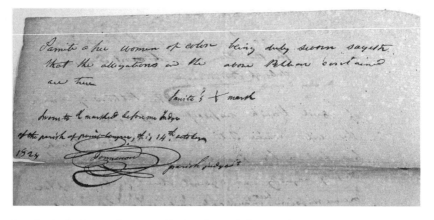

People of color frequently appeared before the antebellum southern courts to give testimony and swear oaths. *Sanite v. Van Winkle*, Pointe Coupee Parish Clerk of the Court's Office, New Roads, Louisiana; photograph by the author.

to defraud them of property. For instance, in an attempt to obtain the land and slaves of their late sister, free black siblings Rosalie, Annette, and Jean François Masse sued five members of the Pierre family, also people of color, who were in possession of their sister's property. The Pierres, they claimed, were not in fact free people and instead were "really slaves for life, altho' they pretend to be free." As the rightful (and free) heirs, they wanted their sister's estate "delivered up" to them. The court found in favor of the Masse family. The Masses certainly had no trouble betraying the Pierres to the authorities when property was on the line.[72]

Surviving as free people of color in the antebellum South was no easy achievement. Black people's freedom was often at risk. The cases involving Stephen Van Winkle, a sheriff in Pointe Coupee Parish, further demonstrate the lengths to which some people would go to separate free people of color from their property. In particular, Van Winkle exploited the tenuous position of free blacks in a slave society and occasionally seized free people to sell as slaves. Consider the situation of Joachim Porche and his wife, Sanite. In the early 1820s, Porche, a free man of color living in Pointe Coupee Parish, ran into some financial trouble and could not meet his obligations. In a process common for the time period, Porche filed a petition in the local court on March 15, 1824, requesting a meeting with his creditors to make arrangements for setting his debts. He had found himself in "unfortunate circumstances," he said, such that it was impossible for him to meet his obligations. He was therefore "willing to abandon his estate to his creditors" and wanted to set up a meeting to divide his property among them. Porche owed his four creditors a total of $604, and he claimed to have $235 in assets, as well as some "moveable and immovable" property that the court could use to settle his obligations. The justice of the peace summoned Porche's creditors to appear in court and issued a temporary stay "in all judicial proceedings against Porche" until a meeting could occur. No meeting took place, however, because the creditors never showed up in court, and Porche's problems went unresolved for another few months. In the meantime, Sheriff Van Winkle began seizing Porche's property and offering it for sale. Porche sued Van Winkle in July 1824 in an effort to stop the seizure and sale of his property, but he lost this lawsuit.

In early September, Porche's wife, Sanite, a free woman of color, initiated lawsuits of her own; Van Winkle had seized her property—property she owned separately from her husband—in order to settle her husband's debts. The court issued injunctions instructing Van Winkle to cease his activities, but Van Winkle ignored these orders. Instead, he seized Sanite as property and advertised her for sale. In early October 1824, Sanite sued Van Winkle for illegally holding her as a slave. In her petition, Sanite claimed to be "inhumanely imprisoned for a debt of her husband." Van Winkle's actions, Sanite insisted, were "against not only the rights of herself but of humanity." Her husband had manumitted her in a New Orleans court three years before, and she provided the court with copies of her free papers. She asked to be released, but a jury found in favor of the sheriff. Although the record is silent on this matter, it is likely that Van Winkle sold her as a slave at a sheriff's auction.[73] Indeed, Van Winkle was an unscrupulous man and part of a notorious kidnapping ring, an operation that involved his father, Jacob Van Winkle (a New Jersey judge), and his father-in-law, Charles Morgan (a former resident of New Jersey and the owner of the enormous Louisiana cotton plantation, Morganza). Morgan and the elder Van Winkle collaborated to export people of color (including kidnapped black children) from New Jersey to Louisiana for sale in the slave pens in New Orleans and Pointe Coupee Parish. Van Winkle and his family increased their wealth by seizing and selling free people.[74]

Yet Van Winkle's schemes sometimes failed. In 1827, for instance, he apprehended and attempted to sell a slave owned by Isabella Hawkins, a free woman of color, to settle the debts of her former master. Hawkins sued Van Winkle to return her property and attempted to harness the power of the courts by requesting an injunction to stop the sale. She lost her lawsuit, at least initially, because Van Winkle claimed she was still enslaved and did not have the standing to sue. Hawkins promptly appealed her case to the state supreme court, and the high court overturned the lower court's decision. Hawkins's status was not in dispute; she was a free woman. "This was not a case of a slave suing for her freedom," the justices opined, "but of a woman in *enjoyment* of it, suing another for property which she alleged belonged to her." Hawkins continued to "enjoy" that property for a number of years to come: to benefit from it, transmit it, secure it, manage it, and sell it.[75] In addition, after Van Winkle released her, she immediately initiated several (and ultimately successful) lawsuits involving ownership, possession, and her relationships to others with respect to property. The sanctity of her property, not her race and status, determined the outcomes of those lawsuits.[76]

Free black people in the antebellum South were sources of tremendous tension: if slavery was the natural state of people of African descent, then free blacks were subversive and dangerous aberrations. Their status as free people in a world where to be black was to be property, however, has rendered their use of the law in their own interests largely invisible to scholars (who instead focus on the role law played in limiting or regulating free people of color). It has also rendered the economic roles they played largely invisible. Free black people performed essential roles in the economy of the Natchez district, roles that provided them with some purchase on personhood, civic inclusion, and equality in the legal arena. It was their property ownership, moreover, that provided them with both access to the courts and the language needed to make their claims.

African Americans' claims to ownership and all that it entailed were all the more powerful because they emerged in the context of black slavery and in spite of white narratives about black dependence. When black people—whose skin color marked them as "natural" slaves—stood up in court before white judges, white juries, and white audiences and made claims to property rights, they spoke in a language that whites had staked as their own. To white slaveholders, private property was sacred. It was inviolable. African-descended people knew this well. As a people with a price, they understood intimately the power of private property. Indeed, it was no accident that Harriet Jacobs began her famous narrative with the words, "I was born a slave." But black people also knew that to protect the sanctity of property and to make a racialized economy palatable to millions of nonslaveholding whites, white slaveholders could be forced to extend the rights of property—the whole constellation of them—to other groups, even people of African descent. For people of color like John Sandy, Augustin Borie, and Isabella Hawkins, property rights were civil rights, and the exercise of those rights by black people could upend the entire social order of the white slaveholders' republic.

6

Subjects of Selfhood

On April 1, 1847, Hannah, Edward, and Rosetta, people of color and residents of Mississippi, sued Andrew Chess, a white man, for their freedom in the circuit court in Claiborne County. In their petition, they claimed that they had long enjoyed the "friendship and protection" of one Thomas Stone, a white man, who helped them "enjoy their rights and privileges" as free people of color "so far as was consistent with the laws of Mississippi." Stone served as their "benefactor," the petitioners relayed, but in January 1838, he had relocated to Georgia and requested that Chess look after their interests. Although he pledged to protect them "in lieu of Thomas Stone," the plaintiffs stated, Chess now "holds and possesses them as his slaves." Chess even composed a fraudulent receipt of sale to support his claim to them as property and continued to "act in oppression of their rights as free people of color." They asked the court to order Chess to "discharge them from the bonds of slavery" and to pay damages in the amount "that the court sees as just."

Unlike in Georgia, Alabama, South Carolina, and Florida, where free blacks needed to secure white guardians to file civil suits on their behalf, administer their estates, and protect them from litigation, Mississippi law did not require that free people of color obtain white guardians to represent their interests.[1] But Claiborne County proved to be a tough and unforgiving place for free black people. For example, while neighboring Adams County was home to more than 250 free people of color (many of whom lived in Natchez and established a strong community there), Claiborne County free blacks did not have such safety in numbers or institutions to provide protection or support. Only forty-two free people of color lived in Claiborne County in

1850.[2] The free blacks of the county were an anomaly among the nearly 11,500 enslaved, and they repeatedly faced persecution from whites. For instance, in 1853, Jeffrey, a free black resident of the county, faced disciplinary action from his church (which admitted both black and white congregants) for "styling himself as a Baptist minister," "teaching strange doctrine" to the black population of Port Gibson, and "other dishonest conduct." After his disciplinary hearing before church officials, the Magnolia Baptist Church "excluded" him from the congregation because he assumed the role of a preacher.[3] While Mississippi state laws required that free people of color periodically register with their local courts, this was rarely enforced. But in 1858, the Claiborne County Board of Police summoned forty free black people to appear before the county court, demanding that they "show to satisfaction" that they were legal residents of the county and the state.[4] Securing a white protector might have been necessary for Hannah's, Edward's, and Rosetta's survival in this slaveholders' regime.

They certainly needed protection from unscrupulous individuals like Chess. In Chess's response to their charges, he stated that he neither "claims title to the said petitioners under the color of a pretended purchase," nor did he "hinder them in their enjoyment of all their rights as free persons of color." Rather, Chess argued that as their "benefactor," he let them live with him and "employed them in his services." In exchange for his "care and attention," he kept all the "proceeds of their labor . . . as compensation." What is more, Chess declared that it was entirely within his rights to keep Hannah, Edward, and Rosetta "in his custody and service until he shall be fully and amply compensated for his trouble and attention in maintaining them." What price he expected the three to pay and for how long, however, was unclear, and the court swiftly intervened to remove them from Chess's clutches. The judge decreed "the defendant had no legal claim or just rights to hold the petitioners in slavery or any manner to restrain them or abridge their exercise of freedom." He ordered that Chess release them "from slavery or servitude" and pay the costs of the suit.[5]

Although denied many legal rights and excluded from formal political arenas, people of color like Hannah, Edward, and Rosetta mobilized the local courts on their own behalf. This chapter examines 128 cases of enslaved people suing for their freedom (lawsuits that recognized or altered the personal status of an individual held in a state of slavery).[6] All but one lawsuit involved a white defendant. Of that total, sixty-one proved successful. In twenty of the lawsuits the court found for the defendant. Twenty-five lawsuits were dismissed without explanation, and in twenty-two instances the outcome is not known. Given the success rate of enslaved people suing in court for their freedom and the fragmentary nature of local legal records from the first half of the nineteenth century more generally, it is quite possible that many of the unknowns were victories as well. It is also possible that in the dismissed cases the plaintiff and the defendant came to an agreement outside the courthouse.

Much of this book focuses on the claims-making of free people of color, as they had legal standing to initiate many more lawsuits in a number of different circumstances. But this book is also a study of African Americans' long history of employing the courts and the legal system to their own benefit. When mapping out the scope, scale, and significance of black litigiousness, it is perhaps easier to focus on free people of color, not least of all because they sued far more often, and in more capacities, than enslaved litigants. The enslaved only had legal standing to initiate freedom suits— and even those opportunities were circumscribed. Yet through freedom suits, we see that it was not just wealthy or property-owning free people of color who had the wherewithal, confidence, networks, or knowledge to sue. Enslaved people also initiated lawsuits in the southern courts—using the same language and strategies deployed by free black people—even though they had far fewer opportunities to approach the bar. Black people's claims-making went deeper than the lawsuits of the free. Indeed, claims about rights are not necessarily conditioned by status; one does not become free and then theorize rights. Enslaved litigants were doing analogous things in court, from leveraging their reputations to crafting their cases to reflect their personal histories and narratives. They also understood the workings of the courts and southern law and approached the courts expecting due process and accountability. Most of all, they envisioned themselves as people with rights (however limited) and knew when those rights were being violated.

Personhood claims—claims to the legal recognition and protection of self-ownership and the rights that accompanied self-possession and self-direction—are most evocative in enslaved people's lawsuits for freedom. As objects of property, slaves did not own themselves, their labor, or their bodies. They could not move freely, contract, or own property. They could not marry without their masters' consent, and their marriages, according to the Louisiana *Civil Code*, "do not produce any of the civil effects which result from such contracts."[7] They did not have standing in court to safeguard their interests. Thus, for white slaveholders, enslaved people's claims to self-ownership, control over their bodies, and the fruits of their own labor proved particularly problematic. Recognizing black people's assertions of legal personhood challenged the law of slavery and the property rights of whites. Nonetheless, when enslaved men and women went to court to assert freedom, they assumed ownership of themselves as legal persons—as subjects of law, not objects of property. On occasion they persuaded the courts to recognize and even accede to their demands.

Enslaved people in the Natchez district exploited narrow escape hatches within the legal system to orchestrate a change in personal status and claim freedom for themselves and their families—often successfully—despite legal restrictions to manumission that increased over time. If they could prove that defendants illegally held them as slaves, they won their lawsuits more often than not. Enslaved litigants sued for their freedom on a number of grounds, from the enforcement of promises of freedom made in their late masters' wills to accusations of kidnapping to safeguarding self-purchase contracts. They employed their knowledge of the law and legal processes and harnessed their considerable community networks—both local and distant—to gain their liberty. Enslaved litigants used every available opening in the law when pressing for freedom and transformed abstract privileges and obligations into social and legal realities. They also engaged in the interpretation of the law—of statutes and of testaments and contracts. By claiming their rights to themselves and their labor, moreover, enslaved people induced the Mississippi and Louisiana courts to act against the economic interests of a slaveholders' republic.

In their lawsuits for freedom, black litigants also made whites accountable to their own language and promises. Whites' language could be authoritative in at least two registers. One of these was the language of the private-law promise (the language of contract and obligations between private parties). This was a language spoken between individuals. But the other authoritative register was the public language of the collectivity, spoken by white people yet binding on the community as a whole. This was the language of statutes and legislation. In both registers, whites made promises to black people— private promises to free them in their will, for instance, or collective promises in the form of statutes protecting free people generally from illegal enslavement. These were promises that black litigants interpreted as legally binding and thus went to the courts to enforce. This chapter, then, also explores white language—in the form of promises—language that black litigants interpreted, leveraged, and even undermined. I begin, however, with a discussion of the legal mechanisms by which enslaved people in the Natchez district sued for their freedom.

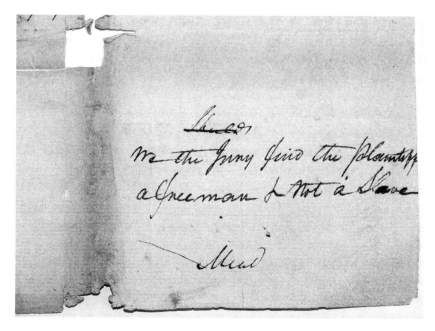

Verdict in Aaron Cooper's freedom suit. While the court records sometimes included
the jury's verdict, they rarely included the names of the jury members. *Cooper v. Briscoe*,
Historic Natchez Foundation, Natchez, Mississippi; photograph by the author.

SUING FOR FREEDOM

For most enslaved men and women in Mississippi and Louisiana, access to
the southern legal system was limited, and law represented an exacting and
menacing presence in their lives. State law often operated as an arm of the
slaveholding class and was enacted to maintain the institution of slavery.
Southern laws denied the enslaved civil and political rights and made them
into property. On occasion, however, enslaved litigants like Hannah, Edward,
and Rosetta mobilized the legal system on their own behalf despite their limited legal rights. For some enslaved people, the courts served as a place to
resolve their grievances and protect their interests—a ritualized space where
the power dynamics and racial hierarchies of daily life in a slaveholder's regime might be briefly suspended. The law, after all, did involve rules, rules that
all members of the community were expected to follow. For some enslaved
people the courts symbolized a site of redress, a notable contrast to the arbitrary punishments meted out by masters, mistresses, and overseers on the
plantation or in the big house. As one scholar of the region put it, "in some
slaves' experience, the law occasionally did what no power in the neighborhood could ever do—bring white men to heel."[8] The rhetoric of the right to

due process of law, as we will see below, riddled their petitions. They may not have always won their lawsuits or achieved their preferred results. Nonetheless, for the enslaved of the Natchez district who sued for their freedom, the courtroom represented an arena of possibility.

Both Mississippi and Louisiana law permitted enslaved people to sue directly for their freedom in the district (Louisiana) and circuit (Mississippi) courts. Article 177 of the 1825 Louisiana *Civil Code* stated: "He [the slave] cannot be a party in any civil action, either as a plaintiff or defendant, *except* when he has to claim or prove his freedom."[9] Similarly, Section 76 of the 1823 Mississippi *Code* read: "Any person, in this state, who shall conceive himself or herself, illegally detained as a slave in the possession of another and claiming his or her freedom, shall proceed by petition to the circuit court of the county, where his or her master or owner shall reside, unless his or her master or owner be a nonresident of this state; and in that case, to the circuit court of any county in this state, where such person may be held in slavery."[10] Suing for freedom was the only time an enslaved person could initiate a civil suit in either Mississippi or Louisiana. Here the law embedded a contradiction, however. To sue, an enslaved person could not really be a slave: as one of the antebellum South's foremost legal authorities, Thomas R. R. Cobb, wrote, "the suit for freedom is allowed only to those who are actually free, and are wrongfully detained in bondage."[11]

When suing for freedom, "wrongfully detained" litigants in Mississippi and Louisiana could sue without the support of a "next friend," and they did not need to use a legal fiction (a fact that is either untrue, nonexistent, or unproven, but is treated as truth under the law). While all slaveholding states permitted those illegally held in bondage to initiate lawsuits for their freedom, a number of states did not allow the enslaved to sue directly without the support of a free white guardian, or a "next friend," as it was often called. In addition, because Natchez district slaves could sue directly, they also did not have to first deploy an action of trespass or a charge of false imprisonment or assault and battery against their owners, who would claim that because the plaintiff was a slave, no trespass or injury had occurred. The court would then bypass the fabricated trespass and agree to make a decision about the plaintiff's personal status. In other words, the chief question in such cases centered on whether or not the alleged false imprisonment was legal (because the plaintiff was a slave).[12]

In Louisiana, enslaved people typically sued for their freedom directly and filed their petitions (usually with the support of a lawyer) in the local district court. Mississippi slaves frequently filed direct suits for freedom in the local circuit courts (the Mississippi equivalent of Louisiana's district court), but they also found other ways to instigate a legal battle over their status. In addition to suing directly, enslaved Mississippians commonly deployed habeas corpus actions to compel the court to initiate examinations of their claims to freedom.[13] When filing habeas corpus petitions, enslaved people demanded that their enslavers bring them before the court and explain why they held them as slaves. The court would then determine whether or not their enslavement (or imprisonment) was lawful. For instance, in his 1833 petition, Stephen, a man of color, claimed that he was "illegally restrained of his liberty and held in custody by Stephen Howard." He asked the court to order a writ of habeas corpus, "whereby the said Stephen Howard may be compelled to bring your petitioner before your Honour or some other judge of the state of Mississippi having jurisdiction in the matter here and explain the cause of his detention." The judge issued the writ and commanded Howard to bring "the body of Stephen a man of color" before the court when it was next in session. The record ends there, however, and Stephen's fate is unknown.[14]

Suspected runaway slaves imprisoned in Mississippi frequently initiated habeas corpus actions to establish their free status and gain their release from jail. In his 1825 petition, James Andre claimed to be a free man from Massachusetts arrested as runaway slave and held in the Natchez jail. He asked to be brought before the judge "to substantiate proof of his freedom." The judge ordered the writ, and Andre gained his freedom after several witnesses testified that he was a free person of color and not a runaway slave.[15] Whether they sued directly or deployed habeas corpus actions, enslaved people in the Natchez district were creative in seeking routes to freedom.

THE POWER OF CONTRACT

White people made promises to black people. Slaveholders' positive good defense of slavery was full of promises and obligations: in exchange for their labor and obedience, owners promised to care for their slaves, provide for them, protect them, teach them, and represent them. Andrew Chess, the self-proclaimed benefactor of Hannah, Edward, and Rosetta, spoke in the language of promises when he told the court in Claiborne County that he kept all of the "proceeds of their labor" in exchange for his "care and attention." A reciprocal relationship of obligations and duties resided at the heart of antebellum masters' paternalism. Through such promises, owners sought to demonstrate to their critics that slavery was a benevolent institution. Promises to represent an enslaved person's interests or vague promises of protection, however, were not legally binding. Thus, enslaved people devised other, extralegal ways to force owners to honor their promises—such as work slowdowns or truancy.

Yet on occasion, enslaved people found ways to make whites legally accountable to their promises and thus their rhetoric: both the private promises whites made in contracts and wills and the public promises made in statutes. Enslaved litigants were well aware of the laws that governed their lives—both the laws of contracts and obligations and the state laws governing manumission and freedom; for to bring a case (or approach a lawyer to help them petition the courts), they had to know that their rights were violated in the first place. Moreover, they seized every available opening in those laws, interpreting them widely, pushing at them, and expanding their boundaries to fit their claims.

Contracts involved promises. Promises made through contracts created obligations and duties enforceable by law. Contracts also entailed personal volition or choice—a choice to incur an obligation and determine the terms without constraint from external forces or coercion. In addition, they signaled reciprocity: those entering into a contract struck a mutual bargain. They represented "a relation of voluntary exchange."[16] Finally, contracts involved claims to personhood. To enter into a contract, one must exercise self-ownership. As one scholar notes, "in order to surrender rights and accept duties, parties to contracts had to be sovereigns of themselves, possessive individuals entitled to their own persons, labor, and faculties."[17] As property, however, slaves could not make contracts. They did not have ownership over their bodies and thus were not entitled to their labor. They could not bargain for themselves or protect those bargains before the courts.

Yet in Louisiana, enslaved people could contract for their freedom. On occasion Louisiana courts recognized those contracts as valid and legally enforceable. When slaves entered into contracts for freedom, they sought to compel the other party (and in some cases, the court) to recognize them as more than just property moving through the southern economy, but as legal persons with choices, rights, and obligations. Perhaps as important, they forced whites to honor their obligations to black people. They sought accountability.

Although people held as slaves in both states could—and did—sue for their freedom, Louisiana slaves had an advantage when seeking legal liberty. While Louisiana denied enslaved people the capacity to contract for wages or enter into marriage contracts, the law allowed slaves to arrange self-purchase contracts. The Louisiana *Civil Code* provided that "the slave is incapable of making any contract, except those which relate to his own emancipation."[18] What is more, slaves' self-purchase contracts were legally binding and thus enforceable at law. A slave's ability to contract for his or her freedom was unique to Louisiana and a legacy of the Spanish legal custom of self-purchase, or *coartación*. Through *coartación* enslaved people could arrange a purchase price for their freedom with their owners and make payments in installment toward it. Throughout the four decades of Spanish rule, hundreds of enslaved people in colonial Louisiana gained their freedom through the practice of *coartación*. After Louisiana joined the federal union, and despite attempts to restrict manumission, Louisiana law permitted slaves to contract for their freedom well into the late antebellum period.[19] It is impossible to know with certainty how many enslaved people in Louisiana took advantage of this provision and arranged to purchase their freedom. If the steady stream of manumissions that occurred in the antebellum period is any indication, however, many contracts for self-purchase probably went smoothly enough. In their study of petitions for manumission to the Police Jury of New Orleans, Laurence Kotlikoff and Anton Rupert discovered 1,780 successful manumissions in the years between 1827 and 1846. The police jury denied the freedom of just ten New Orleans slaves in this twenty-year period, half of them because they were too young to support themselves.[20] Petitioners seeking to manumit slaves in Pointe Coupee and Iberville Parishes found similar success. Only when contracts went awry did lawsuits over self-purchase appear before the local courts.

Louisiana was the only state in which slaves enjoyed the legal capacity to enter into contracts to purchase their freedom.[21] Yet enslaved people in other states on occasion purchased their liberty if their masters permitted it. Elizabeth Keckley—a talented dressmaker and seamstress—arranged to purchase her freedom and the freedom of her son from their St. Louis, Missouri, master for the sum of $1,200. A number of Keckley's St. Louis customers and patrons helped her raise the purchase price, and she later moved to the nation's capital where her clients included Mary Todd Lincoln and other members of the Washington elite.[22] Moses Grandy—an enslaved man in North Carolina—purchased his freedom twice. The first time his master pocketed the purchase price and resold him as a slave. After acquiring his freedom following a second self-purchase agreement, Grandy sought to find and arrange to buy the liberty of all his children. He managed to purchase some of his family and help others enter into agreements with their owners to hire out their time and use the profits to buy their liberty. But of the children and other family members that he could not track down, he said this: "I know nothing of the others, nor am I likely ever to hear of them again."[23]

Although Mississippi law did not protect slaves' contracts for freedom, at least one enslaved person in the Mississippi territory initiated a lawsuit involving a self-purchase agreement. In 1790, Abraham Jones, also known as Sampson, contracted with his owner to purchase his freedom, and although he paid the agreed-on price, Benjamin Ozman, a resident of Natchez, continued to hold him as a slave. In 1800, Jones sued for his freedom in the court of common pleas in Adams County. The record of the lawsuit is fragile and in pieces, and Jones's petition (as well as the outcome) is missing from the file. But other extant materials (including substantial witness testimony) reveal the details of Jones's claim. Several witnesses appeared before the court and professed to have seen a document "confirming the liberty and freedom of the said Negro Sampson" (his freedom papers) and a written self-purchase contract between Jones and his owner, Henry French of Virginia. Per their agreement, Jones arranged to pay French "one hundred and forty pounds Virginia money" for his liberty. After working about eight years as a sawyer and gathering wood in swamps, Jones raised the money to pay his purchase price, and French manumitted him. Jones filed the contract and his freedom papers with Governor Manuel Gayoso, the governor of the region during the Spanish period. But Gayoso misplaced the documents and died of yellow fever in 1799, leaving Jones vulnerable to enslavement. Not long after the disappearance of his paperwork, Ozman claimed Jones as his slave. Ozman did not present any evidence to show that Jones was in fact a slave, however. While the outcome of Jones's case is unknown, the witnesses' testimony in his favor may have convinced the court of his free status.[24] Jones's lawsuit is the only extant Mississippi freedom suit to involve a slave's self-purchase contract; Mississippi law did not protect such agreements.[25] And indeed, it is likely that this case was allowed to proceed because it did not, at bottom, require the court to decide on a self-purchase contract. After all, Jones did not sue his original owner, Henry French, and request that the court enforce their contract; French had honored their agreement and manumitted him. Rather, Jones sued because he was a free man held illegally as a different man's slave.

Even in Louisiana, however, a number of factors limited a slave's self-purchase. Because enslaved people could not force owners to make a sale, their owners had to approve it and permit their slaves to hire themselves out for wages or peddle goods in their spare time for cash. Louisiana law also dictated that slaves could not acquire property without their owners' permission

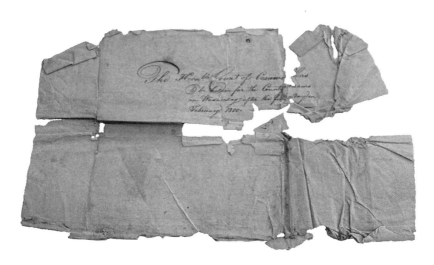

Fragments of Abraham Jones's freedom suit. *Jones v. Ozman*, Historic
Natchez Foundation, Natchez, Mississippi; photograph by the author.

(although enslaved people throughout the region owned and acquired personal property and cash with and without the permission of their owners).
Slaves wanting to purchase their freedom needed skills or goods to sell. Yet
if they could raise the money to purchase their freedom and their owner was
amenable, state law allowed them to contract for their liberty. One study suggests that slaves in New Orleans had the greatest success contracting for their
freedom because they enjoyed more opportunities to work for wages in their
spare time.[26] Enslaved people in the rural areas of Louisiana—areas like the
Natchez district—also made a determined effort to purchase their freedom
and entered into contracts with their owners for their liberty. They too acquired property and cash to buy their freedom.

Deceitful and stingy owners sometimes appropriated the purchase price,
however, and denied the existence of the agreement. When their contracts
fell apart, Louisiana slaves turned to the courts to safeguard the bargains they
had made with their owners and to protect their interests.[27] For example,
on May 6, 1822, Alexander Moore, "commonly called Ellick a free man of
color," sued William Moore, a white man, for his freedom. Alexander claimed
that he had entered into a contract for his freedom with William in 1817, and
William pledged to free him on March 6, 1822. But William continued to detain Alexander "by force of arms," Alexander insisted, and denied "the rights
of your petitioner to his freedom which is fully apparent and manifest by the
annexed document filed with this petition . . . establishing the manumission
of your petitioner." Alexander requested that William "be cited to appear in

the honorable court and decreed and adjudged to desist from further exercise of torturous and unwarranted ownership of your petitioner." Alexander also wanted William to pay damages and the court costs. What is more, because his "liberty" was "in great jeopardy" and "the power of the torturous possessor might place him beyond the reach of the law," law "which protects and secures the rightful freedom of individuals," Alexander asked the court to place him into the hands of a more "suitable person" until the court had decided his case. Alexander, however, did not show up for his court date, and the judge eventually found him in default and dismissed the lawsuit.[28] We can only speculate as to why Alexander did not appear before the court. Perhaps he and William came to an agreement without the court's intervention, or perhaps (as Alexander feared) William carried him outside the jurisdiction of the court. Perhaps he gained his freedom through flight. It is impossible to know.

Yet the language that Alexander used in his petition indicates that he viewed the courtroom as a space to right wrongs done to him and a place to make whites accountable to their promises. He initiated a lawsuit and convinced the judge that not only did he have a case but to set a trial date and order William to appear before the court and answer to his charges. He expected the court to force William to honor his contractual obligations to him and allow him to exercise ownership over his person. After all, as expressed in Alexander's petition, the law "protects and secures the rightful freedom of individuals" like himself.

Some enslaved people suing to enforce contracts also expected the courts to protect their property. In so doing, they sought the ability to direct aspects of their lives and ensure their futures. For instance, Milien, a man of color, petitioned the district court in St. Landry Parish, claiming that in September 1852 he had entered into a contract with his mistress, the late Carmalitte Lacasse, to purchase his freedom for $550. Although he had paid the agreed-on price, the administrator of his mistress's estate, Florian Sonnier, had advertised him for sale at auction, along with "some little property" Milien possessed, including two horses, twelve heads of cattle, and a bale of cotton. He asked the court for a writ of injunction prohibiting Sonnier and his "aiders and abettors" from selling him and his property. Moreover, he wanted the court to enforce the terms of his contract with the late Lacasse, declare him a free man, and allow him to keep his property. The court granted his request for a writ of injunction and ordered the sale be stopped. While Milien was successful in harnessing the power of the state to protect his property (and keep the sheriff from selling it), it is not clear if the court enforced his contract. The final outcome of his lawsuit is missing from the record. Nonetheless, in making claims to himself and "some little property"—property that would help safeguard his future as a free person—Milien conducted himself as a property-owning, rights-bearing person. By granting his request for an injunction, the court acknowledged him as such.[29]

Enslaved people in Louisiana continued to sue to enforce the terms of their self-purchase contracts, and the courts heard such cases well into the 1850s, despite the adoption of further restrictions on manumission. Yet changes in the laws in the years between the time the parties agreed to the self-purchase and payment of the final installment of the purchase price could invalidate the contract altogether. For instance, in 1854, Tom (whom we have encountered in previous chapters) lost his lawsuit for freedom because although he had paid his owner the agreed-on price, the judge declared the case a nonsuit, claiming that the contract did not meet the new state laws governing manumissions. The judge claimed that Tom's master did not post the newly required "bond with good security" to ensure that "the slave if emancipated and allowed to remain in the state, shall not become a public charge." Thus, the contract did not conform to the law, the judge argued, and was now null and void. Tom remained a slave, and it is likely that his owner pocketed the money Tom paid him for his freedom.[30]

WILLS AND HEIRS

When enslaved people sued over breach of contract, they held whites accountable to their own language and agreements. Similarly, enslaved men and women used the courts to enforce the terms of their late owners' wills and tried to compel heirs to keep their late owners' promises. For much of the first half of the nineteenth century, Mississippi and Louisiana law permitted slaveholders to manumit their slaves during the lifetime of the owner and "by a disposition made in prospect of death."[31] Owners regularly provided slaves with their freedom by last will and testament. For example, in his will, Pierre Belly manumitted his slave Ned and instructed his "executors, legatees, and heirs" to free Ned "according to law" and immediately on execution of the will. Belly's estate included few debts and a large amount of property, and his heirs did not contest Ned's manumission.[32] Such transactions often went off without a hitch, particularly if the estate's debts did not exceed its assets and the manumission did not deprive the heirs of their inheritance.

Sometimes, however, executors and heirs ignored the wishes of the deceased and refused to liberate the enslaved people in question. After all, freeing slaves meant the loss of valuable human property. Heirs and executors profited handsomely by keeping in bondage enslaved people who had been freed by will. In other circumstances, jealousy and resentment drove the white families of the dead to thwart the manumission of an enslaved mistress or an enslaved child of the deceased. Freeing slaves also created free blacks, a class of people many southern whites increasingly considered subversive. Moreover, the promise of manumission made in a will did not automatically provide a slave with his or her freedom. Wills had to follow the state laws of succession.[33]

Despite the challenges, slaves promised their freedom by their deceased masters and mistresses sought redress in court and sued heirs and executors for their liberty.[34] Sometimes a lawsuit or the threat of a lawsuit was an effective enough strategy in convincing heirs and executors to free a slave, as Peter, an enslaved man belonging to the late Moses Kirkland, found in 1824. Immediately after Peter petitioned the district court in West Feliciana Parish for his freedom, Kirkland's heirs filed an answer to his petition admitting that Kirkland had freed Peter in his will and promising to liberate him without delay. The court declared Peter a free man and made the defendants pay the costs of the lawsuit.[35]

Typically heirs did not surrender valuable slave property so easily, and they often went to great lengths to hold in bondage slaves who had been bequeathed their freedom. In April 1833, Bob and Milley, two enslaved people freed by will in Adams County, sued their late master's executors for their freedom and the liberty of their seven children. Bob and Milley claimed that their master, Timothy O'Hara, had stipulated in his will that when their youngest child reached ten years of age, the entire family would be freed. O'Hara had instructed his executors to take them to Ohio to free them if Mississippi law did not allow the manumission, and O'Hara had designated funds for that purpose. This precaution proved unnecessary, however, as Mississippi permitted manumission by will until 1842.[36] Yet after his death, Bob and Milley claimed, one of his executors, O'Hara's heir John Nugent, took possession of the family, continued to "fraudulently" hold them "in bondage and slavery . . . as his own absolute property," and "appropriated" their labor "for his own use and the use of his creditors." Nugent's creditors had recently sued him, Bob and Milley told the court, and he had listed them for sale to cover his debts. In addition to their freedom, he owed them $300 that O'Hara had bequeathed to them in his will. They asked the court to declare them free and require Nugent to pay the $300. The court agreed, awarding them their liberty and $300 and condemned Nugent to pay the court costs.[37]

People of African descent—both free and enslaved—endowed their labor with value. Frequently, free people of color sued their employers for back wages, but enslaved people also claimed their right to the ownership of their own labor and demanded back wages—compensation for the time they had worked without pay as slaves. In an effort to retain valuable property, some heirs attempted to keep the provisions of wills secret; slaves labored for years after the death of their owners before they realized they should have been granted their liberty and sued. Mary, an enslaved woman in East Baton Rouge Parish, Louisiana, claimed that she was "ipso facto free" according to the terms of her late master's will. She told the court that her former owner, John Marshall, "conscientiously believing that civil and religious Liberty is the natural right of all men," had bequeathed Mary and her five children to his daughter, Miriam Morris, for a term of five years, after which they were to be liberated. But Miriam and her husband Gerard had left Mary in "complete ignorance of the existence of the will and provisions thereof, and did illegally and fraudulently detain" her in the "bonds of slavery." She should have been freed several years prior. She therefore asked the court to grant her and her children their freedom and sought $2,000 for her "services rendered during the eight or nine years of her illegal detention." The district court found for Mary, granted her and her children their freedom, and ordered the Morris family to pay her $900 in back wages and cover the court costs. While she did not received the $2,000 she asked for, $900 was no small amount (overseers, for instance, worked for about $200 to $300 a year in wages).[38] The money she received would help her in the transition from slavery to freedom and provide some economic and family stability.[39]

While Mississippi law prohibited all individual manumissions in 1842, closing this avenue to freedom, enslaved people in Louisiana continued to benefit from manumission by will and sued to claim freedom on these grounds well into the late 1850s. Slaves suing for the freedom promised them in their late owners' wills continued to be successful, even in the 1850s as tensions over slavery increased. Yet in early 1857, the Louisiana legislature—reflecting lawmakers' fears of slave insurrection and their alarm over the expanding population of free blacks, a population considered by many to be "a plague and a pest in the community"—passed a law banning manumissions entirely.[40]

Enslaved people who filed claims that year to enforce their freedom by will suddenly found themselves on the wrong side of the law. For instance, in June 1857, Irma, an enslaved woman in Iberville Parish, sued John Baptiste Rils, the executor of her late owner's estate, for her freedom. Her former owner's will, Irma claimed, had promised her her liberty, yet Rils had not taken "the legal steps to carry out the provisions of the will." She asked the court to make her free. In his response to Irma's petition, Rils conceded that Irma's late owner had granted her a "bequest for her freedom" in his will; yet "the laws and policies of the state no longer permitted the emancipation of slaves." Indeed, in March 1857, a few short months before Irma sued for her legal liberty, the Louisiana legislature prohibited all emancipations of slaves. Thus, Rils argued, he did not have "the legal power or authority" to free her. The court agreed, dismissing the case as a nonsuit and denying her request to appeal her lawsuit to the Supreme Court of Louisiana.[41] Thus, after early 1857, the Louisiana courts ceased to be a site of legal redress for slaves like Irma seeking their freedom by will.

STATU LIBERI AND THE POYDRAS SLAVES

Those with an intermediate status, in particular, sought to protect their future as free people and made claims that would affect their impending ability to direct their own lives. Contracts for freedom and manumission by will created, in the words of the Louisiana *Civil Code*, "slaves for a time, or *statu liberi*." Louisiana law defined such people as "those who have acquired the right of being free at a time to come, or on a condition which is not fulfilled, or in a certain event which has not happened, but who, in the mean time, remain in a state of slavery."[42] Although temporarily still enslaved, *statu liberi* were no longer without rights. For instance, while they waited out their remaining terms, they could receive property through gift or testament. In the intervening years before they gained their freedom, however, slaves for a time remained vulnerable to the whims of their owners—and especially to sale beyond the jurisdiction of the state. But they also exploited every possible avenue to protect their interests and compel the courts to protect their imminent claims to self-ownership. In ways similar to those who demanded that the courts enforce the terms of their self-purchase contracts, enslaved people sued to protect their rights as *statu liberi* and to prevent others from impeding their future as free people. Such lawsuits could have lasting consequences that reached beyond the courtroom or an individual case; lawsuits initiated by *statu liberi* sometimes induced the courts to act against the economic interests of a slaveholding society, as the litigation involving the Poydras slaves indicates.

Julien Poydras was born on April 3, 1746, and like many other Frenchman of his generation, he immigrated to Louisiana—first to New Orleans, then upriver to Pointe Coupee Parish (one of the oldest permanent European settlements in the region). On arrival in the parish, Poydras promptly set himself up in business as one of the settlement's first merchants. His enterprise grew rapidly, and Poydras invested in transporting merchandise to and from New Orleans and bought considerable acreage in and around Pointe Coupee Parish and a staggering number of slaves. When he died in 1824, Poydras owned no fewer than four plantations and 570 slaves in Pointe Coupee Parish alone (valued at $917,310), as well as considerable holdings up and down the Mississippi River. Poydras never married, but he did leave bequests to several nieces and nephews (some of whom lived in France and never set foot on Louisiana soil). His will, however, proved controversial and was the subject of considerable litigation.[43]

The first person to initiate a lawsuit involving Poydras's will was an unlikely litigant—a slave. In the fall of 1825, Bob Moussa, a man of color, sued Valerian Allain and Villeneuve Leblanc in the district court in West Baton Rouge Parish over a bill of sale that had transferred him, as human property, from Allain to Leblanc. Moussa claimed that the sale violated the terms of his late master's will and his rights as a slave for a time. For most of his twenty-four years, Moussa had belonged to Poydras. Poydras, however, had died the previous year, leaving a will that would be fought over in the Louisiana courts by his slaves and his heirs for decades to come. In his will, Poydras stipulated that his heirs sell each of his six plantations in Pointe Coupee Parish at the time of his death, along with all of his slaves. The purchase of these six plantations and the hundreds of people living and working on them came with strict conditions. Poydras specified that none of the slaves, including their future children, could be sold apart from the plantation on which they resided. They were "to be considered attached" to the plantations and could not be removed from them. In addition, the purchasers were to treat the slaves with "humanity." After twenty-five years, or when the individual bondsperson reached the age of sixty, whichever came first, each slave would be freed. Once free, they could no longer be compelled to work, could remain on the plantation if they chose, and would receive an annual stipend of twenty-five dollars as "relief against the infirmities of age." With this will, the Poydras slaves became *statu liberi*, or slaves for a time.

Some of Poydras's heirs, however, ignored the provisions of the will and sold off much of the property in pieces. Shortly after his death, Allain bought the plantation where Moussa lived and labored (as well as the other 154 slaves living on the plantation). Then, in telling language for a slave, Moussa relayed that, "without any regard or consideration for the conditions [of the will] and the rights of this petitioner," Allain sold him to Leblanc against Moussa's "will and inclination." His rights had been disregarded, he told the court. Worse,

Moussa claimed that he had "good reasons for believing that [Leblanc] intended to carry him out of the state," an action that would endanger his promised freedom and further violate his rights as a *statu liber*. The Louisiana *Civil Code* protected slaves for a time from removal: "The slave for years cannot be transported out of the State. He can appear in court to claim the protection of the laws in cases where there are good reasons for believing that it is intended to carry him out of the State."[44] Moussa asked the court to declare the sale null and void, to "restore" him to his plantation in Pointe Coupee Parish, and to forbid Allain from separating him from the plantation a second time. In short, he wanted his rights (as a *statu liber*) respected.

It would be remiss to underestimate the enormous challenges Moussa faced when lodging a complaint before the court—challenges that other enslaved people similarly confronted when initiating their lawsuits. Moussa had to leave his master's property without permission, secure an attorney to represent him in court, and find a way to compensate his lawyer. Moreover, he defied Allain and Leblanc at great personal risk. Challenging his masters (in public, no less) was dangerous. The consequences of loss could be devastating, perhaps even violent. Beyond these practical concerns, he faced larger structural barriers. Given the racial inequalities embedded in the southern legal system, it is remarkable that he approached the courts at all.

Not surprisingly, Moussa lost. The district court ruled in favor of the defendants, and Moussa appealed his case to the state supreme court, where he lost a second time. The Supreme Court of Louisiana held that because "there is no evidence of even an intention of the defendant Leblanc to transfer the plaintiff" outside "of the jurisdiction of the state," Moussa's rights as a *statu liber* and his future freedom were thus not in danger. The high court affirmed the lower court's decision, and presumably Moussa remained Leblanc's slave. It is unclear if Moussa eventually received the freedom promised him when his term was up. But a man who sued once to settle such matters would likely sue again if frustrated a second time and given the opportunity.[45]

While Moussa failed to obtain redress in court for the personal injustices done to him, his actions were not futile, and they influenced the next round of the battle over Poydras's property. Over the following decade, dozens of enslaved men and women who had once belonged to Poydras learned valuable lessons from Moussa's defeat and used the Louisiana courts to enforce the provisions of their late master's will and to make the heirs accountable to Poydras's promises. Many were successful. The Poydras slaves who sued after Moussa, however, found an important and powerful ally to appear in court and initiate their lawsuits with them—Poydras's nephew, Benjamin Poydras.

Why Benjamin Poydras came to the aid of his uncle's slaves remains a mystery, as he was a large owner of unfree labor himself and freed only four of his own slaves. Benjamin Poydras arrived in Louisiana from France in 1804 with similar ambitions as his uncle, and he too prospered as one of the region's largest merchants and landowners. When he died in 1851, he left behind nine separate tracts of land, land worked by 155 enslaved laborers. In the intervening years, Benjamin Poydras was party to no fewer than 128 lawsuits in Pointe Coupee Parish, including one involving his slave, Baptiste LeRidel's, lawsuit for his freedom (discussed below) and lawsuits against members of his own family for acting against their uncle's wishes. His reasons for helping his uncle's slaves were probably not altruistic, although that was what he claimed. Given the constant litigation between himself and his family members, he may have gotten involved merely to vex his kin.[46]

Nonetheless, with Benjamin Poydras's help, the Poydras slaves fought to impose the finer points of the will—manumission dates, promises for humane treatment, annual stipends, and a stop to sales separating them from the plantations where they lived and labored. The battle began in 1835 when Benjamin Poydras (alongside a slave named Martin and four dozen other enslaved men, women, and children) sued his cousin, Pelagie Garnier Mourain, to enforce the provisions of his uncle's will and to protect the *statu liberi* from "violations" of their rights. In their petition to the district court in Pointe Coupee Parish, Benjamin Poydras and the *statu liberi* claimed that Julien Poydras's will "expressly" ordained that all future purchasers of his plantations could not separate the slaves and sell them apart from the plantations on which they lived. In addition, buyers had to free the slaves after twenty-five years, allow the freed people to remain on the plantation, treat them humanely, and provide them with a twenty-five dollar annual stipend without requiring them to work. Yet the Widow Mourain had purchased at auction one of the plantations and its slaves, and she recently advertised for sale "forty-one or forty-two slaves," each "to be sold individually," the plaintiffs relayed. This proposed sale was an "unjust violation" of the will and a "great injury" to the slaves. They therefore requested an injunction to stop the sale. In this case, the Poydras slaves were on stronger footing than Moussa. Indeed, it is possible that Moussa's case urged the others to engage in the legal interpretation of the nature of property and the words of wills. Their interpretation proved effective; the court found for the plaintiffs and ordered that the injunction be made perpetual. Mourain appealed the case to the Supreme Court of Louisiana, and there she lost a second time.[47]

Over the following decade, dozens of bondspeople who had once belonged to Poydras continued to use the Louisiana courts to enforce the provisions of their late master's will and protect their rights as *statu liberi*. Not only did the Poydras slaves use the courts to challenge their owners, improve their lives, and influence the dispersal of an enormous estate; their litigation also induced the southern legal system to act against its own material interests in favor of their freedom. Many (although not all) won their lawsuits—lawsuits that directly influenced the distribution of more than 2 million dollars in property and ignited future litigation between Poydras's heirs.[48] In addition, perhaps emboldened by such lawsuits, dozens of the Poydras slaves took flight and ran away when it became clear that their rights as *statu liberi* might be violated. Many evaded apprehension indefinitely.[49] Technically, the language of contracts and legally binding promises was language reserved for whites (and white men at that; white married women could not contract). But when people like the Poydras slaves appeared in court, they not only made whites accountable to their promises but also induced the courts to treat them—however temporarily—as partners in a mutual bargain.

BORN FREE

While, on the one hand, enslaved men and women approached the courts to make whites honor their private-law promises (the language of contract and obligations between private parties), they also went to court to make whites accountable to the promises they made through statutes and legislation (the public language of the collectivity, spoken by white men but binding on the larger community). Legislatures, after all, professed to be the voice of the people. When enslaved people made claims to freedom in court, they engaged in a form of statutory interpretation, and in so doing bound whites to their promises and rhetoric.

Mississippi and Louisiana lawmakers intended freedom-suit statutes to protect the rights of free people, such as freeborn people held as slaves, illegally enslaved whites, or kidnapped free blacks. Several such people sued for their liberty: many enslaved people appeared before the Natchez district courts claiming freedom based on statutes protecting the freeborn.[50] In particular, enslaved people in the Natchez district commonly initiated suits for freedom because their mothers were white and thus free. Similar to the statutes of other slaveholding states, the laws of Mississippi and Louisiana determined that slave status followed the condition of mothers (*partus sequitur ventrem*). Only mothers of African descent could be slaves. The children of white mothers (and of free black mothers) were free. Article 183 of the Louisiana *Civil Code*, for example, held that "children born of a mother then in a state of slavery, whether married for not, follow the condition of their mother; they are consequently slaves and belong to the master of their mother."[51]

Yet the presumption of slavery followed people of African descent, and those with white mothers and black fathers or grandparents remained vulnerable to enslavement. As one study has shown, white antebellum Americans "believed that racial identity was obvious" and recognizable "on sight."[52] "Whiteness," like "blackness," involved performance as much as it involved appearance, demonstrating just how uncertain racial identity could be despite white southerners' claims that they "knew" race when they saw it.[53] Nonetheless, appearance made certain people vulnerable. Johnson Woodall's skin color made him an ideal target for unscrupulous individuals looking to profit from his sale and labor. Born free in Kentucky, Woodall was the orphaned son of a white mother and a black father. After the death of his parents, he was apprenticed to a blacksmith until he reached the age of twenty-one. In the intervening years, however, a number of Woodall's masters sold his remaining time to others, and Woodall changed hands frequently. Now Daniel Sexton of Natchez claimed him not as an apprentice, but as a slave for life. In a social order where blackness equaled slavery, the burden was on him to prove his free status. Thus, Woodall sued Sexton for his freedom, claiming that his mother was white. After several witnesses corroborated his story, the court issued a verdict in his favor.[54]

Because of the stigma attached to having sexual relations with a black man, white women sometimes went to great lengths to hide such associations from their families and communities. Their concealment left the children of these unions at risk. Driven by shame after coupling with "a mulatto," Sally Kimberland, a white woman from Kentucky, hid her pregnancy and distanced herself from her mixed-race daughter, Phoebe. Because she lived in a world in which the presumption of slavery followed people of color, Phoebe was at the mercy of individuals who might benefit from her enslavement. While Phoebe and her children were living as free people in Kentucky, several unsavory characters, including Phoebe's white uncle, kidnapped them and sold them into slavery in Mississippi. In May 1826, Phoebe initiated a lawsuit against William Boyer, the man who held her and her children as his slaves. Declaring that they deserved the "liberty guaranteed by the laws of the state," Phoebe asked the court for their freedom; because her mother was a white woman, under

Kentucky state law she was born free.[55] Boyer, however, insisted that Phoebe and her children were born slaves and denied that they were free persons.

Witnesses, however, would clear up the confusion. Phoebe had a murky past and the circumstances of her birth proved difficult to uncover. Her mother, she claimed, took care to "conceal her parentage" resulting from the "disgrace" she faced for having "relations . . . with a negro." Recently, though, Phoebe had met several "respectable persons" who could confirm the details surrounding her birth and prove that she and her children were in fact "free and not slaves." To that end, several white witnesses testified on her behalf. Jeremiah Mathers recounted that the "general report from old settlers and residents in the neighborhood" supported Phoebe's claim to freedom. She was, Mathers informed the court, the child of Sally Kimberland, a white woman, and thus entitled to her liberty. Walter Miles, a resident of Kentucky familiar with Sally Kimberland, divulged that it was "common knowledge in the neighborhood" that Kimberland was Phoebe's mother and a white woman. Miles also testified that slave traders had kidnapped Phoebe and her children, brought them down the Mississippi River, and sold them as slaves. But the rumors about her birth—"general reports from old settlers" about her personal history and genealogy—secured her freedom. With such evidence in her favor, the court found for Phoebe and her children and granted them their liberty.[56]

Other enslaved litigants sued because they had Indian ancestry and were thus born free. Both Mississippi and Louisiana determined that Native Americans, like whites, could not be held as slaves. But in 1828, Elizabeth Mordecai and several of her family members sued for their freedom in Pointe Coupee Parish, claiming to be members of the Creek Nation and therefore illegally enslaved. In their petition, the Mordecai family asserted that they were "born between the headwaters of the Tallapoosa and Chattahoochee Rivers in the Creek Nation of what is commonly called Indians." Roughly "four moons" ago, "while they were pursuing their innocent amusements . . . a band of armed robbers who appeared to be white men feloniously kidnapped them." These men stole them from "their native forests and dear relations, fettered and chained them with irons," and sold them as slaves to one John Baird, a resident of the parish. The Mordecai family demanded their freedom on the grounds that they were Indians and thus could not be enslaved, and they wanted $10,000 in compensation for their trauma. It seems that they received their freedom without a trial, however, as the judge ordered their release, and their attorney requested that the case be dismissed. It did not appear that anyone involved in the trial contested the Mordecais' claim that they were

Indians; their identity was not ambiguous or up for debate. Rather, they were the victims of ruthless kidnappers looking to make a quick profit.[57]

THE OTHER UNDERGROUND RAILROAD

The most common argument used in Natchez district freedom suits entailed kidnapping. Enslaved people in the region filed (at least) thirty-one lawsuits for freedom claiming to be kidnapped free people of color illegally held as slaves. In such cases, the plaintiffs attempted to convince the court to recognize their status as free people and return them a condition of freedom.[58] Nearly all involved people enslaved in Mississippi, and over half were successful.[59] Kidnapping cases did appear in other areas of Louisiana and in numbers greater than what I found in the Natchez district; there was widespread evidence of instances of kidnapping in New Orleans, for example. Like Natchez (the site of nearly all the lawsuits involving kidnapping), New Orleans was home to a large slave market, and perhaps this explains the higher number of kidnapping cases in both slave-trade hubs.[60]

While both Mississippi and Louisiana enacted statutes against kidnapping, the laws were hard to enforce given the voracious demand for enslaved laborers and the greed of those involved in the slave trade. In the first half of the nineteenth century, with the enormous expansion of sugar and cotton production in the Lower South and the rapid growth of a booming internal slave trade, more than a million enslaved men and women were transported from the eastern seaboard to the Old Southwest. Initially slaveholders themselves moved their slaves to the interior. Yet over time, they increasingly relied on slave traders—a new group of merchants whose sole business was to deal in human beings—to build their labor force.[61] The trade in human property to the southern interior also encouraged the kidnapping of free blacks and nearly free people—often indentured servants or "slaves for a time" (those with a fixed number of years to serve before becoming free, such as people promised their freedom by individual manumission or state statute). The abduction of free people of color was an attractive option for slave traders and their agents because it garnered high profits while keeping costs low. The kidnapping of free blacks burgeoned notwithstanding its illegality.[62]

Kidnapping occurred often enough to invoke concern among black people in free states. African American newspapers such as the *Colored American* (published weekly in New York City) routinely warned northern free blacks about the dangers of kidnapping and published entreaties seeking support for the kidnapped. For instance, in 1839, the newspaper printed the following account of a suspected kidnapping of an indentured servant: "*Supposed kidnapping on the North River*—Abram Dument, a colored man, in the service of Ephraim Beach (formerly of this city,) at Catskill, went down to the river on the 25th and has not since been heard of. It is supposed he was decoyed on board a strange [schooner] which was then lying in the river, and which sailed in the night. Several blacks were seen on her deck. Similar occurrences have taken place in that quarter before."[63] *The North Star*, Frederick Douglass's antislavery newspaper, published similar warnings and requests for aid to victims of kidnapping. For instance, in December 1848, the paper printed a news release alerting the local community of a recent kidnapping in Rochester, New York: "Just as we go to press, the particulars of a villainous case of Kidnapping in this city have come to our knowledge. Two coloured young men, in pursuit of work in Duane street, were met this morning by two men, seized from behind, and thrust into a carriage, which drove up on the instant, and one of them was immediately handcuffed; the other was then forced out, and the kidnappers drove off. They were, however, traced to the Philadelphia cars, in which they departed for the South, at 9 A.M. before the alarm could be given."[64] *The North Star, The Colored American*, and other newspapers routinely published these nineteenth-century versions of the modern-day Amber Alert—notices that underscored the problem of the kidnapping of northern free blacks for sale into slavery in the South.

Despite evidence of kidnapping in both Mississippi and Louisiana (and freedom suits involving victims who claimed to be kidnapped), no extant record exists from the Natchez district in which a kidnapper was punished for his or her crime. Kidnapping free blacks and selling them into slavery was a felony in both Mississippi and Louisiana. In Mississippi, for instance, the law held, "Every person who shall, without lawful authority, forcibly seize and confine any other, or shall inveigle or kidnap any other with intent, either, . . . To cause such other person to be sold as a slave, or in any way held to service against his will. . . . Shall, upon conviction, be punished by imprisonment in the penitentiary, not exceeding ten years."[65] But the courts did not appear keen to enforce the law. Some local authorities even facilitated and participated in the kidnapping of free people of color. Charles Morgan, his son-in-law, Stephen Van Winkle, and Stephen's brother, Jacob Van Winkle, were involved in a kidnapping ring and each served (in succession beginning with Morgan) as sheriff of Pointe Coupee Parish.[66]

Once kidnapped and sold into slavery (usually far from friends and family), black people found it hard to escape. Finding allies probably proved difficult, and Mississippi law complicated the process even further by requiring individuals who aided an enslaved person in their lawsuit for freedom to pay the person's owner a $100 fine if the plaintiff lost his or her case.[67] As Solomon Northup, the most famous victim of kidnapping, wrote after the restoration of his freedom and the return to his family, "I doubt not . . . that hundreds of free citizens have been kidnapped and sold into slavery, and are at this moment wearing out their lives on plantations in Texas and Louisiana."[68]

Slave owners were likely unsympathetic to alleged victims of kidnapping. After all, investigating claims of kidnapping (and expending time and money to pursue a victim's claim) was not in accordance with slaveholders' material interests. If freed, the buyer would lose the money they paid to purchase the slave, the lifelong labor of that slave, and the slave's future offspring. Many slaveholders were probably reluctant to believe (or admit) they had been duped into buying a kidnapped free person. Others probably did not care. In nearly all the freedom suits from the Natchez district that involved accusations of kidnapping, the defendants denied such charges and insisted that the plaintiff was a slave for life. For instance, after John Hamm sued James Steele and Charles Green for his freedom in Natchez (claiming to be a kidnapped free man from Maryland), Steele appeared in court to deny Hamm's claim to freedom. Hamm, Steele asserted, was his property and "a slave for life." He had the paper trail to prove it: he purchased Hamm "from Eustis French, who purchased him from Charles B. Green, who purchased him from one Joseph Thompson from Guilford County in the state of North Carolina."[69] With owners denying their freedom (or ignorant of it), it was often up to those illegally held in slavery to seek the means to secure their rightful liberty. The burden of proof in freedom suits was on the enslaved.

Although it was difficult to do so, some people of color found legal remedies for their unjust and illegal enslavement.[70] Kidnapped free black people were cognizant of their statutory rights. Because both Mississippi and Louisiana law permitted people illegally held as slaves to sue for their freedom, and because Mississippi and Louisiana law made kidnapping a felony, victims of kidnapping could and did appeal to the courts. Sometimes the courts lent a sympathetic ear—especially if witnesses came forward to substantiate the claims. For instance, in 1822, Benjamin and Bradford Lewis sued J. W. Clark and David Slater for their freedom in the Superior Court in Natchez. They were free men of color from Indiana, they insisted, who had been "forcibly taken to the state of Tennessee and . . . sold as slaves" to Clark and Slater. Moreover, their captors now conspired to "take them to distant ports [to] dispose of them as slaves for life." Several witnesses from the Natchez region appeared before the court and testified that Benjamin and Bradford were free men from Indiana, "where there is no such thing as slavery." Benjamin and Bradford were apprentices and born free men, the witnesses relayed, and Clark and Slater held them illegally. After hearing such testimony, the jury recognized their status as free people and ordered their release.[71]

Many of the enslaved litigants suing in the Mississippi courts claimed to be free people from states (both free and slave) along the borderland region separating freedom from slavery: Pennsylvania, New Jersey, Maryland, Delaware, Indiana, Illinois, Ohio, and Kentucky. Because of their proximity to slave states and because cities like Baltimore and Philadelphia held large communities of free people of color, free blacks in the border region were easy prey for unscrupulous individuals (and gangs) looking to profit from selling free people into slavery in the Deep South. What is more, the demarcations between slavery and freedom along the border region were not clear-cut. For instance, the parallels between the labor systems on both sides of the Ohio River (work regimes committed to exploiting African-descended people), the omnipresence of white racism in the Old Northwest, and draconian laws bent on controlling the movements and status of people of color complicate the slave/free dichotomy that scholars have long attributed to this region.[72]

Free blacks in the borderland region knew all too well how quickly their status could shift from free to slave. Because the presumption of slavery followed people of African descent, kidnappers could traffic them along the interstate slave trade and sell them as slaves in the Deep South with few questions. Yet several kidnapped people from the borderland region found recourse in the courthouse in Natchez, Mississippi, and sued their captors for their freedom.

In each of these lawsuits, the court made every effort to verify the claims of the alleged victims. In 1817, Elias sued George Bell for his freedom, insisting that he had been kidnapped from Pennsylvania, where he was a free man, born of free parents. Bell, however, kept him in a state of slavery, contrary to his "natural rights." After hearing the testimony from depositions taken on Elias's behalf in Pennsylvania, depositions then sent to Mississippi, the jury issued a verdict in favor of Elias and found him to be a free man.[73] Similarly, Aaron Cooper, a free man from Delaware, sued Parmenas Briscoe for his freedom after being kidnapped by a gang of men and sold into slavery in Natchez. Again, the jury listened to testimony read in open court from depositions taken in Delaware, and again, the jury found Cooper to be a free man.[74] The Mississippi and Louisiana courts routinely sent entreaties (commissions) to justices of the peace or magistrates in other regions and states requesting they take the depositions of locals who might shed light on the circumstances of a given case. Kidnapped people of color may have been strangers in the community and thus at a disadvantage, but sometimes the courts went to great lengths to investigate their stories.[75]

Kidnapping victims did not just stem from the borderland region, however. Free people in the Deep South also fell prey to kidnappers. In 1804, Susey and eighteen other people of color (three families total) sued William Scott and Cuthbert Rees for their freedom. Susey and her co-plaintiffs insisted that Scott and Rees snatched them from their homes in Georgia where they had lived as free people and brought them to Mississippi against their will to sell as slaves. In their answer, Scott and Rees admitted that they had brought the plaintiffs from Georgia to Mississippi with the intention of selling them, but they denied the kidnapping charges and insisted that the plaintiffs were born slaves. What is more, the defendants asserted, as slaves, the plaintiffs did not have the legal standing to "maintain their said action against them." As slaves, they could not bring claims to court. Susey and the others responded by requesting that the court proceed with their case "because they were and always since have been and yet still are free persons." The court agreed to move forward with the lawsuit, and the judge set a trial date and sent a request to Georgia for the depositions of witnesses. The list of court costs included in the record indicates that a trial took place; indeed, there was a two-dollar fee for a final judgment among the documented costs. However, that final judgment is missing from the record, and thus the fate of Susey and the others remains unknown.[76]

The fate of kidnapped indentured servants, in particular, underscores the blurred lines between slavery and freedom and demonstrates how quickly a person's legal status could change with a new master. As unfree laborers (for a specified number of years) their contracts and remaining time could be sold to other masters who might sell them (or hold them) as slaves in the Deep South. John's lawsuit against George Williams was typical. John's story began in New York, where he worked as an indentured servant for almost ten years for one William Helen. Helen then sold John's remaining time to another New York resident, Samuel Haight. Haight transferred John once again, this time to one Thomas McBarney, with whom he served the remaining years of his contract. When it came time to release him, John relayed, "McBarney well knowing your petitioner was entitled to his freedom by the laws of New York did forcibly carry him out of the state" and sold him to William Chambers in Louisville, Kentucky. Chambers then took

John "down the river to Natchez and sold him as a slave for life to George Williams." That John changed hands so many times was likely deliberate, as it obscured his status even further. It was up to him, as a man of color in a world in which blackness denoted slavery, to prove he was free. Once in Mississippi, however, John sued Williams for his freedom. After the jury heard the testimony of several people who knew John in New York (depositions the court requested be taken in New York before a justice of the peace and then sent to Mississippi), they issued a verdict in his favor, found him to be a free man, and ordered Williams to pay the court costs—costs that included John's attorney's fees.[77]

When requesting that the courts enforce freedom-suit and kidnapping statutes, enslaved people demanded more than their freedom. They also used their lawsuits to lay claim to other aspects of self-possession: the right to their bodies and the fruits of their own labor. Some convinced the court to award them back wages for the labor they had performed as slaves. In February 1834, Charles and Betsy (alias Lisette) sued Philip Rocheblanc for their freedom in Iberville Parish, Louisiana. They claimed that for more than six years Rocheblanc had "illegally, forcefully, and unjustly deprived them of their liberty" by keeping them as his slaves. They were free people of color and residents of Illinois, Charles and Betsy told the court, where by "virtue of the Constitution and Laws of the State . . . slavery does not and can not by Law exist." Despite Rocheblanc's knowledge of their free status, he "illegally, fraudulently, secretly, and with the intention of depriving them of their liberty" seized them in St. Louis and brought them to Louisiana where he "kept them in a state of slavery." Rocheblanc had even boasted that "they ought to be free . . . in the presence of witnesses," they told the court. They were "entitled to their liberty" and insisted on "legal redress." In addition to their freedom, they wanted monetary damages for the six years they had labored for Rocheblanc without pay—a total of $900 ($600 for Charles and $300 for Betsy)—and the costs of the lawsuit. The jury found in favor of Charles and Betsy, affirmed their status as free people, and demanded that Rocheblanc pay them $900 and cover the court costs. The court also refused Rocheblanc's motion for a new trial. Charles and Betsy received the "legal redress" they desired, regained control of their own bodies, and received compensation for the years they labored without pay.[78] In this case, Charles and Betsy compelled the court to recognize that even in a society that marked people of African descent as natural slaves, black people could own themselves, and they could also own and direct their labor and endow that labor with value. As freeborn people, the laws of Mississippi guaranteed their rights to their bodies and to their labor, and with their lawsuit Charles and Betsy made whites accountable to those guarantees.

When suing for freedom, enslaved people also capitalized on the laws of other territories, states, and nations. After sojourns on free soil, a number of enslaved people from Louisiana in particular petitioned for their freedom on the grounds that their owners had taken them to a state or country in which slavery did not exist.[79] This argument originated with the famous 1772 British case, *Somerset v. Stewart*, in which James Somerset, an enslaved man of African descent, sought a writ of habeas corpus to prevent his owner, Charles Stewart, from deporting him from England for sale in Jamaica. Somerset's legal team argued that while colonial laws supported slavery, neither English common law nor positive law recognized chattel slavery, thus slaves entering England thereby became free. In his judgment, Lord Mansfield, the chief justice of the Court of King's Bench, held that "the state of slavery is of such a nature, that . . . it must take its rise from positive law," and he ordered Somerset's release.[80] The *Somerset* decision also influenced law in the United States, and it was cited as precedent in American courtrooms up until the 1857 *Dred Scott* decision.[81]

In their lawsuits, Natchez district slaves insisted that once on free soil, the laws of the free state or nation in question operated to free them. On their return to the South from the North or (more commonly) France, enslaved litigants argued, they could not revert to a condition of slavery. Indeed, the Louisiana *Civil Code* held that, "emancipation, once perfected, is irrevocable."[82] In 1843, Baptiste LeRidel sued Benjamin Poydras, a white man from Pointe Coupee Parish, for his freedom on the grounds that he had lived on free soil. In his petition, LeRidel stated that he had left Louisiana in 1822 "with the consent and authorization of Benjamin Poydras." He and Poydras had "sailed from the city of New Orleans to the city of Havre de Grace in the Kingdom of France." Next, they had traveled to Nantes, France, "at which place your petitioner was allowed by the said Poydras to reside during a period of more than nine years, viz. from the year 1822 to the year 1831, at which time he was induced to return to the State of Louisiana." Yet while he lived in France, he had attended "public school" and had served as "an apprentice to learn diverse trades," both at the "request of said Poydras." Importantly, LeRidel insisted, because French law prohibited slavery, "his residence in that country" granted him "all the rights and privileges of a free man." Poydras, however, "persists in holding him in bondage on his plantation." He asked the court to grant him his freedom and ended the petition by signing his name. In his answer, Poydras simply insisted that LeRidel was and always had been his slave and bypassed the question of free soil entirely. Yet several witnesses subpoenaed by the plaintiff, including members of Poydras's own family, appeared before the court and not only confirmed LeRidel's account but also claimed to "know that by the written law of France slavery is declared not to exist." The court issued a verdict in favor of LeRidel and declared him a free man.[83]

In 1846, however, the Louisiana legislature enacted a law designed to close this escape hatch to freedom and declared that time spent in free territory was not grounds for freedom. The law stated that, "From the passage of this act, no slave shall be entitled to his or her freedom, under the pretense that he or she has been, with or without the consent of his or her owner, in a country where slavery does not exist, or in any other States where slavery is prohibited."[84] But Louisiana courts granted freedom to enslaved people who demonstrated that they had lived in free territory before 1846. What is more, courts in the Natchez district also continued to hear such cases into the 1850s, and enslaved litigants continued to have success suing on these grounds.

Although she initiated her freedom suit after the passage of the 1846 act, Marie, a woman of color, found redress in the district court in West Baton Rouge Parish. On September 4, 1848, Marie claimed that in 1831, her owners, Dr. and Mrs. Doussan, had taken her to France where she remained "for about one year and became thereby free." What is more, her owners knew that "slavery is not tolerated in France" and thus (in her mind) consented to her freedom. The Doussans, however, continued to keep her as a slave. In early 1848, she gave the Doussans "a letter" detailing her intentions to hire a lawyer and "claim her freedom." "Because she is good cook," she insisted, and because they did not want to "give her the chance or facility of suing them for her freedom," they had her jailed "every night" to keep a close watch over her. It appears, however, that Marie managed to give them the slip and filed a civil suit against the Doussans in the local court. In their answer to her petition, the Doussans admitted they had taken Marie to France in 1831, "where they remained for about nine months." If this sojourn, the Doussans continued, "entitles the Plaintiff to her freedom, these Respondents will not oppose her claim to be free." But they "deny that she has any claim" to back wages and court costs. A mere three weeks after Marie filed her lawsuit, the judge in West Baton Rouge issued a verdict in her favor and found her a free woman. But he also ordered her to pay the costs of the suit.[85] While Marie gained her freedom, enslaved people in the Natchez district who traveled to or lived on free soil after 1846 found the courts unsympathetic to their claims to freedom.

Marie's lawsuit—and the language she used in her petition—reveals not only her legal consciousness but also her view of herself as a person with rights. Similar to other enslaved people suing for their freedom—and free people of color suing to protect their interests—Marie knew her rights, and she knew the law, both local and international. She knew these rights had been violated, and laws had been broken. She knew how to hire a lawyer, file a claim, and demand redress. The Doussans were well aware of this knowledge and confined her in their home to keep her from the courthouse. Their actions, moreover, point to a contradiction at the heart of southern law: slaves as persons versus property. Marie was the Doussans' property. But they also acknowledged that she could (and did) act as a legal person, and one with volition.

When enslaved people went to court to sue for their freedom, they exercised legal personhood. They insisted on the ownership of their bodies, their labor, and other forms of self-possession. Sometimes they even made claims to property. The enslaved men and women who initiated civil suits for their freedom in the local courts of Mississippi and Louisiana employed their knowledge of the southern legal system to their advantage. When pressing their claims to freedom and personhood, they exploited every possible opening in the law. They also compelled court officials to acknowledge that the stories told by black people—stories that stemmed from their personal histories, genealogies, and accounts of wrong doing—were credible. Indeed, the courts conceded that it might be the white person who lied.

Moreover, enslaved litigants made whites accountable to their own language and obligations. Enslaved people interpreted the promises that white southerners made in contracts, wills, and statutes as legally binding and thus enforceable. They positioned themselves as rights-bearing persons and as such transformed abstractions in the law into realities. Some even secured their freedom, the liberty of their families, and a degree of control over their bodies and their lives. In so doing, they induced white southerners to act against their own material interests and forced them to recognize enslaved litigants as legal subjects—wielders of law, not objects of it.

But their definition of personhood was their own. When enslaved litigants theorized rights and the meanings of personhood and freedom, they did not do so in the image of white men—law's normative person. This was not mimicking or parody; enslaved litigants envisioned and pushed for an idea of freedom, rights, and dignity beyond what white men—and the state—could imagine. Instead, they framed their claims in ways that reflected their own experiences and narratives, drawn from their own histories and perspectives. And they sought to act, in the words of the enslaved litigant Bob Moussa, of their "own will and inclination."[86]

Of course, most enslaved people in the American South did not enter the legal arena as plaintiffs. Yet for a number of enslaved men and women, the courts represented a place to air grievances and redress past wrongs. Their legal action—coupled with the litigiousness of free people of color—points to the depth of legal consciousness in antebellum black communities. While many people of African descent in the slave South could not and did not go to court, the legal activity of people of color—their claims-making and self-advocacy—had a long and robust history, a history that did not begin with the Thirteenth and Fourteenth Amendments and the extension of formal rights. This history, as the next chapter shows, was also multigenerational. Their pre-Emancipation experience with private law, moreover, proved important in the struggle for rights, equal treatment, and racial justice, for it provided future generations of African Americans with a model—with language, knowledge, skills, strategies, networks, and theories—for the long battle ahead.

7

For Family and Property

Southern law circumscribed the family life of people of color in distinct and often violent ways, ranging from authorizing the sale of children and sanctioning the brutal beatings of family members to denying enslaved people legal names and limiting the property and inheritance rights of free blacks. By denying black people the right to legal personhood, white southerners tried to limit African Americans' claims to other features that arose from self-ownership: the right to marry, form families, and inherit and convey property to kin. Yet people of African descent throughout the Natchez district appealed to the legal system to protect their families, as well as their families' property and ability to ensure their futures. They used the courts to register marriages, probate wills, bequeath property, emancipate family members, allocate family resources, and assert their right to family life in myriad other ways.

One of the most pressing issues, perhaps even more pressing than property or personal status, was the family itself. Characteristic of white attempts to socially exclude blacks was to deny them the ability to form households. Nevertheless, black people used the courts to construct stable families. When formal law limited their ability to form families and protect their family's livelihoods and safety, people of color devised ways to circumvent those restrictions. Specifically, in the absence of legal recognition of their families, black people used property ownership to solidify their ties to one another, and they recorded their shared ownership of property and resources in official documents before the courts. Thus, they strengthened the bonds between them.[1]

When using the courts to protect their family, people of color relied on and deployed a well-used model for litigation and claims-making—a model set by fellow black litigants. This model included several tactics for appealing to the bar: they exploited the language of property and law, rhetoric that was recognizable to their audiences and thus usable and effective. They found ways to make others accountable to them: with their stories and reputations and through their networks. They bound people in relationships of obligation to them—bonds that sometimes upended the southern racial hierarchy. They used property ownership and its associated presumptions about independence and reliability to make their claims and, as I demonstrate in what follows, to legitimize and safeguard their families. In so doing, they served as their own advocates, registered their voices in an official, public forum, and laid claim to civic inclusion.

This chapter examines how well the model worked. It follows the formation of one family from Iberville Parish, the Belly family, and their efforts to construct a family before the law and through property ownership. Although denied legal sanction of their family, Pierre Belly, a Frenchman, and Rose, Pierre's "wife" and former slave, used the courts to make their relationship to one another public and official and proclaim their children as their own, and they insisted that the courts recognize them as a lawful family. Their daughters and their descendants would do the same, as would families of color throughout the Natchez district. The Belly family was unique in some ways: they were wealthier than nearly all other free people of color in the region and many of the whites. They were also Afro-French, and as such their connections provided them with some advantages. Their prominence, however, meant that they left behind a particularly rich set of documents, making it possible to trace their history across several generations. Few people of color left such records behind. Yet in their use of the courts, the Bellys drew from a repertoire of strategies deployed by other black people throughout the region. The Belly family employed many of the tactics developed by a wide range of other black litigants (rich and poor, young and old, male and female, and slave and free), tactics that provided their family with legitimacy and security.

PIERRE AND ROSE

Pierre Belly, a Frenchman and Louisiana military officer, planter, and judge, was born in mid-summer 1738 on his family estate in Eyrans, a French village north of Bordeaux. His father, Jean Belly, was a textile merchant of modest income who incurred many debts. When he died in 1758, Jean's wife, Valerie Goyer de la Rochette Belly, and their minor children inherited those debts and were forced to divide his estate with his creditors. Valerie managed to retain real estate and personal property equal to the dowry her family had provided to her and Jean when they married. Through this arrangement, Jean's heirs received the family estate—an estate that eventually passed to Jean Belly *fils*, the eldest son. The agreement between Valerie and her late husbands' creditors also stipulated that she renounce the family's claim to his textile business. Pierre came of age during this unfortunate period, and most likely his father's death, his position as a younger son, and his family's financial problems compelled him to seek new opportunities elsewhere. He set his sights on Louisiana.[2]

Such a move was not unusual. Men down on their luck and looking to profit from the riches of the New World flocked to the colonies. By the time Pierre's father died, French settlement of colonial Louisiana was well established.[3] In 1699, in an effort to control the mouth of the Mississippi River, the French established a beachhead at Biloxi, along the present day Mississippi Gulf Coast, and France began to make a claim to the entire Mississippi Valley and the coast of the Gulf of Mexico between Spain's colonies of New Spain (Mexico) and Florida. The colony of French Louisiana developed slowly, and French control of the region was fragile. Life in lower Louisiana was harsh, especially in the early years, and colonists faced chaotic French rule, hurricanes, outbreaks of disease, and offensives from hostile neighbors.[4] Yet if Pierre—the younger son of a family in decline—survived a yellow fever epidemic or an Indian attack, he might accumulate wealth, especially as the region transitioned to plantation agriculture.

It is unclear when Pierre departed France for Louisiana, and in the years after his father's death, he may have first traveled to other colonies. But by 1774, Pierre resided in Louisiana—now a colony of Spain—unmarried and without his family. In that year, he received a land grant from the Spanish government for a large tract of land in what is now Iberville Parish. He also began serving in the Spanish colonial militia; in 1779 he assisted colonial Governor of Spanish Louisiana, Bernardo de Gálvez, in the Battle of Baton Rouge against the British and commanded a force of 120 men. He retired from the Spanish militia in 1792, but later took up arms against the British once again, this time alongside his sons-in-law in the defense of New Orleans during the War of 1812. In 1805, Pierre also served as one of the first officials appointed to local government in Iberville Parish, and between 1805 and 1807 he served as a civil judge for the parish. He was an educated man and apparently versed in the civil law. Indeed, the inventory of his estate contained a collection of books, including a volume of statutes from the *Civil Code*.[5]

On his arrival in Louisiana, Pierre did what he could not do in France given his family circumstances. He invested in land. In 1774, he received his first tract of land—for 3,756 acres—in the form of a land grant from the Spanish colonial government, and he quickly supplemented this allotment in 1776 with a private purchase of land on the Mississippi River from one Madame Dautrieve.[6] Through private sales, he continued to add to his real-estate holdings along both sides of the Mississippi River.[7] Pierre also received five more land grants (three from the Spanish government and two from the U.S. government) totaling about 4,898 acres. In the years leading to his death, he passed much of his 8,000 acres in Iberville Parish to his family through gifts and sales, and when he died in 1814, he held 5,593 arpents of land.[8] While his primary occupation was that of a planter (he grew staple crops—crops cultivated by slave laborers—and owned a cotton gin and a corn mill), he also supplied the Spanish government with lumber from the forests on his land.[9]

Pierre also invested in slaves; when he died he was the largest slaveholder in the parish.[10] By the time he established his holdings in the rich lands along the Mississippi River in the late eighteenth century, the French and Spanish had imported and enslaved thousands of people of African descent. For most of the Spanish period, enslaved people of African descent made up 55 percent of the total population of lower Louisiana.[11] For instance, in 1763, there were 4,598 slaves in the colony and 3,654 free people. The 1788 census counted 18,737 free people in lower Louisiana and 20,673 enslaved. By 1800, the number of enslaved people grew to 24,264. The total population was 44,116, but that number now included the territory of West Florida.[12] While natural increase accounted for some of this growth, the French and Spanish imported most of their enslaved laborers directly from Africa. Yet smugglers operating in the British Atlantic colonies also began transporting slaves to Louisiana after 1758, and many British merchants supplied Spanish Louisiana with slaves from the British islands.[13]

In 1779, Pierre purchased several slaves from Jamaica. One of them was Rose, a young Nago woman about twelve years of age. Rose arrived in Louisiana on board the ship *La Golondrina* (The Swallow). She was part of a group of thirty slaves sent to Pierre by a business agent. Her arrival marked the beginning of a long relationship with Pierre that lasted nearly thirty-five years and produced six daughters. The two are interred together in a family tomb in St. Raphael Cemetery in Iberville Parish. The circumstances of Pierre and Rose's early relationship are unclear, but in 1784, at approximately seventeen, Rose bore their first child, Rosalie. By this point, Rose was living with Pierre as his wife, and their community accepted them as married. She and

Pierre had five more daughters: Marie Antoinette, Marie Geneviève, Marie Françoise (also called Nanette), Valerie Octavine, and Héloïse. All six survived into adulthood, married, and had families of their own.[14]

Intimate, familial liaisons across the color line like Pierre and Rose's were common in this part of the Louisiana, as was sex (forced, coerced, or consensual) between white men and free and enslaved women of African descent. Interracial sexual connections in Louisiana and in the United States and the Atlantic world more generally ranged from life partnerships that produced children and were familial in nearly every way to (more commonly) violent acts of rape and sexual assault and coercion through which slave owners demonstrated their power. Even seemingly consensual relations between white men and black women were forged in the shadow of slavery and the rampant sexual exploitation of black women. As one scholar astutely argues, "the ways that white men and black women negotiated their relations . . . shared that origin [slavery] and never shed the imbalance of power inherent in it."[15] Indeed, Rose's early relationship with Pierre cannot be extricated from her status as his slave, because to do so would require us to view her as free to make choices.

Pierre and Rose's negotiations over the contours of their relationship cannot be reconstructed without speculation, but for a white man and a black woman to enter a life partnership was not unusual in early Louisiana. The demography of late colonial New Orleans in particular, in which white men far outnumbered white women and free women of color outnumbered free men of color, as well as a rapidly growing slave population, favored relationships between white men and black women.[16] For instance, in New Orleans in 1791, there were 1,474 white men and only 912 white women. Thus, as one study shows, "it was statistically impossible for every New Orleanian to marry within the racial category to which he or she was assigned until well after 1800."[17] Upriver, in the more isolated parishes—such as Iberville and Pointe Coupee—intimate liaisons between people of European, African, and Indian descent flourished. When Pierre settled in Iberville Parish, it was an isolated and often dangerous frontier, and the population of the region, as Gwendolyn Midlo Hall argues, "adapted by creating a flexible, permeable world where human talents and abilities were at a premium."[18] White men in Iberville and Pointe Coupee Parishes frequently entered into conjugal relationships with enslaved women, and they often freed them, lived out their lifetimes with them, provided for and recognized their children by them, and on occasion even openly acknowledged them as their partners.[19] What is more, the formation of such relationships continued in Iberville and Pointe Coupee Parishes in the more settled antebellum period, and they also occurred upriver in Natchez, Mississippi. For instance, in 1836, after the death of his white wife, Charles Poydras, a Pointe Coupee Parish lawyer and sugar planter, entered into a relationship with Marie Calvin, a woman of color, and the two lived together for nearly forty years. Calvin bore Poydras two daughters, and after his death and in accordance with inheritance laws, he bequeathed $6,000 to her and half his remaining estate to their daughter Charlotte (their second daughter, Euphemie, had died at a young age).[20] Adam L. Bingaman, a wealthy Natchez planter, had a long relationship with his slave, Mary Ellen Williams, whom he freed. When he died in 1869, he bequeathed his entire estate to their daughter.[21] Both the law and a culture of white supremacy in Louisiana and Mississippi rendered such families illegitimate, however.

TELLING STORIES IN THE LANGUAGE OF PROPERTY

Technically, families like the Bellys resided in the shadow of the law. No colonial law in Louisiana explicitly prohibited marriages between white men and women of color, but once under the American regime, Louisiana banned marriages between free persons and slaves and free white persons and free persons of color.[22] Yet members of mixed-race families—and people of color in the region more generally—used the law to validate and protect their families and family resources. They did so through stories crafted in the language of property.

The nature of property in the slave South was such that it could be manipulated as a substitute for other kinds of relations. As co-narrators, Pierre and Rose (like other families in the region) used the courts to shape a story about their family—one that undermined the legal apparatus of a slave society designed to prohibit the formation of such families and limit their family's opportunities. Their story began with manumission.

Pierre's first legal act to safeguard his family came on October 3, 1786, when he manumitted Rosalie, his one-year-old daughter by Rose, and Marie Antoinette, their newborn, before a notary and three witnesses in the Iberville Parish court.[23] He also manumitted Marie Françoise (b. 1800) soon after her birth and freed Marie Geneviève (b. 1788) in 1802—on the same day he freed her mother.[24] It is not clear why Pierre held Rose as a slave for nearly twenty-three years; but on July 14, 1802, he appeared in court and provided Rose with her freedom because of "the great love and affection that [he]

holds for her."[25] Pierre and Rose's fifth daughter, Valerie Octavine (b. 1803), and sixth daughter, Héloïse (b. 1805), were born free.

With manumission, Rose and her daughters could enjoy the privileges of the free, legally and culturally. Although limited by their race and gender, they could own and inherit property, marry, and travel freely. Their free status protected them from certain circumstances beyond their control, such as seizure and sale to settle Pierre's debts and sale upon his death by his heirs. As an unmarried woman, moreover, Rose was neither beholden to the laws of marriage and coverture, laws that would otherwise limit her ability to contract, hold and manage property, retain the fruits of her own labor, keep custody of her children, and to sue and be sued. Nor was she bound to obey her husband in all matters. Although race barred Rose from marrying Pierre, she could operate in court and in the economy as a single woman, and she did just that.[26]

As Sally Hemings's relationship with Thomas Jefferson reminds us, not all white slaveholders freed their enslaved consorts. Many slaveholders sold their black mistresses and children. Yet white men throughout the Natchez district petitioned the courts and the state legislatures to manumit their enslaved families. For instance, in 1820, William Johnson, a white man living in Natchez, petitioned the Mississippi legislature for permission to manumit his son, also named William Johnson. He had recently manumitted William's mother, Amy, just over the river in Louisiana, but relayed that he could not manumit William at the same time because he was too young (according to Louisiana law, to be eligible for manumission, one had to be older than thirty). Thus, he asked the legislature to "permit him to make that disposition of his property most agreeable to his feelings & consonant with humanity—the act to give that Liberty to a human being which all are entitled to as a Birthright, & extend the hand of humanity to a rational creature, on whom unfortunately Complexion, Custom, & even Law in this Land of Freedom, has conspired to rivet the fetters of Slavery."[27] After manumitting Amy and his son, the elder William Johnson aided them in their transition, and they continued to use his name. Amy Johnson owned slaves of her own and conducted a successful trade in the Natchez marketplace. The younger William Johnson apprenticed as a barber and quickly rose to the top of the ranks of Natchez's free black community.[28]

Free people of color throughout the region also used the courts to manumit family members and provide them with the benefits of freedom. Many free blacks bought and then freed enslaved friends and family. While laws governing individual manumission grew stricter over time (and eventually both states banned individual manumissions entirely), free black petitioners seeking to manumit their kin and whose slaves met the requirements for manumission did so with relative ease.[29] In particular, individual manumission was commonplace throughout Louisiana. For instance, between 1827 and 1846, the police jury of New Orleans denied only ten petitions for manumission, mostly because the enslaved were very young and could not support themselves. The other 1,780 were successful.[30] Petitioners seeking to manumit slaves in Pointe Coupee and Iberville Parishes found similar success: of the thirty-seven black petitioners who attempted to use the district court to free their slaves (some kin and some not), only three were denied (and these three occurred in late 1856, just before the state legislature banned manumission on any grounds). Twenty-one of these petitioners sought to manumit family members—wives, children, parents, and siblings—and the courts approved each of their requests.[31] What is more, the courts in Iberville and Pointe Coupee Parishes also permitted these newly manumitted people to remain in the state. Manumission laws in both Louisiana and Mississippi (and throughout the South) dictated that all newly freed people leave the state immediately after their manumission. Such policies reflected lawmakers' desire to rid the region of free people of color, often believed to be dangerous and subversive. Yet individual petitioners usually bypassed this requirement by seeking permission for the newly freed to remain in their county and state of residence.

Free blacks in Mississippi also petitioned the state legislature to request a "special act" or law permitting them to manumit their kin. For instance, after working for years to scrape together the purchase price, Jeremiah Gill, a free black man, managed to buy his wife, Amy, and their daughter, Betsey. Because he was "advanced in age" and concerned about their future, he petitioned the Mississippi legislature in 1830 for an "act of emancipation." He feared that on his death, his family might "through tyranick grasp and relentless cupidity of some unfeeling wretch, be deprived of that portion of their liberty, which the sweat of your petitioner's humble brow has purchased for them." Here Gill fused political theory with religion: the sweat of his brow was his safeguard against tyranny. The legislature granted his request and allowed Amy and Betsey to remain in Mississippi.[32] Pierre's manumission of Rose and their daughters formed part of a culture in which both white and black family members appealed to the courts and the state legislature to free their enslaved kin and ensure their (relative) safety.

Pierre and Rose's next step in crafting a legal, or official, story about themselves and the legitimacy of their family was to formalize their relationship. They did this through the adoption of a family name and the transfer of property—processes they documented in court. While Pierre and Rose could not marry, they did take several steps before the law to validate their relationship, steps that provided Rose with security and legal legitimacy. Less than a year after Pierre manumitted Rose, the Louisiana territory passed from the French to the Americans, and in 1803, Louisiana officially banned marriage between free whites and free people of color. Thus, even if Pierre intended to marry Rose legally (which might have been difficult given the racial dynamics and prejudices of a slave society), he no longer could. Yet it appears that Rose was his wife in his eyes, in the eyes of their family, and in the eyes of the community at large. Their relationship was not considered illicit. For three decades, Rose and Pierre lived together openly with their children, and those around them viewed them as husband and wife. No extant records—civil or religious—demonstrate any grievances or even mumblings about Rose and Pierre's relationship. Even five years after Pierre's death, a federal surveyor mentioned the couple offhandedly in his travel journal. He wrote that as part of his duties, he walked "round to ENE in all 7 miles to Bailies plantation a Frenchman who is married to a Negresse a native of Congo."[33] Neither Pierre nor Rose hid their relationship in public or before the law. Instead, they did the opposite.

Both Rose and Pierre affirmed their "marriage" in legal documents in various ways. In particular, Pierre appeared in court frequently to register transfers, donations, and sales of real and personal property to Rose, and in those records the couple made Rose visible as his wife by giving her Pierre's name and affiliating her with his vast estate. In several legal documents involving Rose (some initiated by Pierre and others initiated by Rose), Pierre and Rose gave her name as "Rose Belly" or "commonly called Rose Belly." For instance, when Rose and Pierre appeared together in court to officially and legally acknowledge their daughters, they stated that the girls were born of Rose, "commonly called Rose Belly free negro woman."[34] Their careful adoption of his surname induced other people in their community to refer to her—in legal documents and otherwise—as "Rose Belly" or "Rose, also called Rose Belly free negro woman." Such documents further solidified her free status, giving her ample proof of her freedom if ever anyone questioned it. The adoption of Pierre's name provided Rose with additional legitimacy before their community and relayed the narrative they wanted the community to accept: they were "married."

Women of color in the region frequently adopted the last name of their white partners, often with the clarifier *dite* (meaning "called"). Marianne, a free woman of color and former Jamaican slave, maintained a lifelong relationship with a prominent Frenchman and colonial official from Pointe Coupee

Parish, Antoine Ricard de Rieutard. She took Antoine's last name and was known as Marianne *dite* Ricard. Eventually the *dite* dropped away, as was common with *dite* names (*dit* in the masculine), and she became Marianne Ricard. Their seven children carried the surname Ricard. Although barred from marrying their lovers, women of African descent like Marianne Ricard used *dite* names to solidify (and officially and publicly document) their ties to their partners and their offspring.

Pierre and Rose's story continued with their children. They also maneuvered to undermine the legal and cultural machinery of a slave society by validating their children before the law. In particular, they took several steps to declare Pierre's paternity, actions that provided their daughters with additional inheritance rights and a degree of legitimacy. They began by baptizing five of the girls in the Church of Saint Gabriel in Iberville Parish (Marie Geneviève was baptized in New Orleans), and they recorded the baptisms in several court documents, including an official acknowledgment of their children filed in the Iberville Parish courthouse.[35] While the Catholic Church frowned on unions between white men and black women, and many fathers of mixed-race children hid their identities and paternity, baptismal records in Louisiana were filled with paternal acknowledgments. Emily Clark shows that fathers in New Orleans often "rejected the clergy's offer of a cloak of anonymity and had themselves clearly identified in their children's baptismal and marriage records."[36] Baptism and the identification of Pierre as the girls' father on the official documents were sufficient enough to recognize his mixed-race daughters as his own. Yet Pierre took special care to declare his paternity in multiple sites. He did so in order to provide his children with property claims to his estate.

Pierre also officially recognized his daughters as his "natural children," a legal condition that separated them from the designation of a bastard—a designation that had both social and financial consequences. It removed the stigma of illegitimacy, and it provided them with a claim to his property. Fathers in Louisiana could legally acknowledge their illegitimate children as natural children in several ways: they could appear before a notary with two witnesses and declare their paternity; they could acknowledge their child in baptismal or birth records (something Pierre did as well); and they could recognize their children in public or private writings and educate them as such. Mothers of bastards could declare the paternity of fathers (which gave their offspring the rights of natural children) if they could prove they were living with the father when the children were conceived.[37] White fathers throughout the Natchez district recognized their mixed-race children as natural children. For instance, in the years before he died, the Natchez planter Adam L. Bingaman appeared before a notary to recognize his free black children as his natural children. He later bequeathed his estate to his surviving mixed-race daughter.[38] In 1818, Joseph Decuir, a white planter who amassed substantial holdings in Pointe Coupee Parish and at Cannes Brulees near New Orleans, officially acknowledged his six natural children, five by Françoise Beaulieu, and one by Claire Louise Quevain, both free women of color. Such a move provided his mixed-race children with claims to inheritance. He accumulated an estate worth 1 million dollars and left half of it to his six natural children (the amount permitted by law). In addition to what they inherited from their father, Decuir's sons by Françoise, Antoine and Leufroy, inherited his plantation, Austerlitz, from their mother. They also took his name. With property they received from both their mother and their father, Antoine Decuir (who would later marry Pierre and Rose's granddaughter, Josephine Dubuclet) and Leufroy Decuir became successful and wealthy sugar planters themselves.[39]

Although he had already baptized his daughters and declared his paternity, Pierre appeared before a judge with two witnesses to acknowledge the girls as his natural children, and he recorded the document in the Iberville Parish courthouse in order to protect them against future questions. Importantly, however, Pierre did not appear in the courthouse alone. Rose and Pierre—as co-narrators of their family story—acknowledged the children *together*. In so doing, they declared themselves a couple and a family before the law.

In February 1813, Pierre and Rose went before the parish court judge, John Dutton, who at their request and in their presence wrote the following acknowledgment: "Be it remembered that on this eighth day of February in the year of our Lord one thousand eight hundred and thirteen before me John Dutton, Parish Judge in and for the Parish of Iberville, came and appeared Pierre Belly and Rose commonly called Rose Belly free negro woman; both appearers inhabitants & planters of said Parish of Iberville which said appearers did *jointly and concurrently*, declare, acknowledge and recognize . . . [their children] to be the natural children of the said Pierre Belly and Rose Belly so called, free negro woman. . . . In testimony of all which at the request of said Pierre Belly and Rose Belly so called free negro woman, I, Judge, aforementioned have made this public and authentic act of declaration, acknowledgment and recognition and caused the parties to sign the same in the presence of Joseph Orillion and Joseph Hugat, witnesses."[40] By filing a joint acknowledgment, Pierre and Rose once again made the story of their relationship public and official, declared their children as their own, and insisted that the court recognize them as a lawful family.

When Rosalie, Marie Antoinette, Marie Françoise, Valerie Octavine, Marie Geneviève, and Héloïse became natural children, they also gained additional property rights—specifically, the right to alimony (akin to child support) for their care and claims to inheritance. Louisiana law provided that "nature and humanity establish certain reciprocal duties between fathers and mothers and their natural children," and they must provide these children with "alimony" sufficient for "their board and lodging, and to enable them to learn to read and write, and a trade." If their parents were dead, natural children could seek alimony from their parents' heirs.[41] In addition, unlike bastards, natural children could inherit. Fathers of natural children were limited in what they could bequeath to them, however. At the time that Pierre died, Louisiana law held that if a father had living parents or grandparents (ascendants), he could only bequeath his natural children one-third of his estate. If he had living siblings, his natural children could only inherit one half. Later, in 1825, Louisiana tightened its restrictions, and if the deceased had any legitimate relatives, however distant, natural children could only inherit one-third of their father's estate.[42] Although restricted in what they could inherit, the Belly girls would receive a portion of their father's large estate on his death, something they would not have gotten had they remained bastards in the eyes of the law.[43]

Perhaps because he could not bequeath his entire estate to his children or to Rose, Pierre donated, transferred, and sold some of his property to Rose, his daughters, and his sons-in-law before he died. Just as he did with other documents acknowledging his family, he also carefully recorded these transfers in the Iberville Parish courthouse. In the last years five years of his life, Pierre began to liquidate a portion of his estate, passing it on—in one way or another—to his mixed-race family. While he transferred real estate and slave property to his daughters and sold his son-in-law a tract of land and a number of slaves, Rose was the primary beneficiary.[44] In at least four separate transactions, Pierre donated a plantation and transferred several large, valuable, and productive tracts of land to Rose and made those transfers public and official by recording them in the local courthouse.[45] These donations of real property made Rose—a former slave and an unmarried woman—one of the largest landholders in the parish.

In the absence of legal authorization and recognition of their relationship, the Belly family used property to reinforce and publicly declare their bonds. Formal marriage was impossible for Pierre and Rose, and thus in the eyes of the law, their family was illegitimate. Yet as Dylan Penningroth has argued, "just as families made property, property helped 'make' family."[46] In Pierre and Rose's case, property facilitated the formalization of their familial connections to one another and to their children. Indeed, when Pierre transferred property to Rose and their daughters, he signified their ties to one another, strengthened those bonds through shared ownership, and made those connections official—and public—before the court.

In his will, Pierre provided for Rose, their children, and their heirs for generations to come. When he died in 1814, Pierre was the wealthiest planter and largest land and slave owner in Iberville Parish. The inventory of his estate included 5,593 arpents of land (valued at $40,000), ninety-six slaves (valued at $36,710), a dwelling house, cabins, a corn mill, a cotton gin, crops, cattle and horses, farm implements, furniture, other personal property ranging from china and cotton sheets to silver buckles and pistols, and a total of $3,857 in outstanding debts owed to him. Although limited in what he could give them, Pierre bequeathed much of this estate to Rose and their daughters. In his will Pierre gave Rose (to "enjoy in full property she and her heirs forever") one-fourth "of the net product of all the property and estate which I shall leave at my decease." In "consideration of the love and affection" he bore his six daughters, he bequeathed them one-fourth "of my estate to be equally shared and divided among them and by them and their heirs to be enjoyed forever in full property; for such is my will and intention." As prescribed by law, the remaining half went to his two surviving siblings in France, his brother, Jean, and his sister, Marguerite. In order to divide the property between the heirs, the court ordered the sale of Pierre's estate, which had a total value of $112,282. After Pierre's executors settled his debts and paid the court costs (together totaling $6,328), $105,954 remained for the heirs to divide between them. Pierre's mixed-race family would inherit half of his estate, and it was settled within a few years.[47]

The relative ease with which Rose and her daughters acquired their inheritance reflected the careful steps the couple took to declare the legitimacy of their family before the courts and to protect their family and family resources. Pierre's bequests to Rose and their daughters went unchallenged by his siblings. This was unusual. While white men frequently used their wills to bequeath a portion of their estate to their free black families and manumit their enslaved mistresses and children, white relatives of the deceased often attempted to deny the heirs their portion of the estate or their freedom.[48]

Yet no one challenged the legitimacy of Pierre's relationship to Rose and their children, and his will was not contested. Pierre provided for Rose, their daughters, and their future heirs, and his bequests made them some of the most prosperous people—white or black—in the region.

Rose similarly created bonds through her property and provided for her family after Pierre's death. In the years leading up to her death in August 1828, Rose began donating and selling land and slaves to her daughters.[49] In February 1828, shortly before she died, Rose appeared in the courthouse in Iberville Parish to donate her separate property and the property she inherited from Pierre (which, combined, amounted to several thousand dollars in value and included land, slaves, horses, cattle, and staple crops) to her six daughters. With this gift—officially documented in the courthouse—Rose used property to increase her bonds to her family before the law and provide for their future, just as she and Pierre had done before.[50]

BREAKING (AND MAKING) THE BONDS OF OBLIGATION

Rose benefited from her unofficial marriage to Pierre in a number of ways, materially and personally. Through sales, donations, and bequests, she received a considerable proportion of his estate, an estate large enough to help provide for the family for generations to come. At the eve of the Civil War, the Belly descendants remained some of the wealthiest residents in the parish. According to the 1860 federal census, the value of their combined real and personal property was just under 1 million dollars. This amount was greater than the total worth of all the free blacks in Charleston, South Carolina, and all the free people of color in the entire state of Tennessee.[51] Although Rose arrived in Louisiana as a slave, she and her daughters spent much or all of their lives as free people and enjoyed the benefits and protections of liberty. No other Belly descendant would be born a slave. Prominent white slaveholders such as Joseph Orillion and local officials such as Nathan Meriam served as witnesses and signatories to the land transfers, slave donations, and official acknowledgments Pierre and Rose registered in the Iberville Parish courthouse. By offering their signatures to certificates acknowledging Pierre and Rose's children or deeds transferring the official ownership of land and slaves from Pierre to Rose, Orillion, Meriam, and others recognized Pierre, Rose, and their daughters as a family. The close ties between the Bellys and other prominent men and their families had benefits and provided the Bellys with a broad network of allies. What is more, these relationships proved mutually beneficial, as Rose served as a large-scale creditor to Orillion and others who needed an influx of

ICI REPOSE
PIERRE BELLY,
NÉ À BLAYE EN FRANCE, LE 17 AOÛT
1738. DÉCÉDÉ LE 17 JUIN 1814.

MARIE ROSE BELLY,
NÉE À LA JAMAÏQUE
DÉCÉDÉE LE 14 AOÛT 1828,
ÂGÉE DE 70 ANS.

Pierre and Rose Belly (along with several of their descendants) are interred together in the St. Raphael Cemetery in Iberville Parish, Louisiana. Their family tomb is the largest and the finest in the cemetery. It is also separated from the other tombs and graves by several yards. St. Raphael Cemetery, Iberville Parish, Louisiana; photograph by the author.

capital. In particular, Rose's position as a propertied woman and moneylender allied her family to other Iberville parish families, white and black.

Rose also benefited from being an unmarried woman. As a single woman, she was not beholden to the restrictive laws of husband and wife that limited the rights of married women. Once married, wives forfeited their legal personhood. Under the unity of person principle (coverture) of Anglo-American common law (which governed jurisdictions outside of Louisiana), a married woman's legal existence was incorporated into that of her husband. Husband

and wife merged into one. This principle limited a married woman's ability to act at law. As a *feme covert*, she could not sue or be sued in her own name. She could not enter into contracts, act as an executor, an administrator of an estate, or a legal guardian, and she could not convey the property she brought to her marriage. Once married, a wife's personal property came under her husband's control, and he could spend it, sell it, or appropriate it. A husband could make all managerial decisions regarding his wife's real property, but he could not sell or mortgage it without her consent.[52]

When it came to the rights and duties of husbands and wives, Louisiana's civil-law system, which had its origins in Roman law rather than British common law, shared a great deal with Anglo-American common law. While wives in Louisiana could hold separate property, their husbands enjoyed the exclusive right to manage the property they held in community. Wives could neither enter into contracts without their husbands' permission, nor initiate lawsuits. The Louisiana *Civil Code* was explicit on the subject of marriage and family responsibility. A husband and wife owed each other "fidelity, support and assistance." A wife was "bound" to her husband, who in turn was "obliged to receive her and to furnish her with whatever is required for the conveniences of life, in proportion to his means and conditions."[53] The doctrine of marital unity articulated in the law of both Louisiana and Mississippi mandated a married woman's subservience to her husband.

Thus, Rose avoided many of the inequalities embedded in the southern legal system; instead, she bound others in relationships of obligation to her. As a creditor, she lent large sums of money (ranging from $1,600 to $2,000) to several white men in her community and capitalized on those investments. For instance, in 1813, she loaned Joseph Orillion $2,000, payable over eight years with interest.[54] She also entered into contracts and sued and was sued in her own name.[55] She served as a legal guardian for her minor children, and she bequeathed her property to those she wished.[56] She had exclusive control over her property, real, slave, and personal, and she engaged in business dealings in her own name. When those transactions went awry, she used the courts to recover the debts owed to her.

It is also possible that because of Rose's status as a single woman, landholder, and economic operator in her own right, she escaped some of the other trappings of a patriarchal marriage. In particular, the power dynamics within her particular marriage to Pierre may have differed from other, more traditional and hierarchical southern marriages. The patriarchal household served as the constituent unit of southern society, one in which men grounded their claims to masterhood. While the composition and wealth of southern households differed, male heads of households established their claims to autonomy and power by exerting authority over their dependents (women, children, slaves, and servants). The state recognized and supported the male head as the sole representative of the family in all economic, legal, and political matters. State power derived from a group of patriarchs; and in theory, dependents had no government but the household.[57]

As an able and independent woman and one in control of much of the family resources, Rose likely enjoyed considerable independence. She may have begun her relationship to Pierre as his slave, but soon after she gained her freedom, Rose held much of his property as her own, lent money to powerful men in her community, and operated in the marketplace as a single woman. She was not dependent on Pierre for her livelihood or the livelihood of her daughters. She was not duty bound (or legally bound for that matter) to obey him, either as his slave or his wife. Like all women (white or black) and men of color, she could not vote and thus could not speak for herself in formal political matters, but she did represent herself in the legal and economic arena. Through property-ownership and the independence it provided her, Rose (like other black women in the region) exercised a civic personality and claimed space for herself. Rose also instilled values of property-ownership and female independence in her daughters, as we will see below.

Rose was not the only woman of color in the Natchez district who benefitted materially and personally from an intimate relationship with a white man but avoided the more limiting features of a patriarchal marriage. William Johnson's one-time consort, Amy Johnson, operated as a *feme sole* in the Mississippi economy and owned personal and slave property in her own right. She also initiated lawsuits with some frequency. For instance, in 1816, she sued Alexander Hunter, a white man, for damages after a fight and received $25 in compensation.[58] For the next decade, she approached the local courts several times to fight her battles and sued whites and blacks to recover damages and settle disputes.[59] Women like Rose could not legally marry their intimate partners (and could not claim the protections of legal marriage), but there were advantages to remaining a single woman.

THE NEXT GENERATION

Like their parents and other families of color in the region, the Belly daughters and their husbands, children, grandchildren, and other descendants used property to make family and further solidify their ties to one another. They, too, documented those bonds—both familial and material ties—in multiple ways in the courthouse and weaved together stories about their families and their property. In so doing, they used the legal system to protect their family resources and provide their families with greater security. The Belly daughters—Rosalie, Marie Antoinette, Marie Geneviève, Marie Françoise, Valerie Octavine, and Héloïse—did something their parents could not, however. They married. Their marriages were recognized by law and symbolized their freedom. They chose their partners, formed families, amassed family property, and insisted on their right to safeguard those bonds. Moreover, their marriages to prominent free men of color connected their family to other families (and resources) in the region.

The Belly women married men from similar backgrounds. Each of their husbands, Antoine Dubuclet (married to Rosalie), Pierre St. Luc Ricard (married to Marie Antoinette), Cyprian Ricard (brother of Pierre St. Luc and married to Marie Geneviève), Zacherie Honoré, (married to Marie Françoise), Paulin Verret (married to Valerie Octavine), and George Deslonde (married to Héloïse), shared their wives' Afro-French heritage. For instance, the Ricard brothers were the children of Frenchman Antoine Ricard de Rieutard and Marianne *dite* Ricard, a woman of color. Like their wives, Rose and Pierre's sons-in-laws inherited land, slaves, and other property from their prosperous parents. With the property they inherited and accrued, coupled with their influence, talent for business, and their considerable legal skills, the Belly daughters and their husbands amassed substantial estates. Of the six Louisiana free blacks who owned more than fifty slaves in 1860, four were descendants or married to a descendant of Pierre and Rose.[60]

Through marriage, the Belly women merged their family and their family assets with other prominent, prosperous free families of color in the region. Their children did the same. For instance, Josephine Dubuclet, Rosalie's daughter, married sugar planter and son of Joseph Decuir, Antoine Decuir. Marie Antoinette's son, Antoine Ricard, married Leda Tournoir, a free woman of color from a prominent Afro-French family in Pointe Coupee Parish. Antoine Dubuclet Jr., married Claire Pollard, a wealthy free woman of color from the Decuir and Pollard lines. Pierre and Rose's grandchildren also intermarried; for instance, Pierre Cyprian Ricard, son of Marie Geneviève, married his cousin, Marie Rose Honoré, daughter of Marie Françoise. These marriages connected the Bellys—legally, socially, and economically—to the most prosperous free families of color in Iberville, Pointe Coupee, and West Baton Rouge Parishes, including the Tournoirs, Pollards, Decuirs, Patins, Porches, Severins, Lacours, Juges, Seldens, and Darensbourgs. They also remained geographically close to one another; often their plantations and other tracts of land bordered one another. For instance, Héloïse and Georges Deslonde's plantation, Cedar Grove, abutted land owned by Rosalie and Antoine Dubuclet.[61]

Just as Pierre and Rose had done before them, the Belly descendants and their kin made and strengthened family through property and used the courts to register their connections to one another, protect their assets, and achieve financial security. They did so in myriad ways. They sold, donated, and bequeathed land and slaves between families and recorded those transfers in the courthouse. The conveyance record books from the Iberville Parish courthouse includes hundreds of deeds, certificates, donations, transfers, mortgages, judicial sales, liquidations, partnerships, and agreements between various members of the Belly, Deslonde, Dubuclet, Honoré, Ricard, and Verret families. Indeed, these conveyance records double as a veritable family tree for generations of Belly descendants and related families.

The Bellys did not just participate in the world of gifts; they also participated in the world of loans, much like other free black creditors in the region. The Belly family and their kin entered into business transactions with one another and used the law as a mechanism to safeguard their dealings. For instance, in 1811, Rose Belly lent Jean Baptiste Lorrie, a white man, $1,600. Lorrie secured the loan with a mortgage for a tract of land (valued at $2,000). The debt went unpaid for several years, collecting interest, and in 1816, Rose appeared before the Iberville Parish Court and "transferred and assigned . . . a certain obligation with mortgage" to Antoine Dubuclet, her son-in-law. When the loan came due in 1820 and remained unpaid, Dubuclet sued Lorrie for $1,765, the balance of the loan plus "legal interest." He stood to make a $165 profit. The court found for Dubuclet and ordered that Lorrie pay the amount by October 20, 1820, a mere fourteen days after Dubuclet filed his lawsuit.[62] Both Rose and Dubuclet benefited from this arrangement; Rose recovered the money she lent Lorrie without the hassle of taking him to court herself, and her son-in-law profited from the interest.

The extended Belly family also deepened their bonds to one another in other kinds of transactions involving their assets and the legal system. They offered witness testimony in lawsuits involving contested land and slave sales, damaged or stolen property, and unpaid debts. When Georges Deslonde sued William Love, a white man, for killing his bay mare, his brother-in-law, Antoine Dubuclet, served as a witness for Deslonde, and Deslonde recovered the value of the horse, plus interest.[63] The family guaranteed loans for one another, acted as sureties, and secured bonds for those with outstanding debts or upcoming court dates. Indeed, Zacherie Honoré served as surety for a number of debts involving Maximillian Ricard.[64] They were signatories and witnesses to deeds of sale, acknowledgments, donations and gifts, and marriage contracts. For instance, Antoine Dubuclet and Paulin Verret witnessed Héloïse Belly and Georges Deslonde's marriage contract.[65] They requested that the courts convene official family meetings dedicated to discussing and allocating family resources. Delphine Ricard, the daughter of Marie Geneviève and Cyprian Ricard, petitioned the court in Iberville Parish to request a family meeting to discuss her emancipation from her family (as she was approaching the age of majority) and her share of the family property. Those in attendance included her parents and her uncles.[66] In addition, they also served as the administrators of each other's estates and as guardians and tutors overseeing the property interests of minor children with deceased parents. When those minors needed to go to court to recover debts owed to them, the guardians served as co-plaintiffs.[67]

Free families of color throughout the Natchez district similarly used property to make family. Like the Belly family, they too intermarried and utilized the legal system to protect their family's holdings and to create space for themselves. The Decuir, Porche, and Tournoir families of Pointe Coupee Parish, for instance, enlarged their family resources through marriage and served as sureties, witnesses, guardians, tutors, and executors for one another. They also sold, donated, and bequeathed real, slave, and personal property to various members of their family.[68] Mississippi barber William Johnson and his sister, Adelia Johnson, partnered with other free black families in Natchez. William married Ann Battles of Natchez, daughter of a white planter, Gabriel Tichenor and his former slave, Harriet. Adelia married James Miller, a free black barber and esteemed businessman in Natchez. The Millers and the Johnsons intermingled and intermarried with other prominent free families of color, such as the McCarys, who acquired a significant portion of their prosperity through inheritance from white fathers. The Johnsons, Millers, and McCarys were regular figures in the Natchez courthouse.[69]

INDEPENDENT WOMEN

Family relationships, of course, are sometimes fraught. Just as the Bellys used the courts to make family through property, they also appeared before the bar to fight over it. Even in their disagreements, when appearing in court, they spoke the language of property ownership. For instance, like Rose, the Belly daughters were well versed in the law. Unlike their mother, however, their marital status limited their ability to act at law and in the economy in their own names. Despite their status as legal dependents and in spite of prohibitions against married women's property ownership, however, many married women of color in the Natchez district owned and controlled property and went to court to safeguard it as de facto *femes sole*. What is more, the Belly women sometimes initiated litigation against their own husbands in disagreements over the management and distribution of their family property.

Free black women's lawsuits against their husbands for divorce provide an important framework for understanding how the struggle over autonomy and assets within free black marriages was fought in the terrain of law. For instance, Rosalie, the eldest Belly daughter, sued her husband for a legal separation, insisting that the court protect her from his abuse and ill treatment. Yet as was consistent with many wives' petitions for divorce and separations of property in Louisiana and Mississippi, a good deal of her lawsuit focused on protecting her property from her husband and removing it from his clutches.[70] In 1808, Rosalie appeared before the Iberville parish court claiming that her husband, Antoine Dubuclet, had beaten and whipped her at diverse times during their marriage. Because of his "cruel & malicious" temper, she told the court, she could no longer live with him. Most important, she wanted him out of her house and away from her property, and she demanded alimony sufficient to support her and their children. Louisiana wives like Rosalie could sue their husbands under certain circumstances and sometimes used the courts to leave their marriages. Women could petition for absolute divorce or for separation from bed and board, a legal separation in which neither party could remarry, but in the early antebellum period, women could receive a separation on limited grounds: for adultery, abandonment, or bigamy. Only later did divorce laws expand to include violence and cruelty.[71]

Dubuclet's "cruel & malicious temper" was not sufficient grounds for a legal separation, and given her family's incisive use of the legal system, it is unlikely that Rosalie was ignorant of Louisiana divorce law. But Rosalie deployed other tactics to separate herself from her husband. Such remedies indicate that her first priority was to keep Dubuclet from appropriating her property if she tried to leave him without a legal separation. Indeed, on the same day that Rosalie sued her husband, her father, Pierre, also filed suit against Dubuclet. Like Rosalie, he tried to eject Antoine from the Belly-Dubuclet household, although he used a different tactic. Pierre told the court he allowed Dubuclet to live as a tenant on his plantation "at his will and pleasure," and although he had asked Dubuclet to leave, the younger man had refused. What is more, Dubuclet had possession of four of his slaves. Pierre wanted to evict Dubuclet and reclaim ownership of "his lawful property." In his response, Dubuclet admitted that he was in fact in possession of the plantation and the slaves, but not as a tenant. When he married Rosalie, Dubuclet contended, Pierre had donated the plantation and the slaves to him and his wife. Pierre, he claimed, had no legal grounds to evict him. The court agreed. Dubuclet remained in control of the property, and he and Rosalie remained married. Both Rosalie and her father lost their joint endeavor to rid themselves of Antoine and protect their family property. But battles between married couples involving abuse and resources reminded husbands that their wives were also daughters, and if a husband mismanaged his household, her family might intervene.[72]

Rosalie was not the only Belly daughter to use the courts to attempt to wrest control of her property from her husband. Her sister, Marie Françoise, was more successful. Marie Françoise's lawsuit against her husband underscores the personal autonomy women gained through property ownership. In 1821, she appeared before the district court in Iberville Parish and sued her husband, Zacherie Honoré, for a separation from bed and board and a separation of property. She claimed to have brought four thousand dollars in property to her marriage to Honoré and accumulated another five thousand dollars through gifts, inheritance, and her own industry. But because of his "bad conduct," questionable business practices, and "excesses," this property was in danger. He even spent money allocated for her children's education, she claimed. Therefore, she wanted the court to separate her from bed and board and in property from her husband, allow her to manage her property with the rights of a single woman, and issue a judgment against him for the $9,150 he owed her. While waiting for the court to make its decision, she requested a temporary separation from her husband and asked to reside (along with her children) with her mother, Rose. She also had reason to believe, she relayed, that Honoré "will dispose of all their tangible property," and she requested that the court intervene to keep him from doing so. He had "already spent and gambled away a considerable amount and she is apprehensive," Marie Françoise said, "that if not prevented, that there will not be a sufficiency to satisfy the amount she expects to recover against him." Two white men, including a friend of the family, Joseph Orillion, appeared in court and corroborated Marie Françoise's claims.

That Marie Françoise sued her husband to protect her property and attempt to recover a verdict against him was not unusual. Many married women throughout the Natchez district commonly sued their husbands for separations of property and requested that courts issue injunctions to keep their husbands from selling or wasting their assets.[73] They did so most frequently in Louisiana because Louisiana's civil law protected the separate property of married women beginning in the colonial period, well before Mississippi did. If Louisiana wives believed that their husbands were mismanaging their property or if their husbands' creditors endangered their own assets, they could sue for a separation of property. This separation granted married women the legal rights of single women, allowing them to administer and control their own property free from their husbands' interference.[74] Mississippi did not have a separate property law for wives until 1839, when the state legislature passed one of the nation's first Married Women's Property Acts in response to the national banking crisis of 1837 when an upsurge of bankruptcies threatened the southern economic order. Supported in part by fathers hoping to protect the property they passed to their daughters from unsuccessful husbands, the law protected women and the property they inherited or earned through their own industry and labor from the financial mishaps of their husbands. Moreover, it allowed wives to possess and administer property in their own names free from their husbands' creditors. Even before 1839, some Mississippi wives of means established trust estates administered in equity (chancery) courts, using that vehicle to own and manage property separate from their husbands.[75]

Married women like Marie Françoise were incensed when their husbands made decisions about their property without their authorization, especially when the husband made bad choices or represented his wife's interests poorly. Wives' petitions for separations of property bring this issue to the fore most explicitly because these disputes had an important effect on power relations within marriages, particularly when husbands owned little property of their own and depended on their wives' property to support them. Both white and black women frequently employed the courts to take legal control of the family finances when their husbands could not manage the household themselves. Marie Françoise contended that she had put a great deal of effort into supporting her family and, like so many other wives, stepped in when her husband failed. Her husband, she claimed, contributed nothing to his family. In fact, he gambled away their assets, expected her to provide for him, and accrued significant debt. He squandered the family resources he was supposed to manage prudently, and, as a result, his creditors and their lawyers might seize her property to settle his debts. His bad decisions and rabid creditors endangered her assets. Her husband's poor management even threatened her children's education, and she wanted him as far away from her property as soon as possible. With her family's livelihood on the line, Marie Françoise took decisive action and sued Honoré.[76]

The Louisiana district court judge granted Marie Françoise a separation from bed and board and a separation of property, restored her to the legal status of a single woman, and granted her a judgment against Honoré for $9,150. The court also ordered Honoré to pay the costs of the lawsuit and give her "half of the acquets made during her marriage if there is any."[77] Now Honoré faced another creditor—Marie Françoise—and was obliged to pay his debt to her before paying his other creditors. Moreover, Marie Françoise became the head of her household, and Honoré was now bound in a relationship of obligation to her.[78]

With verdicts in support of industrious wives, judges and juries conceded women's competence. Granting wives legal separations and the right to control their property as *femes sole* indicates that, on some level, the courts found some women proficient household managers. In cases like that of Marie Françoise, it was the wife's property that sustained the household. Wives could plan their children's futures and education, carefully dispense money, manage their finances, and run a household. When granting a woman legal separation from her husband, the courts demonstrated a belief in female self-reliance.[79] Marie Françoise owned considerable property in her own name, operated as a single woman in the Iberville Parish economy, and continued to use the courts to protect her assets. For example, in 1828, she brought a claim against Louis Bousagne, a white man, for the $130 he owed her. She had "contracted to board Bousagne and to furnish him with two horses for the space of one year," but, despite her repeated "demands" for payment, he did not compensate her until she took him to court.[80]

Through her lawsuits, Marie Françoise also exercised a civic identity, and by heading a household, she claimed a space usually reserved for men. Through property ownership, and her use of the courts to protect it, Marie Françoise connected herself to narratives about economic independence and, ultimately, membership in the polity. She may not have had the vote, but it was she who directed her household resources, she who made all familial decisions, and she who represented her family in the public legal arena.

While the Belly daughters made property through family and aligned themselves through marriage with prominent families in three parishes, they were also notably protective of the assets they accrued on their own and inherited from their parents. Indeed, the youngest Belly daughter, Héloïse, appeared to have learned valuable lessons from her sisters regarding the protection of her property. Before she married Georges Deslonde, Héloïse insisted that Deslonde agree to a marriage contract that made the property she brought into her marriage her own and allowed her to manage her assets herself. Héloïse recorded this contract in the courthouse in Iberville Parish.[81]

The wealth and connections enjoyed by Afro-French families like the Bellys provided them certain economic and social advantages. Many gained significant property holdings through inheritance or gifts from French fathers. They were multilingual, literate, and highly educated. The Belly daughters, for instance, hired private tutors for their children and often sent them to France for additional education. Their familial connections to prosperous Frenchmen meant that some of the most prominent members of the white community acted as sureties and witnesses and served as godfathers to their children. Julien Poydras, a wealthy Pointe Coupee planter and politician, was the godfather of Antoine Ricard de Rieutard and Marianne *dite* Ricard's children. Afro-Frenchmen also used militia service as a pathway to elevated status, and they served in unsegregated battalions. The Ricard brothers, Pierre St. Luc and Cyprien, for instance, took up arms alongside whites (including their father-in-law, Pierre Belly) as part of Nathan Meriam's Eighth Regiment during the War of 1812.[82] The Belly descendants and kin traveled widely, and some married cousins in France. Their wealth, education, and connections to other prominent families, white and black, likely protected Afro-French families like the Bellys from some of the worst aspects of a racialized society.

Yet prominent people of color did not receive special treatment before the bar, and the tactics they used in court were not theirs alone. As evidence from the local court records in both Mississippi and Louisiana demonstrates, the lack of such connections and wealth neither impeded other people of color from approaching the legal system in their own interests nor did it bar the courts from hearing their cases and deciding in their favor. People of color throughout the Natchez district initiated lawsuits in the service of their own interests, whether born free or enslaved, of European ancestry or not, or wealthy or living on the margins. Like the Belly family, they used the courts to protect, enhance, recover, and bequeath their property, safeguard their families, ensure their futures, make equal bargains, and claim freedom and the rights and privileges of free people. Through their litigation, they directed their own lives, registered their voices in public, laid claim to legal personhood, and exercised a civic personality. In so doing, they claimed space for themselves in a world of white supremacy and black slavery. Not every person of color—free or enslaved—in the Natchez district went to court and staked their claim. A great many did not. But the ones who did provided other black people with a model (the language, litigation strategies, and claims to inclusion) and an example that they could and would employ in court in the long struggle for equality and rights—a struggle that began well before formal emancipation.

Afterword

FROM PROPERTY TO PLESSY

On July 29, 1872, Josephine Decuir, the granddaughter of Pierre and Rose Belly and the widow of the Louisiana sugar planter Antoine Decuir, sued John G. Benson, the owner and captain of the steamboat *Governor Allen*, for refusing her passage in the ladies' cabin because she was a woman of color. A week prior to filing her lawsuit, she had traveled on the *Governor Allen*, a steamer "engaged in the business of the common carrier of passengers," from New Orleans to her upriver plantation in Pointe Coupee Parish. On boarding the steamboat, she attempted to enter the ladies' cabin but was denied access by the boat's officers and "forced to remain in a small compartment in the rear," a compartment reserved for black people and "without the common conveniences granted to other passengers." Although "willing and able to pay for such privileges as the other cabin passengers had," she was "denied such privileges on account of her race." Decuir claimed that the ship's officers also refused her a seat at the table to eat her meals and only offered her a space on the floor to sleep. Because this "place was public and a place of passage for the officers of the said boat and everyone, and she could not on account of delicacy disrobe herself," she chose instead to sit up all night. Worse, this compartment "exposed her to the vulgar conversation of the crew." She was, she insisted, a well-educated and well-traveled woman, having lived for more than twelve years in Paris, France, and "in all her travels on different steamers and public conveyances both in this country and in Europe" she had never "met a like indignity as on the Steamer Governor Allen." Such treatment was humiliating in the extreme and "occasioned so much mental pain, shame, and mortification that her mind was affected." Importantly, she was "not guilty of any gross, vulgar or disorderly conduct," conduct that would have given the captain legal cause to refuse her "equal rights with the other cabin passengers." Rather, he denied her entry to the ladies' cabin solely because she was a person of color.

In contrast to black litigants in the antebellum period, Decuir deployed the language of equal rights and race. Refusing her a berth in the ladies' cabin, she insisted, constituted "illegal discrimination on account of color." In so doing, the *Governor Allen* violated Louisiana law: in segregating her, the owner of the steamer "denied her the equal rights and privileges granted to all persons under the provisions of Article 13 of the Constitution of Louisiana," a provision that guaranteed all people "equal rights and privileges upon any conveyance of a public character" and held that "all places of business and public resort . . . shall be open to the accommodation and patronage of all persons without distinction or discrimination on account of race or color." For these gross violations of her "equal rights and privileges," she demanded $75,000 in damages. In early 1873, the case went to trial. After listening to the witness testimony, which included several descriptions of the separate accommodations reserved for white and black passengers, accommodations not remotely equal in size, location, or quality, the judge in Orleans Parish issued a verdict for Decuir and granted her $1,000 in damages. According to the court, the material evidence supported her allegations, and the *Governor Allen* violated state law when it refused Decuir the same rights and privileges it accorded to white passengers. Benson appealed, and the Supreme Court of Louisiana affirmed the lower court's decision.

The climate of the postbellum era demanded a new language, one that shifted from property to race. Because they lived in a world of black slaves and white supremacy, Decuir's ancestors and predecessors necessarily exploited the sanctity of property rights as their primary means to access the antebellum courts. Yet in the postwar world, Decuir could make different claims— demanding equal rights generally and an end to discrimination based on race. White southerners' language also changed, however. With Emancipation and in the wake of the Reconstruction Amendments, former slaveholders could not use their own property rights as a means to control, restrict, and extract labor from people of color. In the absence of claims to ownership of black people, they deployed the language of race to deny African Americans access to public accommodations, as well as other rights and privileges. Indeed, as Benson admitted in court, he denied Decuir a cabin because she was "a colored person." His clerk, who dealt with Decuir directly, concurred, and when asked if he wished to sit in an integrated cabin, he testified, "I would not like to be put into the cabin with colored passengers. If they allowed Tom, Dick, or Harry to be set down at a table to eat with me and put into a room with me, I should certainly object to it myself and I judge that other people are a good deal like myself in that respect." It was "custom," he claimed, to segregate black and white passengers, and they did so "for the safety and comfort of their passengers."[1] To be sure, whites in the antebellum period were racist too; but the language of law made available to them and others to "claim judicially what is due" to them had shifted dramatically.[2] No longer did they have to articulate a defense of property that would satisfy nonslaveholding whites (with the corollary effect that property-owning black people might litigate too). Instead, former slaveholders severed the language of rights from its roots in the language of property and grafted rights onto race.

What was "custom" would become law, however, and it would come to be a national, rather than a merely local issue. The United States Supreme Court would soon strike down Louisiana's antidiscrimination law. In 1878, the court overturned the case by a unanimous vote on the grounds that the Louisiana statute violated the commerce clause of the U.S. Constitution: states, the court held, could not regulate common carriers engaged in interstate commerce (the *Governor Allen* traveled between Louisiana and Mississippi). In a decision that would help set the stage for the acceptance of separate-but-equal arguments used in cases like *Plessy v. Ferguson*, the Supreme Court decided that without congressional action, states could not require carriers involved in interstate commerce to provide integrated facilities even for voyages that took place within state borders (as Decuir's had).[3] And by the end of the nineteenth century, every southern state required segregated carriages for white and black passengers in railroad travel and with the new century began to segregate all areas of public life.[4]

When she sued Benson, however, Decuir—the first plaintiff in a constitutional case on racial discrimination in public transit to appear before the U.S. Supreme Court—drew on a rich tradition of black legal advocacy, lessons she had learned from her family and from black litigants throughout the Natchez district. People of African descent in the antebellum South went to court and made claims. They told stories to convey their cases in this public forum, undercutting the assumption that black people were not reliable speakers and thus should remain voiceless. They utilized the framework of reputation (a bedrock of southern social interaction) in making their presentations. They found advocates to present their cases in courts, and they were often successful. They sued over a wide range of issues, from debt actions and disputes involving property to lawsuits over personal status and freedom. And they arranged stable family relationships to protect family networks and property. In so doing, they protected their interests, claimed space for themselves in a violent and exploitative world, and exercised a civic personality. Through their claims-making and self-advocacy, people of color compelled white southerners to hear, recognize, and acknowledge those they regarded as other and inferior. Black litigants learned to make claims about justice, access, membership, self-direction, and civic inclusion in the antebellum era. When they made these claims, they expanded the boundaries of the possible.

This pre-Emancipation experience with private law was important, for it served as preparation for the long battle ahead for full citizenship and equality, a battle that would continue (and continues) to be fought in the nation's courts and beyond. Civil litigation—seemingly mundane lawsuits over property disputes, for divorce, or to recover unpaid loans—is also a significant component of the civil rights and racial justice struggle.[5] For these lawsuits involve claims about who counts, whose voices are worth hearing, and who can and should be included. They are claims on the state and claims to accountability and recognition. They are claims about the protection of human dignity.

Appendix

RESEARCHING
BLACK LITIGANTS

My research in lower court records stored in local courthouse basements and storage sheds in the Natchez district includes more than one thousand cases involving black litigants using law to protect their interests. The bulk of these records involve black plaintiffs and defendants in the civil courts. My dataset also includes some criminal actions, but in the courthouses in which I conducted my research, very few criminal records involving free blacks and slaves have survived. For instance, I found about sixty criminal actions involving free people of color, and most of those are from Adams County, Mississippi (where the records have been far better preserved). In the Louisiana parishes where I conducted research, nearly all of the criminal records from the first half of the nineteenth century have gone missing.

Trial court cases from Iberville and Pointe Coupee Parishes in Louisiana and Adams and Claiborne Counties in Mississippi roughly between 1800 and 1860 represent the bulk of the research materials for this project. In each county/parish courthouse, I began my research with the earliest extant records (this differed with each county, but all opened their doors and started hearing cases and keeping records in the territorial period), and I ended my research when each court closed its doors during the Civil War (when the Union army occupied the region). I chose these four counties because of their centrality to the region and their location along the Mississippi River, but, more important, because the trial court records from this time period still exist in these locations. This is unusual. Many southern courthouses were burned to the ground during the Civil War or suffered from floods that destroyed the early records. In other counties in the region, I found that the early court records had been discarded. Even in the four locations that

I selected for my research, the extant records are in danger of disappearing. For example, during one research trip, I found several boxes of cases in a shed on the outskirts of Plaquemine, Louisiana, where the Iberville Parish Clerk of the Court's office kept old personnel files. The boxes that held these cases and several hundred others from the late eighteenth and early nineteenth centuries had rotted, and the files were strewn all across the dirt floor. Many were mislabeled and placed into parish personnel files from the 1950s and 1960s. I gathered six trash bags full of legal records, brought them back to the clerk's office, dried them out, cleaned them off (as many were covered in bug and rodent feces), relabeling and filing them as best I could. I then took digital photographs of all the cases, as many involved criminal actions against free blacks and slaves. They also included succession records from free black families dating back to the 1770s. These records are still in the possession of the clerk's office, but unfortunately due to space problems may well have been returned to the storage shed.

Over the course of several years, I have developed a method for working with these materials. Because these cases are unpublished and unavailable beyond the county and parish court of origin, I began by traveling to the clerks' offices to locate the extant records. As there is often no index, finding cases that involve free black or enslaved litigants required examining each box or drawer of trial court records beginning with the earliest records and continuing until the beginning of the Civil War. As a research method, sampling every fifth (or tenth) box or drawer of cases would not produce representative results. Many of these records are not organized by date or type, and to get a sense of the presence of black litigants in the antebellum southern courts, the meaning of that presence, and how that presence might change over time, one must look through everything. It makes for a daunting task because it means reading through thousands and thousands of cases. But by law, the Mississippi and Louisiana courts had to identify the race of litigants and witnesses of color with the designation "fpc" if free and "slave" if enslaved. Of course, clerks and lawyers did not always do this. Some of the time court officials neglected to note whether or not the litigants and witnesses were people of color. Yet just because the designation is missing, we cannot assume that the plaintiff or defendant was white. Indeed, black litigants were common, and many sued more than once. Thus, court officials knew or knew of them, and it was not always necessary to designate their race. If the designation was missing, I attempted to ascertain an individual's status in other ways. In particular, enslaved litigants often lacked surnames, and litigious free blacks tended to appear in court repeatedly. If I was unsure of the racial status of a litigant, I cross-checked that person's name with a growing database I have created of free people of color living in Mississippi and Louisiana (data drawn from other court records, local and family histories, and census information). This system was not without its drawbacks, not least of all because people shared common names, such as "Fanny" or "William Johnson," but it did allow me to pinpoint most cases involving black litigants. Once I identified if the particular case involved a person of color, I took digital photographs of the entire case (a time-consuming but important step). Next, I read the case and entered a number of pertinent details into my database, including case number, name of complainant and defendant, filing dates, outcome (if known), race and gender of litigants, names of witnesses, lawyers, and judges, keywords identifying the type of case, and notes about the circumstances of the case. I also created individual files for the photographs of each case, so that later I could find them quickly and read and analyze them without confusion.

The courthouses of the Natchez district contain a significant and largely unexplored archive of black legal action. They also present a host of problems for scholars interested in questions of representivity. For instance, I have found ninety debt actions involving black plaintiffs. The question remains whether this should be understood as few or many, that is, how significant this body of material is with respect to what is "normal" in court, or in southern society more broadly. More to the point, the courtroom records themselves are kept in no reliable order, so we do not know what percentage of the original total is missing or has been discarded. Thus, instead of a quantitative analysis, I have opted for the more qualitative method of close reading. As a corollary, when I present numbers, I give them purely for their heuristic value, rather than using them to prove any points about statistical significance. Nevertheless, these extant cases reveal much about the networks black litigants formed, the language they used to petition the local courts, and the particular dynamics of African Americans' legal claims-making in communities throughout the Natchez district.

To supplement my dataset of cases from these four locations, I examined county court records from nearby parishes and free blacks' petitions to their state legislatures seeking permission to remain in the state or relief from restrictive legislation—records compiled in the Race and Slavery Petitions Project at the University of North Carolina, Greensboro. In addition, I examined extralegal sources such as newspapers, census records, family papers, church records, and slave narratives—records that provide a valuable window through which to view the broader matrix of black people's legal activities. For instance, local newspapers discussed court cases, announced decisions, and reported legal gossip. The personal papers of judges and lawyers prove particularly helpful for understanding the broader circumstances of a given lawsuit, a judge's motivation when deciding a case, or a lawyer's incentive to represent a black client. Many of these collections include testimony, letters to and from clients, judgments, warrants, contracts, depositions, and other legal documents. To broaden my sense of community-level adjudication and relationships, I also turned to church minutes and disciplinary hearings from Baptist, Catholic, Episcopal, and Presbyterian churches in the Natchez district. Finally, slave narratives helped me better understand how enslaved men and women interpreted the power of the southern courts in their lives and why they might turn to law.

Notes

ABBREVIATIONS

CRP HNF Courthouse Records Project, Historic Natchez
Foundation, Natchez, Mississippi

LLMV Louisiana and Lower Mississippi Valley Collection,
Louisiana State University Libraries, Baton Rouge

MBHC Mississippi Baptist Historical Commission,
Mississippi College, Clinton, Mississippi

MDAH Mississippi Department of Archives and History, Jackson, Mississippi

NARA National Archives and Records Administration, Washington, D.C.

NTC Natchez Trace Collection, Dolphe Briscoe Center for
American History, University of Texas at Austin

PAR Petition Analysis Record

RSFB Race, Slavery, and Free Blacks Petitions to Southern Legislatures
and County Courts, 1775–1867, Race and Slavery Petitions Project

INTRODUCTION

1. Witnesses in the civil suit mention pending criminal trials. However, the criminal records from antebellum Pointe Coupee Parish are missing, and thus it is impossible to know what the court charged them with (assault, attempted kidnapping, and so forth) or the outcome.

2. *Joseph v. Calmes et al.*, Records of the Ninth Judicial District Court, #1826, Pointe Coupee Parish Clerk of the Court, New Roads, Louisiana, 1857.

A note on citations and style: I cite the trial court record at the end of my summary of a given case. Because of the fragmentary and disorganized nature of the records (and lack of page numbers), I cite the entire case rather than specific sections of the case.

3. This book is informed by a rich and growing literature that engages lower court records. Much of the current historical scholarship investigating the relationship between

subordinated people and the law in the nineteenth century examines the legal system from the bottom up. Rather than focusing on statutes and appellate court records as the conclusive expression of the law (records that by their very nature tend to exclude the voices of subordinated people), scholars such as Laura Edwards, Ariela Gross, Hendrik Hartog, and Dylan Penningroth (to name but a few) have turned to the trial courts to emphasize how ordinary people (including people of color, poor whites, women, the elderly, and children) participated in and shaped local systems of law and governance. For examples of the growing scholarship on local courts, see Edwards, *The People and Their Peace*; Gross, *Double Character*; Hartog, *Man and Wife in America*; Hartog, *Someday All This Will Be Yours*; W. Johnson, "Inconsistency, Contradiction, and Complete Confusion"; and Penningroth, *The Claims of Kinfolk*. For an excellent discussion of the range of possibilities for examining slave law from the bottom up, see Gross, "Reflections on Law, Culture, and Slavery."

4. For a detailed description of lower court records from antebellum America and the challenges of working with them, see Edwards, *The People and Their Peace*, 22–24.

5. Edwards, *The People and Their Peace*; Gross, *Double Character*; and Turner, "Rights and the Ambiguities of the Law."

6. Ibid.

7. This book builds on and expands the groundbreaking work of Laura Edwards and Ariela Gross. In particular, Edwards and Gross demonstrate the extent to which African Americans (especially slaves) participated in their local legal systems, actions that shaped both the outcomes of cases and southern law more generally. Yet neither Gross nor Edwards focus on black litigants as parties to civil suits; rather, they examine African Americans' more indirect influence on the law and legal system, as well as on informal maneuvering. By contrast, the current study investigates black people's direct and formal use of the courts—hundreds of cases in which free blacks and slaves were parties to civil suits in their own name. See Edwards, *The People and Their Peace*; and Gross, *Double Character*.

8. For some examples of the scholarship on slaves and criminal law, see Flanigan, "Criminal Procedure in Slave Trials in the Antebellum South"; A. Nash, "Fairness and Formalism"; Bardaglio, "Rape and the Law in the Old South"; Ayers, *Vengeance and Justice*; Frazier, *Slavery and Crime in Missouri*; Campbell, *Slavery on Trial*; Hindus, "Black Justice Under White Law"; Hindus, *Prison and Plantation*; and Schwarz, *Twice Condemned*. In addition, when discussing black Americans' interactions with the legal system, recent studies of slavery and race in the antebellum South focus their attention on criminal law and restrictive legislation. For instance, see W. Johnson, *River of Dark Dreams*, chap. 8; Kaye, *Joining Places*, chap. 5; Ely, *Israel on the Appomattox*, chap. 6; and Forret, *Slave against Slave*. Historians examining free people of color's interactions with the southern legal apparatus tend to focus on restrictive legislation and whether or not white officials and communities enforced those laws. For recent work on free blacks and restrictive legislation, see Eslinger, "Free Black Residency in Two Antebellum Virginia Counties"; Nicholls, "Creating Identity"; and Rohrs, "The Free Black Experience in Antebellum Wilmington, North Carolina."

9. As Dan Berger has noted, "the primary institutions of American society—the government, the academy, and the media—have largely defined blackness in and through

criminality." See Berger, *Captive Nation*, 5. On blackness and criminality in antebellum America, see DeLombard, *In the Shadow of the Gallows*.

10. Beginning with the work of John Hope Franklin and in more recent studies by scholars such as Melvin Patrick Ely, Kirt von Daacke, and especially Amrita Chakrabarti Myers, we have seen examples of people of color (and free blacks in particular) using the southern civil courts to expand their liberty. In addition, Johanna Smith's dissertation on community, family, and identity formation traces several free families of color in West Baton Rouge Parish, Louisiana, and provides some examples of free people of color and their use of the law (namely through land and property transfers). While important, these studies do not provide a comprehensive understanding of African Americans' relationship to the antebellum southern civil courts (nor is it their intention to do so). See Franklin, *The Free Negro in North Carolina*; Ely, *Israel on the Appomattox*; von Daacke, *Freedom Has a Face*; and Myers, *Forging Freedom*. On Louisiana, see J. Smith, "Mulatto Bend"; and Brasseaux et al., *Creoles of Color in the Bayou Country*.

In recent years, however, we have seen the development of a rich and promising scholarship on enslaved people's lawsuits for freedom. For some examples, see Grinberg, "Freedom Suits and Civil Law in Brazil and the United States"; Kennington, *In the Shadow of Dred Scott*; Kennington, "Law, Geography, and Mobility"; Schafer, *Becoming Free, Remaining Free*; Schweninger, "Freedom Suits, African American Women, and the Genealogy of Slavery"; Twitty, *Before Dred Scott*; VanderVelde, *Redemption Songs*; and Wong, *Neither Fugitive nor Free*.

Much less is known about the legal claims of free blacks in the antebellum South, however. Martha Jones's work on free people of color's legal action in Maryland and their claims to citizenship is a notable exception. For instance, in her investigation of free blacks' applications for travel permits in antebellum Baltimore, Jones found that African Americans played a central role in the development of antebellum American legal culture. Moreover, these "everyday disputes" informed much broader debates about race, citizenship, freedom, and rights. See M. Jones, "Leave of Court." For a discussion of black citizenship in the wake of the *Dred Scott* decision and African Americans' use of trial courts in the *Dred* years, see M. Jones, "*Hughes v. Jackson*." Other new work suggests that free black people's use of the courts was not unusual. Kenneth Aslakson's examination of the New Orleans City Court between 1806 and 1813 demonstrates that free people of color were litigants in more than 300 of the 3,500 cases that came before the court in that short time period. Indeed, these cases ranged from property disputes to lawsuits over freedom. See Aslakson, *Making Race in the Courtroom*. Emily West's and Ted Maris-Wolf's recent books examine instances in which free people of color petitioned their state legislatures and county courts for enslavement or re-enslavement to shed light on the lengths free blacks went to maintain their familial and community ties. See West, *Family or Freedom*; and Maris-Wolf, *Family Bonds*.

11. I adopt this phrase from Brian P. Owensby's essay on freedom suits in colonial Mexico. He argues that while most slaves did not come before the courts to claim freedom or to seek better treatment, for some enslaved people, "the law represented an arena of countervailing possibility." See Owensby, "How Juan and Leonor Won Their Freedom," 78.

My thinking in this book is influenced by the rich work on the legal claims-making of Indigenous people, people of African descent, and women currently being conducted by historians of Latin America. In particular, I am indebted to the following: Bennett, *Africans in Colonial Mexico*; S. Bryant, "Enslaved Rebels, Fugitives, and Litigants"; de la Fuente, "Slaves and the Creation of Legal Rights in Cuba"; de la Fuente, "Slave Law and Claims-Making in Cuba"; Gross and de la Fuente, "Slaves, Free Blacks, and Race in the Legal Regimes of Cuba, Louisiana, and Virginia"; McKinley, "Fractional Freedoms"; McKinley, "Such Unsightly Unions Could Never Result in Holy Matrimony"; Owensby, "How Juan and Leonor Won Their Freedom"; Premo, "Before the Law"; and Wisnoski, "'It Is Unjust for the Law of Marriage to Be Broken by the Law of Slavery.'"

12. *Dred Scott v. Sandford*, 60 U.S. 393, 406 (1857).

13. Welke, *Law and the Borders of Belonging*, 3; emphasis in the original.

14. Ibid. For a similar definition of personhood, see DeLombard, *In the Shadow of the Gallows*.

15. Welke, *Law and the Borders of Belonging*.

16. Cobb, *An Inquiry into the Law of Negro Slavery*, 83.

17. Ibid., 315.

18. Ibid., 314.

19. Oakes, *Slavery and Freedom*, 69.

20. In her examination of law and governance in the post-Revolutionary Carolinas, Laura Edwards argues that because local authorities worked to "keep the peace" and emphasized social order and community regulation over individual rights, "everyone," including domestic dependents such as wives, slaves, and children, "participated in the identification of offenses, the resolution of conflicts, and the definition of law." Edwards, *The People and Their Peace*, 7. As Edwards shows, even those without individual rights could access (and influence) the local legal system in the name of protecting social and public welfare. Yet the claims many black litigants made in private law disputes—claims to property, recognition, accountability, and personhood—do not fit neatly into appeals to "the peace." By contrast, this book highlights the ways individual litigants forced others to acknowledge the immanent tensions in their legal system, tensions that a concept like "the peace" worked to conceal or deny.

21. An emphasis on the law as an instrument of hegemony—posited by Eugene Genovese in *Roll, Jordon, Roll*—is one of the most influential interpretations of the role of law in the slave South. According to Genovese, the law "constituted a principal vehicle for the hegemony of the ruling class"; slaveholders used the law to retain their power, but it enabled them to "disguise the extent to which state power" rested on force. See Genovese, *Roll, Jordon, Roll*, 25–49, quotes at 26.

22. My thinking here is influenced by Ariela Gross's and Laura Edwards's discussion of "hegemony" and "instrumentalism" in *Slavery and the American South*. As Gross and Edwards demonstrate, trial court records suggest that "the law is not an instrument that can ever be completely captured by one group"; instead, "daily practice makes the law look less definitive and less unified, by emphasizing actual people and all the contradictions that made up their lives." See Gross, "Reflections on Law, Culture, and Slavery"; and Edwards, "Commentary," quotes at 88 and 89, respectively. Indeed, "the law," in Gross's words, "has many makers." Gross, *Double Character*, 158. My own reading of trial court records from the Natchez district supports this position. In addition, Genovese's conception of law as a vehicle of the ruling class presumes that the

power of the planter elite was determinedly established. Trial court records, however, demonstrate that the power of elite white men was under siege—with threats coming from slaves, certainly, but also from their wives (who sued them for divorce and over property) and nonelite whites (who challenged them in myriad ways). Even slave codes themselves—codes dedicated to policing all aspects of black life—underscore masters' fears and anxieties about the power of enslaved people to upset social and racial hierarchies.

23. For another example of how antebellum white southerners' commitment to the protection of private property sometimes limited their ability to enforce white supremacy unilaterally, see B. Jones, *Fathers of Conscience*. On the post-Emancipation South, see Bernstein, "Philip Sober Controlling Philip Drunk"; and Wertheimer, *Law and Society in the South*, chap. 3. On the role private law played in negotiating the tensions between private property and maintaining racial hierarchies in the nineteenth century, see A. Davis, "The Private Law of Race and Sex."

24. In *Masters of Small Worlds*, for instance, Stephanie McCurry argues that planters "could not simultaneously establish the requisite legal and customary basis of household integrity and masters' authority without making more general claims. Rooted in notions of property rights, those claims extended inexorably to the household of every free and propertied man." McCurry, *Masters of Small Worlds*, 16. These rights, however, were also extended to free people of color.

25. On this point, I am grateful for the suggestions of Annette Gordon-Reed. See Annette Gordon-Reed, "Comment," Panel on "Enslaved Women Waging Law in the Nineteenth-Century American South," Society for Historians of the Early American Republic, July 2015, in author's possession. On the enslaved as a "person with a price," see W. Johnson, *Soul by Soul*. On enslaved people's claims to property and the role property ownership played in shaping kinship and community, see Penningroth, *The Claims of Kinfolk*.

26. *Ricard, FWC v. Hubeau, FMC*, Records of the Fourth Judicial District Court, #326, West Baton Rouge Parish Clerk of the Court, Port Allen, Louisiana, 1829. *Salvador v. Turner*, Records of the Fourth Judicial District Court, #1495, Pointe Coupee Parish Clerk of the Court, New Roads, Louisiana, 1844.

27. There is a voluminous historical literature on the Lower Mississippi Valley in the nineteenth century. For some examples, see Broussard, *Stepping Lively in Place*; Gross, *Double Character*; W. Johnson, *River of Dark Dreams*; Kaye, *Joining Places*; Moore, *The Emergence of the Cotton Kingdom in the Old Southwest*; A. Rothman, *Slave Country*; J. Rothman, *Flush Times and Fever Dreams*; and Wayne, *The Reshaping of Plantation Society*.

28. On slavery and the cotton economy, see W. Johnson, *River of Dark Dreams*; and Baptist, *The Half Has Never Been Told*.

29. In recent years, we have seen a number of new works examining slavery's relationship to capitalism, scholarship that positions racial slavery as the key component of early American economic development. Through forced migration, violence, and innovations in work regimes and production, white slave owners squeezed more and more labor from their slaves. Slaves' commodification and toil ensured that the United States would control the global cotton market. Indeed, slave-produced cotton—the ingredient that fueled the Industrial Revolution—guaranteed America's position as

a wealthy global power. See especially Baptist, *The Half Has Never Been Told*. See also Beckert, *Empire of Cotton*; W. Johnson, *River of Dark Dreams*; and J. Rothman, *Flush Times and Fever Dreams*. See also the recent review essay in the *Journal of the Civil War Era*: Nelson, "Who Put Their Capitalism in My Slavery?" Black people themselves, however, remain outsiders to the history of capitalism and slavery and often appear as interchangeable laborers and targets of violence and commodification. Examining African Americans' relationship to this world on their own terms calls into question the capacity of violence and domination to explain the totality of relationships.

30. Grandy, *Narrative of the Life of Moses Grandy*, 7.

31. Louisiana *Civil Code* (1838), Art. 35, p. 8.

32. Berlin, *Slaves without Masters*, chap. 10; Nieman, *Promises to Keep*, 24–29; and Schafer, *Slavery, the Civil Law, and the Supreme Court of Louisiana*, chap. 3.

33. Scholars disagree about the extent to which southern courts provided slaves with procedural rights and fair trials. For instance, Michael Hindus argues that "black justice" may have been "soothing to some slaveholders' consciences, but it was never intended to be just. And just it rarely was." See Hindus, "Black Justice under White Law," 599. For other scholars who argue that slaves in criminal cases did not experience fair trials, see Higginbotham, *In the Matter of Color*; and Higginbotham and Barbara K. Kopytoff, "Property First, Humanity Second." But scholars such as Daniel Flanigan, A. E. Keir Nash, and Peter Bardaglio argue that in criminal proceedings, the law treated slaves with fairness. See Flanigan, "Criminal Procedure in Slave Trials in the Antebellum South"; A. Nash, "Fairness and Formalism in the Trials of Blacks in the State Supreme Courts of the Old South"; and Bardaglio, "Rape and the Law in the Old South." As recent scholarship has shown, southern jurists formed part of a legal system dedicated to protecting white property and as such often granted slaves procedural due process. On this point, see Kaye, *Joining Places*, 168; and Schafer, *Slavery, the Civil Law, and the Supreme Court of Louisiana*, chap 3. See also Forret, *Slave against Slave*, chap. 3.

34. Schafer, *Slavery, the Civil Law, and the Supreme Court of Louisiana*, 64.

35. *Digest of the Laws of Mississippi* (1839), chap. XCII, sec. 59, p. 757. "List of Free Negroes and Free Mulattos," box 2E773, folder 5, NTC.

37. Berlin, *Slaves without Masters*, chap. 10; Nieman, *Promises to Keep*, 26–29; Sydnor, "The Free Negro in Mississippi before the Civil War"; and Sterkx, *The Free Negro in Ante-Bellum Louisiana*.

38. Scholars have long underscored African Americans' agency, resistance, and efforts to define their own lives, beginning with the work of W. E. B. Du Bois and Herbert Aptheker.

39. The rich scholarship on slave families, neighborhoods, religion, cultural practices, politics, and so on similarly shows black people organizing their worlds (as much as they could) on their own terms.

40. W. Johnson, *River of Dark Dreams*, 9. See also W. Johnson, "On Agency." Indeed, several scholars have pointed to the limitations of the concept of agency. For some examples of scholarship on African Americans in the slave South that push beyond the accommodation-and-resistance dialectic and suggest an alternative framework, see Penningroth, *Claims of Kinfolk*; and Kaye, *Joining Places*.

41. My thinking here is influenced by Premo, "Before the Law."

42. For a discussion of the limitations of resistance, agency, and autonomy, and for suggestions on how to move beyond these frameworks, see Kaye, "The Problem of Autonomy."

43. Penningroth, "The Claims of Slaves and Ex-Slaves to Family and Property," 1044.

44. On property as a set of "jural relations" and a "scheme of opposites and correlatives," see Hohfeld, *Fundamental Legal Conceptions*. For a recent discussion of the "bundle of rights" theory of property, see Baron, "Rescuing the Bundle-of-Rights Metaphor."

45. For a discussion of Louisiana's civil-law tradition, see E. Brown, "Legal Systems in Conflict"; Schafer, *Slavery, the Civil Law, and the Supreme Court of Louisiana*; Palmer, *Louisiana*; and Fernandez, *From Chaos to Continuity*.

46. In her study of slavery and law in the American South, Ariela Gross compared breach of warranty suits from antebellum Georgia, Alabama, South Carolina, Mississippi, and Louisiana, with the bulk of her evidence from Mississippi and Louisiana. She, too, found little difference between the common law states and Louisiana's civil law system. As Gross observed, "despite Louisiana's unusual Roman law heritage and its Civil Code, its cases exhibit struggles over the character of slaves and masters remarkably similar to those in common law states." See Gross, *Double Character*, 6–7. For a recent study that also challenges scholars to rethink Louisiana (and New Orleans) exceptionalism, see R. Johnson, *Slavery's Metropolis*. Nonetheless, scholars of Louisiana have long argued that because of its civil-law heritage and the influence of the French and Spanish on its slave system (among other factors), Louisiana was different than the rest of the United States—particularly in its treatment of free people of color. Notably, much of this literature focuses on New Orleans and does not directly compare Louisiana to other regions of the country. For instance, in his recent study of race in the New Orleans courtroom in the territorial period, Kenneth Aslakson argues that Louisiana's free people of color had "uncommon legal rights and privileges," and "enjoyed an unusually privileged position compared with free people of African descent in the rest of the United States" (5). Yet local court records from Mississippi show something different. Indeed, like Louisiana's free black population, Mississippi's free people of color similarly owned property, contracted, moved about freely, and sued whites and other people of color in court. What is more, enslaved people consistently sued for their freedom in Mississippi courts, and more often than not, those courts ruled in their favor. The legal action of free blacks and slaves in both Mississippi and Louisiana did not decrease over time, even as they faced increased restrictions. For a discussion of the literature that argues for Louisiana's uniqueness in regard to people of color, see Aslakson, *Making Race in the Courtroom*, 193n12.

47. On performance in the courtroom, especially of racial categories, see Gross, *What Blood Won't Tell*.

48. My findings about the consistency of black legal action in the antebellum period differ from those of Laura Edwards. Edwards found that by the 1840s, people without formal rights had fewer opportunities to participate in and influence localized law; state leaders and reformers had managed to construct a more centralized legal system—one less invested in the maintenance of "the peace" in local communities and more interested in protecting individual rights. Those without such rights—women, African Americans,

and the poor—no longer had the same access or influence. While in some areas of law, as Edwards aptly demonstrates, African Americans' influence waned after 1840, I have found that their claims to property rights and the constellation of rights related to property rights did not. Instead of being sidelined, black people demanded to be included in the rhetoric of rights-bearing individuals. See Edwards, *The People and Their Peace*, esp. part 3.

CHAPTER 1

1. In this chapter, I follow Natalie Zemon Davis's approach in *Fiction in the Archives* and focus less on the particulars of assault, boundary disputes, or bad business deals and instead concentrate my attentions on the "forming, shaping, and molding elements" of a story and "the crafting of a narrative." N. Davis, *Fiction in the Archives*, 3. See also Peter Brooks's and Paul Gewirtz's exploration of the role of narrative and rhetoric in the law. Like Brooks and Gewirtz, I view laws as "artifacts that reveal a culture, not just policies that shape the culture." Brooks and Gewirtz, *Law's Stories*, 3.

2. Cobb, *An Inquiry into the Law of Negro Slavery*, 233. In most southern states, enslaved people could only offer testimony in cases involving other people of color, most often in criminal cases involving enslaved defendants. However, Ariela Gross shows that while slaves could not testify against whites officially, their testimony came to court through whites' repetition of their words. See Gross, *Double Character*. See also Edwards, *The People and Their Peace*. On masters' views about slaves as liars and tricksters, see Greenberg, "The Nose, the Lie, and the Duel in the Antebellum South"; Gross, *Double Character*; and Osofsky et al., *Puttin' on Ole Massa*.

3. *Digest of the Laws of Mississippi* (1839), chap. XCII, sec. 59, p. 757.

4. Amsterdam and Bruner, *Minding the Law*, 110.

5. Ibid., 117.

6. Cover, "The Supreme Court," 4.

7. Bruner, *Making Stories*, 12.

8. In my thinking here, I am indebted to the work of James C. Scott. In particular, see J. Scott, *Domination and the Arts of Resistance*; and J. Scott, *Weapons of the Weak*.

9. Conley and O'Barr, *Just Words*, 6.

10. Marianne Constable's assertion that "law exists rhetorically" and "its claims often happen through words" influences my thinking on the relationship between law and the language of everyday life (2). Grounding the law in language denies it a special status that makes it impenetrable to nonspecialists. See Constable, *Our Word Is Our Bond*.

11. Macgill and Newmyer, "Legal Education and Legal Thought," 38.

12. Ibid., 40.

13. Anne Twitty has similarly shown that enslaved people were legally savvy and deployed both their understanding of formal law and a creative array of legal strategies to their advantage. How they acquired their legal knowledge is difficult to parse out, but as Twitty demonstrates, they had vast experience with the law and plenty of opportunity to learn through observation. For a description of how enslaved people in antebellum St. Louis gained the knowledge to sue for freedom, see Twitty, *Before Dred Scott*, chap. 2.

14. On the "localized" legal system of the post-Revolutionary South, see Edwards, *The People and Their Peace*. On the county as the central unit of government in the Old South

and the importance of local courts, see Sydnor, *The Development of Southern Sectionalism*, 33–54; Wooster, *The People in Power*, 81–107; Burton, *In My Father's House Are Many Mansions*, 28–30; Bardaglio, *Reconstructing the Household: Families*, chap. 1; and Gross, *Double Character*, 22–46.

15. *William Johnson's Natchez*, 757 (diary entry for Nov. 11, 1850). I am indebted to Gross, *Double Character*, for finding this entry. See Gross, *Double Character*, 26.

16. For a discussion of the role of court week in the culture of the Old South, see Isaac, *The Transformation of Virginia*; Sydnor, *The Development of Southern Sectionalism*, 34–35; G. Johnson, *Ante-Bellum North Carolina*, 148–49, 613–15; Roeber, "Authority, Law, and Custom"; and Gross, *Double Character*, 22–30.

17. For a discussion of African Americans' frequent observation of hearings, trials, and inquests, see Edwards, "Status without Rights"; and Turner, "Rights and the Ambiguities of the Law."

18. Gross, *Double Character*, 23.

19. Edwards, *The People and Their Peace*, 69.

20. On the communication networks of slaves, see Kaye, *Joining Places*; and O'Donovan, "Universities of Social and Political Change." On the flow of information up and down the Mississippi River, see Buchanan, *Black Life on the Mississippi*. On enslaved people's shared knowledge of strategies for suing for freedom, see Kennington, *In the Shadow of Dred Scott*; and Twitty, *Before Dred Scott*.

21. Miller to Johnson, Dec. 2, 1848, W. T. Johnson Collection, Mss. #529, box 1, folder 1, LLMV.

22. William Johnson's Journal, September 5, 1841, W. T. Johnson Collection, Mss. #529, LLMV.

23. On slaves' awareness and understanding of the laws that governed their lives, see Gross, *Double Character*, 41–45; and Twitty, *Before Dred Scott*, chap. 2.

24. *Mississippi Slave Narratives*, 3.

25. For instance, the narratives of Harriet Jacobs, William Wells Brown, and Frederick Douglass underscore the reach of the law in enslaved people's daily lives. See H. Jacobs, *Incidents in the Life of a Slave Girl*; W. Brown, *Narrative of the Life of William W. Brown*; and Douglass, *Narrative of the Life of Frederick Douglass*.

26. See chapter 3 for a discussion of William B. Griffith.

27. Lewis, *Out of the Ditch* (1910), Documenting the American South, University Library, the University of North Carolina at Chapel Hill, 2000, 16–21, quotation at page 21. http://docsouth.unc.edu/neh/lewisj/menu.html.

28. Ibid.

29. See chapter 3 for more on attorneys who represented black clients.

30. False River is an oxbow lake in southeastern Pointe Coupee Parish that was once a part of the main channel of the Mississippi River. It was cut off from the Mississippi around 1722 when flooding cut another channel.

31. Specifically, heads of households, single men, and widows could purchase public land in Michigan, Ohio, Indiana, Illinois, Missouri, Alabama, Mississippi, Louisiana, and Arkansas. See the Preemption Act of 1841, 27th Congress, Ch. 16, 5 Stat. 453 (1841).

32. Ibid.

33. Ibid.; emphasis added.

34. Kantrowitz, *More Than Freedom*, 239–44.

35. Ibid., 240.

36. Even after *Dred Scott*, some African Americans continued to exercise rights associated with citizenship before state courts. For an excellent discussion of black citizenship in the wake of the *Dred Scott* decision, see M. Jones, "*Hughes v. Jackson.*"

37. U.S. Constitution, art. IV, section 2.

38. Kennedy, "*Dred Scott* and African American Citizenship." On free blacks and citizenship before *Dred Scott*, see Allen, *Origins of the Dred Scott Case*, chap. 6; Link, *Creating Citizenship in the Nineteenth-Century South*; M. Jones, "*Hughes v. Jackson*"; Kantrowitz, *More Than Freedom*; Kachun, "From Forgotten Founder to Indispensable Icon"; Parker, *Making Foreigners*, chap. 2; and Perl-Rosenthal, *Citizen Sailors*. See also Hamburger, "Privileges or Immunities"; Novak, "The Legal Transformation of Citizenship in Nineteenth-Century America"; Finkelman, "Prelude to the Fourteenth Amendment"; and Kerber, "The Meanings of Citizenship."

39. D. Brown, "Citizenship, Democracy, and the Structure of Politics in the Old South." Before the Civil War, antebellum Americans tended to associate full citizenship with the franchise. "But," as Kate Masur states, "voting was considered less an individual right than a privilege to which only those with certain kinds of elevated status—property holders or white men, for example—were entitled." Masur, *An Example for All the Land*, 5.

40. Kantrowitz, *More Than Freedom*, 5.

41. Riffel, *Iberville Parish History*, 13–14.

42. For an extended discussion of the Belly family, see chapter 7.

43. *Salvador v. Turner*, Records of the Fourth Judicial District Court, #1495, Pointe Coupee Parish Clerk of the Court, New Roads, Louisiana, 1844.

44. For instance, in 1842, Judge Deblieux purchased 152 acres from the U.S. General Land Office; in 1844, he purchased another 36 acres in partnership with one Joseph Connand. See U.S. Bureau of Land Management, General Land Office Records, 1796–1907, http://www.ancestry.com/.

45. Natchez district courts routinely sent commissions to take depositions from distant witnesses. I discuss this phenomenon in more depth in chapter 3.

46. Northup, *Twelve Years a Slave*.

47. *Elias, man of color v. Bell*, Adams County, Mississippi, 1817, Records of the Circuit Court, Group 1810–19, box 25, file 124, CRP HNF. For other examples of African Americans claiming they had been kidnapped and suing for their freedom (some successfully), see *Mary Ann v. Kempe*, Adams County, Mississippi, 1818, Records of the Circuit Court, Group 1810–19, box 43, file 68, CRP, HNF; *Springer v. Hundley*, Adams County, Mississippi, 1822, Records of the Circuit Court, Group 1820–29, box 13, file 70, CRP, HNF; *Tennet v. Smith*, Adams County, Mississippi, 1823, Records of the Circuit Court, Group 1820–29, box 23, file 56, CRP, HNF; and *Woodall v. Sexton*, Adams County, Mississippi, 1826, Records of the Circuit Court, Group 1820–29, box 37, file 36, CRP, HNF.

48. A. Rothman, *Slave Country*.

49. For a discussion of kidnapping and freedom suits, see chap. 6. On the kidnapping of free African Americans, see Berlin, *Generations of Captivity*, 167–68; Berlin, *The Making of African America*, 102; Bell, "'Thence to Patty Cannon's'"; Deyle, *Carry Me Back*, 17, 29,

39, 178; Gudmestad, *A Troublesome Commerce*, 62, 73–5, 159–60; G. Nash and Soderlund, *Freedom by Degrees*, 196–201; and Wilson, *Freedom at Risk*.

50. On Richard Cooper's background, his material and spiritual life, and his relationship to the Quaker community (and those who helped chase down his son's kidnappers), see Gall et al., "Navigation and Negotiation."

51. Slaveholders were not the only people to wield the stereotype of the debauched "negro trader" to their advantage. African Americans suing for their freedom also employed the image of the slave speculator on their own behalf. In lawsuits involving kidnapping, the slave trader often emerged as the ultimate villain. For instance, in 1828, John Neal, a man of color, claimed that the slave speculator Branch Jordon held him illegally as his slave and sued him for his freedom in Mississippi. In his petition, Neal described Jordan as a "transient person" and a "dealer in slaves." Although he offered no additional proof of his free status, the court granted his request for a writ of habeus corpus. The fact that he was held as a slave by an allegedly dishonest and transient slave speculator may have been sufficient evidence of his kidnapping. *Neal v. Jordon*, Adams County, Mississippi, 1828, Records of the Circuit Court, Group 1820–29, box 56, file 33, CRP, HNF.

52. On slave traders as leaders of their communities, see Tadman, *Speculators and Slaves*, chap 7. On the stereotypes of slave traders and traders as scapegoats, see Deyle, *Carry Me Back*, 9–10; Gudmestad, *A Troublesome Commerce*, 56; and W. Johnson, *Soul by Soul*, 24–25.

53. The court's verdict in favor of Cooper was not unusual. My research includes 128 instances of enslaved people suing for their freedom in the Natchez district. Of that total, sixty-one were successful (about half of the time). For some representative examples of freedom suits, see *Hamm v. Green*, Adams County, Mississippi, 1819, Records of the Circuit Court, Group 1810–19, box 43, file 76, CRP, HNF; *Lewis and Lewis v. Clark and Slater*, Adams County, Mississippi, 1822, Records of the Circuit Court, Group 1820–29, box 13, file 39, CRP, HNF; and *Phoebe, John, and Sally v. Boyer*, Adams County, Mississippi, 1826, Records of the Circuit Court, Group 1820–29, box 34, file 82, CRP, HNF.

54. *Cooper v. Briscoe*, Adams County, Mississippi, 1811, Records of the Circuit Court, Group 1810–19, box 43, file 22, CRP, HNF.

55. After Cooper's trial in Natchez, he returned to Kent County and moved to Camden. The 1820 federal census shows Cooper in Camden with a household of five free persons (two adults and three children) and "engaged in agriculture." Fourth Census of the United States, 1820, Records of the Bureau of the Census, Record Group 29, NARA, http://www.ancestry.com/.

56. Because of its colonial heritage, Louisiana practiced the French legal custom of calling a married woman by her maiden name, often followed by the designation "wife of."

57. Several scholars investigating southern divorce have demonstrated that to be successful, petitioners had to show that they behaved according to the accepted marital/gender conventions of their time. For some examples, see especially Bardaglio, *Reconstructing the Household*; Broussard, "Naked before the Law"; Bynum, *Unruly Women*; Censer, "'Smiling through Her Tears'"; and Edwards, *The People and Their Peace*. Husbands

and wives in northern states used the same tactics when suing their spouses for divorce. They, too, highlighted their ideal spousal behavior to their greater advantage in their divorce petitions. See Basch, *Framing American Divorce*, 99–140; Cott, *Public Vows*, 48–49; and Hartog, *Man and Wife in America*, 93–166. Moreover, this tactic of exhibiting proper behavior when petitioning for a divorce or legal separation dates back to the colonial period, as Cornelia Hughes Dayton demonstrates. See Dayton, *Women before the Bar*.

58. *Brout v. Heno*, Orleans Parish, 1824, in in RSFB, Series II, Part F: Louisiana, PAR #20882047.

59. *Richards v. McDougald*, West Baton Rouge Parish, Louisiana, 1826, in RSFB, Series II, Part F, PAR #20882632. For some examples of women calling on their qualities as ideal wives to sue for divorce in Mississippi, see *McLendon v. McLendon*, Adams County, Mississippi, 1834, Records of the Circuit Court, Group 1830–39, box 17, file 71, CRP, HNF; *Smith v. Smith*, Claiborne County, Mississippi, 1857, Records of the Claiborne County Chancery Court, #6, Claiborne County Courthouse, Port Gibson, Mississippi; *Hoel v. Hoel*, Claiborne County, Mississippi, 1857, Records of the Claiborne County Chancery Court, #9, Claiborne County Courthouse, Port Gibson, Mississippi. For Louisiana, see *Black v. Black*, West Feliciana Parish, Louisiana, 1825, in RSFB, Series II, Part F, PAR #20882519; *Allyn v. Allyn*, West Feliciana Parish, Louisiana, 1829, in RSFB, Series II, Part F, PAR #20882942; *Overbay v. Overbay*, West Feliciana Parish, Louisiana, 1834, in RSFB, Series II, Part F, PAR #20883417.

60. *Bienville v. Bienville*, East Baton Rouge Parish, Louisiana, 1836, in RSFB, Series II, Part F, PAR #20883605.

61. On myths about black women's sexuality, see especially White, *Ar'n't I a Woman?*; and Morgan, *Laboring Women*. For the centrality of gender and sexuality to the development of laws supporting racial slavery, see K. Brown, *Good Wives, Nasty Wenches, and Anxious Patriarchs*.

62. Davis was not the only black woman to depict herself as a chaste and virtuous wife in her divorce petition. Other African-descended women employed this formula too. For instance, see *Walker v. Villiar, her husband*, Records of the Fourth Judicial District Court, #2092, Iberville Parish Clerk of the Court, Plaquemine, Louisiana, 1843; and *Lauvee v. Leblanc*, Records of the Fourth Judicial District Court, #393, Pointe Coupee Parish Clerk of the Court, New Roads, Louisiana, 1819.

63. Louisiana law provided that "the several districts in this state shall have jurisdiction of all suits for the partition or sale of any property lying within the limits of the district where the suit is brought, and held in common between several part owners, or in which several persons may have an interest, . . . notwithstanding any or all of the parties, to be made defendants, be minors, or persons residing without the limits of this state." *Louisiana Digest*, Art. 541, p. 88–89.

64. *Davis v. Edmonds*, St. Landry Parish, Louisiana, 1847, in RSFB, Series II, Part F, PAR #20884719 and PAR #20885023.

65. Constable, *Our Word Is Our Bond*, 42.

66. Suggs, *Whispered Consolations*, 27.

67. Ibid., 28.

68. H. Jacobs, *Incidents in the Life of a Slave Girl*, 5–6; emphasis in original. On the centrality of law in slave narratives, see Suggs, *Whispered Consolations*. On slaves'

awareness of the law and the law's influence over their lives, see Gross, *Double Character*, 41–45.

69. The "Extract" is included in the London edition of Brown's narrative. W. Brown, *Narrative of the Life of William W. Brown*, 148–62.

70. W. Brown, *Clotel; or, The President's Daughter*, 41–42. For a discussion of the importance of law in Jacobs's slave narrative and Brown's novel, see Suggs, *Whispered Consolations*, chap. 1.

71. J. Jacobs, "A True Tale of Slavery," 140, Documenting the American South, University Library, the University of North Carolina at Chapel Hill, 2000. http://docsouth.unc.edu/neh/jjacobs/menu.html.

72. H. Jacobs, *Incidents in the Life of a Slave Girl*, 55.

73. Bibb, *Narrative of the Life and Adventures of Henry Bibb, an American Slave, Written by Himself* (1849), Documenting the American South, University Library, the University of North Carolina at Chapel Hill, 2000, 64, 62. http://docsouth.unc.edu/neh/bibb/menu.html.

74. I am indebted to Sally Engle Merry's exceptional work, *Getting Justice and Getting Even*, for helping me shape my thoughts about the legal consciousness of ordinary people and the ways disputes, in her words, represent "a contest over meanings in which the law provides one possible set of meanings." See Merry, *Getting Justice and Getting Even*, 6.

75. DeLombard, *Slavery on Trial*, 24.

76. Ibid.

77. Ibid.

78. Ibid.

79. *Salvador v. Turner*.

80. Amsterdam and Bruner, *Minding the Law*, 111; emphasis in the original.

CHAPTER 2

1. The final outcome of Fanny's lawsuit is not known. *Fanny v. Gueho*, Records of the Fourth Judicial District Court, #539, Pointe Coupee Parish Clerk of the Court, New Roads, Louisiana, 1822.

2. Edwards, *The People and Their Peace*, chap. 4.

3. Gross, *Double Character*. See also Twitty, "The Court of Public Opinion?"

4. Edwards, *The People and Their Peace*, chap. 4. A number of other scholars have explored the importance of personal reputation and character evidence in the nineteenth-century southern courtroom, especially for subordinated peoples such as African Americans. In some circumstances, as Kirt von Daacke and Ted Maris-Wolf have recently demonstrated, African Americans could rely on their reputations as dependable or upright to circumvent restrictive legislation (such as removal laws). See von Daacke, *Freedom Has a Face*; and Maris-Wolf, *Family Bonds*. In addition, Kelly Kennington demonstrates that a reputation for living as a free person in one's community could influence the outcome of a freedom suit. See Kennington, "'Just as Free as You Are'"; and Kennington, *In the Shadow of Dred Scott*. On reputation and the law more generally, see Friedman, *Guarding Life's Dark Secrets*.

5. Potter, *The South and the Sectional Conflict*, 16.

6. On the importance of personalism to free blacks, see especially von Daacke, *Freedom Has a Face*; and M. Johnson and Roark, *Black Masters*, 96–97.

7. Edwards, *The People and Their Peace*, 102.

8. *State of Mississippi v. Nero*, Adams County, Mississippi, 1818, Records of the Circuit Court, Habeas Corpus files, box 1, CRP, HNF. William Griffith commanded respect in Natchez and throughout the state. He ran the best-regarded law practice in Natchez alongside his partner, John A. Quitman, a man who would later serve as the governor of Mississippi and as a judge on the High Court of Errors and Appeals. Griffith represented dozens of free and enslaved African Americans in cases that ranged from criminal actions to lawsuits for freedom. For other instances in which Griffith represented people of color, see *Elias v. Bell*, Adams County, Mississippi, 1818, Records of the Circuit Court, Group 1810–19, box 35, file 124, CRP, HNF; *de la Croux v. Reinhart*, Adams County, Mississippi, 1822, Records of the Circuit Court, Group 1820–29, box 13, file 77, CRP, HNF; and *Smith v. Welsh*, Adams County, Mississippi, 1827, Records of the Circuit Court, Group 1820–29, box 51, file 77, CRP, HNF.

9. On the narrow space for free blacks within the positive good theory of slavery, see Berlin, *Slaves without Masters*, 188–95.

10. Gould, *Chained to the Rock of Adversity*, xxx.

11. The *Natchez*, March 5, 1831, quoted in Gould, *Chained to the Rock of Adversity*, xxx.

12. Petition of H. L. Foules et al. to the Mississippi State Legislature, 1859, in RSFB, Series I: Legislative Petitions, PAR #11085912.

13. On African Americans' "certificates of character," assurances from whites that the petitioner had a "good" character, see Maris-Wolf, *Family Bonds*, 50–52.

14. Petition of Ann Caldwell to the Mississippi State Legislature, 1859, in RSFB, Series I: Legislative Petitions, PAR #11085923. See also Petition of Agnes Earhart to the Mississippi State Legislature, 1859, in RSFB, Series I: Legislative Petitions, PAR #11085911. On free blacks petitioning to remain in the state and securing the support of white allies by acting respectably, see von Daacke, *Freedom Has a Face*; Maris-Wolf, *Family Bonds*; West, *Family or Freedom*, chaps. 2 and 5; and Wolf, *Almost Free*. On free black women securing the support of white men, see Broussard, "Stepping Lively in Place."

15. Petition of L. G. Rowan et al. to the Mississippi State Legislature, 1830, in RSFB, Series I: Legislative Petitions, PAR #11083008. It is unclear how Caldwell and Barland attained the support of so many white southerners—their petitions collectively contained the signatures of more than one hundred whites. On this, the records remain silent. However, because both women emphasize their reputations for "great industry," it is likely that Caldwell and Barland developed skills that white southerners valued. For instance, it is possible that Caldwell offered her services as a nurse to other white families.

16. Harriet Battles received similar support from those around her when she sought to remain in the state of Mississippi after her owner, Gabriel Tichenor, freed her. Tichenor, who was probably the father of her child, Ann Battles, sold Harriet a tract of land in Natchez for two dollars and continued to offer her his assistance. What is more, in 1832 (twelve years after her manumission) Harriet Battles received a certificate from the Adams County Court permitting her to remain in Mississippi because of her "good character and honest deportment." W. T. Johnson and Family Collection, Mss. #529,

folder 16, LLMV. On Tichenor and Battles, see also Broussard, "Stepping Lively in Place," 28.

17. *Tom v. Porche*, Records of the Ninth Judicial District Court, #1126, Pointe Coupee Parish Clerk of the Court, New Roads, Louisiana, 1854. For a similar example, see *Debby v. Campbell*, Adams County, Mississippi, 1821, Records of the Circuit Court, Group 1820–29, box 6, file 102, CRP, HNF.

18. *Colston v. Littell and Arden*, St. Landry Parish, Louisiana, 1821, in RSFB, Series II, Part F, PAR #20882103.

19. Hayden's petition to the state legislature is missing an outcome, but it is clear from Hayden's slave narrative that the legislature granted his request. Petition of William Hayden to the Mississippi State Legislature, 1829, in RSFB, Series I: Legislative Petitions, PAR #11082904. See also Hayden, *Narrative of William Hayden*. For a similar case, see Petition of William Parker to the Mississippi State Legislature, n.d., in RSFB, Series I: Legislative Petitions, PAR #11000008.

20. On skilled black laborers and their position in the slave South, see M. Johnson and Roark, *Black Masters*, 28, 57–59; and Hanger, *Bounded Lives, Bounded Places*, chap. 2.

21. Bristol, *Knights of the Razor*.

22. Hayden, *Narrative of William Hayden*, 97.

23. W. T. Johnson and Family Collection, Mss. #529, folder 39, Ledger, Feb. 1837 - Oct. 1841, LLMV. See also Davis and Hogan, *The Barber of Natchez*.

24. William Johnson's Journal, September 5, 1841, W. T. Johnson and Family Collection, Mss. #529, LLMV.

25. Quoted in Davis and Hogan, *The Barber of Natchez*, 265–66. See also Natchez *Courier*, June 20, 1851; *The Natchez Free Trader*, June 18, 1851; Woodville *Republican*, June 24, 1851. On William Johnson and his family, see Davis and Hogan, *The Barber of Natchez*; Gould, *Chained to the Rock of Adversity*; and Hogan and Davis, *William Johnson's Natchez*.

26. Davis and Hogan, *The Barber of Natchez*, chap. 22; Hogan and Davis, *William Johnson's Natchez*; and Gross, *Double Character*, 63.

27. Natchez *Courier*, June 20, 1851. See also Davis and Hogan, *The Barber of Natchez*, 265–66; and Gross, *Double Character*, 63.

28. In a letter to Johnson in late 1849, William Moseley wrote that "every honest man knows B. Winn to be a black hearted wretch and those in co. with him no better." Moseley to Johnson, November 28, 1849, W. T. Johnson and Family Collection, Mss. #529, box 1, folder 1, LLMV. Newspaper accounts of Winn's trials echoed Moseley's opinion of Winn. The Natchez *Courier* also implicated Winn as Johnson's murderer and said that he "repeatedly . . . threaten[ed] Johnson's life." See Natchez *Courier*, June 20, 1851.

29. On the circumstances that led to Johnson's death, see Davis and Hogan, *The Barber of Natchez*; and Hogan and Davis, *William Johnson's Natchez*.

30. *State of Mississippi v. Burwell*, Adams County, Mississippi, 1822, Records of the Circuit Court, Group 1820–29, box 12, file 32, CRP, HNF; *State of Mississippi v. Burwell*, Adams County, Mississippi, 1818, Records of the Circuit Court, Group 1810–19, box 40, file 80, CRP, HNF; *State of Mississippi v. Burwell*, Adams County, Mississippi, 1818, Records of the Circuit Court, Group 1810–19, box 40, file 81, CRP, HNF; and *State of Mississippi v. Burwell*, Adams County, Mississippi, 1819, Records of the Circuit Court, Group 1820–29, box 1, file 27, CRP, HNF.

31. *State of Louisiana v. Fleming*, unprocessed materials, Iberville Parish Clerk of the Court, Plaquemine, Louisiana, 1833. For other cases in which free blacks were charged with insulting whites, see *State of Louisiana v. Louise*, unprocessed materials, Iberville Parish Clerk of the Court, Plaquemine, Louisiana, 1842; and *State of Louisiana v. Marguerite and Julian*, unprocessed materials, Iberville Parish Clerk of the Court, Plaquemine, Louisiana, 1842. I found these cases in a storage shed on the outskirts of Plaquemine, Louisiana, where the Iberville Parish Clerk of the Court's office kept old personnel files. For lack of a better, more precise term, I indicate that these records are "unprocessed materials."

32. Debt collectors, court bailiffs, and executioners faced far more vilification than people of other occupations such as farmers and craftspeople because they made arrests, delivered summonses, hanged criminals, seized property, and collected taxes and debts. See Moogk, "'Thieving Buggers' and 'Stupid Sluts,'" 531–33.

33. Petition of John Motton, East Baton Rouge Parish, Louisiana, 1838, in RSFB, Series II, Part F, PAR #20883808.

34. Ibid.

35. Louisiana *Digest* (1842), Art. 40, p. 57.

36. *State of Louisiana v. Fleming*. See also *Byrenheidt v. Fleming*, Records of the Fourth Judicial District Court, #1286, Iberville Parish Clerk of the Court, Plaquemine, Louisiana, 1833. The court found for Byrenheidt and ordered Fleming to pay him $379.00. It appears that Fleming owed lots of people money, as at least nine other white men and women sued Fleming over the course of the next year to recover debts. Fleming only won one of those cases. Still, white men continued to lend him money, testify on his behalf, and posted security bonds for him in his lawsuits. For examples of the lawsuits against Fleming, see *Martin v. Fleming*, Records of the Fourth Judicial District Court, #1405, Iberville Parish Clerk of the Court, Plaquemine, Louisiana, 1834; *Lambremont v. Fleming*, Records of the Fourth Judicial District Court, #1438, Iberville Parish Clerk of the Court, Plaquemine, Louisiana, 1834; and *Leblanc v. Fleming*, Records of the Fourth Judicial District Court, #1439, Iberville Parish Clerk of the Court, Plaquemine, Louisiana, 1834.

37. Davis and Hogan, *The Barber of Natchez*; Gould, *Chained to the Rock of Adversity*; and Hogan and Davis, *William Johnson's Natchez*.

38. 1830 U.S. Census, Iberville, Louisiana, Microfilm Publication M19, Roll 43, NARA. For a description of Lacour's property, see also *Ingledove v. Lacour*, Records of the Fourth Judicial District Court, #1065, Iberville Parish Clerk of the Court, Plaquemine, Louisiana, 1839.

39. For example, see *Lacour v. Landry*, Records of the Fourth Judicial District Court, #1070, Iberville Parish Clerk of the Court, Plaquemine, Louisiana, 1831 (Lacour successfully sued Valerin Landry, a white man, to recover damages for killing his horse); and *Lacour v. Landry*, Records of the Fourth Judicial District Court, #2154, Iberville Parish Clerk of the Court, Plaquemine, Louisiana, 1844 (Lacour successfully recovered a debt from Camile Landry, another white man).

40. *Ingledove v. Lacour*, #1065; and *Ingledove v. Lacour*, Records of the Fourth Judicial District Court, #1745, Iberville Parish Clerk of the Court, Plaquemine, Louisiana, 1840.

41. *Ingledove v. Lacour*, Records of the Fourth Judicial District Court, #1726, Iberville Parish Clerk of the Court, Plaquemine, Louisiana, 1840; *Ingledove v. Lacour*, Records of the Fourth Judicial District Court, #1754, Iberville Parish Clerk of the Court, Plaquemine, Louisiana, 1840.

42. On the importance of witness testimony in local court cases in the nineteenth century, see Edwards, *The People and Their Peace*, chap. 4; and Kennington, *In the Shadow of Dred Scott*.

43. On the importance of reputation in financial matters, see Mann, *Republic of Debtors*. See also W. Johnson, *River of Dark Dreams*, chap. 5.

44. Honor was available to every white man regardless of class. White men of the poorer classes also participated in honor rituals—from brawling and nose-pulling to defending their honor through litigation. However, honor was not equally distributed, as Ingledove found when a black man dishonored him. On southern honor, see especially Wyatt-Brown, *Southern Honor*; and Greenberg, *Honor and Slavery*. On southern honor and the courtroom, see Gross, *Double Character*, chap. 2.

45. On honor and accusations of dishonesty, see Greenberg, "The Nose, the Lie, and the Duel in the Antebellum South"; and Freeman, *Affairs of Honor*, 67.

46. Free blacks were not the only ones who could dishonor whites. Ariela Gross points to the myriad ways the words and actions of slaves might damage a white man's reputation as an apt master and cause others to question his honor. See Gross, *Double Character*, chap. 2.

47. On the enhanced credibility of propertied white men's speech, see Edwards, *The People and Their Peace*, 113.

48. For similar cases in which free black men and women acted decisively in court and property ownership helped determine their reputation, see *Borie v. Lorie*, Records of the Fourth Judicial District Court, #154, Iberville Parish Clerk of the Court, Plaquemine, Louisiana, 1818; *Borie v. Blanchard*, Records of the Fourth Judicial District Court, #463, Iberville Parish Clerk of the Court, Plaquemine, Louisiana, 1824; *Marguerite, FWC v. Janes*, Records of the Fourth Judicial District Court, #1066, Iberville Parish Clerk of the Court, Plaquemine, Louisiana, 1831; and *Marguerite, FWC v. Allain*, Records of the Old Parish Court, #809, Iberville Parish Clerk of the Court, Plaquemine, Louisiana, 1831.

49. For a similar discussion of a black man walking the line between self-assertion and deference when suing a white man, see M. Johnson and Roark, *Black Masters*, 28–29. For some examples of free black people successfully suing whites in Mississippi, see *Black Ben, FMC v. Brooks and Claiborne*, Adams County, Mississippi, 1814, Records of the Circuit Court, Group 1810–19, box 25, file 61, CRP, HNF; *Lewis v. Patterson*, Adams County, Mississippi, 1828, Records of the Circuit Court, Group 1820–29, box 46, file 31, CRP, HNF; and *Hardes v. Mosby*, Adams County, Mississippi, 1835, Records of the Circuit Court, Group 1830–39, box 23, file 11, CRP, HNF. For Louisiana, see *Dubuclet v. Lorrie*, Records of the Fourth Judicial District Court, #228, Iberville Parish Clerk of the Court, Plaquemine, Louisiana, 1820; *Belly v. Bousange*, Records of the Fourth Judicial District Court, #725, Iberville Parish Clerk of the Court, Plaquemine, Louisiana, 1828; *Verret v. Kelly*, Records of the Sixth Judicial District Court, #811, Iberville Parish Clerk of the Court, Plaquemine, Louisiana, 1855.

CHAPTER 3

1. *Corbet v. Duplesis*, Records of the Old Parish Court, unnumbered, Iberville Parish Clerk of the Court, Plaquemine, Louisiana, 1830.

2. The first known African American to practice law was Macon Bolling Allen, who was admitted to the Maine bar in 1844. Prior to the Civil War, a handful of other black lawyers joined Allen, mostly practicing in Massachusetts. See J. Smith, *Emancipation*, chap. 2.

3. *Code of Practice in Civil Cases for the State of Louisiana*, Art. 1, p. 70; emphasis added.

4. Welke, *Law and the Borders of Belonging*, 2.

5. Ibid.

6. Ibid., chap. 1. As Welke states, "Law protected a man's real and personal property through the law of property, his reputation through the law of slander and libel, his 'property' in his wife through the law of coverture, in his children through the law of patriarchy, and in his human chattel through the law of slavery.... The white male citizen took form in a die cast by the dependency and subjectness of women, slaves, free blacks, and Indians." See Welke, "Law, Personhood, and Citizenship in the Long Nineteenth Century," 347.

7. Jefferson, *Notes on the State of Virginia*, Query XIV, 84–85.

8. On black advocacy in the North and white northerners' similarly racist interpretations of it, see DeLombard, *Slavery on Trial*, chap. 4.

9. For a sense of the number of lawyers practicing in the Old Southwest, see Foote, *The Bench and Bar of the South and Southwest*.

10. John A. Quitman letter to his father, May 7, 1821, Claiborne, *Life and Correspondence of John A. Quitman*, 60–61.

11. John A. Quitman letter to his father, January 16, 1822, Claiborne, *Life and Correspondence of John A. Quitman*, 71.

12. Baldwin, *The Flush Times of Alabama and Mississippi*, 34.

13. Ibid.

14. Ibid., 173.

15. Ibid., 174.

16. Ibid., 176.

17. Winchester Family Papers, 1793–1906, box 2E903, folder 1, NTC.

18. Abraham Lincoln letter, December 2, 1858, quoted in Friedman, *A History of American Law*, 606.

19. Thomas Reed Papers, Mss. 783, box 2, folder 15, LLMV.

20. John T. McMurran Papers, Mss. 1403, LLMV. See also Gross, *Double Character*, 29.

21. On legal education in the long nineteenth century, see Macgill and Newmyer, "Legal Education and Legal Thought"; and Konefsky, "The Legal Profession."

22. See Edwards, *The People and Their Peace*, quote at 58.

23. Edward Turner Papers, Mss. 1403, box 1, folder 5, LLMV.

24. Baldwin, *Flush Times of Alabama and Mississippi*, 240.

25. Thomas Reed Papers, Mss. 783, box 1, folder 1, LLMV.

26. Baldwin, *Flush Times of Alabama and Mississippi*, 241. A "chose in action" is the right to sue to recover money, chattels, or a debt, such as the right of an employee to recover unpaid wages.

27. Macgill and Newmyer, "Legal Education and Legal Thought," 38.

28. For examples, see *Duperron, FMC v. Desormes*, Records of the Fourth Judicial District Court, #1558, Pointe Coupee Parish Clerk of the Court, New Roads, Louisiana, 1844; and Petition of Antoinette Colin Lacour, FWC, Records of the Ninth Judicial

District Court, #121, Pointe Coupee Parish Clerk of the Court, New Roads, Louisiana, 1847.

29. For an example of Natham Miriam representing a free woman of color, see *Phillis, FWC v. Langlois*, Records of the Fourth Judicial District Court, #139, Iberville Parish Clerk of the Court, Plaquemine, Louisiana, 1817. For Nichols, see *Honore v. Honore*, Records of the Fourth Judicial District Court, #266, Iberville Parish Clerk of the Court, Plaquemine, Louisiana, 1821.

30. For instance, see *Juge, FMC v. Honore, FMC*, Records of the Ninth Judicial District Court, #25, Pointe Coupee Parish Clerk of the Court, New Roads, Louisiana, 1845; *Juge, FMC v. Duperron, FMC*, Records of the Ninth Judicial District Court, #117, Pointe Coupee Parish Clerk of the Court, New Roads, Louisiana, 1847; *Decuir, FMC v. Duperron, FMC*, Records of the Ninth Judicial District Court, #105, Pointe Coupee Parish Clerk of the Court, New Roads, Louisiana, 1847; and *Decuir, FMC v. Duperron, FMC*, Records of the Ninth Judicial District Court, #279, Pointe Coupee Parish Clerk of the Court, New Roads, Louisiana, 1848.

31. For lawsuits in which Haralson represented Hawkins, see *Hawkins, FWC v. Moore, FWC*, Records of the Early Parish Court, #752, Pointe Coupee Parish Clerk of the Court, New Roads, Louisiana, 1828; *and Hawkins, FWC v. Van Winkle*, Records of the Fourth Judicial District Court, #669, Pointe Coupee Parish Clerk of the Court, New Roads, Louisiana, 1827. For lawsuits in which he represented parties suing her, see *Franchette, FWC v. Hawkins, FWC*, Records of the Fourth Judicial District Court, #807, Pointe Coupee Parish Clerk of the Court, New Roads, Louisiana, 1832.

32. *Grymes and Grymes v. Foster*, Adams County, Mississippi, 1808, Records of the Circuit Court, Group 1800–09, box 32, file 29, CRP, HNF; and *Cooper v. Briscoe*, Adams County, Mississippi, 1811, Records of the Circuit Court, Group 1810–19, box 43, file 22, CRP, HNF.

33. Schafer, *Becoming Free, Remaining Free*, 34.

34. Ibid., chap. 2. Despite rich scholarship on people of African descent and the law generally, few scholars have examined black clients and white attorneys. Ted Maris-Wolf's recent book on free blacks and re-enslavement law in Virginia, however, dedicates a chapter to black clients and their white lawyers. Maris-Wolf shows that Virginia attorneys who represented free blacks in their attempts to remain in the state or in their petitions for enslavement/re-enslavement dutifully followed the law, just as they would for white clients. However, while Maris-Wolf elucidates a number of situations in which a black client would hire a white attorney, in general, attorneys' motivations for taking such cases remain murky. It is clear, however, that these men were not abolitionists, and instead may have accepted black clients because they knew them. See Maris-Wolf, *Family Bonds*, chap. 2. Similarly, Anne Twitty has shown that the lawyers representing enslaved clients suing for their freedom in St. Louis did not appear to be ardent slavery opponents, and regardless of their motives, provided their clients with solid representation. See Twitty, *Before Dred Scott*, chap. 3. For additional insight into lawyers who represented enslaved people suing for freedom in St. Louis, including the fees they charged and the strategies they devised, see Kennington, *In the Shadow of Dred Scott*, chap. 3. See also VanderVelde, *Redemption Songs*, 8–9. For a discussion of lawyers' involvement in a handful of freedom suits from the late eighteenth century, see Honor Sachs, "'Freedom by a Judgment.'"

35. Ariela Gross traces a number of prominent white lawyers in Natchez, Mississippi, men who represented white clients in their lawsuits against other whites and involving slave property. As Gross shows, Natchez attorneys (who often became judges, planters, and politicians) were some of the most influential men in their communities and actively shaped the slave economy and the legal culture of the antebellum South. For more on white lawyers (representing white clients) in Natchez, see Gross, *Double Character*, especially chap. 1.

I have found that the same prominent lawyers that Gross discusses—men like John T. McMurran and John A. Quitman—did not just represent white clients. They also represented black clients (free and enslaved) in a wide range of cases, from freedom suits to debt actions to criminal cases.

36. Similarly, Kelly Kennington has found that representing enslaved people in freedom suits did not damage St. Louis lawyers' reputations or ability to advance politically. See Kennington, *In the Shadow of Dred Scott*, chap. 3.

37. On Quitman and his wealth, see Walther, *The Fire-Eaters*, 85. On McMurran, see Gross, *Double Character*, chap. 1.

38. On Poydras and his wealth, see Costello, *The Life, Family and Legacy of Julien Poydras*, 96–125.

39. Edward Turner, Seventh Census of the United States, 1850, Slave Schedules, United States of America, Bureau of the Census, NARA, http://www.ancestry.com/; William B. Shields, Fourth Census of the United States, 1820, Records of the Bureau of the Census, Record Group 29, NARA, http://www.ancestry.com/; John Dutton, Fourth Census of the United States, 1820, Records of the Bureau of the Census, Record Group 29, NARA, http://www.ancestry.com/.

40. John T. McMurran Papers, Mss. 1403, folder 2: William B. Griffith Estate, LLMV.

41. Claiborne, *Life and Correspondence of John A. Quitman*; Lynch, *The Bench and Bar of Mississippi*, 112; and Walther, *The Fire-Eaters*, 85–86.

42. For instance, see *State v. Burwell*, Adams County, Mississippi, 1818, Records of the Circuit Court, Group 1810–19, box 40, file 80, CRP, HNF; *Milly v. Brown*, Adams County, Mississippi, 1824, Records of the Circuit Court, Group 1820–29, box 28, file 68, CRP, HNF; *Peter, FMC v. Thomas*, Adams County, Mississippi, 1820, Records of the Circuit Court, Group 1810–19, box 33, file 50, CRP, HNF; and *Anthony v. Reed and Carter*, Adams County, Mississippi, 1819, Records of the Circuit Court, Habeas Corpus files, box 1, CRP, HNF.

43. *Hamm v. Green*, Adams County, Mississippi, 1819, Records of the Circuit Court, Group 1810–19, box 43, file 76, CRP, HNF.

44. See chapter 6 for a discussion of kidnapping and freedom suits.

45. See *The Revised Code of the Laws of Mississippi* (1824), Sec. 76, p. 386; and *The Revised Code of the Statute Laws of the State of Mississippi* (1857), Art. 10, p. 236. Enslaved people could also sue directly for their freedom in the Louisiana district courts. See the Louisiana *Civil Code*, Art. 177, p. 28.

46. Foote, *The Bench and Bar of the South and Southwest*, 25.

47. John A. Quitman letter to his father, January 16, 1822, Claiborne, *Life and Correspondence of John A. Quitman*, 71.

48. On a master's duty and burden (as a species of paternalism), see Genovese, *Roll, Jordon, Roll*, 75–86. On southern statesmanship and honor and the role honor played

in the southern courtroom, see Gross, *Double Character*, chaps. 2 and 4. On southern honor more generally, see Wyatt-Brown, *Southern Honor*; Greenberg, *Honor and Slavery*; and Stowe, *Intimacy and Power in the Old South*. For a recent statement on southern paternalism, see Ford, *Deliver Us from Evil*.

49. Claiborne, *Life and Correspondence of John A. Quitman*, 74.

50. Although, as Ariela Gross has shown, enslaved people dishonored white slaveholders in myriad ways. For instance, a slave with a reputation for running away could cause other slaveholders to question his master's ability to control or care for him. For a discussion of the workings of honor and dishonor in the courtroom and slaves' ability to dishonor whites, see Gross, *Double Character*, chaps. 2 and 4.

51. See Patterson, *Slavery and Social Death*; and Oakes, *Slavery and Freedom*, chap. 1.

52. There is a vast and robust literature on slaveholders' ideologies and the intellectual history of white southerners. For a starting point, see O'Brien, *Rethinking the South*; O'Brien, *Conjectures of Order*; Faust, *A Sacred Circle*; Faust, *James Henry Hammond and the Old South*; Fox-Genovese and Genovese, *The Mind of the Master Class*; Oakes, *The Ruling Race*; Oakes, *Slavery and Freedom*; Wyatt-Brown, *Southern Honor*; Greenberg, *Honor and Slavery*; Stowe, *Intimacy and Power in the Old South*; and Ford, *Deliver Us from Evil*.

53. Cobb, *An Inquiry into the Law of Negro Slavery*, 252.

54. For instance, see *Black Ben v. Brooks and Claiborne*, Adams County, Mississippi, 1814, Records of the Circuit Court, Group 1810–19, box 25, file 61, CRP, HNF; and *Johnston v. Hunter*, Adams County, Mississippi, 1816, Records of the Circuit Court, Group 1810–19, box 39, file 69, CRP, HNF.

55. Alonzo Synder Ledger, 1842–1847, Alonzo Snyder Papers, Mss. 655, LLMV.

56. F. H. and Thomas P. Farrar Papers, 1849–1869, box 2E557, NTC.

57. *Viales v. Honore and his wife*, Records of the Fourth Judicial District Court, #115, Iberville Parish Clerk of the Court, Plaquemine, Louisiana, 1816; *Viales v. Rose, FWC*, Records of the Fourth Judicial District Court, #116, Iberville Parish Clerk of the Court, Plaquemine, Louisiana, 1816; and *Viales v. Rosalie and Antoine Dubuclet*, Records of the Fourth Judicial District Court, #118, Iberville Parish Clerk of the Court, Plaquemine, Louisiana, 1816.

58. *John (a negro) v. Williams*, Adams County, Mississippi, 1821, Records of the Circuit Court, Group 1820–29, box 6, file 101, CRP, HNF.

59. *Stumps v. Mardis*, Adams County, Mississippi, 1827, Records of the Circuit Court, Group 1820–29, box 44, file 79, CRP, HNF.

60. For an example of Grayson representing an African American in a freedom suit, see *Hercules (a boy of color) v. Walker*, Adams County, Mississippi, 1824, Records of the Circuit Court, Habeas Corpus files, box 2, CRP, HNF.

61. Norman Davis, Seventh Census of the United States, 1850, Shreveport, Caddo, Louisiana, Records of the Bureau of the Census, Record Group 29, NARA, http://www.ancestry.com/.

62. For instance, see *Colin, FWC v. Ricard, FMC*, Records of the Fourth Judicial District Court, #323, Iberville Parish Clerk of the Court, Plaquemine, Louisiana, 1822.

63. Petition of John L. Collins, West Feliciana Parish, Louisiana, 1830, in RSFB, Series 2, Part F, PAR #20884041. For another case in which an African American man served as an

"agent" and "attorney in fact," see *Brittion v. Brittion*, West Feliciana Parish, Louisiana 1837, in RSFB, Series 2, Part F, PAR #20883729.

64. Gross, *Double Character*, 27.

65. Quitman letter to his father, Jan. 16, 1822, Claiborne, *Life and Correspondence*, 72.

66. Ibid.

67. In both Mississippi and Louisiana, former lawyers filled the judiciary. They attained their positions as judges first by appointment (by the governor of the state) and later by popular election (Mississippi made judicial offices elective in 1832, and Louisiana governors appointed judges until 1852, when the new state constitution provided that voters elect their appellate and inferior court judges). Ariela Gross demonstrates that even after Mississippi elected their judges, "nearly all of the candidates were lawyers." Gross, *Double Character*, 30. On the growth of the elected judiciary, see K. Hall, "The Judiciary on Trial."

68. Gross, *Double Character*, 23.

69. The composition of the juries in most civil cases involving African Americans is difficult to assess, as the trial records rarely listed the names of the jurors. However, Mississippi jurors were male freeholders or householders between twenty-one and sixty. They had to be citizens of the United States and residents of the county, and they could not have been convicted of an "infamous crime." In the event that jurors failed to attend court, the sheriff or another office of the court could convene a bystander jury. *Revised Code of the Statute Laws of the State of Mississippi* (1857), Art. 126, p. 497–98; Art. 153, p. 503–4.

70. Jury trials were rare in Louisiana civil cases (although litigants could request a jury trial in any case but debt recovery). The defendant in debt-recovery cases, however, could request a jury trial if he or she was the victim of fraud. See Louisiana *Code of Practice*, Art. 494, p. 201–202. In Louisiana, jurors were white, male citizens of the state above the age of twenty-one. They could not have been found guilty of a crime punishable by death or hard labor, and they could not be apprentices, servants, or indentures. They also had to have resided in the parish for twelve months and liable to pay taxes. See the *Louisiana Digest* (1841), Art. 1798, p. 275. As in Mississippi, the courts could convene a bystander jury if other jurors failed to come to court. *Louisiana Digest*, Art. 1792, p. 274.

71. See, for instance, *Andre v. State of Mississippi*, Adams County, Mississippi, 1825, Records of the Circuit Court, Habeas Corpus files, box 2, CRP, HNF; and *Elias Wilson (FMC) v. State of Mississippi*, Adams County, Mississippi, 1825, Records of the Circuit Court, Habeas Corpus files, box 2, CRP, HNF.

72. J. Bryant, *Dark Places of the Earth*, quote at 216.

73. Edward Turner Papers, Mss. 1403, box 1, folder 5, LLMV.

74. Ibid.

75. For representative cases involving black litigants who appeared before Judge Turner, see *Woodall v. Sexton*, Adams County, Mississippi, 1826, Records of the Circuit Court, Group 1820–29, box 37, file 36, CRP, HNF; *Lewis, FMC v. Patterson*, Adams County, Mississippi, 1828, Records of the Circuit Court, Group 1820–29, box 46, file 31, CRP, HNF; and *Neal v. Jordon*, Adams County, Mississippi, 1828, Records of the Circuit Court, Group 1820–29, box 56, file 33, CRP, HNF.

76. Jennison, "Rewriting the Free Negro Past."

77. *Salvador v. Turner*, Records of the Fourth Judicial District Court, #1495, Pointe Coupee Parish Clerk of the Court, New Roads, Louisiana, 1844.

78. *Salvador v. Turner*.

79. Kent, *Commentaries on American Law*, vol. 2, 258n.

80. Ibid.

81. For representative lawsuits, see *LeRidel v. Poydras*, Records of the Fourth Judicial District Court, #1433, Pointe Coupee Parish Clerk of the Court, New Roads, Louisiana, 1843; *Juge v. Porche*, Records of the Fourth Judicial District Court, #1445, Pointe Coupee Parish Clerk of the Court, New Roads, Louisiana, 1843; and *Riche, FWC v. Decoux*, Records of the Fourth Judicial District Court, #1572, Pointe Coupee Parish Clerk of the Court, New Roads, Louisiana, 1845.

82. A. Davis, "The Private Law of Race and Sex," 227.

83. Quoted in Oakes, *Slavery and Freedom*, 72. As Oakes demonstrates, "proslavery thought focused most often on the primacy of rights—with particular fidelity to the right of property." Oakes, *Slavery and Freedom*, 174. On the importance of property rights in southern society, see also McCurry, *Masters of Small Worlds*.

84. See, for instance, *Dauphine v. Ricard, et al.*, Records of the Fourth Judicial District Court, #2279, Iberville Parish Clerk of the Court, Plaquemine, Louisiana, 1845; *Grymes and Grymes v. Foster*, Adams County, Mississippi, 1808, Records of the Circuit Court, Group 1800–09, box 32, file 29, CRP, HNF; and *Elias v. Bell*, Adams County, Mississippi, 1817, Records of the Circuit Court, Group 1810–19, box 25, file 124, CRP, HNF.

85. For instance, the attorney Alonzo Snyder notes a commission cost of $47. See Alonzo Snyder Papers, Mss. 655, box 10, folder 4, LLMV. Court costs ranged, especially if a case required a great deal of witness testimony (as witnesses were paid for their mileage), but more witnesses, especially witness testimony taken in distant places, meant higher court costs.

86. On commissions in Louisiana, see Louisiana *Code of Practice* (1861), Art. 425-Art. 440, p. 182–89. On Mississippi, see *Revised Code of the Statute Laws of the State of Mississippi* (1857), Art. 210–221, p. 514–16.

87. For representative freedom suits in which the judge issued a commission, see *Susey et al. v. Scott and Rees*, Adams County, Mississippi, 1805, Records of the Circuit Court, Group 1800–09, box 32, file 14, CRP, HNF; and *Hamm v. Green and Steele*, Adams County, Mississippi, 1819, Records of the Circuit Court, Group 1810–19, box 43, file 76, CRP, HNF. For representative lawsuits in which the court sent a commission in a case other than a freedom suit, see *Pilard, FWC v. Plessy*, Records of the Early Parish Court, #375, Pointe Coupee Parish Clerk of the Court, New Roads, Louisiana, 1812; and *Borie v. Lorie*, Records of the Fourth Judicial District Court, #154, Iberville Parish Clerk of the Court, Plaquemine, Louisiana, 1818. Courts sent commissions at the request of both white and black plaintiffs. For a representative lawsuit in which the court sent a commission at the request of a white plaintiff, see *Belly v. Orillion*, Records of the Fourth Judicial District Court, #125, Iberville Parish Clerk of the Court, Plaquemine, Louisiana, 1817.

88. For instance, see Ferguson, *The Trial in American Life*, 12–13.

89. Edwards, *The People and Their Peace*, 114.

90. My finding that courts readily accepted the testimony of witnesses (often second-hand accounts in which witnesses claimed to have "heard" that a person was born free or

of a white mother) about the genealogies, ancestries, and personal histories of enslaved
people (as well as the stories the enslaved litigants presented themselves) are counter
to the findings of the historian Honor Sachs. In her study of freedom suits in Virginia,
she argues that by the early nineteenth century, the courts expressed reservations about
hearsay and second-hand evidence. See Sachs, "Freedom by a Judgment," 198–201. In the
antebellum Natchez district, by contrast, litigants and witnesses presented this kind of
evidence in many of the extant freedom suits and used it to enslaved litigants' success.

91. *Irwin v. Powell*, West Feliciana Parish, Louisiana, 1837, in RSFB, Series II, Part F, PAR
#20883713.

92. See, for instance, *Franchette (alias Francoise), FWC v. Hawkins, FWC*, Records of
the Early Parish Court, #790, Pointe Coupee Parish Clerk of the Court, New Roads,
Louisiana, 1831.

93. For some instances in black litigants won their lawsuits in Cooley's courtroom,
see *Porche, FWC v. Turner*, Records of the Ninth Judicial District Court, #1064, Pointe
Coupee Parish Clerk of the Court, New Roads, Louisiana, 1854; and *Tournoir, FMC, et
al. v. Honore et al.*, Records of the Fourth Judicial District Court, #1069, Pointe Coupee
Parish Clerk of the Court, New Roads, Louisiana, 1845.

94. See chapter 6 for a discussion of enslaved people contracting for their freedom.

95. See Edwards, *The People and Their Peace*; and Novak, *The People's Welfare*.

96. *Tom v. Porche*, Records of the Ninth Judicial District Court, #1126, Pointe Coupee
Parish Clerk of the Court, New Roads, Louisiana, 1854.

97. In my thinking here, I am inspired by the work of Daniel Sharfstein and
Joshua Rothman. See Sharfstein, *The Invisible Line*; and J. Rothman, *Notorious in the
Neighborhood*.

CHAPTER 4

1. *Lewis, FMC v. Patterson*, Adams County, Mississippi, 1828, Records of the Circuit
Court, Group 1820–29, box 46, file 31, CRP, HNF. Damages in debt-recovery suits were
rare.

2. On the dual nature of debt (as representative of both opportunity and moral or
economic failure), see Balleisen, *Navigating Failure*; and Mann, *Republic of Debtors*.

3. Balleisen, *Navigating Failure*, 27.

4. Atherton, "The Problem of Credit Rating in the Ante-Bellum South," 535. On the
pervasiveness of debt in early America, see Balleisen, *Navigating Failure*; Mann, *Republic
of Debtors*; and Sandage, *Born Losers*. On the Civil War–era South, see Silkenat, *Moments
of Despair*.

5. On the role of credit in the cotton economy of Lower Mississippi Valley, see W.
Johnson, *River of Dark Dreams*; and J. Rothman, *Flush Times and Fever Dreams*.

6. For instance, in her study of mortgages, Bonnie Martin also found examples of
black creditors in rural Louisiana. See B. Martin, "Slavery's Invisible Engine." In her study
of community and identity in rural Louisiana, Johanna Smith also notes a handful of
instances in which free blacks lent money to others. See J. Smith, "Mulatto Bend."

7. See for instance, *Britto v. Pascalin*, Records of the Ninth Judicial District Court, #1833,
Pointe Coupee Parish Clerk of the Court, New Roads, Louisiana, 1857.

8. For instance, in 1813, Rose Belly lent Joseph Orillion, a white man, $2,000 to be paid over eight years. Obligation of Joseph Orillion to Rose Belly, July 26, 1813, Conveyances, Original Acts, vol. E, no. 576, Iberville Parish Clerk of the Court, Plaquemine, Louisiana.

9. Hogan and Davis, *William Johnson's Natchez*, 71.

10. W. T. Johnson Collection, folder 39, "Ledger, Feb. 1837–Oct. 1841," LLMV.

11. Hogan and Davis, *William Johnson's Natchez*, 30.

12. Ibid., 30–31.

13. For instance, see *Pilard, FWC v. Plessy*, Records of the Early Parish Court, #375, Pointe Coupee Parish Clerk of the Court, New Roads, Louisiana, 1812; *Pilard, FWC v. Fruget*, Records of the Early Parish Court, #410, Pointe Coupee Parish Clerk of the Court, New Roads, Louisiana, 1812; and *Pilard, FWC v. Plessy*, Records of the Early Parish Court, #462, Pointe Coupee Parish Clerk of the Court, New Roads, Louisiana, 1812.

14. Silkenat, *Moments of Despair*, 146.

15. Mann, *Republic of Debtors*, 18–29.

16. *Leduff v. Leduff*, Records of the Ninth Judicial District Court, #1998, Pointe Coupee Parish Clerk of the Court, New Roads, Louisiana, 1858. Leduff was a common surname in Pointe Coupee Parish. It is not clear if the two men were related.

17. *Decuir v. Dupperon*, Records of the Ninth Judicial District Court, #548, Pointe Coupee Parish Clerk of the Court, New Roads, Louisiana, 1850.

18. *Margueritte v. Roth*, Records of the Old Parish Court, #1095, Iberville Parish Clerk of the Court, Plaquemine, Louisiana, 1840.

19. *Margueritte v. Allain*, Records of the Old Parish Court, #809, Iberville Parish Clerk of the Court, Plaquemine, Louisiana, 1831.

20. For instance, she sued William Janes twice for the money he owed her for renting her slave, Urbin. See *Margueritte v. Janes*, Records of the Old Parish Court, #805, Iberville Parish Clerk of the Court, Plaquemine, Louisiana, 1831; and *Margueritte v. Janes*, Records of the Old Parish Court, #1066, Iberville Parish Clerk of the Court, Plaquemine, Louisiana, 1831.

21. Debts ranged considerably. Some wealthy black lenders like Rose Belly lent money in the thousands. For instance, see Obligation of Joseph Orillion to Rose Belly, July 26, 1813, Conveyances, Original Acts, vol. E, no. 576, Iberville Parish Clerk of the Court, Plaquemine, Louisiana ($2,000). But others extended a wider range of loans. William Johnson's account books show that he advanced cash to some people like Issac Leum and James Dyer a few dollars at a time. Others borrowed larger amounts. On March 22, 1839, for instance, Johnson lent Robert McCary $200, and he extended loans to others that that same year for up to $350. See W. T. Johnson Collection, vol. 36, Ledger, Feb. 1837-Nov. 1867, LLMV. The extant debt actions involving both white and black lenders show, however, that lawsuits over small amounts (under $100) were not unusual in the Natchez district courts. For examples of cases involving white lenders, see *Hasse v. Leblanc*, Records of the Forth Judicial District Court, #275, Pointe Coupee Parish Clerk of the Court, New Roads, Louisiana, 1815 ($27); and *Layse v. Vaughn*, Adams County, Mississippi, 1820, Records of the Circuit Court, Group 1810–19, box 30, file 47, CRP, HNF ($67). For examples involving black lenders, see *Borie v. Troxler*, Records of the Fourth Judicial District Court, #627, Iberville Parish Clerk of the Court, Plaquemine, Louisiana,

1827 ($59); and *Allain v. Strother*, Records of the Ninth Judicial District Court, #838, Iberville Parish Clerk of the Court, Plaquemine, Louisiana, 1832 ($65).

22. *Phillis, FWC v. Langlois*, Records of the Fourth Judicial District Court, #145, Iberville Parish Clerk of the Court, Plaquemine, Louisiana, 1817.

23. *Phillis, FWC v. Langlois*, Records of the Fourth Judicial District Court, #139, Iberville Parish Clerk of the Court, Plaquemine, Louisiana, 1817.

24. My research includes ninety cases involving free black plaintiffs' attempts to recover loan repayments. Of that total, the court issued a verdict for the plaintiff in seventy of these cases, and in fourteen others the plaintiff and defendant came to an agreement about repayment and dismissed the lawsuit before its conclusion. In four of the lawsuits the verdict is unknown. Only two cases had a verdict for the defendant (both of whom were white). Sixty-one of ninety lawsuits were against white defendants, and the black plaintiffs won all but two of these cases.

25. *Verret v. Kelly*, Records of the Sixth Judicial District Court, #811, Iberville Parish Clerk of the Court, Plaquemine, Louisiana, 1855. For similar cases, see *Handy v. Prudin*, Records of the Fourth Judicial District Court, #545, Pointe Coupee Parish Clerk of the Court, New Roads, Louisiana, 1822; and *Julien, FMC v. Leduff, FMC*, Records of the Ninth Judicial District Court, #1770, Pointe Coupee Parish Clerk of the Court, New Roads, Louisiana, 1857.

26. *Rapp et al. v. Fletcher*, Adams County, Mississippi, 1837, Records of the Circuit Court, Group 1830–39, box 44, file 23, CRP, HNF.

27. For similar cases in which black plaintiffs won in default, see *Pilard (alias Lascabes), FWC v. Fruget*, Records of the Early Parish Court, #410, Pointe Coupee Parish Clerk of the Court, New Roads, Louisiana, 1812; and *Dupperon, FMC v. Major*, Records of the Ninth Judicial District Court, #1116, Pointe Coupee Parish Clerk of the Court, New Roads, Louisiana, 1854.

28. *Borie v. Troxler*, Records of the Fourth Judicial District Court, #627, Iberville Parish Clerk of the Court, Plaquemine, Louisiana, 1827.

29. Plaintiffs in debt-recovery cases, black and white, almost always won. Of the 296 loan-related cases I have found involving black people (as either plaintiffs or defendants), only seven cases had verdicts for the defendant. As Bruce Mann demonstrates, in debt cases throughout the United States in late the eighteenth and early nineteenth centuries, "debtors almost invariably" lost. Mann, *Republic of Debtors*, 21.

30. *Petition of Maximillion Ricard*, FMC, Records of the Fourth Judicial District Court, #324, Iberville Parish Clerk of the Court, Plaquemine, Louisiana, 1823.

31. Balleisen, *Navigating Failure*, 70.

32. On reputation and extending credit, see Mann, *Republic of Debtors*, chap. 1. On the assessment of character and particular character traits in credit relationships, see Olegario, *A Culture of Credit*, chap. 3.

33. Obligation of Joseph Orillion to Rose Belly, July 26, 1813, vol. E, no. 576, Iberville Parish Clerk of the Court, Plaquemine, Louisiana. For an example of Orillion serving as a witness to a legal transaction involving Rose Belly, see Pierre and Rose Belly Acknowledgment of Children, February 8, 1818, Conveyances, Original Acts, vol. E, no. 517, Iberville Parish Clerk of the Court, Plaquemine, Louisiana.

34. Mann, *Republic of Debtors*, 9.

35. Indeed, as Bonnie Martin has shown in her study of mortgages and slave collateral, when borrowing and lending, most did so for economic gain or opportunity. B. Martin, "Slavery's Invisible Economy," 862.

36. *Cambre v. Fleming*, Records of the Fourth Judicial District Court, #1349, Iberville Parish Clerk of the Court, Plaquemine, Louisiana, 1833. For an example of a lawsuit Fleming lost, see *Walton v. Fleming*, Records of the Fourth Judicial District Court, #1399, Iberville Parish Clerk of the Court, Plaquemine, Louisiana, 1834.

37. See, for instance, *Gerard v. Dormenon*, FMC, Records of the Early Parish Court, #909, Pointe Coupee Parish Clerk of the Court, New Roads, Louisiana, 1838; and *Poydras v. Dormenon*, Records of the Ninth Judicial District Court, #68, Pointe Coupee Parish Clerk of the Court, New Roads, Louisiana, 1847.

38. For an example of white men speaking in favor of Fleming's character, see *State of Louisiana v. Fleming*, unprocessed materials, Iberville Parish Clerk of the Court, Plaquemine, Louisiana, 1833.

39. *Folger v. Britto*, Records of the Ninth Judicial District Court, #1994, Pointe Coupee Parish Clerk of the Court, New Roads, Louisiana, 1858.

40. On the assignability of written credit instruments in early America, see Mann, *Republic of Debtors*, 12–18.

41. *Territory of Mississippi v. Miler*, Adams County, Mississippi, 1808, Records of the Circuit Court, Group 1800–09, box 4, file 92, CRP, HNF.

42. *Dubuclet v. Lorrie*, Records of the Fourth Judicial District Court, #228, Iberville Parish Clerk of the Court, Plaquemine, Louisiana, 1820.

43. Mann, *Republic of Debtors*, 15.

44. *Hawkins, FMC v. Rutledge*, Records of the Fifteenth Judicial District Court, #4212, St. Landry Parish Clerk of the Court, Opelousas, Louisiana, 1843. For similar cases, see *Donato, FMC v. Liebenberg*, Records of the Fifteenth Judicial District Court, #7546, St. Landry Parish Clerk of the Court, Opelousas, Louisiana, 1855; and *Donato, FMC v. Gallot, FWC*, Records of the Fifteenth Judicial District Court, #8658, St. Landry Parish Clerk of the Court, Opelousas, Louisiana, 1859.

45. *Borie v. Roth and Roth*, Records of the Fourth Judicial District Court, #478, Iberville Parish Clerk of the Court, Plaquemine, Louisiana, 1824. On mortgaging slaves, see B. Martin, "Slavery's Invisible Engine"; and Kilbourne, *Debt, Investment, Slaves*, chap. 3.

46. *Joseph v. Calmes et al.*, Records of the Ninth Judicial District Court, #1826, Pointe Coupee Parish Clerk of the Court, New Roads, Louisiana, 1857.

47. Balleisen, *Navigating Failure*, 31.

48. Silkenat, *Moments of Despair*, chap. 7.

49. Mann, *Republic of Debtors*, 135.

50. Slaveholders were, of course, also involved in a formal credit and debt economy too. For instance, see Kilbourne, *Debt, Investment, Slaves*.

51. On the comparisons between debt and slavery in early America, see Balleisen, *Navigating Failure*, 165–67; Mann, *Republic of Debtors*, chap 4; and Sandage, *Born Losers*, chap. 7.

52. The *Woodville Republican*, Woodville, Mississippi, February 25, 1851.

53. Balleisen, *Navigating Failure*, 167.

54. *Southern Sentinel*, Plaquemine, Louisiana, August 15, 1857.

55. *Southern Sentinel*, Plaquemine, Louisiana, February 21, 1852.

56. The *Woodville Republican*, Woodville, Mississippi, February 25, 1851.

57. *Lawson v. Brown*, Adams County, Mississippi, 1824, Records of the Circuit Court, Group 1820–29, box 28, file 66, CRP, HNF.

58. *Milly v. Brown*, Adams County, Mississippi, 1823, Records of the Circuit Court, Group 1820–29, box 28, file 69, CRP, HNF.

59. *Elizabeth, a Negro woman v. Williams*, Adams County, Mississippi, 1801, Records of the Circuit Court, Group 1800–09, box 23, file 65, CRP, HNF.

60. A legal fiction is a fact or claim accepted or treated as true (although fictitious), enabling the court to apply a legal rule or resolve a matter.

61. *Code of Practice in Civil Cases for the State of Louisiana* (1861), Art. 1, p. 70.

CHAPTER 5

1. Wright, *Slavery and American Economic Development*, 2. See also Morris, *Southern Slavery and the Law*.

2. Wright, *Slavery and American Economic Development*, 7.

3. Quoted in Oakes, *Slavery and Freedom*, 72.

4. On slavery, liberalism, and property rights, see Oakes, *Slavery and Freedom*, chap. 2.

5. Appleby, *Capitalism and a New Social Order*, 9.

6. Sterkx, *The Free Negro in Ante-Bellum Louisiana*, 172–73.

7. The Johnson family left behind a large collection of documents, including William Johnson's diary and account books, letters between family members, and the family's financial records. See W. T. Johnson and Family Collection, LLMV.

8. Pierre and Rose Belly Acknowledgment of Children, February 8, 1818, Conveyances, Original Acts, vol. E, no. 517, Iberville Parish Clerk of the Court, Plaquemine, Louisiana.

9. Pierre Belly to Rose Belly, February 16, 1809, Conveyances, Original Acts, vol. D, no. 86, Iberville Parish Clerk of the Court, Plaquemine, Louisiana; Pierre Belly to Rose Belly, June 15, 1809, Conveyances, Original Acts, vol. E, no. 29, Iberville Parish Clerk of the Court, Plaquemine, Louisiana; Pierre Belly to Rose Belly, May 1, 1811, Conveyances, Original Acts, vol. E, no. 317, Iberville Parish Clerk of the Court, Plaquemine, Louisiana; and Pierre Belly to Rose Belly, January 1, 2014, Conveyances, Original Acts, vol. F, no. 140, Iberville Parish Clerk of the Court, Plaquemine, Louisiana.

10. Succession of Pierre Belly, Records of the Probate Court, #65, Iberville Parish Clerk of the Court, Plaquemine, Louisiana, 1814.

11. Rose Belly to Rosalie Dubuclet and others, February 2, 1828, Conveyances, Original Acts, vol. L, no. 293, Iberville Parish Clerk of the Court, Plaquemine, Louisiana.

12. Immediately after the Civil War, the Belly descendants became important players in Reconstruction-era politics. Respected in their community, propertied, and well educated, the Belly descendants became leaders in the struggle for racial equality in postbellum Louisiana. Pierre G. Deslonde, a grandson of Pierre and Rose Belly, served as a delegate to the Louisiana Constitutional Convention of 1867–68, a member of the House of Representatives from 1868 to 1870, and the Louisiana secretary of state from 1872 to 1876. Another grandson, Antoine Dubuclet, served as the Louisiana state treasurer

from 1868 to 1878. See Ricard, "Pierre Belly and Rose." For a case study of the Belly family, see chapter 7.

13. Schweninger, *Black Property Owners in the South*, 63.

14. On Bingaman's relationship with Williams, see Broussard, "Stepping Lively in Place," 33.

15. Louisiana *Civil Code*, 1825, arts. 220–30, pp. 100–102. For a description of the process of recognizing children as "natural children," see chapter 7.

16. For examples, see Clark, *The Strange History of the American Quadroon*, chap. 4.

17. *State of Mississippi v. Bartlett*, Warren County, Mississippi, 1843, box 2E938, NTC.

18. Schweninger, "Antebellum Free Persons of Color in Postbellum Louisiana," 347.

19. Petition of Henriette, FWC, Records of the Ninth Judicial District Court, #179, Pointe Coupee Parish Clerk of the Court, New Roads, Louisiana, 1847.

20. Petition of Antoine Dubuclet, Records of the Sixth Judicial District Court, unnumbered, Iberville Parish Clerk of the Court, Plaquemine, Louisiana, 1852.

21. On free black property ownership in the Deep South, see especially Schweninger, *Black Property Owners in the South*; Hanger, *Bounded Lives, Bounded Places*, chap 2; and J. Smith, "Mulatto Bend." A number of scholars have pointed to the role property ownership (both real and personal) played in free black people's pursuit of independence and liberty in the antebellum South. For some recent works, see Ely, *Israel on the Appomattox*; Myers, *Forging Freedom*; and von Daacke, *Freedom Has a Face*. See also Lebsock, *The Free Women of Petersburg*.

22. For a summary of the laws governing the lives of free people of color in the Natchez district, see Sydnor, "The Free Negro in Mississippi before the Civil War"; and Sterkx, *The Free Negro in Ante-Bellum Louisiana*. See also Berlin, *Slaves without Masters*, chap. 10. For a discussion of free people of color's involvement in property disputes in New Orleans between 1806 and 1813, see Aslakson, *Making Race in the Courtroom*, chap. 5.

23. *Black Ben, FMC v. Brooks and Claiborne*, Adams County, Mississippi, 1814, Records of the Circuit Court, Group 1810–19, box 25, file 61, CRP, HNF; and *Ben v. Brooks*, Adams County, Mississippi, 1816, Records of the Circuit Court, Group 1810–19, box 31, file 80, CRP, HNF.

24. *Lacour v. Landry*, Records of the Fourth Judicial District Court, #1070, Iberville Parish Clerk of the Court, Plaquemine, Louisiana, 1831

25. Neglecting to identify a litigant of color appeared to be a common practice in the Natchez district, despite state law requirements. For some instances in which court officials did not identify Britto as a person of color, see *Britto v. Lalande*, Records of the Ninth Judicial District Court, #886, Pointe Coupee Parish Clerk of the Court, New Roads, Louisiana, 1832; and *Britto v. Pascalin*, Records of the Ninth Judicial District Court, #1833, Pointe Coupee Parish Clerk of the Court, New Roads, Louisiana, 1857. For some examples in which court officials did label Britto a person of color, see *Britto, FMC v. Lalande, FMC*, Records of the Ninth Judicial District Court, #1214, Pointe Coupee Parish Clerk of the Court, New Roads, Louisiana, 1854; and *Britto, FMC v. Chustz*, Records of the Ninth Judicial District Court, #1381, Pointe Coupee Parish Clerk of the Court, New Roads, Louisiana, 1855.

26. *Borie v. Lorrie*, Records of the Fourth Judicial District Court, #154, Iberville Parish Clerk of the Court, Plaquemine, Louisiana, 1818. They continued to disagree, however,

and in 1821 Lorrie sued Borie over the gin. But once again they came to an agreement, and Lorrie dismissed the lawsuit. See *Lorrie v. Borie, FMC*, Records of the Fourth Judicial District Court, #255, Iberville Parish Clerk of the Court, Plaquemine, Louisiana, 1821.

27. For example, see *Borie v. Blanchard*, Records of the Fourth Judicial District Court, #463, Iberville Parish Clerk of the Court, Plaquemine, Louisiana, 1824; *Borie v. Roth and Roth*, Records of the Fourth Judicial District Court, #478, Iberville Parish Clerk of the Court, Plaquemine, Louisiana, 1824; *Borie v. Danos*, Records of the Fourth Judicial District Court, #579, Iberville Parish Clerk of the Court, Plaquemine, Louisiana, 1826; and *Borie v. Troxler*, Records of the Fourth Judicial District Court, #627, Iberville Parish Clerk of the Court, Plaquemine, Louisiana, 1827.

28. A. Smith, *Wealth of Nations*, 103.

29. *Cadoret v. Decuir*, Records of the Early Parish Court, #610, Pointe Coupee Parish Clerk of the Court, New Roads, Louisiana, 1821.

30. *Cadoré (Cadoret) v. Demouny et al.*, Records of the Ninth Judicial District Court, #984, Pointe Coupee Parish Clerk of the Court, New Roads, Louisiana, 1853.

31. *Rosalie, FWC v. Duclos*, Records of the Old Parish Court, #1061, Iberville Parish Clerk of the Court, Plaquemine, Louisiana, 1839.

32. Free blacks also sued to protect, retrieve, or recover debts for various types of personal property, as well as for goods and services. For instance, in 1832, Manuel Britto, a Louisiana free man of color, sued another free black man, Charles Lalande, for an $850 debt for "diverse goods, merchandise, and groceries" and received a verdict in his favor when Lalande failed to appear at trial. *Britto v. Lalande*, Records of the Ninth Judicial District Court, #886, Pointe Coupee Parish Clerk of the Court, New Roads, Louisiana, 1832. Britto sued to protect his property and his investments with some frequency. In 1855, for example, Britto brought a claim against Gustave Chustz, a white man, to recover a debt for several pounds of cotton. *Britto, FMC v. Chustz*, Records of the Ninth Judicial District Court, #1381, Pointe Coupee Parish Clerk of the Court, New Roads, Louisiana, 1855. Other free blacks filed claims over horses and cattle. In 1825, Jacob Clark, a free black from Mississippi, sued Thomas Jones, a white man, asserting that Jones had found his missing horse but refused to return it. Jones died, however, before the case reached its conclusion. *Clark v. Jones*, Adams County, Mississippi, 1825, Records of the Circuit Court, Group 1820–29, box 36, file 56, CRP, HNF.

33. On black landownership in the antebellum South, see Ely, *Israel on the Appomattox*, chap. 3; and J. Smith, "Mulatto Bend." In the postwar era, see Petty, *Standing Their Ground*.

34. *Sandy, FMC v. Barnes*, Records of the Third Judicial District Court, #2537, West Feliciana Parish Clerk of the Court, St. Francisville, Louisiana, 1841. For another case involving a land dispute, see *Collins, alias Daves, FWC v. Harbour*, Records of the Ninth Judicial District Court, #584, Pointe Coupee Parish Clerk of the Court, New Roads, Louisiana, 1850.

35. For a discussion of the ways African Americans linked property rights to civil rights in the Jim Crow era, see Connolly, *A World More Concrete*.

36. See Hohfeld, *Fundamental Legal Conceptions*; Banner, *American Property*, chap 3; Baron, "Rescuing the Bundle-of-Rights Metaphor"; Honoré, "Ownership"; and Waldron, *The Rule of Law and the Measure of Property*, 66.

37. Quoted in Banner, *American Property*, 45.

38. For a description of these categories of ownership (management, use, transfer, security, etc.), see Honoré, "Ownership."

39. On property and kinship in African American communities, see Penningroth, *Claims of Kinfolk.*

40. *Salvador v. Turner,* Records of the Fourth Judicial District Court, #1495, Pointe Coupee Parish Clerk of the Court, New Roads, Louisiana, 1844.

41. See, for instance, *Cooper v. Briscoe,* Adams County, Mississippi, 1811, Records of the Circuit Court, Group 1810–19, box 43, file 22, CRP, HNF.

42. *Ricard, FWC v. Hubeau, FMC,* Records of the Fourth Judicial District Court, #326, West Baton Rouge Parish Clerk of the Court, Port Allen, Louisiana, 1829.

43. For instance, some married women petitioned for separations in property from their husbands (which allowed them to own property of their own) and then operated as single women. Others, with varying degrees of success, simply ignored the doctrine of coverture and sued (or attempted to sue) without their husband's explicit consent. Still others hid behind married women's legal incapacities when convenient. See, for example, *Borie v. Roth and Roth,* Records of the Fourth Judicial District Court, #478, Iberville Parish Clerk of the Court, Plaquemine, Louisiana, 1824. As Laura Edwards has recently argued, scholars have placed too great an emphasis on a "literal reading of a particularly restrictive version of coverture" (173), a reading that has "flatten[ed] the complexities of women's legal status at the time" (178). See Edwards, "The Material Conditions of Dependency."

44. Welke, *Law and the Borders of Belonging,* chap 1.

45. *Maria Theresa, FWC v. Martin,* Adams County, Mississippi, 1815, Records of the Circuit Court, Group 1810–19, box 38, file 25, CRP, HNF. The outcome of this lawsuit is unknown.

46. For instance, see *Bossack v. Holden,* Adams County, Mississippi, 1835, Records of the Circuit Court, Group 1830–39, box 24, file 27, CRP, HNF; and *Bossack v. Holden,* Adams County, Mississippi, 1836, Records of the Circuit Court, Group 1830–39, box 41, file 78, CRP, HNF.

47. J. Martin, *Divided Mastery.* On slave rentals, see also Zaborney, *Slaves for Hire.*

48. For more on the conflict between owners and hirers, see J. Martin, *Divided Mastery.*

49. Ibid., 74–86.

50. *Ove v. Lartigue,* Records of the Fourth Judicial District Court, #320, Pointe Coupee Parish Clerk of the Court, New Roads, Louisiana, 1816.

51. *Simien, FWC v. Nicholas, FMC,* St. Landry Parish, 1822.

52. *Margueritte, FWC v. Janes,* Records of the Fourth Judicial District Court, #1066, Pointe Coupee Parish Clerk of the Court, New Roads, Louisiana, 1831.

53. *Porche, FWC v. Cooley,* Records of the Ninth Judicial District Court, #761, Pointe Coupee Parish Clerk of the Court, New Roads, Louisiana, 1851. For a discussion of owners using the courts to help regulate hirers, see J. Martin, *Divided Mastery,* 94–95.

54. *Bonnefoi, FMC v. Labry,* Records of the Ninth Judicial District Court, #2593, Pointe Coupee Parish Clerk of the Court, New Roads, Louisiana, 1860.

55. For a classic account of the free labor ideology, see Foner, *Free Soil, Free Labor, Free Men.*

56. On skilled free blacks in the early American South, see M. Johnson and Roark, *Black Masters*, 28, 57–58; Ely, *Israel on the Appomattox*, chap. 4; and Myers, *Forging Freedom*. On early New Orleans, see Hanger, *Bounded Lives, Bounded Places*, chap. 2.

57. Petition of William Hayden to the Mississippi State Legislature, 1829, in RSFB, Series I: Legislative Petitions, #11082904.

58. Petition of Ann Caldwell to the Mississippi State Legislature, 1859, in RSFB, Series I: Legislative Petitions #11085923.

59. *Hardes v. Mosby*, Adams County, Mississippi, 1835, Records of the Circuit Court, Group 1830–39, box 23, file 11, CRP, HNF. For other examples of free blacks suing whites for back wages and to enforce labor contracts, see *Zenon v. Sicard*, Records of the Fourth Judicial District Court, #621, Pointe Coupee Parish Clerk of the Court, New Roads, Louisiana, 1826; *Mitchell v. Taylor*, Records of the Early Parish Court, #1114, Pointe Coupee Parish Clerk of the Court, New Roads, Louisiana, 1844; *Villiar v. Bristow*, Records of the Fourth Judicial District Court, #1835, Iberville Parish Clerk of the Court, Plaquemine, Louisiana, 1841; and *Dubuclet v. Tenent and Navy*, Records of the Fourth Judicial District Court, #2030, Iberville Parish Clerk of the Court, Plaquemine, Louisiana, 1843.

60. *Decuir, FMC v. Gleason*, Records of the Sixth Judicial District Court, #1254, Iberville Parish, Louisiana, 1859.

61. See *Roth v. Garlick*, Records of the Sixth Judicial District Court, #477, Iberville Parish Clerk of the Court, Plaquemine, Louisiana, 1851; *Roth v. Comeau*, Records of the Sixth Judicial District Court, #1127, Iberville Parish Clerk of the Court, Plaquemine, Louisiana, 1858; and *Roth v. Hebert et al.*, Records of the Sixth Judicial District Court, #1140, Iberville Parish Clerk of the Court, Plaquemine, Louisiana, 1858.

62. *Degruise v. Breaux et al.*, Records of the Sixth Judicial District Court, #1235, Iberville Parish Clerk of the Court, Plaquemine, Louisiana, 1859.

63. On property ownership among American slaves, see especially Penningroth, *The Claims of Kinfolk*; Schweninger, *Black Property Owners in the South, 1790–1915*; and Hilliard, *Masters, Slaves, and Exchange*.

64. Penningroth, *Claims of Kinfolk*.

65. *State of Mississippi v. Smith*, Adams County, Mississippi, 1854, Records of the Circuit Court, Group 1850–59, box 16, file 21, CRP, HNF.

66. *Elizabeth, a Negro woman v. Williams*, Adams County, Mississippi, 1801, Records of the Circuit Court, Group 1800–09, box 23, file 65, CRP, HNF.

67. *Lacroix v. Ricard, FMC*, Records of the Old Parish Court, #586, Iberville Parish Clerk of the Court, Plaquemine, Louisiana, 1822; *Lacroix v. Ricard, FMC*, Records of the Fourth Judicial District Court, no number, Iberville Parish Clerk of the Court, Plaquemine, Louisiana, 1822; *Thompson v. Ricard*, Records of the Fourth Judicial District Court, #363, Iberville Parish Clerk of the Court, Plaquemine, Louisiana, 1823; *Baugnon v. Ricard*, Records of the Fourth Judicial District Court, #364, Iberville Parish Clerk of the Court, Plaquemine, Louisiana, 1823; *Hiriart v. Ricard*, Records of the Fourth Judicial District Court, #365, Iberville Parish Clerk of the Court, Plaquemine, Louisiana, 1823; and Petition of Maximillian Ricard, Records of the Fourth Judicial District Court, #324, Iberville Parish Clerk of the Court, Plaquemine, Louisiana, 1823.

68. *Meyer v. Dupperon, FMC*, Records of the Ninth Judicial District Court, #421, Pointe Coupee Parish Clerk of the Court, New Roads, Louisiana, 1849.

69. *Borie v. Danos and Bush*, Records of the Fourth Judicial District Court, #579, Iberville Parish Clerk of the Court, Plaquemine, Louisiana, 1826.

70. *Wooten v. Harrison*, Records of the Seventh Judicial District Court, #3476, West Feliciana Parish Clerk of the Court, St. Francisville, Louisiana, 1850.

71. *Hicks v. Evans and Ledoux*, Records of the Fifth Judicial District Court, #1635, St. Landry Parish Clerk of the Court, Opelousas, Louisiana, 1830.

72. *Masse et al. v. Pierre et al.*, Records of the Fifth Judicial District Court, #969, St. Landry Parish Clerk of the Court, Opelousas, Louisiana, 1825.

73. Petition of Joachim Porche, Records of the Fourth Judicial District Court, #599, Pointe Coupee Parish Clerk of the Court, New Roads, Louisiana, 1824; *Porche v. Van Winkle*, Records of the Fourth Judicial District Court, #615, Pointe Coupee Parish Clerk of the Court, New Roads, Louisiana, 1824; *Sanite v. Van Winkle*, Records of the Early Parish Court, #658, Pointe Coupee Parish Clerk of the Court, New Roads, Louisiana, 1824; *Sanite v. Van Winkle*, Records of the Early Parish Court, #659, Pointe Coupee Parish Clerk of the Court, New Roads, Louisiana, 1824; and *Sanite v. Van Winkle*, Records of the Fourth Judicial District Court, #623, Pointe Coupee Parish Clerk of the Court, New Roads, Louisiana, 1824.

74. On the Van Winkles (alias Van Wickle) and their slave-trading operation, see Gigantino, "Trading in Jersey Souls"; Pingeon, "An Abominable Business"; and Drake, "Off the Record."

75. *Hawkins v. Van Winkle*, Records of the Fourth Judicial District Court, #669, Pointe Coupee Parish Clerk of the Court, New Roads, Louisiana, 1827; emphasis added.

76. For instance, see *Hawkins, FWC v. Moore, FWC*, Records of the Early Parish Court, #752, Pointe Coupee Parish Clerk of the Court, New Roads, Louisiana, 1828; and *Hawkins v. Reed*, Records of the Early Parish Court, #774, Pointe Coupee Parish Clerk of the Court, New Roads, Louisiana, 1831.

CHAPTER 6

1. Louisiana law also did not require free people of color to obtain a white guardian. But in several southern states, free blacks were considered children in the eyes of the law and were required to obtain white guardians. In 1810, for instance, the Georgia legislature passed an act stipulating that all free blacks apply to the county court to obtain a white guardian to oversee their interests. The parties also had to appear before the court annually and register. See *Acts of the General Assembly of the State of Georgia*, 120.

2. The total population of Claiborne County in 1850 was 14,941, 11,450 of whom were slaves. Historical Census Browser, University of Virginia Library, 2004, http://mapserver.lib.virginia.edu/php/state.php.

3. Minute Book of Magnolia Baptist Church, Claiborne County, Mississippi, September 1852 to August 1875, box 86, MBHC.

4. "List of Free Negroes and Free Mulattos," box 2E773, folder 5, NTC.

5. *Hannah, Edward, and Rosetta, v. Chess*, Claiborne County, 1847, Records of the Circuit Court, Port Gibson, Mississippi. For a similar case in which free blacks in Claiborne County fell victim to enslavement by their supposed protector and sued for

their freedom, see *Chaney et al. v. Kinley*, Claiborne County, 1835, Records of the Circuit Court, Port Gibson, Mississippi.

6. This number probably does not account for all of the freedom claims in the region, such as those lost from the record, and it cannot account for those that were summarily rejected.

7. Louisiana *Civil Code*, Art. 183, p. 28.

8. Kaye, *Joining Places*, 172.

9. See the Louisiana *Civil Code*, Art. 177, p. 28; emphasis added.

10. See *The Revised Code of the Laws of Mississippi* (1824), Sec. 76, p. 386. Such laws remained in force throughout the antebellum period. For instance, see *The Revised Code of the Statute Laws of the State of Mississippi* (1857), Art. 10, p. 236.

11. Cobb, *An Inquiry into the Law of Negro Slavery*, 252. Slaves had an ambiguous status in southern jurisprudence. They were at once people and property: the law recognized slaves as persons in criminal law (and punished them as people) but viewed them as property in civil law. Civil law, then, aimed to suppress bondspeople's personality. In Daniel Flanigan's words, "A slave could not own a horse, but he could surely steal one." See Flanigan, "Criminal Procedure in Slave Trials in the Antebellum South," 537. Yet Ariela Gross uses lower court records, warranty cases in particular, to disrupt this person-versus-property dichotomy. For example, when buyers found "defects" in their human property (such as habitual running away), they might sue for a breach of warranty as they would for other property. But unlike with cases involving horses and other types of property, Gross found that in warranty cases involving slaves, the parties in the courtroom brought into question enslaved people's moral character. In so doing, they recognized slave personality in civil cases, cases where, in Gross's words, "slaves were most property-like" (3). Gross, *Double Character*, 3–5.

12. Schafer, *Becoming Free, Remaining Free*, 3. For a description of how enslaved people initiated freedom suits through charges of assault and battery and false imprisonment, see Kennington, "Law, Geography, and Mobility," 580–81.

13. I did not find any examples of enslaved Louisianans initiating habeas corpus actions in the Natchez district.

14. Petition of Stephen, Warren County, Mississippi, 1833, NTC. For other examples of enslaved people's habeas actions and freedom claims, see *Donnerson v. Chapman and Terrell*, Adams County, Mississippi, 1823, Records of the Circuit Court, Group 1820–29, box 46, file 11, CRP, HNF; and *Rebecca v. Jones*, Adams County, Mississippi, 1828, Records of the Circuit Court, Habeas Corpus files, box 2, CRP, HNF.

15. *Andre v. The State of Mississippi*, Adams County, Mississippi, 1825, Records of the Circuit Court, Habeas Corpus files, box 2, CRP, HNF. For other examples of free people of color held as runaway slaves and suing for their freedom, see *State of Mississippi v. Grayson*, Adams County, Mississippi, 1821, Records of the Circuit Court, Habeas Corpus files, box 5, CRP, HNF; *State of Mississippi v. Kiah*, Adams County, Mississippi, 1821, Records of the Circuit Court, Habeas Corpus files, box 5, CRP, HNF; and *State of Mississippi v. Lewis*, Adams County, Mississippi, 1841, Records of the Circuit Court, Habeas Corpus files, box 3, CRP, HNF.

16. Stanley, *From Bondage to Contract*, 3.

17. Ibid.

18. Louisiana *Civil Code*, Art. 174, p. 27.

19. On Louisiana slaves' ability to contract for their freedom, see Schafer, *Becoming Free, Remaining Free*, chap. 3. On enslaved people and *coartación* in the Spanish period, see Spear, "'Using the Facilities Conceded to Her by Law.'" On enslaved people's routes to freedom in colonial New Orleans, see Hanger, *Bounded Lives, Bounded Places*, chap. 1. On the legacy of *coartación* in Louisiana, see Gross and de la Fuente, "Slaves, Free Blacks, and Race in the Legal Regimes of Cuba, Louisiana, and Virginia"; and Schafer, *Slavery, the Civil Law, and the Supreme Court of Louisiana*. For an excellent analysis of enslaved people creating and shaping the law of *coartación* in Cuba, see de la Fuente, "Slaves and the Creation of Legal Rights in Cuba."

20. Kotlikoff and Rupert, "The Manumission of Slaves in New Orleans."

21. Schafer, *Slavery, the Civil Law, and the Supreme Court of Louisiana*, 224.

22. Keckley, *Behind the Scenes; or, Thirty Years a Slave, and Four Years in the White House* (1868), Documenting the American South, University Library, the University of North Carolina at Chapel Hill, 1999, http://docsouth.unc.edu/neh/keckley/keckley.html.

23. Grandy, *Narrative of the Life of Moses Grandy, Late a Slave in the United States of America* (1843), Documenting the American South, University Library, the University of North Carolina at Chapel Hill, 1996, http://docsouth.unc.edu/fpn/grandy/grandy.html.

24. *Jones v. Ozman*, Adams County, Mississippi, 1800, Records of the Circuit Court, Group 1800–09, box 23, file 56, CRP, HNF.

25. It is possible that additional archival research in courthouses in other regions of Mississippi will reveal similar cases, but Jones's lawsuit is the only one of this nature from Adams and Claiborne Counties.

26. Schafer, *Becoming Free, Remaining Free*, 45.

27. Judith Schafer found several instances in which the Supreme Court of Louisiana heard the appeals of slaves attempting to gain their liberty by enforcing their self-purchase contracts with their owners. The formula for success in these cases appears to have been producing a written contract as evidence of the contract. Many with only verbal contracts lost their appeals. See Schafer, *Slavery, the Civil Law, and the Supreme Court of Louisiana*, 224–34; and Schafer, *Becoming Free, Remaining Free*, chap. 3.

28. *Moore v. Moore*, St. Landry Parish, Louisiana, 1822, in RSFB, Series II, Part F, PAR #2088214.

29. *Milien v. Sonnier*, St. Landry Parish, Louisiana, 1855, in RSFB, Series II, Part F, PAR #20885503.

30. *Tom v. Porche*, Records of the Ninth Judicial District Court, #1126, Pointe Coupee Parish Clerk of the Court, New Roads, Louisiana, 1854. For a similar case, see *Pauline v. Hubert and Moore*, Records of the Ninth Judicial District Court, #1850, Pointe Coupee Parish Clerk of the Court, New Roads, Louisiana, 1857.

31. Louisiana *Civil Code*, Art. 184, p. 29. Mississippi allowed manumission by will until 1842. See *An Act to Amend the Several Acts of this State in Relation to Free Negroes and Mulattoes*, Feb. 26, 1842, *Laws of the State of Mississippi*, 69–71.

32. Succession of Pierre Belly, Records of the Probate Court, #65, Iberville Parish Clerk of the Court, Plaquemine, Louisiana, 1814.

33. Schafer, *Slavery, the Civil Law, and the Supreme Court of Louisiana*, 201–2.

34. In her study of freedom suits in St. Louis, Lea VanderVelde follows the fate of the slaves of Milton Duty, who sued for their freedom after their master freed them in his will. See VanderVelde, *Redemption Songs*, chap. 12.

35. *Peter v. Bradford et al.*, West Feliciana Parish, Louisiana, 1827 in RSFB, Series II, Part F, PAR #20882728.

36. In early 1842, Mississippi law banned private manumissions. The law held that, "Hereafter it shall not be lawful for any person, by last will or testament, to make any device or bequest of any slave or slaves for the purpose of emancipation, or to direct that any slave or slaves shall be removed from this state for the purpose of emancipation elsewhere." *An Act to Amend the Several Acts of this State in Relation to Free Negroes and Mulattoes, Feb. 26, 1842*, p. 69–71.

37. *Bob and Milley v. Nugent et al.*, Iberville Parish, Louisiana, 1833, in RSFB, Series II, Part F, PAR #20883304. For a similar case, see *Steer v. Steer*, East Baton Rouge, 1819, in RSFB, Series II, Part F, PAR #20881917.

38. Louis Cadoret, for instance, sued the owner of a plantation for $300 in back wages, the amount he was to be paid for one year's employment as an overseer. *Cadoret v. Decuir*, Records of the Early Parish Court, #610, Pointe Coupee Parish Clerk of the Court, New Roads, Louisiana, 1821.

39. *Mary v. Morris et al.*, East Baton Rouge Parish, Louisiana, 1830, in RSFB, Series II, Part F, PAR #20883001.

40. *New Orleans Daily Picayune*, March 8, 1856, quoted in Schafer, *Becoming Free, Remaining Free*, 82. For the act of the Louisiana legislature, see "An Act to Prohibit the Emancipation of Slaves," Act of March 6, 1857, *Louisiana Acts, 1857*, p. 55.

41. *Irma (a slave) v. Rils*, Records of the Sixth Judicial District Court, #977, Iberville Parish Clerk of the Court, Plaquemine, Louisiana, 1857. Similarly, see *Pauline v. Hubert and Moore*.

42. Louisiana *Civil Code*, Art. 37, p. 8. See also Palmer, *Through the Codes Darkly*, 149–52.

43. On Julien Poydras, see Costello, *The Life, Family and Legacy of Julien Poydras*.

44. Louisiana *Civil Code*, Art. 194, p. 30. Louisiana law protected *statu liberi* in other ways as well: they could acquire property through donation (although a curator would oversee that property until they acquired their freedom, and the children of a slave mother born after she became a *statu liber* would gain their freedom at the same time as their mothers (even if their mothers died). Louisiana *Civil Code*, Arts. 193 and 196, p. 30.

45. *Moussa v. Allain*, West Baton Rouge Parish, Louisiana, 1825, in RSFB, Series II, Part F, PAR #20882524. The record of the appeal is included with the trial court record (as was typical), but the supreme court case spells Moussa's name as Moosa.

46. On the life of Benjamin Poydras, see Costello, *The Life, Family and Legacy of Julien Poydras*.

47. *Poydras and slaves v. Mourain*, Records of the Fourth Judicial District Court, #877, Pointe Coupee Parish Clerk of the Court, New Roads, Louisiana, 1835.

48. For another successful case in which Benjamin Poydras and several slaves sued to enforce the provisions of Julien Poydras's will, see *Poydras et al. v. Taylor et al.*, Records of the Fourth Judicial District Court, #896, Pointe Coupee Parish Clerk of the Court, New Roads, Louisiana, 1835; for an example in which the plaintiffs lost their lawsuit, see

Poydras v. Bonneau and Delamare, Records of the Fourth Judicial District Court, #1100, Pointe Coupee Parish Clerk of the Court, New Roads, Louisiana, 1839. For other cases in which the Poydras slaves sued to enforce their former owner's will, see Costello, *The Life, Family and Legacy of Julien Poydras*, 127–36.

49. For a lawsuit in which an owner of some of the Poydras slaves sued a free black woman for harboring his property, see *Leblanc v. Chalinette, FWC*, Records of the Fourth Judicial District Court, #971, Pointe Coupee Parish Clerk of the Court, New Roads, Louisiana, 1837. On the Poydras runaways more generally, see Costello, *The Life, Family and Legacy of Julien Poydras*, 129–31.

50. Claiming to have been born free was a common argument in freedom suits in other regions too, as Anne Twitty shows in her study of freedom suits in antebellum St. Louis. At least seventy-one enslaved plaintiffs in St. Louis initiated suits for their freedom on the grounds that they were freeborn. Twitty, *Before Dred Scott*, 16.

51. Louisiana *Civil Code*, Art. 183, p. 28.

52. Gross, *What Blood Won't Tell*, 48.

53. Ibid.

54. *Woodall v. Sexton*, Adams County, Mississippi, 1826, Records of the Circuit Court, Group 1820–29, box 37, file 36, CRP, HNF.

55. *A Digest of the Statute Law of Kentucky*, chapter CLXXIV, Sec. 1, p. 1149–50.

56. *Phoebe, John, and Sally v. Boyer*, Adams County, Mississippi, 1826, Records of the Circuit Court, Group 1820–29, box 34, file 82, CRP, HNF.

57. *Mordecai et al. v. Baird*, Records of the Fourth Judicial District Court, #713, Pointe Coupee Parish Clerk of the Court, New Roads, Louisiana, 1828. For other examples of litigants claiming freedom through Indian ancestry (in Virginia and Kentucky), see Sachs, "'Freedom by a Judgment."

58. Free people of color held as runaway slaves and suing for their freedom represented the second most common type of freedom suit in Mississippi (involving eighteen lawsuits). The remaining litigants (both in Mississippi and Louisiana) used a number of different arguments to sue for freedom, which I detail throughout.

59. Sixteen out of thirty-one won their cases (52 percent); ten either lost or the case was dismissed for some unspecified reason; and in five cases the verdict is missing and the outcome unknown. Twenty-seven of these cases involved people enslaved in Mississippi, and the other four involved Louisiana slaves.

60. On New Orleans and kidnapping, see Schafer, *Becoming Free, Remaining Free*, chap. 7; and Aslakson, *Making Race in the Courtroom*, chap. 6.

61. See Berlin, *Generations of Captivity*, chap. 4; and Berlin, chap. 3. For more on the internal slave trade, see Deyle, *Carry Me Back*; Gudmestad, *A Troublesome Commerce*; W. Johnson, *Soul by Soul*; A. Rothman, *Slave Country*; and W. Johnson, *The Chattel Principle*.

62. On the kidnapping of free African Americans, see Richard Bell, "'Thence to Patty Cannon's'"; Berlin, *Generations of Captivity*, 167–68; Berlin, *The Making of African America*, 102; Deyle, *Carry Me Back*, 17, 29, 39, 178; Gigantino, "Trading in Jersey Souls"; Gudmestad, *A Troublesome Commerce*, 62, 73–5, 159–60; Pingeon, "An Abominable Business"; Schafer, *Becoming Free, Remaining Free*, chap. 7; Wilson, *Freedom at Risk*; and Winch, "Philadelphia and the Other Underground Railroad." On the abduction of a freed woman's children in wartime New Orleans, see A. Rothman, *Beyond Freedom's Reach*.

63. "Supposed Kidnapping of the North River," *Colored American*, November 23, 1839.

64. "Kidnapping," *North Star*, December 29, 1848.

65. *The Statutes of the State of Mississippi* (1840), 697. In Louisiana, the law held, "If any person or persons shall, without due process of law, seize and forcibly confine or inveigle or kidnap any negro, mulatto, or other person of colour not being a slave, with intent to send him within or out of this state against his will, or shall conspire with any other person or persons, or aid, abate, assist, command or procure any other person to commit the said offence, such person or persons so offending, shall, on conviction of any of the said offences, be fined or imprisoned, or both, at the discretion of the court before which such conviction shall be heard, such fine not to exceed one thousand dollars, and such imprisonment not to exceed fourteen years at hard labour or otherwise." *A General Digest of the Acts of the Legislature of Louisiana*, 398–99.

66. On the Van Winkles (alias Van Wickle), kidnapping, and their slave-trading operations, see Gigantino, "Trading in Jersey Souls"; Pingeon, "An Abominable Business"; and Drake, "Off the Record."

67. The statute held, "If any person or persons shall be found aiding, abetting or maintaining any person in the prosecution of a suit upon a petition as aforesaid, and such person or persons shall fail to establish his, her, or their claim to freedom, person so found aiding, abetting or maintaining, shall forfeit and pay to the owner of such slave, or to the person who shall prosecute for the same, the sum of one hundred dollars for every person so complaining; to be recovered by action of debt, in any circuit court within this state; and moreover, be liable to an action on the case for damages arising therefrom to the party grieved thereby." *The Revised Code of the Laws of Mississippi* (1824), 387. I have not found evidence of this statute being enforced in the Natchez district, however.

68. Northup, *Twelve Years a Slave*.

69. *Hamm v. Green and Steele*, Adams County, Mississippi, 1819, Records of the Circuit Court, Group 1810–19, box 43, file 76, CRP, HNF.

70. For an example of an enslaved family suing for freedom on the grounds of kidnapping in antebellum St. Louis, see VanderVelde, *Redemption Songs*, chap. 5.

71. *Lewis and Lewis v. Clark and Slater*, Adams County, Mississippi, 1822, Records of the Circuit Court, Group 1820–29, box 13, file 39, CRP, HNF.

72. Salafia, *Slavery's Borderland*. See also Kennington, "Law, Geography, and Mobility."

73. *Elias, man of color v. Bell*, Adams County, Mississippi, 1817, Records of the Circuit Court, Group 1810–19, box 25, file 133, CRP, HNF.

74. *Cooper v. Briscoe*, Adams County, Mississippi, 1812, Records of the Circuit Court, Group 1810–19, box 43, file 22, CRP, HNF. For a similar case involving a kidnapping from the borderland region, see *Hamm v. Green and Steele*, Adams County, Mississippi, 1819, Records of the Circuit Court, Group 1810–19, box 43, file 76, CRP, HNF.

75. On courts issuing commissions to take the testimony of long distance witnesses, see chapter 3.

76. *Susey et al. v. Scott and Rees*, Adams County, Mississippi, 1805, Records of the Circuit Court, Group 1800–09, box 32, file 14, CRP, HNF.

77. *John (a negro) v. Williams*, Adams County, Mississippi, 1821, Records of the Circuit Court, Group 1820–29, box 6, file 101, CRP, HNF. For a similar case, see *Mary Ann v. Kempe*,

Adams County, Mississippi, 1820, Records of the Circuit Court, Group 1820–29, box 6, file 37, CRP, HNF.

78. *Charles and Betsy v. Rocheblanc*, Records of the Fourth Judicial District Court, #1387, Iberville Parish Clerk of the Court, Plaquemine, Louisiana, 1834.

79. I did not find any extant Mississippi freedom suits that involved arguments about time spent in free territory. Free soil arguments, however, appear to be common in freedom suits. For instance, Kelly Kennington demonstrates that time spent in free territory (usually Illinois) was the most common claim in St. Louis, Missouri, freedom suits. See Kennington, *In the Shadow of Dred Scott*. See also Twitty, *Before Dred Scott*; and VanderVelde, *Redemption Songs*, chap. 4. As Judith Schafer demonstrates, slaves suing for their freedom in the New Orleans district courts also used free soil arguments. See Schafer, *Becoming Free, Remaining Free*, chap. 1. On the principle of free soil, see Peabody and Grinberg, "Free Soil."

80. *Somerset v. Stewart*, 1772, 89 ER, 499.

81. Peabody and Grinberg, "Free Soil," 331–22. On the application of *Somerset* to American law, see Finkelman, *An Imperfect Union*; and Wong, *Neither Fugitive nor Free*. On *Somerset v. Stewart*, see Van Cleve, "*Somerset's Case* and Its Antecedents in Imperial Perspective."

82. On this point, see Schafer, *Becoming Free, Remaining Free*, 15; and Louisiana *Civil Code*, Art. 185, p. 9.

83. *LeRidel v. Poydras*, Records of the Fourth Judicial District Court, #1433, Pointe Coupee Parish Clerk of the Court, New Roads, Louisiana, 1843.

84. "An Act to Protect the Rights of Slaveholders in the State of Louisiana, May 30, 1846," *Louisiana Acts, 1846*, p. 163.

85. *Marie v. Doussan*, West Baton Rouge Parish, 1848, in RSFB, Series II, Part F, PAR # 20884843. For a similar case, see *Angelina, colored woman v. Parlange*, Records of the Ninth Judicial District Court, #824, Pointe Coupee Parish Clerk of the Court, New Roads, Louisiana, 1852.

86. *Moussa v. Allain*.

CHAPTER 7

1. This chapter builds on Dylan Penningroth's work on the meaning of property and ownership to African Americans and the networks and relationships property helped create. Because southern law did not protect the slaves' economy, Penningroth examines the extralegal ways antebellum slaves made, acquired, and bequeathed property. By contrast, I discuss the ways black people used the legal system to protect their property and the ways that the legal recognition of that property helped forge relationships between people. See Penningroth, *The Claims of Kinfolk*.

2. Ricard, "Pierre Belly and Rose," 13.

3. The French regime in the Province of Louisiana began with the first explorations in the 1670s, and it ended with the final handover of the territory to Spain (lower Louisiana) and England (upper Louisiana) at the end of the French and Indian War. France regained sovereignty of the western part of the territory in 1800 but sold it to the United States in the Louisiana Purchase of 1803. During Pierre Belly's lifetime, the lower Mississippi Valley passed through French, Spanish, and American hands.

4. G. Hall, *Africans in Colonial Louisiana*, chap. 1.

5. Ricard, "Pierre Belly and Rose," 13–14; and Riffel, *Iberville Parish History*, 166–67. For legal proceedings in which Belly served as judge, see "Lawsuits, April 1805-August 1805," unprocessed materials, Iberville Parish Clerk of the Court, Plaquemine, Louisiana. For Belly's estate records, see Succession of Pierre Belly, Records of the Probate Court, #65, Iberville Parish Clerk of the Court, Plaquemine, Louisiana, 1814.

6. Madame Dautrieve to Pierre Belly, December 10, 1802, Conveyances, Original Acts, vol. A-1, no. 7, Iberville Parish Clerk of the Court, Plaquemine, Louisiana.

7. For instance, see Joseph Roth to Pierre Belly, September 24, 1782, Conveyances, Original Acts, vol. A-1, no. 53, Iberville Parish Clerk of the Court, Plaquemine, Louisiana.

8. One arpent was roughly equivalent to one acre.

9. Ricard, "Pierre Belly and Rose," 13–14; Riffel, *Iberville Parish History*, 166–67; Succession of Pierre Belly. On Belly as a sugar planter and for some details on his family, see Russell, "Cultural Conflicts and Common Interests."

10. Belly's estate included ninety-six slaves. See Succession of Pierre Belly. For examples of Belly purchasing slaves, see Louis Judice to Pierre Belly, August 29, 1789, Conveyances, Original Acts, vol. A-1, no. 180, Iberville Parish Clerk of the Court, Plaquemine, Louisiana; and George Depassua to Pierre Belly, November 1, 1808, Conveyances, Original Acts, vol. D, no. 58, Iberville Parish Clerk of the Court, Plaquemine, Louisiana.

11. G. Hall, *Africans in Colonial Louisiana*, 278.

12. Ibid., 278–79. For the slave and free populations of lower Louisiana between 1763 and 1800, see especially figure 8, p. 279.

13. Ibid., chap. 9.

14. Ricard, "Pierre Belly and Rose."

15. Clark, *The Strange History of the American Quadroon*, 100. On the range of sexual relationships across the color line in the antebellum South, see especially J. Rothman, *Notorious in the Neighborhood*; and Hodes, *White Women, Black Men*.

16. Clark, *The Strange History of the American Quadroon*, chap. 4. Early in the colonial period, French men and Indian women also engaged in intimate relationships, and these cross-cultural connections worried French colonial officials to such a degree that they attempted to import French women to the colony in an effort to solve the problem. See Spear, *Race, Sex, and Social Order in Early New Orleans*, chap. 1.

17. Clark, *The Strange History of the American Quadroon*, 101.

18. G. Hall, *Africans in Colonial Louisiana*, 238.

19. Ibid., 239–42. White men in the region entered into similar partnerships with Indian women as well. But as the population of native peoples diminished in the region, cross-cultural intimate relationships between black women and white men grew.

20. Costello, *A History of Pointe Coupee Parish*, 102–3.

21. On Bingaman and Williams, see Broussard, "Stepping Lively in Place," 33.

22. Clark, *The Strange History of the American Quadroon*, 101. See also the Louisiana *Civil Code*, 1825, art. 95, p. 77.

23. Manumission of Rosalie and Marie Antoinette, Oct. 3, 1786, Conveyances, Original Acts, vol. E. no. 93, p. 119–120, Iberville Parish Clerk of the Court, Plaquemine, Louisiana.

24. Manumission of Geneviève, July 14, 1802, Conveyances, Original Acts, vol. E. no. 28, Iberville Parish Clerk of the Court, Plaquemine, Louisiana.

25. Manumission of Rose, July 14, 1802, Conveyances, Original Acts, vol. E. no. 27, Iberville Parish Clerk of the Court, Plaquemine, Louisiana.

26. For a discussion of women and manumission (especially the role of reproduction and childbirth in the struggle for freedom) in Maryland in the eighteenth and nineteenth centuries, see Millward, *Finding Charity's Folk.*

27. Petition of William Johnson to the Mississippi State Legislature, 1820, in RSFB, Series I: Legislative Petitions, PAR #11082002.

28. W. T. Johnson and Family Collection, LLMV. On familial slaveholding of free people of color in antebellum Louisiana, see Sharafi, "Slaves and Slavery of Marie Claire Chabert."

29. Mississippi law permitted individual manumissions until 1842. Louisiana law allowed manumissions under specific circumstances until early 1857, when the Louisiana legislature passed a law banning manumissions entirely. For the Mississippi law, see *An Act to Amend the Several Acts of this State in Relation to Free Negroes and Mulattoes, Feb. 26, 1842* (539–40). For the act of the Louisiana legislature, see "An Act to Prohibit the Emancipation of Slaves," Act of March 6, 1857, *Louisiana Acts, 1857,* p. 55.

30. Kotlikoff and Rupert, "The Manumission of Slaves in New Orleans, 1827–1846."

31. For a representative example, Petition of Nanette, FWC, and Antoine Lacour, FMC, Records of the Old Parish Court, #732, Iberville Parish Clerk of the Court, Plaquemine, Louisiana, 1829.

32. Petition of Jeremiah Gill to the Mississippi State Legislature, 1830, in RSFB, Series I: Legislative Petitions, PAR #11083005.

33. Quoted in Ricard, "Pierre Belly and Rose," 14.

34. Pierre and Rose Belly Acknowledgment of Children, February 8, 1818, Conveyances, Original Acts, vol. E, no. 517, Iberville Parish Clerk of the Court, Plaquemine, Louisiana.

35. Pierre and Rose Belly Acknowledgment of Children, February 8, 1818, Conveyances, Original Acts, vol. E, no. 517, Iberville Parish Clerk of the Court, Plaquemine, Louisiana.

36. Clark, *The Strange History of the American Quadroon,* 101.

37. Louisiana *Civil Code,* 1825, arts. 220–230, pp. 100–102.

38. Broussard, "Stepping Lively in Place," 33.

39. Costello, *A History of Pointe Coupee Parish,* 101.

40. Pierre and Rose Belly Acknowledgment of Children, February 8, 1818, Conveyances, Original Acts, vol. E, no. 517, Iberville Parish Clerk of the Court, Plaquemine, Louisiana; emphasis added.

41. Louisiana *Civil Code,* 1825, arts. 254–62, pp. 105.

42. Ibid., arts. 911–27, pp. 234–37; and Clark, *The Strange History of the American Quadroon,* 110.

43. On mixed-race inheritance involving enslaved beneficiaries, see B. Jones, *Fathers of Conscience.*

44. For instance, see Pierre Belly to Antione Dubuclet, March 3, 1808, Conveyances, Original Acts, vol. D, no. 5, Iberville Parish Clerk of the Court, Plaquemine, Louisiana.

45. Pierre Belly to Rose Belly, February 16, 1809, Conveyances, Original Acts, vol. D, no. 86, Iberville Parish Clerk of the Court, Plaquemine, Louisiana; Pierre Belly to Rose Belly, June 15, 1809, Conveyances, Original Acts, vol. E, no. 29, Iberville Parish Clerk of the Court, Plaquemine, Louisiana; Pierre Belly to Rose Belly, May 1, 1811, Conveyances, Original Acts, vol. E, no. 317, Iberville Parish Clerk of the Court, Plaquemine, Louisiana; and Pierre Belly to Rose Belly, January 1, 2014, Conveyances, Original Acts, vol. F, no. 140, Iberville Parish Clerk of the Court, Plaquemine, Louisiana.

46. Penningroth, *The Claims of Kinfolk*. On free people of color in colonial New Orleans and the ties created by succession, see J. Johnson, "Death Rites as Birthrights in Atlantic New Orleans."

47. Succession of Pierre Belly.

48. Schafer, "'Open and Notorious Concubinage.'" See also A. Davis, "The Private Law of Race and Sex"; and B. Jones, *Fathers of Conscience*.

49. For instance, see Rose, FWC to Octavine Belly, wife of Paulin Verret, June 25, 1818, Conveyances, Original Acts, vol. F, no. 634, Iberville Parish Clerk of the Court, Plaquemine, Louisiana.

50. Rose Belly to Rosalie Dubuclet and others, February 2, 1828, Conveyances, Original Acts, vol. L, no. 293, Iberville Parish Clerk of the Court, Plaquemine, Louisiana.

51. This number only includes the immediate family. If the holdings of the families related to the Bellys by marriage (such as the Decuirs and the Tournoirs) then their worth would increase even more significantly. Ricard, "Pierre Belly and Rose," 15.

52. On the legal rights of wives, see Salmon, *Women and the Law of Property in Early America*, chap. 2; and Basch, *In the Eyes of the Law*, chap. 1.

53. See *The Digest of Laws Now in Force in the Territory of New Orleans*; and Upton and Jennings, *The Civil Code of the State of Louisiana, with Annotations*.

54. See Obligation of Joseph Orillion to Rose Belly, July 26, 1813, Conveyances, Original Acts, vol. E, no. 576, Iberville Parish Clerk of the Court, Plaquemine, Louisiana. Rose also lent other Iberville Parish men large sums of money. See also *Dubuclet v. Lorrie*, Records of the Fourth Judicial District Court, #228, Iberville Parish Clerk of the Court, Plaquemine, Louisiana, 1820.

55. For instance, see *Viales v. Rose Belly, FWC*, Records of the Fourth Judicial District Court, #116, Iberville Parish Clerk of the Court, Plaquemine, Louisiana, 1816.

56. On Rose petitioning the court in Iberville Parish to serve as a legal guardian for her minor children, see Succession of Pierre Belly. For an example of Rose donating a significant portion of her property to her daughters, see Rose Belly to Rosalie Dubuclet and others.

57. Bardaglio, *Reconstructing the Household*, 27.

58. See *Johnson v. Hunter*, Adams County, Mississippi, 1816, Records of the Circuit Court, Group 1810–19, box 36, file 69, CRP, HNF.

59. In 1814, Amy Johnson sued another white man for $1,000 damages for whipping and beating her and kicking her while she lay on the ground. The outcome of that case is not known. See *Amey v. Davis*, Adams County, Mississippi, 1814, Records of the Circuit Court, Group 1810–19, box 30, file 15, CRP, HNF. She also sued Arthur Mitchum, a free black man, for damages for assault. While she won that case, the court only granted her one cent in damages and probably viewed the charges as frivolous. See *Johnson v. Mitchum*,

Adams County, Mississippi, 1822, Records of the Circuit Court, Group 1820–29, box 12, file 96, CRP, HNF.

60. Ricard, "Pierre Belly and Rose," 15–16.

61. See Johanna Smith's dissertation for details about some of these family networks and others free families of color in West Baton Rouge Parish. J. Smith, "Mulatto Bend."

62. *Dubuclet v. Lorrie*, Records of the Fourth Judicial District Court, #228, Iberville Parish Clerk of the Court, Plaquemine, Louisiana, 1820.

63. *Deslonde, FMC v. Love*, Records of the Old Parish Court, #829, Iberville Parish Clerk of the Court, Plaquemine, Louisiana, 1831.

64. For instance, see *Colin, FWC v. Ricard, FMC*, Records of the Fourth Judicial District Court, #323, Iberville Parish Clerk of the Court, Plaquemine, Louisiana, 1822.

65. Héloïse Belly and Georges Deslonde Marriage Contract, September 10, 1822, Conveyances, Original Acts, vol. L, no. 293, Iberville Parish Clerk of the Court, Plaquemine, Louisiana.

66. Petition of Delphine Ricard, FWC and Minor, Records of the Fourth Judicial District Court, #1324, Iberville Parish Clerk of the Court, Plaquemine, Louisiana, 1833; and Record of a Ricard Family Meeting, April 13, 1833, vol. N, no. 473, Iberville Parish Clerk of the Court, Plaquemine, Louisiana.

67. See, for instance, *Heirs of the Widow Maximillian Ricard v. Hiriart*, Records of the Fourth Judicial District Court, #1180, Iberville Parish Clerk of the Court, Plaquemine, Louisiana, 1832.

68. For example, see Succession of Marie Croizet Tournoir, FWC, Records of the Ninth Judicial District Court, #2473, Pointe Coupee Parish Clerk of the Court, New Roads, Louisiana, 1859; and Succession of Adeline Decuir, FWC, Records of the Ninth Judicial District Court, #2493, Pointe Coupee Parish Clerk of the Court, New Roads, Louisiana, 1860.

69. See W. T. Johnson and Family Collection, LLMV.

70. On married women's property in Mississippi, see Broussard, "Naked before the Law."

71. A liberalization of divorce law occurred throughout the United States during the antebellum period, especially between 1830 and 1860, and both Mississippi and Louisiana increasingly expand the grounds for divorce. By the late antebellum period, the grounds for divorce or a legal separation included insanity or idiocy, impotence at the time of marriage, criminal activity on the part of the spouse, habitual drunkenness, nonsupport, and cruelty. With the exception of South Carolina, which did not allow for divorce until after the Civil War, the South saw increasingly liberalized divorce laws throughout the early nineteenth century. The liberalization of divorce law was consistent throughout much of the nation in the early nineteenth century. See Censer, "'Smiling through Her Tears.'"

72. *Belly Dubuclet v. Dubuclet*, Records of the Old Parish Court, #71, Iberville Parish Clerk of the Court, Plaquemine, Louisiana, 1808; and *Belly v. Dubuclet*, Records of the Old Parish Court, #70, Iberville Parish Clerk of the Court, Plaquemine, Louisiana, 1808.

73. Married women in Louisiana, both white and black, consistently sued their husbands for separations of property, and courts frequently issued verdicts in their favor. For instance, see *Sloan v. Sloan*, East Baton Rouge Parish, Louisiana, 1842, in RSFB, Series

II, Part F, PAR #20884219; *Stuart v. Stuart*, East Baton Rouge Parish, Louisiana, 1843, in RSFB, Series II, Part F, PAR #20884302; *Martin v. Martin*, East Baton Rouge Parish, Louisiana, 1846, in RSFB, Series II, Part F, PAR #20884628; *Scudder v. Scudder*, East Baton Rouge Parish, Louisiana, 1851, in RSFB, Series II, Part F, PAR #20885110;

74. Louisiana law stipulated that a married couple's property was divided into separate property and common property. The property that either party brought into the marriage or acquired during the marriage through inheritance constituted the separate property of a spouse. Any other property acquired during the marriage was common property. A wife could hold property separate from her husband if she had stipulated this in her marriage contract. A wife's separate property was both dotal, the property that she brought to the husband to help bear the expenses of the marriage, and extra-dotal, property that formed no part of the dowry. A husband had the right to administer the dowry and the community property, but the wife had the right to manage her extra-dotal property if she had so stipulated in her marriage contract. If a wife believed her husband endangered her property, she could petition the district court for a separation of property from her husband. If granted, she could administer this property (property she brought to the marriage or acquired during the marriage) as her separate property. Once separated in property from her husband, her husband's creditors could not seize it to settle his debts. Furthermore, if a wife received a divorce or a separation from bed and board, she would also receive a separation of property, restoring her to the legal status of a single woman. Upton and Jennings, *The Civil Code of the State of Louisiana*; and Phillips, comp, *The Revised Statutes of Louisiana*.

75. *Digest of the Laws of Mississippi*, "An Act for the protection and preservation of the rights and property of Married Women," 23rd sess., Jan. 1839. On the Mississippi Married Women's Property Act, see Broussard, "Naked before the Law."

76. For similar examples of Louisiana wives accusing their husbands of being incapable of managing the family finances, see *Bell v. Bell*, Iberville Parish, Louisiana, 1842, in RSFB, Series II, Part F, PAR #20884205; *Brown v. Brown*, Iberville Parish, Louisiana, 1847, in RSFB, Series II, Part F, PAR #20884734; *Matherine v. Matherine*, Iberville Parish, Louisiana, in RSFB, Series II, Part F, PAR # 0884826; *Reid v. Reid*, Iberville Parish, Louisiana, 1848, in RSFB, Series II, Part F, PAR #20884842; *Hutchinson v. Hutchinson*, Pointe Coupee Parish, Louisiana, 1827, in RSFB, Series II, Part F, PAR #20882710; *McKinney v. McKinney*, Pointe Coupee Parish, Louisiana, 1837, in RSFB, Series II, Part F, PAR #20883720; *Tardy v. Tardy*, Pointe Coupee Parish, Louisiana, 1842, in RSFB, Series II, Part F, PAR #20884412; and *Dozier v. Dozier*, Pointe Coupee Parish, Louisiana, 1855, in RSFB, Series II, Part F, PAR #20885523. Women in Mississippi made similar accusations against their husbands when petitioning the chancery courts to intervene when their husbands' mismanagement endangered their property or their husbands did not adhere to the property stipulations in their marriage contracts. See, for example, *Lanier v. Lanier*, Wilkinson County, Mississippi, 1846, Records of the Vice Chancery Court, #13, CRP, HNF; *Carter v. Carter*, Wilkinson County, Mississippi, 1847, Records of the Vice Chancery Court, #60, CRP, HNF; and *Fletcher v. Fletcher*, Adams County, Mississippi, 1856, Records of the Vice Chancery Court, #859, CRP, HNF.

77. *Honoré v. Honoré*, Records of the Fourth Judicial District Court, #266, Iberville Parish Clerk of the Court, Plaquemine, Louisiana, 1821.

78. For similar cases in which wives became creditors of their husbands, see *Kirkland v. Kirkland*, West Feliciana Parish, Louisiana, 1827, in RSFB, Series II, Part F, PAR #20882727; *Richardson v. Richardson*, West Feliciana Parish, Louisiana, 1833, in RSFB, Series II, Part F, PAR #20883309; *Chestnut v. Chestnut*, West Feliciana Parish, Louisiana, 1848, in RSFB, Series II, Part F, PAR #20884808; *Hamilton v. Hamilton*, West Feliciana Parish, Louisiana, 1848, in RSFB, Series II, Part F, PAR #20884815; *Glaze v. Glaze*, West Feliciana Parish, Louisiana, 1849, in RSFB, Series II, Part F, PAR #20884917; *Kimball v. Kimball*, St. Landry Parish, Louisiana, 1822, in RSFB, Series II, Part F, PAR #20882224; *Richard v. Richard*, St Landry Parish, Louisiana, 1828, in RSFB, Series II, Part F, PAR #20882824; *Lessassier v. Lessassier*, St Landry Parish, Louisiana, 1830, in RSFB, Series II, Part F, PAR #20883009; *Leger v. Leger*, St. Landry Parish, Louisiana, 1840, in RSFB, Series II, Part F, PAR #20884011; and *Provost v. Provost*, St. Landry Parish, Louisiana, 1841, in RSFB, Series II, Part F, PAR #20884125.

79. On this point, see Censer, "Smiling through Her Tears," 42–43.

80. *Belly v. Bousange*, Records of the Fourth Judicial District Court, #725, Iberville Parish Clerk of the Court, Plaquemine, Louisiana, 1828.

81. Héloïse Belly and George Deslonde Marriage Contract, September 10, 1822, vol. L, no. 293, Iberville Parish Clerk of the Court, Plaquemine, Louisiana.

82. Riffel, *Iberville Parish History*, 13–14.

AFTERWORD

1. *Decuir v. Benson*, 27 La. Ann. 1 (1875), Historical Archives of the Supreme Court of Louisiana, Earl K. Long Library, the University of New Orleans, Louisiana. On Decuir and making claims through the rubric of "public rights," see R. Scott, "Public Rights and Private Commerce." On Decuir and injury to her status, see Welke, *Recasting American Liberty*, 302–3.

2. *Code of Practice in Civil Cases for the State of Louisiana* (1861), Art. 1, p. 70.

3. *Hall v. Decuir*, 95 U.S. 485 (1878). When Benson died, his administer, Eliza Hall, continued the case on his behalf.

4. Welke, *Recasting American Liberty*, 348.

5. Forthcoming work by Dylan Penningroth and Melissa Milewski on African Americans and the law in the post–Civil War era also elucidates the connections between the fight for racial justice and the civil litigation. Lessons, I believe, black people learned long before formal emancipation. Crystal N. Feimster's forthcoming work on African Americans' use of military commissions during the Civil War also suggests a long history of appealing to the law for redress. See Penningroth, "Doing Civil Rights: African Americans and the Law, 1800–1970," manuscript in progress; Milewski, "Litigating across the Color Line: Civil Cases between Black and White Southerners from the End of Slavery to Civil Rights," manuscript in progress; and Feimster, "'Truth Be Told': Mutiny and Rape at Fort Jackson, Louisiana," unpublished manuscript, in author's possession.

Bibliography

UNPUBLISHED PRIMARY SOURCES

Trial Court Records

Claiborne County Clerk of the Court, Port Gibson, Mississippi
    Records of the Chancery Court
    Records of the Circuit Court
    Minute Books
    Unprocessed Materials
Historic Natchez Foundation, Natchez, Mississippi (Adams County)
    Records of the Circuit Court, Courthouse Records Project
    Records of the Circuit Court, Habeas Corpus Files, Courthouse Records Project
    Records of the Orphans Court, Courthouse Records Project
    Records of the Vice Chancery Court, Courthouse Records Project
    Minute Books
    Unprocessed Materials
Iberville Parish Clerk of the Court, Plaquemine, Louisiana
    Conveyances, Original Acts
    Probate Successions
    Records of the Fifth Judicial District Court
    Records of the Fourth Judicial District Court
    Records of the Old Parish Court
    Records of the Sixth Judicial District Court
    Records of the Probate Court
    Unprocessed Materials
Library of Congress, Washington, D.C.
    Race, Slavery, and Free Blacks, Series I: Petitions to Southern Legislatures, 1777–1867.
        Bethesda, Md.: University Publications of America, 1998. Microfilm edition.

Race, Slavery, and Free Blacks, Series II: Petitions to Southern County Courts, 1777–1867, Part A: Georgia, Florida, Alabama, and Mississippi. Bethesda, Md.: LexisNexis, 2003. Microfilm edition.

Race, Slavery, and Free Blacks, Series II: Petitions to Southern County Courts, 1777–1867, Part F: Louisiana. Bethesda, Md.: LexisNexis, 2005. Microfilm edition.

Louisiana State Archives, Baton Rouge, Louisiana
 St. Landry Parish Court Documents.

Pointe Coupee Parish Clerk of the Court, New Roads, Louisiana
 Original Acts
 Records of the Early Parish Court
 Records of the Fourth Judicial District Court
 Records of the Ninth Judicial District Court
 Unprocessed Materials

West Baton Rouge Parish Clerk of the Court, Port Allen, Louisiana
 Records of the Fourth Judicial District Court

West Feliciana Parish Clerk of the Court, St. Francisville, Louisiana
 Records of the Third Judicial District Court

Manuscript Sources

Dolphe Briscoe Center for American History, University of Texas, Austin
 Natchez Trace Collection
  Adair vs. Wilkinson Case Records, 1819–1820
  Adams County, Mississippi Records
  Adams, Robert H., Papers, 1820–1834
  Adler, Bennett, Deposition, 1856
  Allen, Jr., Henry S., Papers, 1857–1858
  Archer, Richard Thomas, Family Papers, 1790–1919
  Arthur, Isham, Papers, 1812
  Balfour, William L., Papers, 1841–1863
  Bank of the State of Mississippi Records, 1804–1846
  Barnes-Willis Family Papers, 1793–1840
  Beall, Andrew, Papers, 1801–1804
  Bellinor, Stephen, Letter
  Billingslea, Sarah, Papers, 1844–1891
  Bodley, John F., Papers, 1839–1844
  Bowie Family Papers, 1807–1861
  Briscoe, William, Papers, 1808–1859
  Broughton, Edward, Papers, 1819–1825
  Browder, Frederick A., Papers, 1814–1835
  Brown, Albert Gallatin, Papers, 1844–1853
  Brown, James N., Papers, 1855–1878
  Brown, Patrick, Papers, 1811–1812
  Brownie, John, Papers, 1805–1807

Buckhorn Plantation Records, 1833–1855

Buckner, Robert H., Papers, 1829–1842

Buford, Thomas, 1814–1815

Buie, Angus, Family Papers, 1808–1830

Bullock, Stephen, Papers, 1805–1817

Burns, John and Sarah, Contract, 1806

Cameron, Joel, Papers, 1832

Carney, Arthur, Papers, 1800–1829

Chamberlain-Hyland-Gould Family Papers, 1805–1886

Chambers, Rowland, Papers, 1839–1871

Church Family Papers, 1854–1862

Claiborne, John Frances Hamtramck, Papers, 1828–1838

Cochran, Robert, Papers, 1838–1858

Cox, James, Papers, 1818

Crutcher-Shannon Family Papers, 1822–1905

Cummins, John, Papers, 1811

Davidson, John A., Papers, 1819

Davis, Joseph Emory, Papers, 1824–1880

Davis, Samuel, Legal Documents, 1821

Dayton Family Papers, 1798–1835

Dearmond, Elizabeth, Family Papers, 1827–1848

Devenport, Joseph, Papers, 1855–1865

Douglass, James S., Papers, 1835–1840

Downes, James M., Papers, 1843

Downing, Thomas, Papers, 1811–1815

Dunlap, James, Papers, 1804–1825

Dunbar, Robert C. and Sarah W., Papers, 1804–1854

Duncan Family Papers, 1826–1881

Dutton, John, Papers, 1789–1890

Elliot, Henry T., Papers, 1853–1854

Farrar, F. H. and Thomas P., Papers, 1849–1869

Freeland (Thomas) Deposition

Kiger Family Papers, 1820, 1841–1885

Lane, Edmund M., Papers, 1840–1882

Lane, John and John A., Papers

Lapice, P. M., Letters

McCaleb, David, Papers, 1819–1823, 1850

Minor Family Papers, 1783–1852

Moore, Robert, Papers, 1826–1836

Natchez Trace Civil War Collection 1861–1865

Natchez Trace Crime and Punishment Collection, 1819–1876

Natchez Trace Imprint and Newspaper Collection

Natchez Trace Map Collection

Natchez Trace Pamphlet and Serials Collection

Natchez Trace Collection Photographs, ca. 1855–1920
Natchez Trace Provisional and Territorial Records, 1759–1813
Natchez Trace Slaves and Slavery Collection, 1793–1864
Natchez Trace Small Manuscript Collection
Natchez Trace Collection Supplement, 1775–1965
Noland, Pearce, Family Papers, 1856–1865
Norrell, Levi, Papers, 1819–1832
Sharkey, William Lewis, Papers, 1823–1881
Tinsler, Henry, Court Documents, 1854
Winchester Family Papers, 1783–1906
Other Collections
Littlefield Map Collection
Littlefield Rare Book and Pamphlet Collection
Littlefield Southern Newspaper Collection
Morrow, William H., Collection
Murray, John R., Papers, 1855–1857
Ellis, Powhatan, Papers, 1811–1835
Ramsdell, Charles, Microfilm Collection
Earl K. Long Library, University of New Orleans, Louisiana
Historical Archives of the Supreme Court of Louisiana
Hill Memorial Library, Louisiana State University, Baton Rouge
Louisiana and Lower Mississippi Valley Collection
Adams County, Mississippi, Court Minutes
Bass-Farrar Family Papers, 1829–1917, Mss. 4907
Chelette, Atala, and Family Papers, Mss. 979
Concordia Parish Records, Mss. 55, 79
Conner, Lemuel Parker, and Family Papers, Mss. 1403
Court Records of East Baton Rouge Parish
East Feliciana Parish Marriage Bonds, Licenses, and Certificates, Mss. 1100
East Feliciana Parish Papers, 1822–1869, Mss. 0893
Elam, James E., Letter Book, Mss. 672, 2464
Farrar, Alexander K., Papers, 1804–1931, Mss. 782, 1348
Johnson, William T., Memorial Collection, 1793–1937, Mss. 529, 561, 597, 770, 926, 1093
John R. Lynch, John R., Papers, Mss. 3928
McMurran, John, T., Papers, Mss. 1403
Meullion Family Papers, Mss. 243, 294
Natchez Court Records, 1767–1805
Quitman, John A., Papers, 1823–1872, Mss. 1403, 1431, 1471, 1595, 1723
Reed, Thomas, Papers, Mss. 783
Saint James Parish Justice of the Peace Ledger, Mss. 4802
Shields, Joseph, D., Papers, Mss. 390, 1526, 1542, 1709, 1821, 1996, 2053
Snyder, Alonzo, Papers, 1779–1919, Mss. 655
Turnbull, Dudley, and Family Papers, Mss. 2907
Turner, Edward, Family Papers, 1767–1878, Mss. 1403

WPA Collection
  Historical Records Survey Transcriptions of Louisiana Police Jury Records
The Historic New Orleans Collection
  Cane River Collection, 1817–1859
Mississippi Baptist Historical Commission, Mississippi College, Clinton, Mississippi
  Minute Book of the Forest Hill Baptist Church, Warren County, MS, 1838, 1840–1860,
    1894, vol. 1
  Minute Book of the Magnolia Baptist Church, Claiborne County, MS, 1852–1875
  Minute Book of the Old Salem Church, Jefferson County, MS, 1832–1855
  Minutes of the Fellowship Baptist Church, Jefferson County, MS, 1815–1834
  Records of the Woodville Baptist Church, Wilkinson County, MS, 1853–1976, vol. 1
Mississippi Department of Archives and History, Jackson, Mississippi
  Ash, Harry C. Manuscript
  Baker, Otis T., Family Papers, 1822–1909
  Baptist Church of Christ at Jerusalem, Amite County, MS, 1812–1889
  Christ Church Records, Jefferson County, MS, 1826–1966
  Claiborne, J. F. H., Collection, 1707–1881
  County Court Case File Collection
  Court Case File Collection
  County Records on Microfilm
  Drake, Benjamin M. and Family Papers, 1805–1914
  Drake-Satterfield Family Papers, 1812–1950
  East Fork Baptist Church Records, 1830–1946
  Ebenezer Baptist Church Records, 1806–1975
  Ellis, Powhatan, Papers, 1814–1832
  Hamilton, Charles D., Family Papers, 1858–1870
  Hawkins, Henry G. Papers, 1842–1935
  Johnson, William, Papers, 1811–1859
  Lewis, Seth, Memoirs
  Nutt Family Collection, 1810–1937
  Pine Ridge Presbyterian Church Records, 1807–1966
  Prentiss, Seargent Smith, Papers, 1842–1845
  Records of the First Presbyterian Church, Natchez, MS, 1817–1902
  Records of the First Presbyterian Church, Vicksburg, MS, undated, 1826–1967
  Quitman, John A., Papers, 1812–1860
  Rodney Presbyterian Church Records, 1852–1919
  Sharkey, William L., Papers, 1841–1865
  St. Alban's Episcopal Church Records, Warren County, MS, 1857–1920
  St. Paul's Episcopal Church Records, Woodville, MS, 1823–1868
  Zion Hill Baptist Church, Minutes, 1811–1979
National Archives and Records Administration, Washington, D.C.
  Federal Census, 1790–1890
  Federal Census, Slave Schedules, 1850, 1860
  Records of the Internal Revenue Service
  U.S. Bureau of Land Management, General Land Office Records

Hall v. Decuir, 95 U.S. 485 (1878)
Somerset v. Stewart, 89 ER, 499 (1772)

The Preemption Act of 1841, 27th Congress, Ch. 16, 5 Stat. 453 (1841)
U.S. Constitution, Art. IV

Legal Codes, Digests, Treatises, and Other Materials

A General Digest of the Acts of the Legislature of Louisiana, Passed from the Year 1804–1827, inclusive, and in force at this last period with an appendix and general index. New Orleans: Benjamin Levy, Bookseller and Stationer, 1828.

Acts of the General Assembly of the State of Georgia; Passed at Milledgeville, at the Annual Session, in November and December, 1810. Milledgeville, Ga., 1811.

Acts Passed at the First Session of the First Legislature of the State of Louisiana: begun and held in the City of New Orleans, on the 9th day of February, 1846. New Orleans: W. Van Benthuysen & P. Besancon Jr., 1846.

Acts Passed by the Third Legislature of the State of Louisiana, at its second session, held and begun in the town of Baton Rouge, on the 19th of January, 1857. New Orleans: J. Claiborne, 1857.

Alden, T. J. Fox, and J. A. Van Hoesen, comps. *A Digest of the Laws of Mississippi.* New York: Alexander S. Gould, 1839.

Bullard, Henry A., and Thomas Curry, comps. *A New Digest of the Statute Laws of the State of Mississippi.* New Orleans: E. Johns and Co., 1842.

Catterall, Helen Tunnicliff, ed. *Judicial Cases Concerning American Slavery and the Negro,* Vol. 3. New York: Octagon Books, Inc., 1968.

Civil Code of the State of Louisiana. Published by a Citizen of the United States, 1825.

Cobb, Thomas R. R. *An Inquiry into the Law of Negro Slavery in the United States of America: To which Is Prefixed, an Historical Sketch of Slavery.* Vol. 1. Philadelphia, Savannah, Ga.: T. & J. W. Johnson & Co.; W. T. Williams, 1858.

The Digest of Laws Now in Force in the Territory of New Orleans. St. Louis: Joseph Charles, 1808.

Howard, V. E., and A. Hutchinson, comps. *Statutes of the State of Mississippi of a Public and General Nature.* New Orleans: E. Johns and Co., 1840.

Greiner, Meinrad. *The Louisiana Digest, embracing the laws of the legislature of a general nature, enacted from the year 1804 to 1841, inclusive, and in force at this last period.* New Orleans: B. Levy, 1841.

Kent, James. *Commentaries on American Law,* Vol. 2. 2nd ed. New York: O. Halsted, 1832.

Laws of the State of Mississippi; Passed at a Regular Biennial Session of the Legislature, Held in the City of Jackson in January and February A. D. 1842. Jackson, Miss.: C. M. Price & G. R. Fall, 1842.

Morgan, Thomas Gibbes, comp. *Civil Code for the State of Louisiana, with the Statutory Amendments, from 1825 to 1853, inclusive.* New Orleans: J. B. Steel, 1853.

———. *Code of Practice in Civil Cases for the State of Louisiana, with the Statutory Amendments, from 1825 to 1853.* New Orleans: J. B. Steel, 1861.

Phillips, U. B., comp. *The Revised Statutes of Louisiana.* New Orleans, John Claiborne, 1856.

The Revised Code of the Statute Laws of the State of Mississippi. Jackson, Miss.: E. Barksdale, 1857.

The Revised Code of the Laws of Mississippi, in Which Are Comprised All Such Acts of the General Assembly, of a Public Nature, As Were In Force At the End of the Year 1823, with a General Index. Natchez, Miss.: Francis Baker, 1824.

Swigert, Jacob, and William Little. *A Digest of the Statute Law of Kentucky.* Frankfort: Kendall and Russell, 1822.

Transcriptions of Parish Records of Louisiana: No. 24 Iberville Parish (Plaquemine), Series 1, Police Jury Minutes, vol. 1, 1850–1862. Prepared by the Historical Records Survey Program, Works Projects Administration, 1840.

Upton, Wheelock S., and Needler R. Jennings. *The Civil Code of the State of Louisiana, with Annotations.* New Orleans: E. Johns and Co., 1838.

Narratives, Letters, Diaries, and Other Materials

Baldwin, Joseph G., *The Flush Times of Alabama and Mississippi: A Series of Sketches.* 1853. New York: Hill and Wang, 1957.

Bibb, Henry. *Narrative of the Life and Adventures of Henry Bibb, an American Slave, Written by Himself.* New York, 1849.

———. *Clotel; or, The President's Daughter.* Introduction by Hilton Als. New York: The Modern Library, 2000.

Brown, William Wells. *Narrative of the Life of William W. Brown, an American Slave.* London: Charles Gilpen, 1850.

Claiborne, John Francis Hamtramck. *Life and Correspondence of John A. Quitman, Major-General, U.S.A., and Governor of the State of Mississippi.* Volume 1. New York, 1860.

Diocese of Baton Rouge, Catholic Church Records. Volumes 2–10: Pointe Coupee Records. Baton Rouge, La.: Diocese of Baton Rouge, Department of Archives, 1978.

Douglass, Frederick. *Narrative of the Life of Frederick Douglass, an American Slave.* Boston: Antislavery Office, 1845.

Hayden, William. *Narrative of William Hayden, Containing a Faithful Account of His Travels for a Number of Years, Whilst a Slave, in the South.* Philadelphia: Rhistoric Publications, 1969.

Hogan, William Ransom, and Edwin Adams Davis, eds. *William Johnson's Natchez: The Ante-Bellum Diary of a Free Negro.* Baton Rouge: Louisiana State University Press, 1951.

Fitzhugh, George. *Sociology for the South; or, The Failure of Free Society.* Richmond, Va.: A. Morris, 1854.

Foote, Henry Stuart. *The Bench and Bar of the South and Southwest.* St. Louis: Soule, Thomas, and Wentworth, 1876.

Grandy, Moses. *Narrative of the Life of Moses Grandy; Late a Slave in the United States of America.* Boston: O. Johnson, 1844.

Jacobs, Harriet A. *Incidents in the Life of a Slave Girl*. Edited by Jean Fagan Yellin. Cambridge, Mass.: Harvard University Press, 2000.

Jacobs, John S. "A True Tale of Slavery." *The Leisure Hour: A Family Journal of Instruction and Recreation* 479 (February 1861): 85–87, 108–10, 125–27, 139–41.

Jefferson, Thomas. *Notes on the State of Virginia*. Philadelphia: R. T. Rawle, 1801.

Keckley, Elizabeth. *Behind the Scenes; or, Thirty Years a Slave, and Four Years in the White House*. New York. G. W. Carleton & Co., 1868.

Lewis, J. Vance. *Out of the Ditch: A True Story of an Ex Slave*. Houston: Rein & Sons Co., 1910.

Lynch, James. *The Bench and Bar of Mississippi*. New York: E. J. Hale & Son Publishers, 1881.

Mississippi Slave Narratives: A Folk History of Slavery from Interviews with Former Slaves. Bedford, Mass.: Applewood Books, 2006.

Northup, Solomon. *Twelve Years a Slave: Narrative of Solomon Northup, a Citizen of New-York, Kidnapped in Washington City in 1841, and Rescued in 1853, from a Cotton Plantation Near the Red River, in Louisiana*. Auburn, N.Y.: Derby and Miller, 1853.

Toulmin, Harry. *The Magistrates' Assistant*. Natchez, Miss.: Samuel Terrell, 1807.

NEWSPAPERS AND PERIODICALS

Ariel (Miss.)

Baton Rouge Gazette

The Colored American (N.Y.)

Democratic Advocate (La.)

Feliciana Democrat (La.)

Free Trader (Miss.)

Freedom's Journal (N.Y.)

Mississippi State Gazette

Mississippi Statesman

Natchez

Natchez Courier and Journal

Natchez Daily Courier

Natchez Gazette

Natchez Weekly Courier

The National Era (D.C.)

New Orleans Daily Picayune

Niles Register (Md.)

The North Star (N.Y.)

Port Gibson Correspondent (Miss.)

Republican (Miss.)

Southern Sentinel (La.)

Semi-Weekly Mississippian

Weekly Advocate (N.Y.)

UNPUBLISHED PAPERS

Gall, Michael J., et al. "Navigation and Negotiation: Adaptive Strategies of a Free African American Family in Central Delaware." Paper presented to the Middle Atlantic Archeological Conference, March 2014, Langhorne, Pa.

Kennington, Kelly M. "'Just as Free as You Are': Individual Lives, Local Communities, and the Establishment of Freedom in the Law." Paper presented at the annual meeting of the American Society for Legal History, St. Louis, November 8–11, 2012.

Twitty, Anne S. "The Court of Public Opinion? Masters, Slaves, and Character Evidence in the St. Louis Circuit Court's Freedom Suits." Paper presented at the annual meeting of the American Historical Association, New Orleans, Louisiana, January 3–6, 2013.

Allen, Austin. *Origins of the Dred Scott Case: Jacksonian Jurisprudence and the Supreme Court, 1837–1857*. Athens: University of Georgia Press, 2006.

Amsterdam, Anthony G., and Jerome S. Bruner. *Minding the Law*. Cambridge, Mass.: Harvard University Press, 2000.

Appleby, Joyce Oldham. *Capitalism and a New Social Order: The Republican Vision of the 1790s*. New York: New York University Press, 1984.

Aslakson, Kenneth R. *Making Race in the Courtroom: The Legal Construction of Three Races in Early New Orleans*. New York: New York University Press, 2014.

Atherton, Lewis E. "The Problem of Credit Rating in the Ante-Bellum South." *Journal of Southern History* 12, no. 4 (November 1946): 534–56.

Ayers, Edward L. *Vengeance and Justice: Crime and Punishment in the Nineteenth Century American South*. New York: Oxford University Press, 1984.

Balleisen, Edward J. *Navigating Failure: Bankruptcy and Commercial Society in Antebellum America*. Chapel Hill: University of North Carolina Press, 2001.

Banner, Stuart. *American Property: A History of How, Why, and What We Own*. Cambridge, Mass.: Harvard University Press, 2011.

Baptist, Edward E. *Creating an Old South: Middle Florida's Plantation Frontier before the Civil War*. Chapel Hill: University of North Carolina Press, 2002.

———. *The Half Has Never Been Told: Slavery and the Making of American Capitalism*. New York: Basic Books, 2014.

Bardaglio, Peter W. "Rape and the Law in the Old South: 'Calculated to Excite Indignation in Every Heart.'" *Journal of Southern History* 60, no. 4 (November 1994): 749–72.

———. *Reconstructing the Household: Families, Sex, and the Law in the Nineteenth-Century South*. Chapel Hill: University of North Carolina Press, 1995.

Baron, Jane B. "Rescuing the Bundle-of-Rights Metaphor in Property Law." *University of Cincinnati Law Review* 82 (2014): 57–101.

Basch, Norma. *Framing American Divorce: From the Revolutionary Generation to the Victorians*. Berkeley: University of California Press, 1999.

———. *In the Eyes of the Law: Women, Marriage, and Property in Nineteenth-Century New York*. Ithaca, N.Y.: Cornell University Press, 1982.

Beckert, Sven. *Empire of Cotton: A Global History*. New York: Knopf, 2014.

Bell, Richard. "'Thence to Patty Cannon's': Gender, Family, and the Reverse Underground Railroad." *Slavery & Abolition* 37, no. 1 (2016): 661–79.

Bennett, Herman L. *Africans in Colonial Mexico: Absolutism, Christianity, and Afro-Creole Consciousness, 1570–1640*. Bloomington: Indiana University Press, 2003.

Bercaw, Nancy, ed. *Gender and the Southern Body Politic: Essays and Comments*. Jackson: University Press of Mississippi, 2000.

Berger, Dan. *Captive Nation: Black Prison Organizing in the Civil Rights Era*. Chapel Hill: University of North Carolina Press, 2014.

Berlin, Ira. *Generations of Captivity: A History of African-American Slaves*. Cambridge, Mass.: Belknap Press of Harvard University Press, 2003.

———. *The Making of African America: The Four Great Migrations*. New York: Viking, 2010.

————. *Many Thousands Gone: The First Two Centuries of Slavery in North America.* Cambridge, Mass.: Belknap Press of Harvard University Press, 1998.

————. *Slaves without Masters: The Free Negro in the Antebellum South.* New York: Vintage Books, 1976.

Berlin, Ira, and Philip D. Morgan, eds. *Cultivation and Culture: Labor and the Shaping of Slave Life in the Americas.* Charlottesville: University Press of Virginia, 1993.

Bernstein, David E. "Philip Sober Controlling Philip Drunk: Buchanan v. Warley in Historical Perspective." *Vanderbilt Law Review* 51, no. 4 (May 1998): 798–879.

Block, Sharon. *Rape and Sexual Power in Early America.* Chapel Hill: University of North Carolina Press, 2006.

Bodenhamer, David J., and James W. Ely, eds. *Ambivalent Legacy: A Legal History of the South.* Jackson: University Press of Mississippi, 1984.

Bogger, Tommy. *Free Blacks in Norfolk, Virginia, 1790–1860: The Darker Side of Freedom.* Charlottesville: University Press of Virginia, 1997.

Bolton, Charles C. *Poor Whites of the Antebellum South: Tenants and Laborers in Central North Carolina and Northeast Mississippi.* Durham, N.C.: Duke University Press, 1994.

Boylan, Anne M. *The Origins of Women's Activism: New York and Boston, 1797–1840.* Chapel Hill: University of North Carolina Press, 2002.

Brasseaux, Carl A. *Creoles of Color in the Bayou Country.* Jackson: University Press of Mississippi, 1996.

Brazy, Martha Jane. *An American Planter: Stephen Duncan of Antebellum Natchez and New York.* Baton Rouge: Louisiana State University Press, 2006.

Bristol, Douglas Walter. *Knights of the Razor: Black Barbers in Slavery and Freedom.* Baltimore, Md.: Johns Hopkins University Press, 2009.

Brooks, Peter, and Paul D. Gewirtz, eds. *Law's Stories: Narrative and Rhetoric in the Law.* New Haven, Conn.: Yale University Press, 1996.

Broussard, Joyce. "Naked before the Law." In *Mississippi Women: Their Histories, Their Lives,* edited by Elizabeth Anne Payne, 57–76. Athens: University of Georgia Press, 2010.

————. "Stepping Lively in Place: The Free Black Women of Antebellum Natchez." In *Mississippi Women: Their Histories, Their Lives,* edited by Elizabeth Anne Payne, 22–38. Athens: University of Georgia Press, 2010.

————. *Stepping Lively in Place: The Not-Married Free Women of Civil War–Era Natchez, Mississippi.* Athens: University of Georgia Press, 2016.

Brown, David. "Citizenship, Democracy, and the Structure of Politics in the Old South: John Calhoun's Conundrum." In *Creating Citizenship in the Nineteenth-Century South,* edited by William A. Link, 84–108. Gainesville: University Press of Florida, 2013.

Brown, Elizabeth Gaspar. "Legal Systems in Conflict: Orleans Territory 1804–1812." *American Journal of Legal History* 1, no. 1 (January 1957): 35–75.

Brown, Kathleen M. *Good Wives, Nasty Wenches, and Anxious Patriarchs: Gender, Race, and Power in Colonial Virginia.* Chapel Hill: University of North Carolina Press, 1996.

Bruner, Jerome S. *Making Stories: Law, Literature, Life.* New York: Farrar, Straus, and Giroux, 2002.

Bryant, Jonathan M. *Dark Places of the Earth: The Voyage of the Slave Ship Antelope.* New York: Norton, 2015.

Bryant, Sherwin K. "Enslaved Rebels, Fugitives, and Litigants: The Resistance Continuum in Colonial Quito." *Colonial Latin American Review* 13, no. 1 (June 2004): 7–46.

Buchanan, Thomas C. *Black Life on the Mississippi: Slaves, Free Blacks, and the Western Steamboat World*. Chapel Hill: University of North Carolina Press, 2004.

Buckley, Thomas E. *The Great Catastrophe of My Life: Divorce in the Old Dominion*. Chapel Hill: University of North Carolina Press, 2002.

Burton, Orville Vernon. *In My Father's House Are Many Mansions: Family and Community in Edgefield, South Carolina*. Chapel Hill: University of North Carolina Press, 1985.

Bynum, Victoria E. *Unruly Women: The Politics of Social and Sexual Control in the Old South*. Chapel Hill: University of North Carolina Press, 1992.

Campbell, James M. *Slavery on Trial: Race, Class, and Criminal Justice in Antebellum Richmond, Virginia*. Gainesville: University Press of Florida, 2007.

Camp, Stephanie M. H. *Closer to Freedom: Enslaved Women and Everyday Resistance in the Plantation South*. Chapel Hill: University of North Carolina Press, 2004.

Cecil-Fronsman, Bill. *Common Whites: Class and Culture in Antebellum North Carolina*. Lexington: University Press of Kentucky, 1992.

Censer, Jane Turner. "'Smiling through Her Tears': Ante-Bellum Southern Women and Divorce." *American Journal of Legal History* 25, no. 1 (January 1981): 24–47.

Chused, Richard H. *Private Acts in Public Places: A Social History of Divorce in the Formative Era of American Family Law*. Philadelphia: University of Pennsylvania Press, 1994.

Clark, Emily. *The Strange History of the American Quadroon: Free Women of Color in the Revolutionary Atlantic World*. Chapel Hill: University of North Carolina Press, 2013.

Cleve, George Van. "Somerset's Case and Its Antecedents in Imperial Perspective." *Law and History Review* 24, no. 3 (September 2006): 601–46.

Conley, John M., and William M. O'Barr. *Just Words: Law, Language, and Power*. 2nd ed. Chicago: University of Chicago Press, 2005.

Connolly, N. D. B. *A World More Concrete: Real Estate and the Remaking of Jim Crow South Florida*. Chicago: University of Chicago Press, 2014.

Constable, Marianne. *Our Word Is Our Bond: How Legal Speech Acts*. Stanford, Calif.: Stanford University Press, 2014.

Costello, Brian J. *A History of Pointe Coupee Parish, Louisiana*. Pointe Coupee Parish, La.: B. J. Costello, 1999.

———. *The Life, Family and Legacy of Julien Poydras*. John and Noelie Laurent Ewing, 2001.

Cott, Nancy F. *The Bonds of Womanhood: "Woman's Sphere" in New England, 1780–1835*. New Haven: Yale University Press, 1977.

———. *Public Vows: A History of Marriage and the Nation*. Cambridge, Mass.: Harvard University Press, 2000.

Cover, Robert. "The Supreme Court, 1982 Term—Foreword: Nomos and Narrative." *Harvard Law Review* 97, no. 1 (November 1983): 4–68.

Daacke, Kirt von. *Freedom Has a Face: Race, Identity, and Community in Jefferson's Virginia*. Charlottesville: University of Virginia Press, 2012.

Daniels, Christine, and Michael V. Kennedy, eds. *Over the Threshold: Intimate Violence in Early America*. New York: Routledge, 1999.

Davis, Adrienne D. "The Private Law of Race and Sex: An Antebellum Perspective." *Stanford Law Review* 51, no. 2 (January 1999): 221–88.

Davis, Edwin Adams, and William Ransom Hogan. *The Barber of Natchez, Wherein a Slave Is Freed and Rises to a Very High Standing; Wherein the Former Slave Writes a Two-Thousand-Page Journal about His Town and Himself; Wherein the Free Negro Diarist Is Appraised in Terms of His Friends, His Code, and His Community's Reaction to His Wanton Murder.* Baton Rouge: Louisiana State University Press, 1954.

Davis, Natalie Zemon. *Fiction in the Archives: Pardon Tales and Their Tellers in Sixteenth-Century France.* Stanford, Calif.: Stanford University Press, 1987.

Davis, Ronald L. F. *The Black Experience in Natchez, 1720–1880: Natchez, National Historical Park, Mississippi.* Denver, Colo.: US Dept. of the Interior, National Park Service, Denver Service Center, 1993.

———. *Good and Faithful Labor: From Slavery to Sharecropping in the Natchez District, 1860–1890.* Westport, Conn.: Greenwood Press, 1982.

Dayton, Cornelia Hughes. *Women before the Bar: Gender, Law, and Society in Connecticut, 1639–1789.* Chapel Hill: University of North Carolina Press, 1995.

DeLombard, Jeannine Marie. *In the Shadow of the Gallows: Race, Crime, and American Civic Identity.* Philadelphia: University of Pennsylvania Press, 2012.

———. *Slavery on Trial: Law, Abolitionism, and Print Culture.* Chapel Hill: University of North Carolina Press, 2007.

Deyle, Steven. *Carry Me Back: The Domestic Slave Trade in American Life.* New York: Oxford University Press, 2005.

Drake, Jarrett. "Off the Record: The Production of Evidence in Nineteenth-Century New Jersey." *New Jersey Studies: An Interdisciplinary Journal* 1, no. 1 (Summer 2015): 104–25.

Edwards, Laura F. "Commentary." In *Slavery and the American South: Essays and Commentaries*, edited by Winthrop D. Jordan, 82–92. Jackson: University Press of Mississippi, 2003.

———. "Enslaved Women and the Law: Paradoxes of Subordination in the Post-Revolutionary Carolinas." *Slavery & Abolition* 26, no. 2 (2005): 305–23.

———. *Gendered Strife and Confusion: The Political Culture of Reconstruction.* Urbana: University of Illinois Press, 1997.

———. "The Material Conditions of Dependency: The Hidden History of Free Women's Control of Property in the Early Nineteenth-Century South." In *Signposts: New Directions in Southern Legal History*, edited by Sally E. Hadden and Patricia H. Minter, 171–92. Athens: University of Georgia Press, 2013.

———. *The People and Their Peace: Legal Culture and the Transformation of Inequality in the Post-Revolutionary South.* Chapel Hill: University of North Carolina Press, 2009.

———. "Status without Rights: African Americans and the Tangled History of Law and Governance in the Nineteenth-Century U.S. South." *American Historical Review* 112, no. 2 (April 2007): 365–93.

Ely, Melvin Patrick. *Israel on the Appomattox: A Southern Experiment in Black Freedom from 1790s through the Civil War.* New York: Knopf, 2004.

Eslinger, Ellen. "Free Black Residency in Two Antebellum Virginia Counties: How the Laws Functioned." *Journal of Southern History* 79, no. 2 (May 2013): 262–98.

Faust, Drew Gilpin. *A Sacred Circle: The Dilemma of the Intellectual in the Old South, 1840–1860.* Baltimore: Johns Hopkins University Press, 1977.

———. *James Henry Hammond and the Old South: A Design for Mastery*. Baton Rouge: Louisiana State University Press, 1982.

Fede, Andrew. *People without Rights: An Interpretation of the Fundamentals of the Law of Slavery in the U.S. South*. New York: Garland, 1992.

———. *Roadblocks to Freedom: Slavery and Manumission in the United States South*. New Orleans: Quid Pro Books, 2012.

Ferguson, Robert A. *The Trial in American Life*. Chicago: University of Chicago Press, 2007.

Fernandez, Mark F. *From Chaos to Continuity: The Evolution of Louisiana's Judicial System, 1712–1862*. Baton Rouge: Louisiana State University Press, 2001.

Finkelman, Paul. *An Imperfect Union: Slavery, Federalism, and Comity*. Chapel Hill: University of North Carolina Press, 1980.

———. "Prelude to the Fourteenth Amendment: Black Legal Rights in the Antebellum North." *Rutgers Law Journal* 17 (1986): 415–82.

Flanigan, Daniel J. *The Criminal Law of Slavery and Freedom, 1800–1868*. New York: Garland, 1987.

———. "Criminal Procedure in Slave Trials in the Antebellum South." *Journal of Southern History* 40, no. 4 (November 1974): 537–64.

Follett, Richard J. *The Sugar Masters: Planters and Slaves in Louisiana's Cane World, 1820–1860*. Baton Rouge: Louisiana State University Press, 2005.

Foner, Eric. *Free Soil, Free Labor, Free Men: The Ideology of the Republican Party before the Civil War*. New York: Oxford University Press, 1970.

Ford, Lacy K. *Deliver Us from Evil: The Slavery Question in the Old South*. New York: Oxford University Press, 2009.

Forret, Jeff. *Race Relations at the Margins: Slaves and Poor Whites in the Antebellum Southern Countryside*. Baton Rouge: Louisiana State University Press, 2006.

———. *Slave against Slave: Plantation Violence in the Old South*. Baton Rouge: Louisiana State University, 2015.

Forret, Jeff, and Christine E. Sears. *New Directions in Slavery Studies: Commodification, Community, and Comparison*. Baton Rouge: Louisiana State University Press, 2015.

Fox-Genovese, Elizabeth. *The Mind of the Master Class: History and Faith in the Southern Slaveholders' Worldview*. New York: Cambridge University Press, 2005.

———. *Within the Plantation Household: Black and White Women of the Old South*. Chapel Hill: University of North Carolina Press, 1988.

Franklin, John Hope. *The Free Negro in North Carolina, 1790–1860*. Chapel Hill: University of North Carolina Press, 1943.

Frazier, Harriet C. *Slavery and Crime in Missouri, 1773–1865*. Jefferson, N.C.: McFarland, 2001.

Freeman, Joanne B. *Affairs of Honor: National Politics in the New Republic*. New Haven, Conn.: Yale University Press, 2001.

Friedman, Lawrence M. *Crime and Punishment in American History*. New York: Basic Books, 1993.

———. *A History of American Law, Revised Edition*. New York: Simon and Schuster, 2010.

Friedman, Lawrence Meir. *Contract Law in America: A Social and Economic Case Study*. Madison: University of Wisconsin Press, 1965.

———. *Guarding Life's Dark Secrets: Legal and Social Controls over Reputation, Propriety, and Privacy*. Stanford, Calif.: Stanford University Press, 2007.

Fuente, Alejandro de la. "Slave Law and Claims-Making in Cuba: The Tannenbaum Debate Revisited." *Law and History Review* 22, no. 2 (July 2004): 339–69.

———. "Slaves and the Creation of Legal Rights in Cuba: Coartación and Papel." *Hispanic American Historical Review* 87, no. 4 (November 2007): 659–92.

Genovese, Eugene D. *Roll, Jordan, Roll: The World the Slaves Made*. New York: Vintage Books, 1976.

Gigantino, James J., II. "Trading in Jersey Souls: New Jersey and the Interstate Slave Trade." *Pennsylvania History: A Journal of Mid-Atlantic Studies* 77, no. 3 (July 2010): 281–302.

Gould, Virginia Meacham, ed. *Chained to the Rock of Adversity: To Be Free, Black and Female in the Old South*. Athens: University of Georgia Press, 1998.

Gowing, Laura. *Domestic Dangers: Women, Words, and Sex in Early Modern London*. Oxford: Oxford University Press, 1996.

Greenberg, Kenneth S. *Honor and Slavery: Lies, Duels, Noses, Masks, Dressing as a Woman, Gifts, Strangers, Humanitarianism, Death, Slave Rebellions, the Proslavery Argument, Baseball, Hunting, and Gambling in the Old South*. Princeton, N.J.: Princeton University Press, 1996.

———. "The Nose, the Lie, and the Duel in the Antebellum South." *American Historical Review* 95, no. 1 (February 1990): 57–74.

Grinberg, Keila. "Freedom Suits and Civil Law in Brazil and the United States." *Slavery & Abolition* 22, no. 3 (December 2001): 66–82.

Gross, Ariela J. *Double Character: Slavery and Mastery in the Antebellum Southern Courtroom*. Princeton, N.J.: Princeton University Press, 2000.

———. "Reflections on Law, Culture, and Slavery." In *Slavery and the American South: Essays and Commentaries*, edited by Winthrop D. Jordan, 57–82. Jackson: University Press of Mississippi, 2003.

———. *What Blood Won't Tell: A History of Race on Trial in America*. Cambridge, Mass.: Harvard University Press, 2008.

Gross, Ariela J., and Alejandro de la Fuente. "Slaves, Free Blacks, and Race in the Legal Regimes of Cuba, Louisiana, and Virginia: A Comparison." *North Carolina Law Review* 91 (2013): 1699–1757.

Grossberg, Michael, and Christopher Tomlins. *The Cambridge History of Law in America*. Vol. 2. New York: Cambridge University Press, 2008.

Gudmestad, Robert H. *A Troublesome Commerce: The Transformation of the Interstate Slave Trade*. Baton Rouge: Louisiana State University Press, 2003.

Guest, Anthony Gordon. *Oxford Essays in Jurisprudence, a Collaborative Work*. London: Oxford University Press, 1961.

Hadden, Sally E., and Patricia H. Minter. *Signposts: New Directions in Southern Legal History*. Athens: University of Georgia Press, 2013.

Hall, Gwendolyn Midlo. *Africans in Colonial Louisiana: The Development of Afro-Creole Culture in the Eighteenth Century*. Baton Rouge: Louisiana State University Press, 1992.

Hall, Kermit L. "The Judiciary on Trial: State Constitutional Reform and the Rise of an Elected Judiciary, 1876–1860." *Historian* 45, no. 3 (1983): 337–54.

Hamburger, Philip. "Privileges or Immunities." *Northwestern University Law Review* 105, no. 1 (2011): 61–147.

Haney-López, Ian. *White by Law: The Legal Construction of Race.* New York: New York University Press, 2006.

Hanger, Kimberly S. *Bounded Lives, Bounded Places: Free Black Society in Colonial New Orleans, 1769–1803.* Durham, N.C.: Duke University Press, 1997.

Hartigan-O'Connor, Ellen. *The Ties That Buy: Women and Commerce in Revolutionary America.* Philadelphia: University of Pennsylvania Press, 2009.

Hartog, Hendrik. *Man and Wife in America: A History.* Cambridge, Mass.: Harvard University Press, 2000.

———. *Someday All This Will Be Yours: A History of Inheritance and Old Age.* Cambridge, Mass.: Harvard University Press, 2012.

Higginbotham, A. Leon. *In the Matter of Color: The Colonial Period.* New York: Oxford University Press, 1978.

Higginbotham, A. Leon, Jr., and Barbara K. Kopytoff. "Property First, Humanity Second: The Recognition of the Slave's Human Nature in Virginia Civil Law." *Ohio State Law Journal* 50 (1989): 511–40.

Hilliard, Kathleen M. *Masters, Slaves, and Exchange: Power's Purchase in the Old South.* New York: Cambridge University Press, 2014.

Hindus, Michael S. "Black Justice under White Law: Criminal Prosecutions of Blacks in Antebellum South Carolina." *Journal of American History* 63, no. 3 (December 1976): 575–99.

———. *Prison and Plantation: Crime, Justice, and Authority in Massachusetts and South Carolina, 1767–1878.* Chapel Hill: University of North Carolina Press, 1980.

Hodes, Martha Elizabeth. *White Women, Black Men: Illicit Sex in the Nineteenth-Century South.* New Haven, Conn.: Yale University Press, 1997.

Hohfeld, Wesley Newcomb. *Fundamental Legal Conceptions as Applied in Judicial Reasoning: And Other Legal Essays.* New Haven: Yale University Press, 1919.

Honoré, A. M. "Ownership." In *Oxford Essays in Jurisprudence*, edited by Anthony Gordon Guest, 112–28. Oxford: Oxford University Press, 1961.

Isaac, Rhys. *The Transformation of Virginia, 1740–1790.* Chapel Hill: University of North Carolina Press, 1982.

Isham, Edward. *The Confessions of Edward Isham: A Poor White Life of the Old South.* Athens: University of Georgia Press, 1998.

Jacobs, Meg, William J. Novak, and Julian E. Zelizer, eds. *The Democratic Experiment: New Directions in American Political History.* Princeton, N.J.: Princeton University Press, 2003.

Jacobsohn, Gary J., and Susan Dunn, eds. *Diversity and Citizenship: Rediscovering American Nationhood.* Lanham, Md.: Rowman and Littlefield, 1996.

Jennison, Watson. "Rewriting the Free Negro Past: Joseph Lumpkin, Proslavery Ideology, and Citizenship in Antebellum Georgia." In *Creating Citizenship in the Nineteenth-Century South*, edited by William A. Link, 41–63. Gainesville: University Press of Florida, 2013.

Johnson, Guion Griffis. *Ante-Bellum North Carolina: A Social History.* Chapel Hill: University of North Carolina Press, 1937.

Johnson, Jessica Marie. "Death Rites as Birthrights in Atlantic New Orleans: Kinship and Race in the Case of María Teresa v. Perine Dauphine." *Slavery & Abolition* 36, no. 2 (2015): 233–56.

Johnson, Michael P., and James L. Roark. *Black Masters: A Free Family of Color in the Old South*. New York: Norton, 1986.

Johnson, Rashauna. *Slavery's Metropolis: Unfree Labor in New Orleans during the Age of Revolutions*. New York: Cambridge University Press, 2016.

Johnson, Walter. "Inconsistency, Contradiction, and Complete Confusion: The Everyday Life of the Law of Slavery." *Law & Social Inquiry* 22, no. 2 (April 1997): 405–33.

———. "On Agency." *Journal of Social History* 37, no. 1 (October 2003): 113–24.

———. *River of Dark Dreams: Slavery and Empire in the Cotton Kingdom*. Cambridge, Mass.: Belknap Press of Harvard University Press, 2013.

———. *Soul by Soul: Life inside the Antebellum Slave Market*. Cambridge, Mass.: Harvard University Press, 1999.

———, ed. *The Chattel Principle: Internal Slave Trades in the Americas*. New Haven, Conn.: Yale University Press, 2004.

Jones, Bernie D. *Fathers of Conscience: Mixed-Race Inheritance in the Antebellum South*. Athens: University of Georgia Press, 2009.

Jones, Martha S. "*Hughes v. Jackson*: Race and Rights beyond Dred Scott." *North Carolina Law Review* 91 (2013): 1757–84.

———. "Leave of Court: African American Claims-Making in the Era of *Dred Scott v. Sanford*." In *Contested Democracy: Freedom, Race, and Power in American History*, edited by Manisha Sinha and Penny M. Von Eschen, 54–74. New York: Columbia University Press, 2007.

———. "Time, Space, and Jurisdiction in Atlantic World Slavery: The Volunbrun Household in Gradual Emancipation New York." *Law and History Review* 29, no. 4 (November 2011): 1031–60.

Jordan, Winthrop D., ed. *Slavery and the American South: Essays and Commentaries*. 2000. Jackson: University Press of Mississippi, 2003.

Kachun, Mitch. "From Forgotten Founder to Indispensable Icon: Crispus Attucks, Black Citizenship, and Collective Memory, 1770–1865." *Journal of the Early Republic* 29, no. 2 (July 2009): 249–86.

Kantrowitz, Stephen. *More Than Freedom: Fighting for Black Citizenship in a White Republic, 1829–1889*. New York: Penguin, 2012.

Kaye, Anthony E. *Joining Places: Slave Neighborhoods in the Old South*. Chapel Hill: University of North Carolina Press, 2007.

———. "The Problem of Autonomy: Toward a Postliberal History." In *New Directions in Slavery Studies: Commodification, Community, and Comparison*, edited by Jeff Forret and Christine E. Sears, 150–75. Baton Rouge: Louisiana State University Press, 2015.

Kennedy, Randell. "Dred Scott and African American Citizenship." In *Diversity and Citizenship: Rediscovering American Nationhood*, edited by Gary J. Jacobsohn and Susan Dunn, 101–21. Lanham, Md.: Rowman and Littlefield, 1996.

Kennington, Kelly M. *In the Shadow of Dred Scott: St. Louis Freedom Suits and the Legal Culture of Slavery in Antebellum America*. Athens: University of Georgia Press, 2017.

———. "Law, Geography, and Mobility: Suing for Freedom in Antebellum St. Louis." *Journal of Southern History* 80, no. 3 (2014): 575–604.

Kerber, Linda K. "The Meanings of Citizenship." *Journal of American History* 84, no. 3 (December 1997): 833–54.

———. *No Constitutional Right to Be Ladies: Women and the Obligations of Citizenship.* New York: Hill and Wang, 1998.

Kilbourne, Richard Holcombe. *Debt, Investment, Slaves: Credit Relations in East Feliciana Parish, Louisiana, 1825–1885.* Tuscaloosa: University of Alabama Press, 1995.

Konefsky, Alfred S. "The Legal Profession: From the Revolution to the Civil War." In *The Cambridge History of Law in America*, 2:68–105. New York: Cambridge University Press, 2008.

Kotlikoff, Laurence J., and Anton J. Rupert. "The Manumission of Slaves in New Orleans, 1827–1846." *Southern Studies* 19 (Summer 1980): 172–81.

Lebsock, Suzanne. *The Free Women of Petersburg: Status and Culture in a Southern Town, 1784–1860.* New York: W. W. Norton, 1984.

Link, William A., ed. *Creating Citizenship in the Nineteenth-Century South.* Gainesville: University Press of Florida, 2013.

Macgill, Hugh, C., and R. Kent Newmyer. "Legal Education and Legal Thought, 1790–1920." In *The Cambridge History of Law in America*, edited by Michael Grossberg and Christopher Tomlins, 2:36–67. New York: Cambridge University Press, 2008.

Mann, Bruce H. *Republic of Debtors: Bankruptcy in the Age of American Independence.* Cambridge, Mass.: Harvard University Press, 2002.

Maris-Wolf, Ted. *Family Bonds: Free Blacks and Re-enslavement Law in Antebellum Virginia.* Chapel Hill: University of North Carolina Press, 2015.

Martin, Bonnie. "Slavery's Invisible Engine: Mortgaging Human Property." *Journal of Southern History* 76, no. 4 (November 2010): 817–66.

Martin, Jonathan D. *Divided Mastery: Slave Hiring in the American South.* Cambridge, Mass.: Harvard University Press, 2004.

Masur, Kate. *An Example for All the Land: Emancipation and the Struggle over Equality in Washington, D.C.* Chapel Hill: University of North Carolina Press, 2010.

McCurry, Stephanie. *Masters of Small Worlds: Yeoman Households, Gender Relations, and the Political Culture of the Antebellum South Carolina Low Country.* New York: Oxford University Press, 1995.

McKinley, Michelle A. "Fractional Freedoms: Slavery, Legal Activism, and Ecclesiastical Courts in Colonial Lima, 1593–1689." *Law and History Review* 28, no. 3 (August 2010): 749–90.

———. "Such Unsightly Unions Could Never Result in Holy Matrimony: Mixed-Status Marriages in Seventeenth-Century Colonial Lima." *Yale Journal of Law and the Humanities* 22 (2010): 217–55.

Merry, Sally Engle. *Getting Justice and Getting Even: Legal Consciousness among Working-Class Americans.* Chicago: University of Chicago Press, 1990.

Milewski, Melissa. "From Slave to Litigant: African Americans in Court in the Postwar South, 1865–1920." *Law and History Review* 30, no. 3 (2012): 723–69.

Millward, Jessica. *Finding Charity's Folk: Enslaved and Free Black Women in Maryland.* Athens: University of Georgia Press, 2015.

Moogk, Peter N. "'Thieving Buggers' and 'Stupid Sluts': Insults and Popular Culture in New France." *William and Mary Quarterly*, 3rd ser., 36, no. 4 (October 1979): 524–47.

Moore, John Hebron. *The Emergence of the Cotton Kingdom in the Old Southwest: Mississippi, 1770–1860*. Baton Rouge: Louisiana State University Press, 1988.

Morgan, Jennifer L. *Laboring Women: Reproduction and Gender in New World Slavery*. Philadelphia: University of Pennsylvania Press, 2004.

Morris, Thomas D. *Southern Slavery and the Law, 1619–1860*. Chapel Hill: University of North Carolina Press, 1996.

Myers, Amrita Chakrabarti. *Forging Freedom: Black Women and the Pursuit of Liberty in Antebellum Charleston*. Chapel Hill: University of North Carolina Press, 2011.

Nash, A. E. Keir. "Fairness and Formalism in the Trials of Blacks in the State Supreme Courts of the Old South." *Virginia Law Review* 56, no. 1 (February 1970): 64–100.

Nash, Gary B., and Jean R. Soderlund. *Freedom by Degrees: Emancipation in Pennsylvania and Its Aftermath*. New York: Oxford University Press, 1991.

Nelson, Scott Reynolds. "Who Put Their Capitalism in My Slavery?" *Journal of the Civil War Era* 5, no. 2 (2015): 289–310.

Nicholls, Michael L. "Creating Identity: Free Blacks and the Law." *Slavery & Abolition* 35, no. 2 (April 2014): 214–33.

Nieman, Donald G. *Promises to Keep: African-Americans and the Constitutional Order, 1776 to the Present*. New York: Oxford University Press, 1991.

Novak, William J. "The Legal Transformation of Citizenship in Nineteenth-Century America." In *The Democratic Experiment: New Directions in American Political History*, edited by Meg Jacobs, William J. Novak, and Julian E. Zelizer, 84–119. Princeton, N.J.: Princeton University Press, 2003.

———. *The People's Welfare: Law and Regulation in Nineteenth-Century America*. Chapel Hill: University of North Carolina Press, 1996.

Oakes, James. *The Ruling Race: A History of American Slaveholders*. New York: Knopf, 1982.

———. *Slavery and Freedom: An Interpretation of the Old South*. New York: W. W. Norton, 1990.

O'Brien, Michael. *Conjectures of Order: Intellectual Life and the American South, 1810–1860*. Chapel Hill: University of North Carolina Press, 2004.

———. *Rethinking the South: Essays in Intellectual History*. Baltimore, Md.: Johns Hopkins University Press, 1988.

O'Donovan, Susan Eva. "Universities of Social and Political Change: Slaves in Jail in Antebellum America." In *Buried Lives: Incarcerated in Early America*, edited by Michele Lise Tarter and Richard Bell, 124–46. Athens: University of Georgia Press, 2012.

Olegario, Rowena. *A Culture of Credit: Embedding Trust and Transparency in American Business*. Cambridge, Mass.: Harvard University Press, 2006.

Osofsky, Gilbert, Henry Bibb, William Wells Brown, and Solomon Northup. *Puttin' on Ole Massa: The Slave Narratives of Henry Bibb, William Wells Brown, and Solomon Northup*. New York: Harper & Row, 1969.

Owensby, Brian P. "How Juan and Leonor Won Their Freedom: Litigation and Liberty in Seventeenth-Century Mexico." *Hispanic American Historical Review* 85, no. 1 (February 2005): 39–80.

Palmer, Vernon V., ed. *Louisiana: Microcosm of a Mixed Jurisdiction*. Durham, N.C.: Carolina Academic Press, 1999.

———. *Through the Codes Darkly: Slave Law and Civil Law in Louisiana*. Clark, N.J.: Lawbook Exchange, 2012.

Parker, Kunal Madhukar. *Making Foreigners: Immigration and Citizenship Law in America, 1600–2000*. New York: Cambridge University Press, 2015.

Patterson, Orlando. *Slavery and Social Death: A Comparative Study*. Cambridge, Mass.: Harvard University Press, 1982.

Peabody, Sue, and Keila Grinberg. "Free Soil: The Generation and Circulation of an Atlantic Legal Principle." *Slavery & Abolition* 32, no. 3 (September 2011): 331–39.

Penningroth, Dylan C. *The Claims of Kinfolk: African American Property and Community in the Nineteenth-Century South*. Chapel Hill: University of North Carolina Press, 2003.

———. "The Claims of Slaves and Ex-Slaves to Family and Property: A Transatlantic Comparison." *American Historical Review* 112, no. 4 (2007): 1039–69.

Perl-Rosenthal, Nathan. *Citizen Sailors: Becoming American in the Age of Revolution*. Cambridge, Mass.: The Belknap Press of Harvard University Press, 2015.

Petty, Adrienne Monteith. *Standing Their Ground: Small Farmers in North Carolina since the Civil War*. New York: Oxford University Press, 2013.

Pingeon, Frances D. "An Abominable Business: The New Jersey Slave Trade, 1818." *New Jersey History* 109, no. 3–4 (Fall/Winter 1991): 15–35.

Potter, David Morris. *The South and the Sectional Conflict*. Baton Rouge: Louisiana State University Press, 1968.

Premo, Bianca. "Before the Law: Women's Petitions in the Eighteenth-Century Spanish Empire." *Comparative Studies in Society and History* 53, no. 2 (April 2011): 261–89.

Ricard, Jr., Ulysses R. "Pierre Belly and Rose: More Forgotten People." *Chicory Review* 1, no. 1 (1988): 2–18.

Riffel, Judy, ed. *Iberville Parish History*. Baton Rouge, La.: Comité des archives de la Louisiane, 1985.

Roeber, A. G. "Authority, Law, and Custom: The Rituals of Court Day in Tidewater, Virginia, 1720 to 1750." *William and Mary Quarterly*, 3rd ser,, 37, no. 1 (January 1980): 29–52.

Rohrs, Richard C. "The Free Black Experience in Antebellum Wilmington, North Carolina: Refining Generalization about Race Relations." *Journal of Southern History* 78, no. 3 (August 2012): 615–38.

Rothman, Adam. *Beyond Freedom's Reach: A Kidnapping in the Twilight of Slavery*. Cambridge, Mass.: Harvard University Press, 2015.

———. *Slave Country: American Expansion and the Origins of the Deep South*. Cambridge, Mass.: Harvard University Press, 2005.

Rothman, Joshua D. *Flush Times and Fever Dreams: A Story of Capitalism and Slavery in the Age of Jackson*. Athens: University of Georgia Press, 2012.

———. *Notorious in the Neighborhood: Sex and Families across the Color Line in Virginia, 1787–1861*. Chapel Hill: University of North Carolina Press, 2003.

Russell, Sarah. "Cultural Conflicts and Common Interests: The Making of the Sugar Planter Class in Louisiana, 1795–1853." Ph.D. diss., University of Maryland, 2000.

Sachs, Honor. "'Freedom by a Judgment': The Legal History of an Afro-Indian Family." *Law and History Review* 30, no. 1 (February 2012): 173–203.

Salafia, Matthew. *Slavery's Borderland: Freedom and Bondage along the Ohio River.* Philadelphia: University of Pennsylvania Press, 2013.

Salmon, Marylynn. *Women and the Law of Property in Early America.* Chapel Hill: University of North Carolina Press, 1986.

Sandage, Scott A. *Born Losers: A History of Failure in America.* Cambridge, Mass.: Harvard University Press, 2005.

Schafer, Judith K. "'Open and Notorious Concubinage': The Emancipation of Slave Mistresses by Will and the Supreme Court in Antebellum Louisiana." *Louisiana History: The Journal of the Louisiana Historical Association* 28, no. 2 (April 1987): 165–82.

Schafer, Judith Kelleher. *Becoming Free, Remaining Free: Manumission and Enslavement in New Orleans, 1846–1862.* Baton Rouge: Louisiana State University, 2003.

———. *Slavery, the Civil Law, and the Supreme Court of Louisiana.* Baton Rouge: Louisiana State University Press, 1994.

Schwarz, Phillip J. *Twice Condemned: Slaves and the Criminal Laws of Virginia, 1705–1865.* Baton Rouge: Louisiana State University Press, 1988.

Schweninger, Loren. "Antebellum Free Persons of Color in Postbellum Louisiana." *Louisiana History: The Journal of the Louisiana Historical Association* 30, no. 4 (October 1989): 345–64.

———. *Black Property Owners in the South, 1790–1915.* Urbana: University of Illinois Press, 1990.

———. *Families in Crisis in the Old South: Divorce, Slavery, and the Law.* Chapel Hill: University of North Carolina Press, 2012.

———. "Freedom Suits, African American Women, and the Genealogy of Slavery." *William and Mary Quarterly* 71, no. 1 (January 2014): 35–62.

Scott, James C. *Domination and the Arts of Resistance: Hidden Transcripts.* New Haven, Conn.: Yale University Press, 1990.

———. *Weapons of the Weak: Everyday Forms of Peasant Resistance.* New Haven, Conn.: Yale University Press, 1985.

Scott, Rebecca J., and Jean M. Hébrard. *Freedom Papers: An Atlantic Odyssey in the Age of Emancipation.* Cambridge, Mass.: Harvard University Press, 2012.

Scott, Rebecca J. "Paper Thin: Freedom and Re-enslavement in the Diaspora of the Haitian Revolution." *Law and History Review* 29, no. 4 (November 2011): 1061–87.

———. "Public Rights and Private Commerce: A Nineteenth-Century Atlantic Creole Itinerary." *Current Anthropology* 48, no. 2 (2007): 237–56.

Sharafi, Mitra. "The Slaves and Slavery of Marie Claire Chabert: Familial Black Slaveholding in Antebellum Louisiana." *Journal of Civil Law Studies* 4, no. 1 (May 2011): 187–216.

Sharfstein, Daniel J. *The Invisible Line: Three American Families and the Secret Journey from Black to White.* New York: Penguin, 2011.

Silkenat, David. *Moments of Despair: Suicide, Divorce, and Debt in Civil War Era North Carolina.* Chapel Hill: University of North Carolina Press, 2011.

Sinha, Manisha, and Penny M. Von Eschen, eds. *Contested Democracy: Freedom, Race, and Power in American History.* New York: Columbia University Press, 2007.

Smith, Adam. *An Inquiry into the Nature and Causes of the Wealth of Nations*. Hartford,
Conn.: Printed for Oliver D. Cooke, 1804.

Smith, J. Clay. *Emancipation: The Making of the Black Lawyer, 1844–1944*. Philadelphia:
University of Pennsylvania Press, 1993.

Smith, Johanna Lee Davis. "Mulatto Bend: Free People of Color in Rural Louisiana,
1763–1865." Ph.D. diss., Tulane University, 2012.

Spear, Jennifer M. *Race, Sex, and Social Order in Early New Orleans*. Baltimore, Md.: Johns
Hopkins University Press, 2009.

———. "'Using the Facilities Conceded to Her by Law': Slavery, Law, and Agency
in Spanish New Orleans, 1763–1803." In *Signposts: New Directions in Southern Legal
History*, edited by Sally E. Hadden and Patricia H. Minter, 65–84. Athens: University of
Georgia Press, 2012.

Stanley, Amy Dru. *From Bondage to Contract: Wage Labor, Marriage, and the Market in the
Age of Slave Emancipation*. New York: Cambridge University Press, 1998.

Sterkx, H. E. *The Free Negro in Ante-Bellum Louisiana*. Rutherford, N.J.: Fairleigh
Dickinson University Press, 1972.

Stowe, Steven M. *Intimacy and Power in the Old South: Ritual in the Lives of the Planters*.
Baltimore, Md.: Johns Hopkins University Press, 1987.

Suggs, Jon Christian. *Whispered Consolations: Law and Narrative in African American Life*.
Ann Arbor: University of Michigan Press, 2000.

Swain, Martha H., Elizabeth Anne Payne, and Marjorie Julian Spruill. *Mississippi Women:
Their Histories, Their Lives*. Athens: University of Georgia Press, 2010.

Sydnor, Charles S. *The Development of Southern Sectionalism, 1819–1848*. Baton Rouge:
Louisiana State University Press, 1948.

———. "The Free Negro in Mississippi before the Civil War." *American Historical Review*
32, no. 4 (July 1927): 769–88.

Tadman, Michael. *Speculators and Slaves: Masters, Traders, and Slaves in the Old South*.
Madison: University of Wisconsin Press, 1989.

Tarter, Michele Lise, and Richard Bell. *Buried Lives: Incarcerated in Early America*. Athens:
University of Georgia Press, 2012.

Turner, Felicity. "Rights and the Ambiguities of the Law: Infanticide in the Nineteenth-
Century U.S. South." *Journal of the Civil War Era* 4, no. 3 (September 2014): 350–72.

Twitty, Anne Silverwood. *Before Dred Scott: Slavery and Legal Culture in the American
Confluence, 1787–1857*. New York: Cambridge University Press, 2016.

———. "Slavery and Freedom in the American Confluence, From the Northwest
Ordinance to Dred Scott." Ph.D. diss., Princeton University, 2010.

Van Cleve, George. "*Somerset's Case* and Its Antecedents in Imperial Perspective (Forum:
Somerset's Case Revisited)." *Law and History Review* 24, no. 3 (2006): 601–45.

VanderVelde, Lea. *Redemption Songs: Suing for Freedom before Dred Scott*. New York:
Oxford University Press, 2014.

Wahl, Jenny Bourne. *The Bondsman's Burden: An Economic Analysis of the Common Law of
Southern Slavery*. New York: Cambridge University Press, 1998.

Waldron, Jeremy. *The Rule of Law and the Measure of Property*. Cambridge: Cambridge
University Press, 2012.

Walther, Eric H. *The Fire-Eaters*. Baton Rouge: Louisiana State University Press, 1992.

Wayne, Michael. *The Reshaping of Plantation Society: The Natchez District, 1860–80.* Urbana: University of Illinois Press, 1990.

Welch, Kimberly. "Black Litigiousness and White Accountability: Free Blacks and the Rhetoric of Reputation in the Antebellum Natchez District." *Journal of the Civil War Era* 5, no. 3 (September 2015): 372–98.

Welke, Barbara Young. *Law and the Borders of Belonging in the Long Nineteenth-Century United States.* New York: Cambridge University Press, 2010.

———. "Law, Personhood, and Citizenship in the Long Nineteenth Century: The Borders of Belonging." In *The Cambridge History of Law in America*, vol. 2, edited by Michael Grossberg and Christopher Tomlins, 345–86. New York: Cambridge University Press, 2008.

———. *Recasting American Liberty: Gender, Race, Law, and the Railroad Revolution, 1865–1920.* Cambridge: Cambridge University Press, 2001.

Wertheimer, John. *Law and Society in the South: A History of North Carolina Court Cases.* Lexington: University Press of Kentucky, 2009.

West, Emily. *Family or Freedom: People of Color in the Antebellum South.* Lexington: University Press of Kentucky, 2012.

White, Deborah Gray. *Ar'n't I a Woman? Female Slaves in the Plantation South.* New York: Norton, 1985.

Wilson, Carol. *Freedom at Risk: The Kidnapping of Free Blacks in America, 1780–1865.* Lexington: University Press of Kentucky, 1994.

Winch, Julie. "Philadelphia and the Other Underground Railroad." *Pennsylvania Magazine of History and Biography* 111, no. 1 (January 1987): 3–25.

Wisnoski, Alexander L. "'It Is Unjust for the Law of Marriage to Be Broken by the Law of Slavery': Married Slaves and Their Masters in Early Colonial Lima." *Slavery & Abolition* 35, no. 2 (April 2014): 234–52.

Wolf, Eva Sheppard. *Almost Free: A Story about Family and Race in Antebellum Virginia.* Athens: University of Georgia Press, 2012.

Wong, Edlie L. *Neither Fugitive Nor Free: Atlantic Slavery, Freedom Suits, and the Legal Culture of Travel.* New York: New York University Press, 2009.

Wooster, Ralph A. *The People in Power: Courthouse and Statehouse in the Lower South, 1850–1860.* Knoxville: University of Tennessee Press, 1969.

Wright, Gavin. *Slavery and American Economic Development.* Baton Rouge: Louisiana State University Press, 2013.

Wyatt-Brown, Bertram. *Southern Honor: Ethics and Behavior in the Old South.* New York: Oxford University Press, 1982.

Young, Jeffrey Robert. *Domesticating Slavery: The Master Class in Georgia and South Carolina, 1670–1837.* Chapel Hill: University of North Carolina Press, 1999.

Zaborney, John J. *Slaves for Hire: Renting Enslaved Laborers in Antebellum Virginia.* Baton Rouge: Louisiana State University Press, 2012.

Index

Page numbers in italics refer to illustrations.

and, 189–91, 265n79; of Hamm, 91–93, 98, 185; kidnapping and, 180, 181–85, 186–88, 263n59; mechanisms of suing for, 165–67, 260n11; narratives and, 43–49, 237n53; wills and heirs and, 174–76. *See also specific plaintiffs of*

Free papers, 4, 18, 31

Free soil arguments, 189–91, 265n79

French, Henry, 170

French Louisiana, 195, 265n3

Gálvez, Bernardo de, 195

Garnishments, 127

Gayoso, Manuel, 170

Genovese, Eugene, 230–31nn21–22

Genre of law, 21–22, 35–36

Gewirtz, Paul D., 234n1

Gift giving as a loan disguise, 116, 117, 128

Gill, Jeremiah, 200

Gleason, Patrick, 153

Goit, Levi, 43

Gourgis, Louis, 151

Government structure and legal system, 30–31

Governor Allen, 219–20, 221

Grandy, Moses, 16, 169–70

Grayson, Spenser M., 95–97

Green, Charles B., 91, 94, 185

Green, Edmund, 82–83

Griffith, William B., 90–91, 94, 103, 240n8; representation of blacks by, 33, 34, 65–66, 91–93, 94, 95, 132

Gross, Ariela, 228n7; on judges, 248n67; law and, 230n22, 233n46, 260n11; on Natchez attorneys, 246n35; on reputation and honor, 243n46, 247n50; on testimony, 234n2

Grymes, Coleman, 89

Grymes, London, 89

Guardians, white, 161–62, 166, 259n1

Gueho, Francois, 60–62

Habeas corpus, 82, 97, 167, 189, 260n13

Haight, Samuel, 187

Hall, Gwendolyn Midlo, 197

Hamm, John, 91–93, 98, 185

Hann, Jonathan, 47

Hannah, Edward, and Rosetta freedom suit, 161, 162, 167

Hanson, Thomas, 43

Haralson, A. D. M., 4, 5

Haralson, Archibald, 60–62, 89

Hardes, John, 153

Harrison (indentured black man), 95–97

Harrison, George, 156

Hawk, Joseph, 155

Hawkins, Cupid, 126

Hawkins, Isabella, 89, 159–60

Hayden, William, 68–70, 153, 241n19

Hegemony, law and, 13, 230–31nn21–22

Heirs and manumission, 173–75, 177, 178–79

Helen, William, 187

Heno, Ursin, 51

Hicks, Rachel, 156–57

Hierarchies: racial, 65, 74–75, 93, 104–5, 130; social (*See* Social hierarchy)

Hindus, Michael, 232n33

Hiring out slaves, 150–52

Holden, John, 150

Honor, 56, 62, 79–80, 93–94, 128, 243nn44–46, 247n50

Honoré, Marie Françoise. *See* Belly, Marie Françoise

Honoré, Marie Rose, 210

Honoré, Zacherie, 210, 211, 214, 215–16

Household managers, women as, 216

Howard, Stephen, 167

Hubeau, Charles, 148

Hunter, Alexander, 209

Husbands, wives suing of, 49–54, 213–16, 269n73, 270n76

Hypersexuality of black females, 52–53, 54

Identifying litigants as black, 140, 255n25

Incidents in the Life of a Slave Girl (Jacobs), 55–56

Indebtedness, 116, 127–28, 129–30. *See also* Debt

Independence: debt and, 130; property and, 134, 136, 144–45, 148–49, 209

Language of the collectivity, public, 164, 180

Language of the private-law promise, 164, 180

Lapice, Peter, 76

Lartigue, Arnaud, 150–51

Law, 20–21; on alimony, 204; blacks' knowledge of, 32–33, 72, 132, 136, 163–64, 191, 234n13; culture and, 234n1; as a discourse, 29–30, 58–59, 234n10; on equality, 220; on family and inheritance, 204; in France, 189; on free blacks, 17–18, 66, 259n1; on freedom suits, 93, 166, 180, 185–86, 189–90; hegemony and, 13, 230–31nn21–22; on kidnapping, 184–85, 264n65; lawyers knowledge of, 30, 85, 86–88; on manumission, 67, 168, 173–74, 175, 190, 262n36, 267n29; on marriage and coverture, 148–49, 163, 198, 199, 207–8, 244n6, 257n43, 270n74; on property, 154, 170, 214–15, 238n63, 270n74; on self-purchase, 169, 173; in slave narratives, 55–58; on slaves, 12, 16–17, 56–58, 178, 180–81, 190; on speech, 74–75; on testifying against whites, 71; as a unified set of principles, 87; on vagrancy, 65; on white guardians, 161. *See also* Language of law

Law Office of J. Vance Lewis, 35

Lawson, David, 131

Law students, 30, 86–88

Lawyers: black, 33–34, 82, 244n2; fees of, 94–95, 96; knowledge of laws of, 30, 85, 86–88; as planters and slaveholders, 90, 99. *See also* Bar, Natchez district; *specific lawyers*

Leake, Walter, 90

Leblanc, Alexander, 60

Leblanc, Villeneuve, 177–78

Leduff, John Baptiste, 119

Leduff, Oscar, 119

Legal fiction, 132, 156, 166, 254n60

Legal personhood. *See* Personhood

LeRidel, Baptiste, 179, 189–90

Leum, Isaac, 118, 251n21

Lewis, Ben, 115

Lewis, Benjamin and Bradford, 185–86

Lewis, Doc, 33–34

Lewis, J. Vance, 33–34, 35

Liens, 119, 126

Lincoln, Abraham, 86–87

Litigators, blacks as, 9–10, 11–12

Littell, Moses, 68

Loan executions, 124–27

Locations for conducting law business, 32

Locke, John, 101–2

Loreno, Domingo, 131, 155–56

Lorrie, Jean Baptiste, 126, 140–41, 211, 255–56n26

Louisiana, colonial, 195–97, 265n3

Louisiana law, 20–21, 233n46; on equality, 220; on family and inheritance, 204; on free blacks, 17–18, 66, 259n1; on freedom suits, 166, 180, 189, 190; on manumission, 67, 176, 190, 199–200, 267n29; on marriage, 163, 198, 208, 270n74; on property, 154, 170, 214–15, 238n63, 270n74; on self-purchase, 169, 173; on slaves, 16–17, 56, 178, 181; *statu liberi*, 176, 262n44. *See also* Law

Louisiana Purchase, 265n3

Love, William, 211

Lowber, Jonathan, 43

Lumpkin, Joseph, 103

Mann, Bruce, 252n29

Mansfield, Lord, 189

Manumission of slaves, 31, 32, 169; advocacy and, 97–98, 109–10; law on, 67, 168, 173–74, 175, 190, 262n36, 267n29; property and, 136, 137, 139; reputation and, 67; that are family, 198–200; Turner and, 102; in wills, 205. *See also* Freedom suits

Mardis, Abner, 95–97

Margueritte (free black woman), 120, 151, 251n20

Maria Theresa (free black woman), 150

Marie (enslaved woman), 190–91

Maris-Wolf, Ted, 229n10, 239n4, 245n34

Marriage: family and, 210, 212; formalizing, 201, 202, 205; of free blacks, 10;

interracial, 32, 137, 196, 198, 201; law on, 148–49, 163, 198, 199, 207–8, 244n6, 257n43, 270n74; property and, 148, 208, 215, 216, 270n74, 270n76; of slaves, 163
Married Women's Property Acts, 215
Marshall, John, 175
Martin, Bonnie, 250n6, 253n35
Martin, Josiah, 150
Martin, Robert, 43–44, 46–49
Mary (enslaved woman), 175
Masse family, 158
Masters of Small Worlds (McCurry), 231n24
Masur, Kate, 236n39
Mathers, Jeremiah, 182
McBarney, Thomas, 187
McCary, Robert, 251n21
McClellan, Margaret, 50
McCurry, Stephanie, 231n24
McGuire, Elizabeth, 91
McMurran, John T., 87, 90–91, 246n35
Mead, Cowls, 89
Membership in the polity and community, 11–12, 15, 38, 94, 216, 222; language and storytelling and, 20, 40, 46, 49; property and, 135, 146, 147–48, 149. *See also* Civic inclusion
Meriam, Nathan, 88, 206, 217
Method of research, 21–22, 223–26
Meyer, Jacob, 156
Miler, George, 125
Miles, Walter, 182
Milewski, Melissa, 271n5
Miller, James, 212
Miller, Lavinia, 32
Miller, William, 118
Milly (enslaved woman), 130–33
Minor, John, 68–70
Mississippi law, 20–21; on free blacks, 17, 66; on freedom suits, 93, 166, 180; on kidnapping, 184–85; on manumission, 67, 200, 262n36, 267n29; on marriage, 208; on property, 154, 215; on self-purchase, 173; on slaves, 16–17, 161; on testifying against whites, 71
Mitchum, Arthur, 268n59

Mixed-race children, 137–38, 202–4
Monopoly of truth by race, 107, 108, 111, 122
Monroe, James, 68, 89
Moore, Alexander, 171–72
Moore, William, 171–72
Mordecai, Elizabeth, 182–83
Morgan, Charles, 159, 184
Morgan, Thomas Jefferson, 106, 107–8
Morris, Miriam, 175
Mortgages, 126
Mosby, William, 153
Moseley, William, 241n28
Motton, John, 74–75
Mourain, Pelagie Garnier, 179
Moussa, Bob, 177–78, 179–80, 192, 262n45
Mutual obligation, 70
Myths of black female promiscuity, 52

Nanly, William, 50
Narrative of the Life of William W. Brown, An American Slave (Brown), 56, 239n69
Narratives, 27–29, 54–55, 234n1; advocacy and, 106; boundaries of, 35–36; centrality of law in, 55–59, 235n25; in *Cooper v. Briscoe*, 43, 45–47, 48; in *Davis v. Edmonds*, 49–54; knowledge and, 32–33, 235n25; membership and citizenship and, 14–15, 40–41, 135, 146, 149, 216; property and, 134, 135, 140–44, 146, 148–49, 156; in *Salvador v. Turner*, 39, 40–41; of virtue and reputation, 51–53, 64
Natchez, Miss., 16
Natchez district, 2, 15–16. *See also* Bar, Natchez district
Native Americans, 41, 182
Natural children, 138, 202–3, 204
Naturalization Act of 1790, 39
Natural law, 101
Natural rights, 100, 101–2, 143, 175
Neal, John, 237n51
Ned (enslaved man), 173
Nero (free black man), 65–66
New Orleans, La., 171, 183, 197
Next friends, 161–62, 166, 259n1
Nicholas, Jacques, 151

Runaway slaves, 3–4, 6, 18, 167, 263n58
Rupert, Anton, 169
Russell, Mary, 50
Rutledge, James, 126

Sachs, Honor, 250n90
Salvador, Pierre, 15, 36–39, 40–42, 54, 58, 103, 147
Sandy, John, 145–47, 148–49
Sanite (free black woman), 158, 158–59
Schafer, Judith Kelleher, 89, 261n27, 265n79
Scholarship on subordinated people and the legal system, 227–28n3
Scott, William, 187
Segregation, 220–21
Selective law enforcement, 65, 70, 73
Self-determination, 147
Self-ownership and possession, 168, 188, 191, 193; advocacy and, 103, 104, 105, 110; personhood and, 11, 104, 163–64. *See also* Freedom suits
Self-purchase agreements, 109, 164, 169–73, 261n27
Separate-but-equal, 221
Separation from bed and board, 49, 51, 213, 214, 215, 270n74
Separation of property suits, 53–54, 214–15, 270n74
Sexton, Daniel, 181
Sexuality of black females, 52–53
Sexual relations, interracial, 144, 181, 197, 266n16
Shields, William B., 44, 89, 90, 92
Simien, Marie, 151
Single women, rights of, 139, 148, 207–9, 215, 257n43, 270n74
Skills and labor as a form of property, 136, 143–44, 152–54
Skills and occupations of free blacks, 138, 152–53
Slater, David, 185–86
Slave codes, 9, 16–17, 56, 231n22
Slave hiring, 150–52
Slaveholders: debt and, 253n50; distancing selves from slave traders, 48; free blacks

as, 139, 149–52; honor and, 93, 247n50; kidnapping and, 185; lawyers as, 89–90; manumission and, 173, 199; of Natchez district, 16–17; property rights and, 13–14, 102, 160; storytelling and, 27–28. *See also specific slaveholders*
Slavery: black race suitability for, 47–48; law and, 12, 16–17, 55–58, 178, 180–81, 190; in Natchez district, 15–17, 231n29; presumption of, 3–4, 181, 186; property rights and, 105, 134, 249n83; territorial expansion and, 41; on trial, 57–58. *See also* Slave codes; Slaveholders; Slaves; Slave trade
Slavery of indebtedness, 129–30
Slaves: as collateral, 117, 126–27, 253n35; court appearances of, 31–32; debt recovery and, 130–33; economy of, 154–56, 160; free blacks' ownership of, 139, 149–52; hiring out, 150–52; as litigants for freedom, 161–92; marriage of, 163; own trials of, 33, 34; as parties to suits, 132; patrols of, 3, 6, 17, 32, 33; population of, 196; property and, 13–14, 20, 42, 102, 149–52, 172–73; as property owners, 154–56, 170–71; rights of, 12; runaway, 3–4, 6, 18, 167, 263n58; for a time, 176, 177–80, 183, 262n44. *See also* Manumission of slaves; Slavery; Slave trade
Slave trade, 16, 45, 48, 100–101, 183, 196, 237n51
Smith, Adam, 143
Smith, Daniel, 155
Smith, Eliza, 50
Smith, Johanna, 229n10, 250n6
Snyder, Alonzo, 95, 249n85
Social hierarchy, 11, 230n20; advocacy and, 93; auction block and, 127–28; debt and, 116, 133; reputation and, 62, 63–65, 74–75
Social institutions, 9, 31
Social order: debt actions and, 116, 127–30, 133; free blacks and, 12, 66.136; language and, 65; property rights and, 160
Somerset, James, 189
Somerset v. Stewart, 189
Sonnier, Florian, 172

Sources of research, 223–26
Southern Sentinel, 129–30
Space, crafting of by blacks, 19–20
Spanish Louisiana, 20–21, 169, 195–97, 265n3
Special tribunals, 17
Speech of blacks, laws on, 74–75
Spousal behavior, 51–52, 237–38n57
Standards for legal education, 86
Standards of behavior, 53, 63, 65, 73, 81
State of nature, 102
Statistical analysis and sampling of court records, 8
Statu liberi, 176, 177–80, 183, 262n44
Steele, James H., 91, 185
Stereotypes: of black women, 52, 54–55; of slave traders, 48, 237n51; use of by blacks, 72–73
Stewart, Charles, 189
Stone, Thomas, 161
Storytelling, 27–29, 35, 54–55, 59, 63, 106–7. *See also* Narratives
Students of law, 30, 86–88
Subordination, 19; debt and, 116, 128–29; narratives and, 28, 29, 55; reputation and, 63, 72, 76
Suggs, Jon-Christian, 55
Sureties, 98, 211, 212, 217
Surget family, 16
Susey (free black woman), 187
Sutton, William, 91–92
Swain, John, 39

Taylor, James, 107–8
Testifying against whites, 16, 18, 21, 28, 71, 155, 234n2
Theft, 79, 125, 153, 155
Tichenor, Gabriel, 76, 212, 240n16
Tom (enslaved man), 67, 108–10, 173
Tournoir, Leda, 210
Transylvania University, 86, 87
Trapper, Jean, 140
Trial of Rev. Benjamin, 34
Troxeler, George, 121
Truth: race monopoly on, 107, 108, 111, 122; storytelling and, 19, 28, 35, 58, 107

Turner, Edward, 87, 90, 94, 100–103, 104, 110
Turner, John C., 36–39, 40–42, 54–55, 103
Twitty, Anne, 234n13, 245n34, 263n50
Tyler, John, 36, 41

U.S. Supreme Court, 221

Vagrancy laws, 18
Van Winkle, Jacob, 159, 184
Van Winkle, Stephen, 158–60, 184
Verret, Paulin, 121, 210, 212
Verret, Valerie Octavine. *See* Belly, Valerie Octavine
Viales, Lewis, 95
Von Daacke, Kirt, 229n10, 239n4
Voting rights, 40, 236n39
Vulnerability of blacks, 156–60

Warren, John A., 5, 127
Wealth of Nations (Smith), 143
Welke, Barbara Young, 11, 83, 244n6
Westward expansion, 41, 45
White supremacy: credit and, 124, 128–29, 130; protection of property and, 13–14, 80–81; rhetoric of, 63–64, 72–73, 75
Williams, George, 95, 187–88
Williams, Maria, 131, 155–56
Williams, Mary Ellen, 137–38, 198
Wills: back wages and, 154; manumission and, 173–76, 177, 178–80, 261n31, 262n36; of Pierre Belly, 205–6; property and, 205
Winchester, George, 86
Winn, Baylor, 71–72, 241n28
Wives: property and, 148–49, 207–8, 214–16, 257n43, 270n74; suing husbands, 213–16, 269n73, 270n76
Women, free black: as household managers, 216; occupations of, 138, 152–53; property and, 139, 148–49. *See also specific women*
Woodall, Johnson, 181
Woodville Republican, 130
Wooten, Ellen, 156–57
Wright, Perry, 42–43